STANDARDS OF PROFESSIONAL CONDUCT
FOR LAWYERS AND JUDGES

STANDARDS OF
PROFESSIONAL CONDUCT
FOR LAWYERS AND JUDGES

Compiled by

Norman Redlich
Dean and Judge Edward Weinfeld
Professor of Law
New York University School of Law

Little, Brown and Company   Boston and Toronto

Library of Congress Catalog Card No. 83-082696

ISBN No. 0-316-73658-9

Fourth Printing

HAM
Published simultaneously in Canada
by Little, Brown & Company (Canada) Limited

Printed in the United States of America

SUMMARY OF CONTENTS

PART I

STANDARDS FOR LAWYERS

PART II

STANDARDS FOR JUDGES

PART I

STANDARDS FOR LAWYERS

A.B.A. MODEL CODE OF PROFESSIONAL RESPONSIBILITY*

In effect as of August 1983

PREAMBLE[1]

The continued existence of a free and democratic society depends upon recognition of the concept that justice is based upon the rule of law grounded in respect for the dignity of the individual and his capacity through reason for enlightened self-government.[2] Law so grounded makes justice possible, for only through such law does the dignity of the individual attain respect and protection. Without it, individual rights become subject to unrestrained power, respect for law is destroyed, and rational self-government is impossible.

Lawyers, as guardians of the law, play a vital role in the preservation of society. The fulfillment of this role requires an understanding by lawyers of their relationship with and function in our legal system.[3] A consequent obligation of lawyers is to maintain the highest standards of ethical conduct.

In fulfilling his professional responsibilities, a lawyer necessarily assumes various roles that require the performance of many difficult tasks. Not every situation which he may encounter can be foreseen,[4] but fundamental ethical

---

1. The footnotes are intended merely to enable the reader to relate the provisions of this Model Code to the ABA Canons of Professional Ethics adopted in 1908, as amended, the Opinions of the ABA Committee on Professional Ethics, and a limited number of other sources; they are not intended to be an annotation of the views taken by the ABA Special Committee on Evaluation of Ethical Standards. Footnotes citing ABA Canons refer to the ABA Canons of Professional Ethics, adopted in 1908, as amended.

2. *Cf.* ABA CANONS, Preamble.

3. "[T]he lawyer stands today in special need of a clear understanding of his obligations and of the vital connection between these obligations and the role his profession plays in society." *Professional Responsibility: Report of the Joint Conference*, 44 A.B.A.J. 1159, 1160 (1958).

4. "No general statement of the responsibilities of the legal profession can encompass all the situations in which the lawyer may be placed. Each position held by him makes its own peculiar demands. These demands the lawyer must clarify for himself in the light of the particular role in which he serves." *Professional Responsibility: Report of the Joint Conference*, 44 A.B.A.J. 1159, 1218 (1958).

principles are always present to guide him. Within the framework of these principles, a lawyer must with courage and foresight be able and ready to shape the body of the law to the ever-changing relationships of society.[5]

The Model Code of Professional Responsibility points the way to the aspiring and provides standards by which to judge the transgressor. Each lawyer must find within his own conscience the touchstone against which to test the extent to which his actions should rise above minimum standards. But in the last analysis it is the desire for the respect and confidence of the members of his profession and of the society which he serves that should provide to a lawyer the incentive for the highest possible degree of ethical conduct. The possible loss of that respect and confidence is the ultimate sanction. So long as its practitioners are guided by these principles, the law will continue to be a noble profession. This is its greatness and its strength, which permit of no compromise.

PRELIMINARY STATEMENT

In furtherance of the principles stated in the Preamble, the American Bar Association has promulgated this Model Code of Professional Responsibility, consisting of three separate but interrelated parts: Canons, Ethical Considerations, and Disciplinary Rules.[6] The Model Code is designed to be adopted by appropriate agencies both as an inspirational guide to the members of the profession and as a basis for disciplinary action when the conduct of a lawyer falls below the required minimum standards stated in the Disciplinary Rules.

Obviously the Canons, Ethical Considerations, and Disciplinary Rules cannot apply to non-lawyers; however, they do define the type of ethical conduct that the public has a right to expect not only of lawyers but also of their non-professional employees and associates in all matters pertaining to professional employment. A lawyer should ultimately be responsible for the

---

5. "The law and its institutions change as social conditions change. They must change if they are to preserve, much less advance, the political and social values from which they derive their purposes and their life. This is true of the most important of legal institutions, the profession of law. The profession, too, must change when conditions change in order to preserve and advance the social values that are its reasons for being." Cheatham, *Availability of Legal Services: The Responsibility of the Individual Lawyer and the Organized Bar*, 12 U.C.L.A. L. REV. 438, 440 (1965).

6. The Supreme Court of Wisconsin adopted a Code of Judicial Ethics in 1967. "The code is divided into standards and rules, the standards being statements of what the general desirable level of conduct should be, the rules being particular canons, the violation of which shall subject an individual judge to sanctions." In re Promulgation of a Code of Judicial Ethics, 36 Wis. 2d 252, 255, 153 N.W. 2d 873, 874 (1967).

The portion of the Wisconsin Code of Judicial Ethics entitled "Standards" states that "[t]he following standards set forth the significant qualities of the ideal judge. . . ." *Id.*, 36 Wis. 2d at 256, 153 N.W. 2d at 875. The portion entitled "Rules" states that "[t]he court promulgates the following rules because the requirements of judicial conduct embodied therein are of sufficient gravity to warrant sanctions if they are not obeyed. . . ." *Id.*, 36 Wis. 2d at 259, 153 N.W. 2d at 876.

conduct of his employees and associates in the course of the professional representation of the client.

The Canons are statements of axiomatic norms, expressing in general terms the standards of professional conduct expected of lawyers in their relationships with the public, with the legal system, and with the legal profession. They embody the general concepts from which the Ethical Considerations and the Disciplinary Rules are derived.

The Ethical Considerations are aspirational in character and represent the objectives toward which every member of the profession should strive. They constitute a body of principles upon which the lawyer can rely for guidance in many specific situations.[7]

The Disciplinary Rules, unlike the Ethical Considerations, are mandatory in character. The Disciplinary Rules state the minimum level of conduct below which no lawyer can fall without being subject to disciplinary action. Within the framework of fair trial,[8] the Disciplinary Rules should be uniformly applied to all lawyers,[9] regardless of the nature of their professional

7. "Under the conditions of modern practice it is peculiarly necessary that the lawyer should understand, not merely the established standards of professional conduct, but the reasons underlying these standards. Today the lawyer plays a changing and increasingly varied role. In many developing fields the precise contribution of the legal profession is as yet undefined." *Professional Responsibility: Report of the Joint Conference*, 44 A.B.A.J. 1159 (1958).

"A true sense of professional responsibility must derive from an understanding of the reasons that lie back of specific restraints, such as those embodied in the Canons. The grounds for the lawyer's peculiar obligations are to be found in the nature of his calling. The lawyer who seeks a clear understanding of his duties will be led to reflect on the special services his profession renders to society and the services it might render if its full capacities were realized. When the lawyer fully understands the nature of his office, he will then discern what restraints are necessary to keep that office wholesome and effective." *Id.*

8. "Disbarment, designed to protect the public, is a punishment or penalty imposed on the lawyer. . . . He is accordingly entitled to procedural due process, which includes fair notice of the charge." In re Ruffalo, 390 U.S. 544, 550, 20 L. Ed. 2d 117, 122 88 S. Ct. 1222, 1226 (1968), *rehearing denied*, 391 U.S. 961, 20 L. Ed. 2d 874, 88 S. Ct. 1833 (1968).

"A State cannot exclude a person from the practice of law or from any other occupation in a manner or for reasons that contravene the Due Process or Equal Protection Clause of the Fourteenth Amendment. . . . A State can require high standards of qualification . . . but any qualification must have a rational connection with the applicant's fitness or capacity to practice law." Schware v. Bd. of Bar Examiners, 353 U.S. 232, 239, 1 L. Ed. 2d 796, 801-02, 77 S. Ct. 752, 756 (1957).

"[A]n accused lawyer may expect that he will not be condemned out of a capricious self-righteousness or denied the essentials of a fair hearing." Kingsland v. Dorsey, 338 U.S. 318, 320, 94 L. Ed. 123, 126, 70 S. Ct. 123, 124-25 (1949).

"The attorney and counsellor being, by the solemn judicial act of the court, clothed with his office, does not hold it as a matter of grace and favor. The right which it confers upon him to appear for suitors, and to argue causes, is something more than a mere indulgence, revocable at the pleasure of the court, or at the command of the legislature. It is a right of which he can only be deprived by the judgment of the court, for moral or professional delinquency." Ex parte Garland, 71 U.S. (4 Wall.) 333, 378-79, 18 L. Ed. 366, 370 (1866).

See generally Comment, *Procedural Due Process and Character Hearings for Bar Applicants*, 15 STAN. L. REV. 500 (1963).

9. "The canons of professional ethics must be enforced by the Courts and must be respected by members of the Bar if we are to maintain public confidence in the integrity and impartiality of the administration of justice." In re Meeker, 76 N. M. 354, 357, 414 P.2d 862, 864 (1966), *appeal dismissed*, 385 U.S. 449 (1967).

activities.[10] The Model Code makes no attempt to prescribe either disciplinary procedures or penalties[11] for violation of a Disciplinary Rule,[12] nor does it undertake to define standards for civil liability of lawyers for professional conduct. The severity of judgment against one found guilty of violating a Disciplinary Rule should be determined by the character of the offense and the attendant circumstances.[13] An enforcing agency, in applying the Disciplinary Rules, may find interpretive guidance in the basic principles embodied in the Canons and in the objectives reflected in the Ethical Considerations.

CANON 1
A LAWYER SHOULD ASSIST IN MAINTAINING THE INTEGRITY AND COMPETENCE OF THE LEGAL PROFESSION

Ethical Considerations

EC 1-1 A basic tenet of the professional responsibility of lawyers is that every person in our society should have ready access to the independent

---

10. See ABA CANON 45.

11. "Other than serving as a model or derivative source, the American Bar Association Model Code of Professional Responsibility plays no part in the disciplinary proceeding, except as a guide for consideration in adoption of local applicable rules for the regulation of conduct on the part of legal practitioners." ABA COMM. ON PROFESSIONAL ETHICS, INFORMAL OPINION NO. 1420 (1978) [hereinafter each Formal Opinion is cited as "*ABA Opinion*"]. For the purposes and intended effect of the American Bar Association Model Code of Professional Responsibility and of the opinions of the Standing Committee on Ethics and Professional Responsibility, see Informal Opinion No. 1420.

"There is generally no prescribed discipline for any particular type of improper conduct. The disciplinary measures taken are discretionary with the courts, which may disbar, suspend, or merely censure the attorney as the nature of the offense and past indicia of character may warrant." Note, 43 CORNELL L.Q. 489, 495 (1958).

12. The Model Code seeks only to specify conduct for which a lawyer should be disciplined by courts and governmental agencies which have adopted it. Recommendations as to the procedures to be used in disciplinary actions are within the jurisdiction of the American Bar Association Standing Committee on Professional Discipline.

13. "The severity of the judgment of this court should be in proportion to the gravity of the offenses, the moral turpitude involved, and the extent that the defendant's acts and conduct affect his professional qualifications to practice law." Louisiana State Bar Ass'n v. Steiner, 204 La. 1073, 1092-93, 16 So. 2d 843, 850 (1944) Higgins, J., concurring in decree).

"Certainly an erring lawyer who has been disciplined and who having paid the penalty has given satisfactory evidence of repentance and has been rehabilitated and restored to his place at the bar by the court which knows him best ought not to have what amounts to an order of permanent disbarment entered against him by a federal court solely on the basis of an earlier criminal record and without regard to his subsequent rehabilitation and present good character. . . . We think, therefore, that the district court should reconsider the appellant's application for admission and grant it unless the court finds it to be a fact that the appellant is not presently of good moral or professional character." In re Dreier, 258 F.2d 68, 69-70 (3d Cir. 1958).

professional services of a lawyer of integrity and competence. Maintaining the integrity and improving the competence of the bar to meet the highest standards is the ethical responsibility of every lawyer.

EC 1-2   The public should be protected from those who are not qualified to be lawyers by reason of a deficiency in education[1] or moral standards[2] or of other relevant factors[3] but who nevertheless seek to practice law. To assure the maintenance of high moral and educational standards of the legal profession, lawyers should affirmatively assist courts and other appropriate bodies in promulgating, enforcing, and improving requirements for admission to the bar.[4] In like manner, the bar has a positive obligation to aid in the continued improvement of all phases of pre-admission and post-admission legal education.

EC 1-3   Before recommending an applicant for admission, a lawyer should satisfy himself that the applicant is of good moral character. Although a

1. "[W]e cannot conclude that all educational restrictions [on bar admission] are unlawful. We assume that few would deny that a grammar school education requirement, before taking the bar examination, was reasonable. Or that an applicant had to be able to read or write. Once we conclude that *some* restriction is proper, then it becomes a matter of degree — the problem of drawing the line. . . .
"We conclude the fundamental question here is whether Rule IV, Section 6 of the Rules Pertaining to Admission of Applicants to the State Bar of Arizona is 'arbitrary, capricious and unreasonable.' We conclude an educational requirement of graduation from an accredited law school is not." Hackin v. Lockwood, 361 F.2d 499, 503-4 (9th Cir. 1966), cert. denied, 385 U.S. 960, 17 L. Ed.2d 305, 87 S. Ct. 396 (1966).

2. "Every state in the United States, as a prerequisite for admission to the practice of law, requires that applicants possess 'good moral character.' Although the requirement is of judicial origin, it is now embodied in legislation in most states." Comment, *Procedural Due Process and Character Hearings for Bar Applicants*, 15 STAN. L. REV. 500 (1963).
"Good character in the members of the bar is essential to the preservation of the integrity of the courts. The duty and power of the court to guard its portals against intrusion by men and women who are mentally and morally dishonest, unfit because of bad character, evidenced by their course of conduct, to participate in the administrative law, would seem to be unquestioned in the matter of preservation of judicial dignity and integrity." In re Monaghan, 126 Vt. 53, 222 A.2d 665, 670 (1966).
"Fundamentally, the question involved in both situations [*i.e.* admission and disciplinary proceedings] is the same — is the applicant for admission or the attorney sought to be disciplined a fit and proper person to be permitted to practice law, and that usually turns upon whether he has committed or is likely to continue to commit acts of moral turpitude. At the time of oral argument the attorney for respondent frankly conceded that the test for admission and for discipline is and should be the same. We agree with this concession." Hallinan v. Comm. of Bar Examiners, 65 Cal.2d 447, 453, 421 P.2d 76, 81, 55 Cal.Rptr. 228, 233 (1966).

3. "Proceedings to gain admission to the bar are for the purpose of protecting the public and the courts from the ministrations of persons unfit to practice the profession. Attorneys are officers of the court appointed to assist the court in the administration of justice. Into their hands are committed the property, the liberty and sometimes the lives of their clients. This commitment demands a high degree of intelligence, knowledge of the law, respect for its function in society, sound and faithful judgment and, above all else, integrity of character in private and professional conduct." In re Monaghan 126 Vt. 53, 222 A.2d 665, 676 (1966) (Holden, C.J., dissenting).

4. "A bar composed of lawyers of good moral character is a worthy objective but it is unnecessary to sacrifice vital freedoms in order to obtain that goal. It is also important both to society and the bar itself that lawyers be unintimidated — free to think, speak, and act as members of an Independent Bar." Konigsberg v. State Bar, 353 U.S. 252, 273, 1 L. Ed. 2d 810, 825, 77 S. Ct. 722, 733 (1957).

lawyer should not become a self-appointed investigator or judge of applicants for admission, he should report to proper officials all unfavorable information he possesses relating to the character or other qualifications of an applicant.[5]

EC 1-4   The integrity of the profession can be maintained only if conduct of lawyers in violation of the Disciplinary Rules is brought to the attention of the proper officials. A lawyer should reveal voluntarily to those officials all unprivileged knowledge of conduct of lawyers which he believes clearly to be in violation of the Disciplinary Rules.[6] A lawyer should, upon request serve on and assist committees and boards having responsibility for the administration of the Disciplinary Rules.[7]

EC 1-5   A lawyer should maintain high standards of professional conduct and should encourage fellow lawyers to do likewise. He should be temperate and dignified, and he should refrain from all illegal and morally reprehensible conduct.[8] Because of his position in society, even minor violations of law by a lawyer may tend to lessen public confidence in the legal profession. Obedience to law exemplifies respect for law. To lawyers especially, respect for the law should be more than a platitude.

EC 1-6   An applicant for admission to the bar or a lawyer may be unqualified, temporarily or permanently, for other than moral and educational reasons, such as mental or emotional instability. Lawyers should be diligent in taking steps to see that during a period of disqualification such person is not granted a license or, if licensed, is not permitted to practice.[9] In like manner,

5. *See* ABA CANON 29.

6. ABA CANON 28 designates certain conduct as unprofessional and then states that: "A duty to the public and to the profession devolves upon every member of the Bar having knowledge of such practices upon the part of any practitioner immediately to inform thereof, to the end that the offender may be disbarred." ABA CANON 29 states a broader admonition: "Lawyers should expose without fear or favor before the proper tribunals corrupt or dishonest conduct in the profession."

7. "It is the obligation of the organized Bar and the individual lawyer to give unstinted cooperation and assistance to the highest court of the state in discharging its function and duty with respect to discipline and in purging the profession of the unworthy." *Report of the Special Committee on Disciplinary Procedures*, 80 A.B.A. REP. 463, 470 (1955).

8. *Cf.* ABA CANON 32.

9. "We decline, on the present record, to disbar Mr. Sherman or to reprimand him — not because we condone his actions, but because, as heretofore indicated, we are concerned with whether he is mentally responsible for what he has done.

"The logic of the situation would seem to dictate the conclusion that, if he was mentally responsible for the conduct we have outlined, he should be disbarred: and, if he was not mentally responsible, he should not be permitted to practice law.

"However, the flaw in the logic is that he may have been mentally irresponsible [at the time of his offensive conduct] . . . , and, yet, have sufficiently improved in the almost two and one-half years intervening to be able to capably and competently represent his clients. . . .

"We would make clear that we are satisfied that a case has been made against Mr. Sherman, warranting a refusal to permit him to further practice law in this state unless he can establish his mental irresponsibility at the time of the offenses charged. The burden of proof is upon him.

"If he establishes such mental irresponsibility, the burden is then upon him to establish his present capability to practice law." In re Sherman, 58 Wash. 2d 1, 6-7, 354 P.2d 888, 890 (1960), *cert. denied*, 371 U.S. 951, 9 L. Ed. 2d 499, 83 S. Ct. 506 (1963).

when the disqualification has terminated, members of the bar should assist such person in being licensed, or, if licensed, in being restored to his full right to practice.

Disciplinary Rules

DR 1-101   Maintaining Integrity and Competence of the Legal Profession

(A)   A lawyer is subject to discipline if he has made a materially false statement in, or if he has deliberately failed to disclose a material fact requested in connection with, his application for admission to the bar.[10]

(B)   A lawyer shall not further the application for admission to the bar of another person known by him to be unqualified in respect to character, education, or other relevant attribute.[11]

DR 1-102   Misconduct

(A)   A lawyer shall not:
  (1)   Violate a Disciplinary Rule.
  (2)   Circumvent a Disciplinary Rule through actions of another.[12]
  (3)   Engage in illegal conduct involving moral turpitude.[13]

10. "This Court has the inherent power to revoke a license to practice law in this State, where such license was issued by this Court, and its issuance was procured by the fraudulent concealment, or by the false and fraudulent representation by the applicant of a fact which was manifestly material to the issuance of the license." North Carolina ex rel. Attorney General v. Gorson, 209 N.C. 320, 326, 183 S.E. 392, 395 (1936), *cert. denied*, 298 U.S. 662, 80 L. Ed. 1387, 56 S. Ct. 752 (1936).

See also Application of Patterson, 318 P.2d 907, 913 (Or. 1957), *cert. denied*, 356 U.S. 947, 2 L. Ed. 2d 822, 78 S. Ct. 795 (1958).

11. *See* ABA CANON 29.

12. In *ABA Opinion* 95 (1933), which held that a municipal attorney could not permit police officers to interview persons with claims against the municipality when the attorney knew the claimants to be represented by counsel, the Committee on Professional Ethics said:

"The law officer is, of course, responsible for the acts of those in his department who are under his supervision and control. *Opinion 85. In re Robinson*, 136 N.Y.S. 548 (affirmed 209 N. Y. 354-1912) held that it was a matter of disbarment for an attorney to adopt a general course of approving the unethical conduct of employees of his client, even though he did not actively participate therein.

" '. . . The attorney should not advise or sanction acts by his client which he himself should not do.' *Opinion 75*."

13. "The most obvious non-professional ground for disbarment is conviction for a felony. Most states make conviction for a felony grounds for automatic disbarment. Some of these states, including New York, make disbarment mandatory upon conviction for *any* felony while others require disbarment only for those felonies which involve moral turpitude. There are strong arguments that some felonies, such as involuntary manslaughter, reflect neither on an attorney's fitness, trustworthiness, nor competence and, therefore, should not be grounds for disbarment, but most states tend to disregard these arguments and, following the common law

(4) Engage in conduct involving dishonesty, fraud, deceit, or misrepresentation.

(5) Engage in conduct that is prejudicial to the administration of justice.

(6) Engage in any other conduct that adversely reflects on his fitness to practice law.[14]

DR 1-103 Disclosure of Information to Authorities

(A) A lawyer possessing unprivileged knowledge of a violation of DR 1-102 shall report such knowledge to a tribunal or other authority empowered to investigate or act upon such violation.[15]

---

rule, make disbarment mandatory on conviction for any felony." Note, 43 CORNELL L.Q. 489, 490 (1958).

"Some states treat conviction for misdemeanors as grounds for automatic disbarment. . . . However, the vast majority, accepting the common law rule, require that the misdemeanor involve moral turpitude. While the definition of moral turpitude may prove difficult, it seems only proper that those minor offenses which do not affect the attorney's fitness to continue in the profession should not be grounds for disbarment. A good example is an assault and battery conviction which would not involve moral turpitude unless done with malice and deliberation." Id. at 491.

"The term 'moral turpitude' has been used in the law for centuries. It has been the subject of many decisions by the courts but has never been clearly defined because of the nature of the term. Perhaps the best general definition of the term 'moral turpitude' is that it imparts an act of baseness, vileness or depravity in the duties which one person owes to another or to society in general, which is contrary to the usual, accepted and customary rule of right and duty which a person should follow. 58 C.J.S. at page 1201. Although offenses against revenue laws have been held to be crimes of moral turpitude, it has also been held that the attempt to evade the payment of taxes due to the government or any subdivision thereof, while wrong and unlawful, does not involve moral turpitude. 58 C.J.S. at page 1205." Comm. on Legal Ethics v. Scheer, 149 W. Va. 721, 726-27, 143 S.E.2d 141, 145 (1965).

"The right and power to discipline an attorney, as one of its officers, is inherent in the court. . . . This power is not limited to those instances of misconduct wherein he has been employed, or has acted, in a professional capacity; but, on the contrary, this power may be exercised where his misconduct outside the scope of his professional relations shows him to be an unfit person to practice law." In re Wilson, 391 S.W.2d 914, 917-18 (Mo. 1965).

14. "It is a fair characterization of the lawyer's responsibility in our society that he stands 'as a shield,' to quote Devlin, J., in defense of right and to ward off wrong. From a profession charged with these responsibilities there must be exacted those qualities of truthspeaking, of a high sense of honor, of granite discretion, of the strictest observance of fiduciary responsibility, that have, throughout the centuries, been compendiously described as 'moral character.'" Schware v. Bd. of Bar Examiners, 353 U.S. 232, 247 1 L. Ed. 2d 796, 806, 77 S. Ct. 752, 761 (1957) (Frankfurter, J., concurring).

"Particularly applicable here is Rule 4.47 providing that 'A lawyer should always maintain his integrity; and shall not willfully commit any act against the interest of the public; nor shall he violate his duty to the courts or his clients; *nor shall he, by any misconduct, commit any offense against the laws of Missouri or the United States of America, which amounts to a crime involving acts done by him contrary to justice, honesty, modesty or good morals*; nor shall he be guilty of any other misconduct whereby, for the protection of the public and those charged with the administration of justice, he should no longer be entrusted with the duties and responsibilities belonging to the office of an attorney.'" In re Wilson, 391 S.W.2d 914, 917 (Mo. 1965).

15. *See* ABA CANON 29; *cf.* ABA CANON 28.

(B)   A lawyer possessing unprivileged knowledge or evidence concerning another lawyer or a judge shall reveal fully such knowledge or evidence upon proper request of a tribunal or other authority empowered to investigate or act upon the conduct of lawyers or judges.[16]

CANON 2
A LAWYER SHOULD ASSIST THE LEGAL PROFESSION IN FULFILLING ITS DUTY TO MAKE LEGAL COUNSEL AVAILABLE

Ethical Considerations

EC 2-1   The need of members of the public for legal services[1] is met only if they recognize their legal problems, appreciate the importance of seeking assistance,[2] and are able to obtain the services of acceptable legal counsel.[3] Hence, important functions of the legal profession are to educate laymen to recognize their problems, to facilitate the process of intelligent selection of lawyers, and to assist in making legal services fully available.[4]

---

16. *Cf.*ABA CANONS 28 and 29.

1. "Men have need for more than a system of law; they have need for a system of law which functions, and that means they have need for lawyers." Cheatham, *The Lawyer's Role and Surroundings*, 25 ROCKY MT. L. REV. 405 (1953).

2. "Law is not self-applying; men must apply and utilize it in concrete cases. But the ordinary man is incapable. He cannot know the principles of law or the rules guiding the machinery of law administration; he does not know how to formulate his desires with precision and to put them into writing; he is ineffective in the presentation of his claims." *Id.*

3. "This need [to provide legal services] was recognized by . . . Mr. [Lewis F.] Powell [Jr., President, American Bar Association, 1963-64], who said: 'Looking at contemporary America realistically, we must admit that despite all our efforts to date (and these have not been insignificant), far too many persons are not able to obtain equal justice under law. This usually results because their poverty or their ignorance has prevented them from obtaining legal counsel.' " Address by E. Clinton Bamberger, Association of American Law Schools 1965 Annual Meeting, Dec. 28, 1965, in PROCEEDINGS, PART II, 1965, 61, 63-64 (1965).

"A wide gap separates the need for legal services and its satisfaction, as numerous studies reveal. Looked at from the side of the layman, one reason for the gap is poverty and the consequent inability to pay legal fees. Another set of reasons is ignorance of the need for and the value of legal services, and ignorance of where to find a dependable lawyer. There is fear of the mysterious processes and delays of the law, and there is fear of overreaching and overcharging by lawyers, a fear stimulated by the occasional exposure of shysters." Cheatham, *Availability of Legal Services: The Responsibility of the Individual Lawyer and of the Organized Bar*, 12 U.C.L.A. L. REV. 438 (1965).

4. "It is not only the right but the duty of the profession as a whole to utilize such methods as may be developed to bring the services of its members to those who need them, so long as this can be done ethically and with dignity." *ABA Opinion* 320 (1968).

"[T]here is a responsibility on the bar to make legal services available to those who need them. The maxim, 'privilege brings responsibilities,' can be expanded to read, exclusive privilege to render public service brings responsibility to assure that the service is available to those in need of it." Cheatham, *Availability of Legal Services: The Responsibility of the Individual Lawyer and of the Organized Bar*, 12 U.C.L.A. L. REV. 438, 443 (1965).

11

Recognition of Legal Problems

EC 2-2   The legal profession should assist laypersons to recognize legal problems because such problems may not be self-revealing and often are not timely noticed. Therefore, lawyers should encourage and participate in educational and public relations programs concerning our legal system with particular reference to legal problems that frequently arise. Preparation of advertisements and professional articles for lay publications[5] and participation in seminars, lectures, and civic programs should be motivated by a desire to educate the public to an awareness of legal needs and to provide information relevant to the selection of the most appropriate counsel rather than to obtain publicity for particular lawyers. The problems of advertising on television require special consideration, due to the style, cost, and transitory nature of such media. If the interests of laypersons in receiving relevant lawyer advertising are not adequately served by print media and radio advertising, and if adequate safeguards to protect the public can reasonably be formulated, television advertising may serve a public interest.

EC 2-3   Whether a lawyer acts properly in volunteering in-person advice to a layperson to seek legal services depends upon the circumstances.[6] The giving of advice that one should take legal action could well be in fulfillment of the duty of the legal profession to assist laypersons in recognizing legal problems.[7] The advice is proper only if motivated by a desire to protect one who does not recognize that he may have legal problems or who is ignorant of his legal rights or obligations. It is improper if motivated by a desire to obtain personal benefit, secure personal publicity, or cause legal action to be taken merely to harass or injure another. A lawyer should not initiate an

---

"The obligation to provide legal services for those actually caught up in litigation carries with it the obligation to make preventive legal advice accessible to all. It is among those unaccustomed to business affairs and fearful of the ways of the law that such advice is often most needed. If it is not received in time, the most valiant and skillful representation in court may come too late." *Professional Responsibility: Report of the Joint Conference*, 44 A.B.A.J. 1159, 1216 (1958).

5. "A lawyer may with propriety write articles for publications in which he gives information upon the law. . . ." ABA CANON 40.

6. *See* ABA CANON 28.

7. This question can assume constitutional dimensions: "We meet at the outset the contention that 'solicitation' is wholly outside the area of freedoms protected by the First Amendment. To this contention there are two answers. The first is that a State cannot foreclose the exercise of constitutional rights by mere labels. The second is that abstract discussion is not the only species of communication which the Constitution protects; the First Amendment also protects vigorous advocacy, certainly of lawful ends, against governmental intrusion. . . .

"However valid may be Virginia's interest in regulating the traditionally illegal practice of barratry, maintenance and champerty, that interest does not justify the prohibition of the NAACP activities disclosed by this record. Malicious intent was of the essence of the common-law offenses of fomenting or stirring up litigation. And whatever may be or may have been true of suits against governments in other countries, the exercise in our own, as in this case of First Amendment rights to enforce Constitutional rights through litigation, as a matter of law, cannot be deemed malicious." NAACP v. Button, 371 U.S. 415, 429, 439-40, 9 L. Ed. 2d 405, 415-16, 422, 83 S. Ct. 328, 336, 341 (1963).

in-person contact with a non-client, personally or through a representative, for the purpose of being retained to represent him for compensation.

EC 2-4   Since motivation is subjective and often difficult to judge, the motives of a lawyer who volunteers in-person advice likely to produce legal controversy may well be suspect if he receives professional employment or other benefits as a result.[8] A lawyer who volunteers in-person advice that one should obtain the services of a lawyer generally should not himself accept employment, compensation, or other benefit in connection with that matter. However, it is not improper for a lawyer to volunteer such advice and render resulting legal services to close friends, relatives, former clients (in regard to matters germane to former employment), and regular clients.[9]

EC 2-5   A lawyer who writes or speaks for the purpose of educating members of the public to recognize their legal problems should carefully refrain from giving or appearing to give a general solution applicable to all apparently similar individual problems,[10] since slight changes in fact situations may require a material variance in the applicable advice; otherwise, the public may be misled and misadvised. Talks and writings by lawyers for laypersons should caution them not to attempt to solve individual problems upon the basis of the information contained therein.[11]

Selection of a Lawyer

EC 2-6   Formerly a potential client usually knew the reputations of local lawyers for competency and integrity and therefore could select a practitioner in whom he had confidence. This traditional selection process worked

---

8. It is disreputable for an attorney to breed litigation by seeking out those who have claims for personal injuries or other grounds of action in order to secure them as clients, or to employ agents or runners, or to reward those who bring or influence the bringing of business to his office. . . . Moreover, it tends quite easily to the institution of baseless litigation and the manufacture of perjured testimony. From early times, this danger has been recognized in the law by the condemnation of the crime of common barratry, or the stirring up of suits or quarrels between individuals at law or otherwise." In re Ades, 6 F.Supp. 467, 474-75 (D. Mary. 1934).

9. "Rule 2.
    "§a. . . .
        "[A] member of the State Bar shall not solicit professional employment by
        "(1) Volunteering counsel or advice except where ties of blood relationship or trust make it appropriate." CAL. BUSINESS AND PROFESSIONS CODE §6076 (West 1962).

10. "Rule 18 . . . A member of the State Bar shall not advise inquirers or render opinions to them through or in connection with a newspaper, radio or other publicity medium of any kind in respect to their specific legal problems, whether or not such attorney shall be compensated for his services." CAL. BUSINESS AND PROFESSIONS CODE §6076 (West 1962).

11. "In any case where a member might well apply the advice given in the opinion to his individual affairs, the lawyer rendering the opinion [concerning problems common to members of an association and distributed to the members through a periodic bulletin] should specifically state that this opinion should not be relied on by any member as a basis for handling his individual affairs, but that in every case he should consult his counsel. In the publication of the opinion the association should make a similar statement." ABA Opinion 273 (1946).

well because it was initiated by the client and the choice was an informed one.

EC 2-7   Changed conditions, however, have seriously restricted the effectiveness of the traditional selection process. Often the reputations of lawyers are not sufficiently known to enable laypersons to make intelligent choices.[12] The law has become increasingly complex and specialized. Few lawyers are willing and competent to deal with every kind of legal matter, and many laypersons have difficulty in determining the competence of lawyers to render different types of legal services. The selection of legal counsel is particularly difficult for transients, persons moving into new areas, persons of limited education or means, and others who have little or no contact with lawyers.[13] Lack of information about the availability of lawyers, the qualifications of particular lawyers, and the expense of legal representation leads laypersons to avoid seeking legal advice.

EC 2-8   Selection of a lawyer by a layperson should be made on an informed basis. Advice and recommendation of third parties — relatives, friends, acquaintances, business associates, or other lawyers — and disclosure of relevant information about the lawyer and his practice may be helpful. A layperson is best served if the recommendation is disinterested and informed. In order that the recommendation be disinterested, a lawyer should not seek to influence another to recommend his employment. A lawyer should not compensate another person for recommending him, for influencing a prospective client to employ him, or to encourage future recommendations.[14] Advertisements and public communications, whether in law lists, telephone directories, newspapers, other forms of print media, television or radio, should be formulated to convey only information that is necessary to make an appropriate selection. Such information includes: (1) office information, such as, name, including name of law firm and names of professional associates; addresses; telephone numbers; credit card acceptability; fluency in foreign languages; and office hours; (2) relevant biographical information; (3) description of the practice, but only by using designations and definitions authorized by [the agency having jurisdiction of the subject under state law], for example, one or more fields of law in which the lawyer or law firm practices; a statement that practice is limited to one or more fields of law; and/or a statement that the lawyer or law firm specializes in a particular field of law practice, but only by using designations, definitions and standards authorized by [the agency having jurisdiction of the subject

---

12. "A group of recent interrelated changes bears directly on the availability of legal services. . . . [One] change is the constantly accelerating urbanization of the country and the decline of personal and neighborhood knowledge of whom to retain as a professional man." Cheatham, *Availability of Legal Services: The Responsibility of the Individual Lawyer and of the Organized Bar*, 12 U.C.L.A. L. REV. 438, 440 (1965).

13. *Cf.* Cheatham, *A Lawyer When Needed: Legal Services for the Middle Classes*, 63 COLUM. L. REV. 973, 974 (1963).

14. *See* ABA CANON 28.

under state law]; and (4) permitted fee information. Self-laudation should be avoided.

Selection of a Lawyer: Lawyer Advertising

EC 2-9 The lack of sophistication on the part of many members of the public concerning legal services, the importance of the interests affected by the choice of a lawyer and prior experience with unrestricted lawyer advertising, require that special care be taken by lawyers to avoid misleading the public and to assure that the information set forth in any advertising is relevant to the selection of a lawyer. The lawyer must be mindful that the benefits of lawyer advertising depend upon its reliability and accuracy. Examples of information in lawyer advertising that would be deceptive include misstatements of fact, suggestions that the ingenuity or prior record of a lawyer rather than the justice of the claim are the principal factors likely to determine the result, inclusion of information irrelevant to selecting a lawyer, and representations concerning the quality of service, which cannot be measured or verified. Since lawyer advertising is calculated and not spontaneous, reasonable regulation of lawyer advertising designed to foster compliance with appropriate standards serves the public interest without impeding the flow of useful, meaningful, and relevant information to the public.

EC 2-10 A lawyer should ensure that the information contained in any advertising which the lawyer publishes, broadcasts or causes to be published or broadcast is relevant, is disseminated in an objective and understandable fashion, and would facilitate the prospective client's ability to compare the qualifications of the lawyers available to represent him. A lawyer should strive to communicate such information without undue emphasis upon style and advertising stratagems which serve to hinder rather than to facilitate intelligent selection of counsel. Because technological change is a recurrent feature of communications forms, and because perceptions of what is relevant in lawyer selection may change, lawyer advertising regulations should not be cast in rigid, unchangeable terms. Machinery is therefore available to advertisers and consumers for prompt consideration of proposals to change the rules governing lawyer advertising. The determination of any request for such change should depend upon whether the proposal is necessary in light of existing Code provisions, whether the proposal accords with standards of accuracy, reliability and truthfulness, and whether the proposal would facilitate informed selection of lawyers by potential consumers of legal services. Representatives of lawyers and consumers should be heard in addition to the applicant concerning any proposed change. Any change which is approved should be promulgated in the form of an amendment to the Code so that all lawyers practicing in the jurisdiction may avail themselves of its provisions.

EC 2-11   The name under which a lawyer conducts his practice may be a factor in the selection process.[15] The use of a trade name or an assumed name could mislead laypersons concerning the identity, responsibility, and status of those practicing thereunder.[16] Accordingly, a lawyer in private practice should practice only under a designation containing his own name, the name of a lawyer employing him, the name of one or more of the lawyers practicing in a partnership, or, if permitted by law, the name of a professional legal corporation, which should be clearly designated as such. For many years some law firms have used a firm name retaining one or more names of deceased or retired partners and such practice is not improper if the firm is a bona fide successor of a firm in which the deceased or retired person was a member, if the use of the name is authorized by law or by contract, and if the public is not misled thereby.[17] However, the name of a partner who withdraws from a firm but continues to practice law should be omitted from the firm name in order to avoid misleading the public.

EC 2-12   A lawyer occupying a judicial, legislative, or public executive or administrative position who has the right to practice law concurrently may allow his name to remain in the name of the firm if he actively continues to practice law as a member thereof. Otherwise, his name should be removed from the firm name,[18] and he should not be identified as a past or present member of the firm; and he should not hold himself out as being a practicing lawyer.

EC 2-13   In order to avoid the possibility of misleading persons with whom he deals, a lawyer should be scrupulous in the representation of his professional status.[19] He should not hold himself out as being a partner or associate of a law firm if he is not one in fact,[20] and thus should not hold

15. *Cf. ABA Opinion* 303 (1961).
16. *See* ABA CANON 33.
17. *Id.*

"The continued use of a firm name by one or more surviving partners after the death of a member of the firm whose name is in the firm title is expressly permitted by the Canons of Ethics. The reason for this is that all of the partners have by their joint and several efforts over a period of years contributed to the good will attached to the firm name. In the case of a firm having widespread connections, this good will is disturbed by a change in firm name every time a name partner dies, and that reflects a loss in some degree of the good will to the building up of which the surviving partners have contributed their time, skill and labor through a period of years. To avoid this loss the firm name is continued, and to meet the requirements of the Canon the individuals constituting the firm from time to time are listed." *ABA Opinion* 267 (1945).

"Accepted local custom in New York recognizes that the name of a law firm does not necessarily identify the individual members of the firm, and hence the continued use of a firm name after the death of one or more partners is not a deception and is permissible. . . . The continued use of a deceased partner's name in the firm title is not affected by the fact that another partner withdraws from the firm and his name is dropped, or the name of the new partner is added to the firm name." *Opinion* No. 45, Committee on Professional Ethics, New York State Bar Ass'n, 39 N.Y.St.B.J. 455 (1967).

Cf. ABA Opinion 258 (1943).
18. *Cf. ABA* CANON 33 and *ABA Opinion* 315 (1965).
19. *Cf. ABA Opinions* 283 (1950) and 81 (1932).
20. *See ABA Opinion* 316 (1967).

himself out as a partner or associate if he only shares offices with another lawyer.[21]

EC 2-14 In some instances a lawyer confines his practice to a particular field of law.[22] In the absence of state controls to insure the existence of special competence, a lawyer should not be permitted to hold himself out as a specialist or as having official recognition as a specialist, other than in the fields of admiralty, trademark, and patent law where a holding out as a specialist historically has been permitted. A lawyer may, however, indicate in permitted advertising, if it is factual, a limitation of his practice or one or more particular areas or fields of law in which he practices using designations and definitions authorized for that purpose by [the state agency having jurisdiction]. A lawyer practicing in a jurisdiction which certifies specialists must also be careful not to confuse laypersons as to his status. If a lawyer discloses areas of law in which he practices or to which he limits his practice, but is not certified in [the jurisdiction], he, and the designation authorized in [the jurisdiction], should avoid any implication that he is in fact certified.

EC 2-15 The legal profession has developed lawyer referral systems designed to aid individuals who are able to pay fees but need assistance in locating lawyers competent to handle their particular problems. Use of a lawyer referral system enables a layman to avoid an uninformed selection of a lawyer because such a system makes possible the employment of competent lawyers who have indicated an interest in the subject matter involved. Lawyers should support the principle of lawyer referral systems and should encourage the evolution of other ethical plans which aid in the selection of qualified counsel.

Financial Ability to Employ Counsel: Generally

EC 2-16 The legal profession cannot remain a viable force in fulfilling its role in our society unless its members receive adequate compensation for services rendered, and reasonable fees[23] should be charged in appropriate

21. "The word 'associates' has a variety of meanings. Principally through custom the word when used on the letterheads of law firms has come to be regarded as describing those who are employees of the firm. Because the word has acquired this special significance in connection with the practice of the law the use of the word to describe lawyer relationships other than employer-employee is likely to be misleading." In re Sussman and Tanner, 241 Ore. 246, 248, 405 P.2d 355, 356 (1965).

According to *ABA Opinion* 310 (1963), use of the term "associates" would be misleading in two situations: (1) where two lawyers are partners and they share both responsibility and liability for the partnership; and (2) where two lawyers practice separately, sharing no responsibility or liability, and only share a suite of offices and some costs.

22. "For a long time, many lawyers have, of necessity, limited their practice to certain branches of law. The increasing complexity of the law and the demand of the public for more expertness on the part of the lawyer has, in the past few years — particularly in the last ten years — brought about specialization on an increasing scale." *Report of the Special Committee on Specialization and Specialized Legal Services*, 79 A.B.A. REP. 582, 584 (1954).

23. *See* ABA CANON 12.

cases to clients able to pay them. Nevertheless, persons unable to pay all or a portion of a reasonable fee should be able to obtain necessary legal services,[24] and lawyers should support and participate in ethical activities designed to achieve that objective.[25]

Financial Ability to Employ Counsel: Persons Able to Pay Reasonable Fees

EC 2-17   The determination of a proper fee requires consideration of the interests of both client and lawyer.[26] A lawyer should not charge more than a reasonable fee,[27] for excessive cost of legal service would deter laymen from utilizing the legal system in protection of their rights. Furthermore, an excessive charge abuses the professional relationship between lawyer and client. On the other hand, adequate compensation is necessary in order to enable the lawyer to serve his client effectively and to preserve the integrity and independence of the profession.[28]

EC 2-18   The determination of the reasonableness of a fee requires consideration of all relevant circumstances,[29] including those stated in the Disciplinary Rules. The fees of a lawyer will vary according to many factors, including the time required, his experience, ability, and reputation, the nature of the employment, the responsibility involved, and the results obtained. It is a commendable and long-standing tradition of the bar that special consideration is given in the fixing of any fee for services rendered a brother lawyer or a member of his immediate family.

EC 2-19   As soon as feasible after a lawyer has been employed, it is desirable that he reach a clear agreement with his client as to the basis of the fee charges to be made. Such a course will not only prevent later misunderstanding but will also work for good relations between the lawyer and the client. It is usually beneficial to reduce to writing the understanding of the parties regarding the fee, particularly when it is contingent. A lawyer should be mindful that many persons who desire to employ him may have had little or no experience with fee charges of lawyers, and for this reason he should

---

24. *Cf.* ABA CANON 12.

25. "If there is any fundamental proposition of government on which all would agree, it is that one of the highest goals of society must be to achieve and maintain equality before the law. Yet this ideal remains an empty form of words unless the legal profession is ready to provide adequate representation for those unable to pay the usual fees." *Professional Representation: Report of the Joint Conference,* 44 A.B.A.J. 1159, 1216 (1958).

26. *See* ABA CANON 12.

27. *Cf.* ABA CANON 12.

28. "When members of the Bar are induced to render legal services for inadequate compensation, as a consequence the quality of the service rendered may be lowered, the welfare of the profession injured and the administration of justice made less efficient." *ABA Opinion* 302 (1961).

Cf. ABA Opinion 307 (1962).

29. *See* ABA CANON 12.

explain fully to such persons the reasons for the particular fee arrangement he proposes.

EC 2-20   Contingent fee arrangements[30] in civil cases have long been commonly accepted in the United States in proceedings to enforce claims. The historical bases of their acceptance are that (1) they often, and in a variety of circumstances, provide the only practical means by which one having a claim against another can economically afford, finance, and obtain the services of a competent lawyer to prosecute his claim, and (2) a successful prosecution of the claim produces a *res* out of which the fee can be paid.[31] Although a lawyer generally should decline to accept employment on a contingent fee basis by one who is able to pay a reasonable fixed fee, it is not necessarily improper for a lawyer, where justified by the particular circumstances of a case, to enter into a contingent fee contract in a civil case with any client who, after being fully informed of all relevant factors, desires that arrangement. Because of the human relationships involved and the unique character of the proceedings, contingent fee arrangements in domestic relation cases are rarely justified. In administrative agency proceedings contingent fee contracts should be governed by the same consideration as in other civil cases. Public policy properly condemns contingent fee arrangements in criminal cases, largely on the ground that legal services in criminal cases do not produce a *res* with which to pay the fee.

EC 2-21   A lawyer should not accept compensation or any thing of value incident to his employment or services from one other than his client without the knowledge and consent of his client after full disclosure.[32]

EC 2-22   Without the consent of his client, a lawyer should not associate in a particular matter another lawyer outside his firm. A fee may properly be divided between lawyers[33] properly associated if the division is in proportion to the services performed and the responsibility assumed by each lawyer[34] and if the total fee is reasonable.

30. *See* ABA CANON 13; *see also* MACKINNON, CONTINGENT FEES FOR LEGAL SERVICES (1964) (A report of the American Bar Foundation).
"A contract for a reasonable contingent fee where sanctioned by law is permitted by *Canon 13*, but the client must remain responsible to the lawyer for expenses advanced by the latter. 'There is to be no barter of the privilege of prosecuting a cause for gain in exchange for the promise of the attorney to prosecute at his own expense.' (Cardozo, C. J. in Matter of Gilman, 251 N.Y. 265, 270-271.)" *ABA Opinion* 246 (1942).
31. *See* Comment, *Providing Legal Services for the Middle Class in Civil Matters: The Problem, the Duty and a Solution*, 26 U. PITT. L. REV. 811, 829 (1965).
32. *See* ABA CANON 38.
"Of course, as . . . [Informal Opinion 679] points out, there must be full disclosure of the arrangement [that an entity other than the client pays the attorney's fee] by the attorney to the client. . . ." *ABA Opinion* 320 (1968).
33. "Only lawyers may share in . . . a division of fees, but . . . it is not necessary that both lawyers be admitted to practice in the same state, so long as the division was based on the division of services or responsibility." *ABA Opinion* 316 (1967).
34. *See* ABA CANON 34.
"We adhere to our previous rulings that where a lawyer merely brings about the employment of another lawyer *but renders no service and assumes no responsibility in the matter*, a division of the latter's fee is improper. (*Opinions 18 and 153*)."

EC 2-23   A lawyer should be zealous in his efforts to avoid controversies over fees with clients[35] and should attempt to resolve amicably any differences on the subject.[36] He should not sue a client for a fee unless necessary to prevent fraud or gross imposition by the client.[37]

Financial Ability to Employ Counsel: Persons Unable to Pay Reasonable Fees

EC 2-24   A layman whose financial ability is not sufficient to permit payment of any fee cannot obtain legal services, other than in cases where a contingent fee is appropriate, unless the services are provided for him. Even a person of moderate means may be unable to pay a reasonable fee which is large because of the complexity, novelty, or difficulty of the problem or similar factors.[38]

EC 2-25   Historically, the need for legal services of those unable to pay reasonable fees has been met in part by lawyers who donated their services

---

"It is assumed that the bar, generally, understands what acts or conduct of a lawyer may constitute 'services' to a client within the intendment of *Canon 12*. Such acts or conduct invariably, if not always, involve 'responsibility' on the part of the lawyer, whether the word 'responsibility' be construed to denote the possible resultant legal or moral liability on the part of the lawyer to the client or to others, or the onus of deciding what should or should not be done in behalf of the client. The word 'services' in *Canon 12* must be construed in this broad sense and may apply to the selection and retainer of associate counsel as well as to other acts or conduct in the client's behalf." *ABA Opinion* 204 (1940).

35. *See* ABA CANON 14.
36. *Cf. ABA Opinion* 320 (1968).
37. *See* ABA CANON 14.

"Ours is a learned profession, not a mere money-getting trade.... Suits to collect fees should be avoided. Only where the circumstances imperatively require, should resort be had to a suit to compel payment. And where a lawyer does resort to a suit to enforce payment of fees which involves a disclosure, he should carefully avoid any disclosure not clearly necessary to obtaining or defending his rights." *ABA Opinion* 250 (1943).

But cf. ABA Opinion 320 (1968).

38. "As a society increases in size, sophistication and technology, the body of laws which is required to control that society also increases in size, scope and complexity. With this growth, the law directly affects more and more facets of individual behavior, creating an expanding need for legal services on the part of the individual members of the society.... As legal guidance in social and commercial behavior increasingly becomes necessary, there will come a concurrent demand from the layman that such guidance be made available to him. This demand will not come from those who are able to employ the best legal talent, nor from those who can obtain legal assistance at little or no cost. It will come from the large 'forgotten middle income class,' who can neither afford to pay proportionately large fees nor qualify for ultra-low-cost services. The legal profession must recognize this inevitable demand and consider methods whereby it can be satisfied. If the profession fails to provide such methods, the laity will." Comment, *Providing Legal Services for the Middle Class in Civil Matters: The Problem, the Duty and a Solution*, 26 U. PITT. L. REV. 811, 811-12 (1965).

"The issue is not whether we shall do something or do nothing. The demand for ordinary everyday legal justice is so great and the moral nature of the demand is so strong that the issue has become whether we devise, maintain, and support suitable agencies able to satisfy the demand or, by our own default, force the government to take over the job, supplant us, and ultimately dominate us." Smith, *Legal Service Offices for Persons of Moderate Means*, 1949 WIS L. REV. 416, 418 (1949).

or accepted court appointments on behalf of such individuals. The basic responsibility for providing legal services for those unable to pay ultimately rests upon the individual lawyer, and personal involvement in the problems of the disadvantaged can be one of the most rewarding experiences in the life of a lawyer. Every lawyer, regardless of professional prominence or professional workload, should find time to participate in serving the disadvantaged. The rendition of free legal services to those unable to pay reasonable fees continues to be an obligation of each lawyer, but the efforts of individual lawyers are often not enough to meet the need.[39] Thus it has been necessary for the profession to institute additional programs to provide legal services.[40] Accordingly, legal aid offices[41] lawyer referral services, and other related programs have been developed, and others will be developed, by the profession.[42] Every lawyer should support all proper efforts to meet this need for legal services.[43]

39. "Lawyers have peculiar responsibilities for the just administration of the law, and these responsibilities include providing advice and representation for needy persons. To a degree not always appreciated by the public at large, the bar has performed these obligations with zeal and devotion. The Committee is persuaded, however, that a system of justice that attempts, in mid-twentieth century America, to meet the needs of the financially incapacitated accused through primary or exclusive reliance on the uncompensated services of counsel will prove unsuccessful and inadequate. . . . A system of adequate representation, therefore, should be structured and financed in a manner reflecting its public importance. . . . We believe that fees for private appointed counsel should be set by the court within maximum limits established by the statute." Report of the Att'y Gen's Comm. on Poverty and the Administration of Criminal Justice 41-43 (1963).

40. "At present this representation [of those unable to pay usual fees] is being supplied in some measure through the spontaneous generosity of individual lawyers, through legal aid societies, and — increasingly — through the organized efforts of the Bar. If those who stand in need of this service know of its availability and their need is in fact adequately met, the precise mechanism by which this service is provided becomes of secondary importance. It is of great importance, however, that both the impulse to render this service, and the plan for making that impulse effective, should arise within the legal profession itself." *Professional Responsibility: Report of the Joint Conference*, 44 A.B.A.J. 1159, 1216 (1958).

41. "Free legal clinics carried on by the organized bar are not ethically objectionable. On the contrary, they serve a very worthwhile purpose and should be encouraged." *ABA Opinion* 191 (1939).

42. "Whereas the American Bar Association believes that it is a fundamental duty of the bar to see to it that all persons requiring legal advice be able to attain it, irrespective of their economic status. . . .

"Resolved, that the Association approves and sponsors the setting up by state and local bar associations of lawyer referral plans and low-cost legal service methods for the purpose of dealing with cases of persons who might not otherwise have the benefit of legal advice. . . ." *Proceedings of the House of Delegates of the American Bar Association*, Oct. 30, 1946, 71 A.B.A. REP. 103, 109-10 (1946).

43. "The defense of indigent citizens, without compensation, is carried on throughout the country by lawyers representing legal aid societies, not only with the approval, but with the commendation of those acquainted with the work. Not infrequently services are rendered out of sympathy or for other philanthropic reasons, by individual lawyers who do not represent legal aid societies. There is nothing whatever in the Canons to prevent a lawyer from performing such an act, nor should there be." *ABA Opinion* 148 (1935).

Acceptance and Retention of Employment

EC 2-26   A lawyer is under no obligation to act as adviser or advocate for every person who may wish to become his client; but in furtherance of the objective of the bar to make legal services fully available, a lawyer should not lightly decline proffered employment. The fulfillment of this objective requires acceptance by a lawyer of his share of tendered employment which may be unattractive both to him and the bar generally.[44]

EC 2-27   History is replete with instances of distinguished and sacrificial services by lawyers who have represented unpopular clients and causes. Regardless of his personal feelings, a lawyer should not decline representation because a client or a cause is unpopular or community reaction is adverse.[45]

EC 2-28   The personal preference of a lawyer to avoid adversary alignment against judges, other lawyers,[46] public officials, or influential members of the community does not justify his rejection of tendered employment.

EC 2-29   When a lawyer is appointed by a court or requested by a bar association to undertake representation of a person unable to obtain counsel, whether for financial or other reasons, he should not seek to be excused from undertaking the representation except for compelling reasons.[47] Compelling reasons do not include such factors as the repugnance of the subject matter of the proceeding, the identity[48] or position of a person involved in the case, the belief of the lawyer that the defendant in a criminal proceed-

---

44. *But cf.* ABA CANON 31.

45. "One of the highest services the lawyer can render to society is to appear in court on behalf of clients whose causes are in disfavor with the general public." *Professional Responsibility: Report of the Joint Conference,* 44 A.B.A.J. 1159, 1216 (1958).

One author proposes the following proposition to be included in "A Proper Oath for Advocates": "I recognize that it is sometimes difficult for clients with unpopular causes to obtain proper legal representation. I will do all that I can to assure that the client with the unpopular cause is properly represented, and that the lawyer representing such a client receives credit from and support of the bar for handling such a matter." Thode, *The Ethical Standard for the Advocate,* 39 TEXAS L. REV. 575, 592 (1961).

"§6068.... It is the duty of an attorney: ...

"(h) Never to reject, for any consideration personal to himself, the cause of the defenseless or the oppressed." CAL. BUSINESS AND PROFESSIONS CODE §6068 (West 1962). Virtually the same language is found in the Oregon statutes at ORE. REV. STATS. Ch. 9 §9.460(8).

See Rostow, *The Lawyer and His Client,* 48 A.B.A.J. 25 and 146 (1962).

46. *See* ABA CANONS 7 and 29.

"We are of the opinion that it is not professionally improper for a lawyer to accept employment to compel another lawyer to honor the just claim of a layman. On the contrary, it is highly proper that he do so. Unfortunately, there appears to be a widespread feeling among laymen that it is difficult, if not impossible, to obtain justice when they have claims against members of the Bar because other lawyers will not accept employment to proceed against them. The honor of the profession, whose members proudly style themselves officers of the court, must surely be sullied if its members bind themselves by custom to refrain from enforcing just claims of laymen against lawyers." ABA Opinion 144 (1935).

47. ABA CANON 4 uses a slightly different test, saying, "A lawyer assigned as counsel for an indigent prisoner ought not to ask to be excused for any trivial reason...."

48. *Cf.* ABA CANON 7.

ing is guilty,[49] or the belief of the lawyer regarding the merits of the civil case.[50]

EC 2-30 Employment should not be accepted by a lawyer when he is unable to render competent service[51] or when he knows or it is obvious that the person seeking to employ him desires to institute or maintain an action merely for the purpose of harassing or maliciously injuring another.[52] Likewise, a lawyer should decline employment if the intensity of his personal feeling, as distinguished from a community attitude, may impair his effective representation of a prospective client. If a lawyer knows a client has previously obtained counsel, he should not accept employment in the matter unless the other counsel approves[53] or withdraws, or the client terminates the prior employment.[54]

EC 2-31 Full availability of legal counsel requires both that persons be able to obtain counsel and that lawyers who undertake representation complete the work involved. Trial counsel for a convicted defendant should continue to represent his client by advising whether to take an appeal and, if the appeal is prosecuted, by representing him through the appeal unless new counsel is substituted or withdrawal is permitted by the appropriate court.

EC 2-32 A decision by a lawyer to withdraw should be made only on the basis of compelling circumstances,[55] and in a matter pending before a tribunal he must comply with the rules of the tribunal regarding withdrawal. A lawyer should not withdraw without considering carefully and endeavoring to minimize the possible adverse effect on the rights of his client and the

---

49. *See* ABA CANON 5.

50. Dr. Johnson's reply to Boswell upon being asked what he thought of "Supporting a cause which you know to be bad" was: "Sir, you do not know it to be good or bad till the Judge determines it. I have said that you are to state facts fairly; so that your thinking, or what you call knowing, a cause to be bad, must be from reasoning, must be from supposing your arguments to be weak and inconclusive. But, Sir, that is not enough. An argument which does not convince yourself, may convince the Judge to whom you urge it: and if it does convince him, why, then, Sir, you are wrong, and he is right." 2 Boswell, The Life of Johnson 47-48 (Hill ed. 1887).

51. "The lawyer deciding whether to undertake a case must be able to judge objectively whether he is capable of handling it and whether he can assume its burdens without prejudice to previous commitments. . . ." *Professional Responsibility: Report of the Joint Conference,* 44 A.B.A.J. 1158, 1218 (1958).

52. "The lawyer must decline to conduct a civil cause or to make a defense when convinced that it is intended merely to harass or to injure the opposite party or to work oppression or wrong." ABA CANON 30.

53. *See* ABA CANON 7.

54. *Id.*

"From the facts stated we assume that the client has discharged the first attorney and given notice of the discharge. Such being the case, the second attorney may properly accept employment. *Canon 7; Opinions 10, 130, 149.*" ABA Opinion 209 (1941).

55. *See* ABA CANON 44.

"I will carefully consider, before taking a case, whether it appears that I can fully represent the client within the framework of law. If the decision is in the affirmative, then it will take extreme circumstances to cause me to decide later that I cannot so represent him." Thode, *The Ethical Standard for the Advocate,* 39 TEXAS L. REV. 575, 592 (1961) (from "A Proper Oath for Advocates").

possibility of prejudice to his client[56] as a result of his withdrawal. Even when he justifiably withdraws, a lawyer should protect the welfare of his client by giving due notice of his withdrawal,[57] suggesting employment of other counsel, delivering to the client all papers and property to which the client is entitled, cooperating with counsel subsequently employed, and otherwise endeavoring to minimize the possibility of harm. Further, he should refund to the client any compensation not earned during the employment.[58]

EC 2-33 As a part of the legal profession's commitment to the principle that high quality legal services should be available to all, attorneys are encouraged to cooperate with qualified legal assistance organizations providing prepaid legal services. Such participation should at all times be in accordance with the basic tenets of the profession: independence, integrity, competence and devotion to the interests of individual clients. An attorney so participating should make certain that his relationship with a qualified legal assistance organization in no way interferes with his independent, professional representation of the interests of the individual client. An attorney should avoid situations in which officials of the organization who are not lawyers attempt to direct attorneys concerning the manner in which legal services are performed for individual members, and should also avoid situations in which considerations of economy are given undue weight in determining the attorneys employed by an organization or the legal services to be performed for the member or beneficiary rather than competence and quality of service. An attorney interested in maintaining the historic traditions of the profession and preserving the function of a lawyer as a trusted and independent advisor to individual members of society should carefully assess such factors when accepting employment by, or otherwise participating in, a particular qualified legal assistance organization, and while so participating should adhere to the highest professional standards of effort and competence.

Disciplinary Rules

DR 2-101 Publicity

(A) A lawyer shall not, on behalf of himself, his partner, associate or any other lawyer affiliated with him or his firm, use or participate in the use of any form of public communication containing a false, fraudulent, misleading, deceptive, self-laudatory or unfair statement or claim.

56. *ABA Opinion* 314 (1965) held that a lawyer should not disassociate himself from a cause when "it is obvious that the very act of disassociation would have the effect of violating *Canon* 37."
57. ABA CANON 44 enumerates instances in which ". . . the lawyer may be warranted in withdrawing on due notice to the client, allowing him time to employ another lawyer."
58. *See* ABA CANON 44.

(B)   In order to facilitate the process of informed selection of a lawyer by potential consumers of legal services, a lawyer may publish or broadcast, subject to DR 2-103, the following information in print media distributed or over television or radio broadcast in the geographic area or areas in which the lawyer resides or maintains offices or in which a significant part of the lawyer's clientele resides, provided that the information disclosed by the lawyer in such publication or broadcast complies with DR 2-101(A), and is presented in a dignified manner:

(1)   Name, including name of law firm and names of professional associates; addresses and telephone numbers;

(2)   One or more fields of law in which the lawyer or law firm practices, a statement that practice is limited to one or more fields of law, or a statement that the lawyer or law firm specializes in a particular field of law practice, to the extent authorized under DR 2-105;

(3)   Date and place of birth;

(4)   Date and place of admission to the bar of state and federal courts;

(5)   Schools attended, with dates of graduation, degrees and other scholastic distinctions;

(6)   Public or quasi-public offices;

(7)   Military service;

(8)   Legal authorships;

(9)   Legal teaching positions;

(10)   Memberships, offices, and comittee assignments, in bar associations;

(11)   Membership and offices in legal fraternities and legal societies;

(12)   Technical and professional licenses;

(13)   Memberships in scientific, technical and professional associations and societies;

(14)   Foreign language ability;

(15)   Names and addresses of bank references;

(16)   With their written consent, names of clients regularly represented;

(17)   Prepaid or group legal services programs in which the lawyer participates;

(18)   Whether credit cards or other credit arrangements are accepted;

(19)   Office and telephone answering service hours;

(20)   Fee for an initial consultation;

(21)   Availability upon request of a written schedule of fees and/or an estimate of the fee to be charged for specific services;

(22)   Contingent fee rates subject to DR 2-106(C), provided that the statement discloses whether percentages are computed before or after deduction of costs;

(23) Range of fees for services, provided that the statement discloses that the specific fee within the range which will be charged will vary depending upon the particular matter to be handled for each client and the client is entitled without obligation to an estimate of the fee within the range likely to be charged, in print size equivalent to the largest print used in setting forth the fee information;

(24) Hourly rate, provided that the statement discloses that the total fee charged will depend upon the number of hours which must be devoted to the particular matter to be handled for each client and the client is entitled to without obligation an estimate of the fee likely to be charged, in print size at least equivalent to the largest print used in setting forth the fee information;

(25) Fixed fees for specific legal services,* the description of which would not be misunderstood or be deceptive, provided that the statement discloses that the quoted fee will be available only to clients whose matters fall into the services described and that the client is entitled without obligation to a specific estimate of the fee likely to be charged in print size at least equivalent to the largest print used in setting forth the fee information.

(C) Any person desiring to expand the information authorized for disclosure in DR 2-101(B), or to provide for its dissemination through other forums may apply to [the agency having jurisdiction under state law]. Any such application shall be served upon [the agencies having jurisdiction under state law over the regulation of the legal profession and consumer matters] who shall be heard, together with the applicant, on the issue of whether the proposal is necessary in light of the existing provisions of the Code, accords with standards of accuracy, reliability and truthfulness, and would facilitate the process of informed selection of lawyers by potential consumers of legal services. The relief granted in response to any such application shall be promulgated as an amendment to DR 2-101(B), universally applicable to all lawyers.**

(D) If the advertisement is communicated to the public over television or radio, it shall be prerecorded, approved for broadcast by the lawyer, and a recording of the actual transmission shall be retained by the lawyer.

(E) If a lawyer advertises a fee for a service, the lawyer must render that service for no more than the fee advertised.

(F) Unless otherwise specified in the advertisement if a lawyer publishes any fee information authorized under DR 2-101(B) in a publication

---

*The agency having jurisdiction under state law may desire to issue appropriate guidelines defining "specific legal services."

**The agency having jurisdiction under state law should establish orderly and expeditious procedures for ruling on such applications.

that is published more frequently than one time per month, the lawyer shall be bound by any representation made therein for a period of not less than 30 days after such publication. If a lawyer publishes any fee information authorized under DR 2-101(B) in a publication that is published once a month or less frequently, he shall be bound by any representation made therein until the publication of the succeeding issue. If a lawyer publishes any fee information authorized under DR 2-101(B) in a publication which has no fixed date for publication of a succeeding issue, the lawyer shall be bound by any representation made therein for a reasonable period of time after publication but in no event less than one year.

(G) Unless otherwise specified, if a lawyer broadcasts any fee information authorized under DR 2-101(B), the lawyer shall be bound by any representation made therein for a period of not less than 30 days after such broadcast.

(H) This rule does not prohibit limited and dignified identification of a lawyer as a lawyer as well as by name:

    (1) In political advertisements when his professional status is germane to the political campaign or to a political issue.

    (2) In public notices when the name and profession of a lawyer are required or authorized by law or are reasonably pertinent for a purpose other than the attraction of potential clients.

    (3) In routine reports and announcements of a bona fide business, civic, professional, or political organization in which he serves as a director or officer.

    (4) In and on legal documents prepared by him.

    (5) In and on legal textbooks, treatises, and other legal publications, and in dignified advertisements thereof.

(I) A lawyer shall not compensate or give any thing of value to representatives of the press, radio, television, or other communication medium in anticipation of or in return for professional publicity in a news item.

DR 2-102   Professional Notices, Letterheads and Offices.

(A) A lawyer or law firm shall not use or participate in the use of professional cards, professional announcement cards, office signs, letterheads, or similar professional notices or devices, except that the following may be used if they are in dignified form:

    (1) A professional card of a lawyer identifying him by name and as a lawyer, and giving his addresses, telephone numbers, the name of his law firm, and any information permitted under DR 2-105. A professional card of a law firm may also give the

names of members and associates. Such cards may be used for identification.

(2) A brief professional announcement card stating new or changed associations or addresses, change of firm name, or similar matters pertaining to the professional offices of a lawyer or law firm, which may be mailed to lawyers, clients, former clients, personal friends, and relatives.[59] It shall not state biographical data except to the extent reasonably necessary to identify the lawyer or to explain the change in his association, but it may state the immediate past position of the lawyer.[60] It may give the names and dates of predecessor firms in a continuing line of succession. It shall not state the nature of the practice except as permitted under DR 2-105.[61]

(3) A sign on or near the door of the office and in the building directory identifying the law office. The sign shall not state the nature of the practice, except as permitted under DR 2-105.

(4) A letterhead of a lawyer identifying him by name and as a lawyer, and giving his addresses, telephone numbers, the name of his law firm, associates and any information permitted under DR 2-105. A letterhead of a law firm may also give the names of members and associates,[62] and names and dates relating to deceased and retired members.[63] A lawyer may be designated "Of Counsel" on a letterhead if he has a continuing relationship with a lawyer or law firm, other than as a partner or associate. A lawyer or law firm may be designated as "General Counsel" or by similar professional reference on stationery of a client if he or the firm devotes a substantial amount of professional time in the representation of that client.[64] The letterhead of a law firm may give the names and dates of predecessor firms in a continuing line of succession.

---

59. *See ABA Opinion* 301 (1961).

60. "[I]t has become commonplace for many lawyers to participate in government service; to deny them the right, upon their return to private practice, to refer to their prior employment in a brief and dignified manner, would place an undue limitation upon a large element of our profession. It is entirely proper for a member of the profession to explain his absence from private practice, where such is the primary purpose of the announcement, by a brief and dignified reference to the prior employment.

". . . [A]ny such announcement should be limited to the immediate past connection of the lawyer with the government, made upon his leaving that position to enter private practice." *ABA Opinion* 301 (1961).

61. *See ABA Opinion* 251 (1943).

62. "Those lawyers who are working for an individual lawyer or a law firm may be designated on the letterhead and in other appropriate places as 'associates'." *ABA Opinion* 310 (1963).

63. *See* ABA CANON 33.

64. *But see ABA Opinion* 285 (1951).

(B)   A lawyer in private practice shall not practice under a trade name, a name that is misleading as to the identity of the lawyer or lawyers practicing under such name, or a firm name containing names other than those of one or more of the lawyers in the firm, except that the name of a professional corporation of professional association may contain "P.C." or "P.A." or similar symbols indicating the nature of the organization, and if otherwise lawful a firm may use as, or continue to include in, its name the name or names of one or more deceased or retired members of the firm or of a predecessor firm in a continuing line of succession.[65] A lawyer who assumes a judicial, legislative, or public executive or administrative post or office shall not permit his name to remain in the name of a law firm or to be used in professional notices of the firm during any significant period in which he is not actively and regularly practicing law as a member of the firm,[66] and during such period other members of the firm shall not use his name in the firm name or in professional notices of the firm.[67]

(C)   A lawyer shall not hold himself out as having a partnership with one or more other lawyers or professional corporations unless they are in fact partners.[68]

(D)   A partnership shall not be formed or continued between or among lawyers licensed in different jurisdictions unless all enumerations of the members and associates of the firm on its letterhead and in other permissible listings make clear the jurisdictional limitations on those members and associates of the firm not licensed to practice in all listed jurisdictions;[69] however, the same firm name may be used in each jurisdiction.

(E)   Nothing contained herein shall prohibit a lawyer from using or permitting the use of, in connection with his name, an earned degree or title derived therefrom indicating his training in the law.

65. *See* ABA CANON 33; *cf. ABA Opinions* 318 (1967), 267 (1945), 219 (1941), 208 (1940), 192 (1939), 97 (1933), and 6 (1925).

66. *ABA Opinion* 318 (1967) held, "anything to the contrary in Formal Opinion 315 or in the other opinions cited notwithstanding that: "Where a partner whose name appears in the name of a law firm is elected or appointed to high local, state or federal office, which office he intends to occupy only temporarily, at the end of which time he intends to return to his position with the firm, and provided that he is not precluded by holding such office from engaging in the practice of law and does not in fact sever his relationship with the firm but only takes a leave of absence, and provided that there is no local law, statute or custom to the contrary, his name may be retained in the firm name during his term or terms of office, but only if proper precautions are taken not to mislead the public as to his degree of participation in the firm's affairs."

Cf. ABA Opinion 143 (1935), New York County Opinion 67, and New York City Opinions 36 and 798; *but cf. ABA Opinion* 192 (1939) and Michigan Opinion 164.

67. *Cf.* ABA CANON 33.

68. *See ABA Opinion* 277 (1948); *cf.* ABA CANON 33 and *ABA Opinions* 318 (1967), 126 (1935), 115 (1934), 106 (1934), and i 1383 (1977).

69. *See ABA Opinions* 318 (1967) and 316 (1967); *cf.* ABA CANON 33.

DR 2-103   Recommendation of Professional Employment[70]

(A) A lawyer shall not, except as authorized in DR 2-101(B), recommend employment as a private practitioner,[71] of himself, his partner, or associate to a layperson who has not sought his advice regarding employment of a lawyer.[72]

(B) A lawyer shall not compensate or give anything of value to a person or organization to recommend or secure his employment[73] by a client, or as a reward for having made a recommendation resulting in his employment[74] by a client, except that he may pay the usual and reasonable fees or dues charged by any of the organizations listed in DR 2-103(D).

(C) A lawyer shall not request a person or organization to recommend or promote the use of his services or those of his partner or associate, or any other lawyer affiliated with him or his firm, as a private practitioner,[75] except as authorized in DR 2-101, and except that

    (1) He may request referrals from a lawyer referral service operated, sponsored, or approved by a bar association and may pay its fees incident thereto.[76]

    (2) He may cooperate with the legal service activities of any of the offices or organizations enumerated in DR 2-103(D) (1) through (4) and may perform legal services for those to whom he was recommended by it to do such work if:

        (a) The person to whom the recommendation is made is a member or beneficiary of such office or organization; and

---

70. *Cf.* ABA CANON 28.

71. "We think it clear that a lawyer's seeking employment in an ordinary law office, or appointment to a civil service position, is not prohibited by . . . [Canon 27]." *ABA Opinion* 197 (1939).

72. "[A] lawyer may not seek from persons not his clients the opportunity to perform . . . a [legal] check-up." *ABA Opinion* 307 (1962).

73. *Cf.* ABA *Opinion* 78 (1932).

74. " 'No financial connection of any kind between the Brotherhood and any lawyer is permissible. No lawyer can properly pay any amount whatsoever to the Brotherhood or any of its departments, officers or members as compensation, reimbursement of expenses or gratuity in connection with the procurement of a case.' " In re Brotherhood of R. R. Trainmen, 13 Ill. 2d 391, 398, 150 N. E.2d 163, 167 (1958), *quoted in* In re Ratner, 194 Kan. 362, 372, 399 P.2d 865, 873 (1965).

See ABA *Opinion* 147 (1935).

75. "This Court has condemned the practice of ambulance chasing through the media of runners and touters. In similar fashion we have with equal emphasis condemned the practice of direct solicitation by a lawyer. We have classified both offenses as serious breaches of the Canons of Ethics demanding severe treatment of the offending lawyer." State v. Dawson, 111 So. 2d 427, 431 (Fla. 1959).

76. "Registrants [of a lawyer referral plan] may be required to contribute to the expense of operating it by a reasonable registration charge or by a reasonable percentage of fees collected by them." *ABA Opinion* 291 (1956).

Cf. ABA *Opinion* 227 (1941).

(b)   The lawyer remains free to exercise his independent professional judgment on behalf of his client.

(D)   A lawyer or his partner or associate or any other lawyer affiliated with him or his firm may be recommended, employed or paid by, or may cooperate with, one of the following offices or organizations that promote the use of his services or those of his partner or associate or any other lawyer affiliated with him or his firm if there is no interference with the exercise of independent professional judgment in behalf of his client:

(1)   A legal aid office or public defender office:

(a)   Operated or sponsored by a duly accredited law school.

(b)   Operated or sponsored by a bona fide nonprofit community organization.

(c)   Operated or sponsored by a governmental agency.

(d)   Operated, sponsored, or approved by a bar association.[77]

(2)   A military legal assistance office.

(3)   A lawyer referral service operated, sponsored, or approved by a bar association.

(4)   Any bona fide organization that recommends, furnishes or pays for legal services to its members or beneficiaries[78] provided the following conditions are satisfied:

(a)   Such organization, including any affiliate, is so organized and operated that no profit is derived by it from the rendition of legal services by lawyers, and that, if the organization is organized for profit, the legal services are not rendered by lawyers employed, directed, supervised or selected by it except in connection with matters where such organization bears ultimate liability of its member or beneficiary.

(b)   Neither the lawyer, nor his partner, nor associate, nor any other lawyer affiliated with him or his firm, nor any non-lawyer, shall have initiated or promoted such organization for the primary purpose of providing financial or other benefit to such lawyer, partner, associate or affiliated lawyer.

(c)   Such organization is not operated for the purpose of procuring legal work or financial benefit for any lawyer as a private practioner outside of the legal services program of the organization.

(d)   The member or beneficiary to whom the legal services are furnished, and not such organization, is recognized as the client of the lawyer in the matter.

77. Cf. ABA Opinion 148 (1935).
78. United Mine Workers v. Ill. State Bar Ass'n., 389 U.S. 217, 19 L. Ed. 2d 426, 88 S. Ct. 353 (1967); Brotherhood of R.R. Trainmen v. Virginia, 371 U.S. 1, 12 L. Ed. 2d 89, 84 S. Ct. 1113 (1964); NAACP v. Button, 371 U.S. 415, 9 L. Ed. 2d 405, 83 S. Ct. 328 (1963). Also see ABA Opinion 332 (1973) and 333 (1973).

    (e)   Any member or beneficiary who is entitled to have legal services furnished or paid for by the organization may, if such member or beneficiary so desires, select counsel other than that furnished, selected or approved by the organization for the particular matter involved; and the legal service plan of such organization provides appropriate relief for any member or beneficiary who asserts a claim that representation by counsel furnished, selected or approved would be unethical, improper or inadequate under the circumstances of the matter involved and the plan provides an appropriate procedure for seeking such relief.

    (f)   The lawyer does not know or have cause to know that such organization is in violation of applicable laws, rules of court and other legal requirements that govern its legal service operations.

    (g)   Such organization has filed with the appropriate disciplinary authority at least annually a report with respect to its legal service plan, if any, showing its terms, its schedule of benefits, its subscription charges, agreements with counsel, and financial results of its legal service activities or, if it has failed to do so, the lawyer does not know or have cause to know of such failure.

(E)   A lawyer shall not accept employment when he knows or it is obvious that the person who seeks his services does so as a result of conduct prohibited under this Disciplinary Rule.

DR 2-104   Suggestion of Need of Legal Services[79,80]

(A)   A lawyer who has given in-person unsolicited advice to a layperson that he should obtain counsel or take legal action shall not accept employment resulting from that advice,[81] except that:

    (1)   A lawyer may accept employment by a close friend, relative, former client (if the advice is germane to the former employment), or one whom the lawyer reasonably believes to be a client.[82]

---

79. "If a bar association has embarked on a program of institutional advertising for an annual legal check-up and provides brochures and reprints, it is not improper to have these available in the lawyer's office for persons to read and take." *ABA Opinion* 307 (1962).

Cf. ABA Opinion 121 (1934).

80. ABA CANON 28.

81. *Cf. ABA Opinions* 229 (1941) and 173 (1937).

82. "It certainly is not improper for a lawyer to advise his regular clients of new statutes, court decisions, and administrative rulings, which may affect the client's interests, provided the communication is strictly limited to such information. . . .

"When such communications go to concerns or individuals other than regular clients of the lawyer, they are thinly disguised advertisements for professional employment, and are obviously improper." *ABA Opinion* 213 (1941).

(2)   A lawyer may accept employment that results from his participation in activities designed to educate laypersons to recognize
legal problems, to make intelligent selection of counsel, or to
utilize available legal services if such activities are conducted or
sponsored by a qualified legal assistance organization.

(3)   A lawyer who is recommended, furnished or paid by a qualified
legal assistance organization enumerated in DR 2-103(D) (1)
through (4) may represent a member or beneficiary thereof, to
the extent and under the conditions prescribed therein.

(4)   Without affecting his right to accept employment, a lawyer
may speak publicly or write for publication on legal topics[83] so
long as he does not emphasize his own professional experience
or reputation and does not undertake to give individual advice.

(5)   If success in asserting rights or defenses of his client in litigation
in the nature of a class action is dependent upon the joinder of
others, a lawyer may accept, but shall not seek, employment
from those contacted for the purpose of obtaining their
joinder.[84]

DR 2-105   Limitation of Practice[85]

(A)   A lawyer shall not hold himself out publicly as a specialist, as practicing in certain areas of law or as limiting his practice permitted under
DR 2-101(B), except as follows:

(1)   A lawyer admitted to practice before the United States Patent
and Trademark Office may use the designation "Patents," "Patent Attorney," "Patent Lawyer," or "Registered Patent Attorney" or any combination of those terms, on his letterhead and
office sign.

(2)   A lawyer who publicly discloses fields of law in which the lawyer
or the law firm practices or states that his practice is limited to
one or more fields of law shall do so by using designations and
definitions authorized and approved by [the agency having jurisdiction of the subject under state law].

"It is our opinion that where the lawyer has no reason to believe that he has been supplanted
by another lawyer, it is not only his right, but it might even be his duty to advise his client of
any change of fact or law which might defeat the client's testamentary purpose as expressed in
the will.

"Periodic notices might be sent to the client for whom a lawyer has drawn a will, suggesting
that it might be wise for the client to reexamine his will to determine whether or not there has
been any change in his situation requiring a modification of his will." *ABA Opinion* 210 (1941).
   Cf. ABA CANON 28.
   83. *Cf. ABA Opinion* 168 (1937).
   84. *But cf. ABA Opinion* 111 (1934).
   85. *See* ABA CANON 45; cf. ABA CANONS 43, and 46.

    (3)   A lawyer who is certified as a specialist in a particular field of law or law practice by [the authority having jurisdiction under state law over the subject of specialization by lawyers] may hold himself out as such, but only in accordance with the rules prescribed by that authority.[86]

DR 2-106 Fees for Legal Services[87]

(A)   A lawyer shall not enter into an agreement for, charge, or collect an illegal or clearly excessive fee.[88]

(B)   A fee is clearly excessive when, after a review of the facts, a lawyer of ordinary prudence would be left with a definite and firm conviction that the fee is in excess of a reasonable fee. Factors to be considered as guides in determining the reasonableness of a fee include the following:

    (1)   The time and labor required, the novelty and difficulty of the questions involved, and the skill requisite to perform the legal service properly.

    (2)   The likelihood, if apparent to the client, that the acceptance of the particular employment will preclude other employment by the lawyer.

    (3)   The fee customarily charged in the locality for similar legal services.

    (4)   The amount involved and the results obtained.

    (5)   The time limitations imposed by the client or by the circumstances.

    (6)   The nature and length of the professional relationship with the client.

    (7)   The experience, reputation, and ability of the lawyer or lawyers performing the services.

    (8)   Whether the fee is fixed or contingent.[89]

---

86. This provision is included to conform to action taken by the ABA House of Delegates at the Mid-Winter Meeting, January, 1969.

87. *See* ABA CANON 12.

88. The charging of a "clearly excessive fee' is a ground for discipline. State ex rel. Nebraska State Bar Ass'n. v. Richards. 165 Neb. 80, 90, 84 N.W.2d 136, 143 (1957).

"An attorney has the right to contract for any fee he chooses so long as it is not excessive (see Opinion 190), and this Committee is not concerned with the amount of such fees unless so excessive as to constitute a misappropriation of the client's funds (see Opinion 27)." *ABA Opinion* 320 (1968).

Cf. ABA Opinions 209 (1940), 190 (1939), and 27 (1930) and State ex rel. Lee v. Buchanan, 191 So.2d 33 (Fla. 1966).

89. *Cf.* ABA CANON 13; *see generally* MACKINNON, CONTINGENT FEES FOR LEGAL SERVICES (1964) (*A Report of the American Bar Foundation*).

(C)   A lawyer shall not enter into an arrangement for, charge, or collect a contingent fee for representing a defendant in a criminal case.[90]

DR 2-107   Division of Fees Among Lawyers

(A)   A lawyer shall not divide a fee for legal services with another lawyer who is not a partner in or associate of his law firm or law office, unless:
   (1)   The client consents to employment of the other lawyer after a full disclosure that a division of fees will be made.
   (2)   The division is made in proportion to the services performed and responsibility assumed by each.[91]
   (3)   The total fee of the lawyers does not clearly exceed reasonable compensation for all legal services they rendered the client.[92]

(B)   This Disciplinary Rule does not prohibit payment to a former partner or associate pursuant to a separation or retirement agreement.

DR 2-108   Agreements Restricting the Practice of a Lawyer

(A)   A lawyer shall not be a party to or participate in a partnership or employment agreement with another lawyer that restricts the right of a lawyer to practice law after the termination of a relationship created by the agreement, except as a condition to payment of retirement benefits.[93]

90. "Contingent fees, whether in civil or criminal cases, are a special concern of the law. . . .
"In criminal cases, the rule is stricter because of the danger of corrupting justice. The second part of Section 542 of the Restatement [of Contracts] reads; 'A bargain to conduct a criminal case . . . in consideration of a promise of a fee contingent on success is illegal. . . .' " Peyton v. Margiotti; 398 Pa. 86, 156 A.2d 865, 967 (1959).
"The third area of practice in which the use of the contingent fee is generally considered to be prohibited is the prosecution and defense of criminal cases. However, there are so few cases, and these are predominantly old, that it is doubtful that there can be said to be any current law on the subject. . . . In the absence of cases on the validity of contingent fees for defense attorneys, it is necessary to rely on the consensus among commentators that such a fee is void as against public policy. The nature of criminal practice itself makes unlikely the use of contingent fee contracts." MACKINNON, CONTINGENT FEES FOR LEGAL SERVICES 52 (1964) (A Report of the American Bar Foundation).
91. See ABA CANON 34 and ABA Opinions 316 (1967) and 294 (1958); see generally ABA Opinions 265 (1945), 204 (1940), 190 (1939), 171 (1937), 153 (1936), 97 (1933), 63 (1932), 28 (1930), 27 (1930), and 18 (1930).
92. "Canon 12 contemplates that a lawyer's fee should not exceed the value of the services rendered. . . .
"Canon 12 applies, whether joint or separate fees are charged [by associate attorneys] . . . ." ABA Opinion 204 (1940).
93. "[A] general covenant restricting an employed lawyer, after leaving the employment, from practicing in the community for a stated period, appears to this Committee to be an unwarranted restriction on the right of a lawyer to choose where he will practice and inconsistent with our professional status. Accordingly, the Committee is of the opinion it would be

(B)   In connection with the settlement of a controversy or suit, a lawyer shall not enter into an agreement that restricts his right to practice law.

DR 2-109   Acceptance of Employment

(A)   A lawyer shall not accept employment on behalf of a person if he knows or it is obvious that such person wishes to:
  (1)   Bring a legal action, conduct a defense, or assert a position in litigation, or otherwise have steps taken for him, merely for the purpose of harassing or maliciously injuring any person.[94]
  (2)   Present a claim or defense in litigation that is not warranted under existing law, unless it can be supported by good faith argument for an extension, modification, or reversal of existing law.

DR 2-110   Withdrawal from Employment[95]

(A)   In general.
  (1)   If permission for withdrawal from employment is required by the rules of a tribunal, a lawyer shall not withdraw from employment in a proceeding before that tribunal without its permission.
  (2)   In any event, a lawyer shall not withdraw from employment until he has taken reasonable steps to avoid foreseeable prejudice to the rights of his client, including giving due notice to his client, allowing time for employment of other counsel, delivering to the client all papers and property to which the client is entitled, and complying with applicable laws and rules.
  (3)   A lawyer who withdraws from employment shall refund promptly any part of a fee paid in advance that has not been earned.
(B)   Mandatory withdrawal.
      A lawyer representing a client before a tribunal, with its permission if required by its rules, shall withdraw from employment, and a lawyer representing a client in other matters shall withdraw from employment, if:

---

improper for the employing lawyer to require the covenant and likewise for the employed lawyer to agree to it." *ABA Opinion* 300 (1961).

94. *See* ABA CANON 30.

"*Rule 13....* A member of the State Bar shall not accept employment to prosecute or defend a case solely out of spite, or solely for the purpose of harassing or delaying another...." CAL. BUSINESS AND PROFESSIONS CODE §6067 (West 1962).

95. *Cf.* ABA CANON 44.

(1) He knows or it is obvious that his client is bringing the legal action, conducting the defense, or asserting a position in the litigation, or is otherwise having steps taken for him, merely for the purpose of harassing or maliciously injuring any person.

(2) He knows or it is obvious that his continued employment will result in violation of a Disciplinary Rule.[96]

(3) His mental or physical condition renders it unreasonably difficult for him to carry out the employment effectively.

(4) He is discharged by his client.

(C) Permissive withdrawal.[97]

If DR 2-110 (B) is not applicable, a lawyer may not request permission to withdraw in matters pending before a tribunal, and may not withdraw in other matters, unless such request or such withdrawal is because:

(1) His client:
   (a) Insists upon presenting a claim or defense that is not warranted under existing law and cannot be supported by good faith argument for an extension, modification, or reversal of existing law.[98]
   (b) Personally seeks to pursue an illegal course of conduct.
   (c) Insists that the lawyer pursue a course of conduct that is illegal or that is prohibited under the Disciplinary Rules.
   (d) By other conduct renders it unreasonably difficult for the lawyer to carry out his employment effectively.
   (e) Insists, in a matter not pending before a tribunal, that the lawyer engage in conduct that is contrary to the judgment and advice of the lawyer but not prohibited under the Disciplinary Rules.
   (f) Deliberately disregards an agreement or obligation to the lawyer as to expenses or fees.

(2) His continued employment is likely to result in a violation of a Disciplinary Rule.

(3) His inability to work with co-counsel indicates that the best interests of the client likely will be served by withdrawal.

(4) His mental or physical condition renders it difficult for him to carry out the employment effectively.

(5) His client knowingly and freely assents to termination of his employment.

(6) He believes in good faith, in a proceeding pending before a tribunal, that the tribunal will find the existence of other good cause for withdrawal.

96. *See also* Code of Professional Responsibility, DR 5-102 and DR 5-105.
97. *Cf.* ABA CANON 4.
98. *Cf.* Anders v. California, 386 U.S. 738, 18 L. Ed. 2d 493, 87 S. Ct. 1396 (1967), *rehearing denied*, 388 U.S. 924, 18 L. Ed. 2d 1377, 87 S. Ct. 2094 (1967).

CANON 3
A LAWYER SHOULD ASSIST IN PREVENTING THE UNAUTHORIZED PRACTICE OF LAW

Ethical Considerations

EC 3-1   The prohibition against the practice of law by a layman is grounded in the need of the public for integrity and competence of those who undertake to render legal services. Because of the fiduciary and personal character of the lawyer-client relationship and the inherently complex nature of our legal system, the public can better be assured of the requisite responsibility and competence if the practice of law is confined to those who are subject to the requirements and regulations imposed upon members of the legal profession.

EC 3-2   The sensitive variations in the considerations that bear on legal determinations often make it difficult even for a lawyer to exercise appropriate professional judgment, and it is therefore essential that the personal nature of the relationship of client and lawyer be preserved. Competent professional judgment is the product of a trained familiarity with law and legal processes, a disciplined, analytical approach to legal problems, and a firm ethical commitment.

EC 3-3   A non-lawyer who undertakes to handle legal matters is not governed as to integrity or legal competence by the same rules that govern the conduct of a lawyer. A lawyer is not only subject to that regulation but also is committed to high standards of ethical conduct. The public interest is best served in legal matters by a regulated profession committed to such standards.[1] The Disciplinary Rules protect the public in that they prohibit a lawyer from seeking employment by improper overtures, from acting in cases of divided loyalties, and from submitting to the control of others in the exercise of his judgment. Moreover, a person who entrusts legal matters to a lawyer is protected by the attorney-client privilege and by the duty of the lawyer to hold inviolate the confidences and secrets of his client.

EC 3-4   A layman who seeks legal services often is not in a position to judge whether he will receive proper professional attention. The entrustment of a legal matter may well involve the confidences, the reputation, the property, the freedom, or even the life of the client. Proper protection of members of the public demands that no person be permitted to act in the

---

1. "The condemnation of the unauthorized practice of law is designed to protect the public from legal services by persons unskilled in the law. The prohibition of lay intermediaries is intended to insure the loyalty of the lawyer to the client unimpaired by intervening and possibly conflicting interests." Cheatham, *Availability of Legal Services: The Responsibility of the Individual Lawyer and of the Organized Bar,* 12 U.C.L.A. L. REV. 438, 439 (1965).

confidential and demanding capacity of a lawyer unless he is subject to the regulations of the legal profession.

EC 3-5   It is neither necessary nor desirable to attempt the formulation of a single, specific definition of what constitutes the practice of law.[2] Functionally, the practice of law relates to the rendition of services for others that call for the professional judgment of a lawyer. The essence of the professional judgment of the lawyer is his educated ability to relate the general body and philosophy of law to a specific legal problem of a client; and thus, the public interest will be better served if only lawyers are permitted to act in matters involving professional judgment. Where this professional judgment is not involved, non-lawyers, such as court clerks, police officers, abstracters, and many governmental employees, may engage in occupations that require a special knowledge of law in certain areas. But the services of a lawyer are essential in the public interest whenever the exercise of professional legal judgment is required.

EC 3-6   A lawyer often delegates tasks to clerks, secretaries, and other lay persons. Such delegation is proper if the lawyer maintains a direct relationship with his client, supervises the delegated work, and has complete professional responsibility for the work product.[3] This delegation enables a lawyer to render legal service more economically and efficiently.

EC 3-7   The prohibition against a non-lawyer practicing law does not prevent a layman from representing himself, for then he is ordinarily exposing only himself to possible injury. The purpose of the legal profession is to

2. What constitutes unauthorized practice of the law in a particular jurisdiction is a matter for determination by the courts of that jurisdiction." *ABA Opinion 198 (1939).*

"In the light of the historical development of the lawyer's functions, it is impossible to lay down an exhaustive definition of 'the practice of law' by attempting to enumerate every conceivable act performed by lawyers in the normal course of their work." State Bar of Arizona v. Arizona Land Title & Trust Co., 90 Ariz., 76, 87, 366 P.2d 1, 8-9 (1961), *modified*, 91 Ariz. 293, 371 P.2d 1020 (1962).

3. "A lawyer can employ lay secretaries, lay investigators, lay detectives, lay researchers, accountants, lay scriveners, nonlawyer draftsmen or nonlawyer researchers. In fact, he may employ nonlawyers to do any task for him except counsel clients about law matters, engage directly in the practice of law, appear in court or appear in formal proceedings a part of the judicial process, so long as it is he who takes the work and vouches for it to the client and becomes responsible to the client." *ABA Opinions 316 (1967).*

ABA Opinion 316 (1967) also stated that if a lawyer practices law as part of a law firm which includes lawyers from several states, he may delegate tasks to firm members in other states so long as he "is the person who, on behalf of the firm, vouched for the work of all of the others and, with the client and in the courts, did the legal acts defined by that state as the practice of law."

"A lawyer cannot delegate his professional responsibility to a law student employed in his office. He may avail himself of the assistance of the student in many of the fields of the lawyer's work, such as examination of case law, finding and interviewing witnesses, making collections of claims, examining court records, delivering papers, conveying important messages, and other similar matters. But the student is not permitted, until he is admitted to the Bar, to perform the professional functions of a lawyer, such as conducting court trials, giving professional advice to clients or drawing legal documents for them. The student in all his work must act as agent for the lawyer employing him, who must supervise his work and be responsible for his good conduct." *ABA Opinions* 85 (1932).

make educated legal representation available to the public; but anyone who does not wish to avail himself of such representation is not required to do so. Even so, the legal profession should help members of the public to recognize legal problems and to understand why it may be unwise for them to act for themselves in matters having legal consequences.

EC 3-8   Since a lawyer should not aid or encourage a layman to practice law, he should not practice law in association with a layman or otherwise share legal fees with a layman.[4] This does not mean, however, that the pecuniary value of the interest of a deceased lawyer in his firm or practice may not be paid to his estate or specified persons such as his widow or heirs.[5] In like manner, profit-sharing retirement plans of a lawyer or law firm which include non-lawyer office employees are not improper.[6] These limited exceptions to the rule against sharing legal fees with laymen are permissible since they do not aid or encourage laymen to practice law.

EC 3-9   Regulations of the practice of law is accomplished principally by the respective states.[7] Authority to engage in the practice of law conferred in any jurisdiction is not per se a grant of the right to practice elsewhere, and it is improper for a lawyer to engage in practice where he is not permitted by law or by court order to do so. However, the demands of business and the mobility of our society pose distinct problems in the regulation of the practice of law by the states.[8] In furtherance of the public interest, the legal profession should discourage regulation that unreasonably imposes territo-

4. "No division of fees for legal services is proper, except with another lawyer . . ." ABA CANON 34. Otherwise, according to *ABA Opinion* 316 (1967), "[t]he Canons of Ethics do not examine into the method by which such persons are remunerated by the lawyer. . . . They may be paid a salary, a per diem charge, a flat fee, a contract price, etc."
See ABA CANONS 33 and 47.

5. "Many partnership agreements provide that the active partners, on the death of any one of them, are to make payments to the estate or to the nominee of a deceased partner on a pre-determined formula. It is only where the effect of such an arrangement is to make the estate or nominee a member of the partnership along with the surviving partners that it is prohibited by *Canon 34*. Where the payments are made in accordance with a pre-existing agreement entered into by the deceased partner during his lifetime and providing for a fixed method for determining their amount based upon the value of services rendered during the partner's lifetime and providing for a fixed period over which the payments are to be made, this is not the case. Under these circumstances, whether the payments are considered to be delayed payment of compensation earned but withheld during the partner's lifetime, or whether they are considered to be an approximation of his interest in matters pending at the time of his death, is immaterial. In either event, as Henry S. Drinker says in his book, LEGAL ETHICS, at page 189: 'It would seem, however, that a reasonable agreement to pay the estate a proportion of the receipts for a reasonable period is a proper practical settlement for the lawyer's services to his retirement or death.'" *ABA Opinion* 308 (1963).

6. *Cf. ABA Opinion* 311 (1964).

7. "That the States have broad power to regulate the practice of law is, of course, beyond question." United Mine Workers v. Ill. State Bar Ass'n, 389 U.S. 217, 222 (1967).
"It is a matter of law, not of ethics, as to where an individual may practice law. Each state has its own rules." *ABA Opinion* 316 (1967).

8. "Much of clients' business crosses state lines. People are mobile, moving from state to state. Many metropolitan areas cross state lines. It is common today to have a single economic and social community involving more than one state. The business of a single client may involve legal problems in several states." *ABA Opinion* 316 (1967).

rial limitations upon the right of a lawyer to handle the legal affairs to obtain the services of a lawyer of his choice in all matters including the presentation of a contested matter in a tribunal before which the lawyer is not permanently admitted to practice.[9]

Disciplinary Rules

DR 3-101   Aiding Unauthorized Practice of Law[10]

(A)   A lawyer shall not aid a non-lawyer in the unauthorized practice of law.[11]

(B)   A lawyer shall not practice law in a jurisdiction where to do so would be in violation of regulations of the profession in that jurisdiction.[12]

DR 3-102   Dividing Legal Fees with a Non-Lawyer

(A)   A lawyer or law firm shall not share legal fees with a non-lawyer,[13] except that:
    (1)   An agreement by a lawyer with his firm, partner, or associate may provide for the payment of money, over a reasonable period of time after his death, to his estate or to one or more specified persons.[14]
    (2)   A lawyer who undertakes to complete unfinished legal business of a deceased lawyer may pay to the estate of the deceased lawyer that proportion of the total compensation which fairly represents the services rendered by the deceased lawyer.

9. "[W]e reaffirmed the general principle that legal services to New Jersey residents with respect to New Jersey matters may ordinarily be furnished only by New Jersey counsel; but we pointed out that there may be multistate transactions where strict adherence to this thesis would not be in the public interest and that, under the circumstances, it would have been not only more costly to the client but also 'grossly impractical and inefficient' to have had the settlement negotiations conducted by separate lawyers from different states." In re Estate of Waring, 47 N.J. 367, 376, 221 A.2d 193, 197 (1966).
    Cf. ABA Opinion 316 (1967).
    10. Conduct permitted by the Disciplinary Rules of Canons 2 and 5 does not violate DR 3-101.
    11. *See* ABA CANON 47.
    12. It should be noted, however, that a lawyer may engage in conduct, otherwise prohibited by this Disciplinary Rule, where such conduct is authorized by preemptive federal legislation. *See* Sperry v. Florida, 373 U.S. 379, 10 L. Ed. 2d 428, 83 S. Ct. 1322 (1963).
    13. *See* ABA CANON 34 and *ABA Opinions* 316 (1967), 180 (1938), and 48 (1931).
    "The receiving attorney shall not under any guise or form share his fee for legal services with a lay agency, personal or corporate, without prejudice, however, to the right of the lay forwarder to change and collect from the creditor proper compensation for non-legal services rendered by the law [*sic*] forwarder which are separate and apart from the services performed by the receiving attorney." *ABA Opinion* 294 (1958).
    14. *See* ABA *Opinion* 266 (1945).

(3)   A lawyer or law firm may include nonlawyer employees in a compensation or retirement plan, even though the plan is based in whole or in part on a profit-sharing arrangement,[15] providing such plan does not circumvent another Disciplinary Rule.[16]

DR 3-103   Forming a Partnership with a Non-Lawyer

(A)   A lawyer shall not form a partnership with a non-lawyer if any of the activities of the partnership consist of the practice of law.[17]

CANON 4
A LAWYER SHOULD PRESERVE THE CONFIDENCES AND SECRETS OF A CLIENT

Ethical Considerations

EC 4-1   Both the fiduciary relationship existing between lawyer and client and the proper functioning of the legal system require the preservation by the lawyer of confidences and secrets of one who has employed or sought to employ him.[1] A client must feel free to discuss whatever he wishes with his

15. *Cf. ABA Opinion* 311 (1964).
16. *See ABA Opinion* i1440.
17. *See* ABA CANON 33; *cf. ABA Opinions* 239 (1942) and 201 (1940).
ABA Opinion 316 (1967) states that lawyers licensed in different jurisdictions may, under certain conditions, enter "into an arrangement for the practice of law" and that a lawyer licensed in State A is not, for such purpose, a layman in State B.
1. *See* ABA CANONS 6 and 37 and *ABA Opinion* 287 (1953).
"The reason underlying the rule with respect to confidential communications between attorney and client is well stated in MECHEM ON AGENCY, 2d Ed., Vol. 2, §2297, as follows: 'The purposes and necessities of the relation between a client and his attorney require, in many cases, on the part of the client, the fullest and freest disclosures to the attorney of the client's objects, motives and acts. This disclosure is made in the strictest confidence, relying upon the attorney's honor and fidelity. To permit the attorney to reveal to others what is so disclosed, would be not only a gross violation of a sacred trust upon his part, but it would utterly destroy and prevent the usefulness and benefits to be derived from professional assistance. Based upon considerations of public policy, therefore, the law wisely declares that all confidential communications and disclosures, made by a client to his legal adviser for the purpose of obtaining his professional aid or advice, shall be strictly privileged; — that the attorney shall not be permitted, without the consent of his client, — and much less will he be compelled — to reveal or disclose communications made to him under such circumstances." *ABA Opinion* 250 (1943).
"While it is true that complete revelation of relevant facts should be encouraged for trial purposes, nevertheless an attorney's dealings with his client, if both are sincere, and if the dealings involve more than mere technical matters, should be immune to discovery proceedings. There must be freedom from fear of revealment of matters disclosed to an attorney because of the peculiarly intimate relationship existing." Ellis-Foster Co. v. Union Carbide & Carbon Corp., 159 F.Supp. 917, 919 (D.N.J. 1958).
Cf. ABA Opinions 314 (1965), 274 (1946), and 268 (1945).

lawyer and a lawyer must be equally free to obtain information beyond that volunteered by his client.[2] A lawyer should be fully informed of all the facts of the matter he is handling in order for his client to obtain the full advantage of our legal system. It is for the lawyer in the exercise of his independent professional judgment to separate the relevant and important from the irrelevant and unimportant. The observance of the ethical obligation of a lawyer to hold inviolate the confidences and secrets of his client not only facilitates the full development of facts essential to proper representation of the client but also encourages laymen to seek early legal assistance.

EC 4-2   The obligation to protect confidences and secrets obviously does not preclude a lawyer from revealing information when his client consents after full disclosure,[3] when necessary to perform his professional employment, when permitted by a Disciplinary Rule, or when required by law. Unless the client otherwise directs, a lawyer may disclose the affairs of his client to partners or associates of his firm. It is a matter of common knowledge that the normal operation of a law office exposes confidential professional information to non-lawyer employees of the office, particularly secretaries and those having access to the files; and this obligates a lawyer to exercise care in selecting and training his employees so that the sanctity of all confidences and secrets of his clients may be preserved. If the obligation extends to two or more clients as to the same information, a lawyer should obtain the permission of all before revealing the information. A lawyer must always be sensitive to the rights and wishes of his client and act scrupulously in the making of decisions which may involve the disclosure of information obtained in his professional relationship.[4] Thus, in the absence of consent of his client after full disclosure, a lawyer should not associate another lawyer in the handling of a matter; nor should he, in the absence of consent, seek counsel from another lawyer if there is a reasonable possibility that the identity of the client or his confidences or secrets would be revealed to such lawyer. Both social amenities and professional duty should cause a lawyer to shun indiscreet conversations concerning his clients.

2. "While it is the great purpose of law to ascertain the truth, there is the countervailing necessity of insuring the right of every person to freely and fully confer and confide in one having knowledge of the law, and skilled in its practice, in order that the former may have adequate advice and a proper defense. This assistance can be made safely and readily available only when the client is free from the consequences of apprehension of disclosure by reason of the subsequent statements of the skilled lawyer. Baird v. Koerner, 279 F.2d 623, 629-30 (9th Cir. 1960).
    Cf. ABA Opinion 150 (1936).
3. "Where . . . [a client] knowingly and after full disclosure participates in a [legal fee] financing plan which requires the furnishing of certain information to the bank, clearly by his conduct he has waived any privilege as to that information." ABA Opinion 320 (1968).
4. "The lawyer must decide when he takes a case whether it is a suitable one for him to undertake and after this decision is made, he is not justified in turning against his client by exposing injurious evidence entrusted to him. . . . [D]oing something intrinsically regrettable, because the only alternative involves worse consequences, is a necessity in every profession." WILLISTON, LIFE AND LAW 271 (1940).
    Cf. ABA Opinions 177 (1938) and 83 (1932).

EC 4-3   Unless the client otherwise directs, it is not improper for a lawyer to give limited information from his files to an outside agency necessary for statistical, bookkeeping, accounting, data processing, banking, printing, or other legitimate purposes, provided he exercises due care in the selection of the agency and warns the agency that the information must be kept confidential.

EC 4-4   The attorney-client privilege is more limited than the ethical obligation of a lawyer to guard the confidences and secrets of his client. This ethical precept, unlike the evidentiary privilege, exists without regard to the nature or source of information or the fact that others share the knowledge. A lawyer should endeavor to act in a manner which preserves the evidentiary privilege; for example, he should avoid professional discussions in the presence of persons to whom the privilege does not extend. A lawyer owes an obligation to advise the client of the attorney-client privilege and timely to assert the privilege unless it is waived by the client.

EC 4-5   A lawyer should not use information acquired in the course of the representation of a client to the disadvantage of the client and a lawyer should not use, except with the consent of his client after full disclosure, such information for his own purposes.[5] Likewise, a lawyer should be diligent in his efforts to prevent the misuse of such information by his employees and associates.[6] Care should be exercised by a lawyer to prevent the disclosure of the confidences and secrets of one client to another,[7] and no employment should be accepted that might require such disclosure.

EC 4-6   The obligation of a lawyer to preserve the confidences and secrets of his client continues after the termination of his employment.[8] Thus a lawyer should not attempt to sell a law practice as a going business because, among other reasons, to do so would involve the disclosure of confidences and secrets.[9] A lawyer should also provide for the protection of the confidences and secrets of his client following the termination of the practice of the lawyer, whether termination is due to death, disability, or retirement. For example, a lawyer might provide for the personal papers of the client to be returned to him and for the papers of the lawyer to be delivered to another lawyer or to be destroyed. In determining the method of disposition, the instructions and wishes of the client should be a dominant consideration.

5. *See* ABA CANON 11.
6. *See* ABA CANON 37.
7. *See* ABA CANONS 6 and 37.
"[A]n attorney must not accept professional employment against a client or a former client which will, or even *may* require him to use confidential information obtained by the attorney in the course of his professional relations with such client regarding the subject matter of the employment . . . ." *ABA Opinion* 165 (1936).
8. *See* ABA CANON 37.
"Confidential communications between an attorney and his client, made because of the relationship and concerning the subject-matter of the attorney's employment, are generally privileged from disclosure without the consent of the client, and this privilege outlasts the attorney's employment. *Canon 37.*" *ABA Opinion* 154 (1936).
9. *Cf. ABA Opinion* 266 (1945).

Disciplinary Rules

DR 4-101 Preservation of Confidences and Secrets of a Client[10]

(A) "Confidence" refers to information protected by the attorney-client privilege under applicable law, and "secret" refers to other information gained in the professional relationship that the client has requested be held inviolate or the disclosure of which would be embarrassing or would be likely to be detrimental to the client.

(B) Except when permitted under DR 4-101 (C), a lawyer shall not knowingly:

    (1) Reveal a confidence or secret of his client.[11]

    (2) Use a confidence or secret of his client to the disadvantage of the client.

    (3) Use a confidence or secret of his client for the advantage of himself[12] or of a third person,[13] unless the client consents after full disclosure.

(C) A lawyer may reveal:

    (1) Confidences or secrets with the consent of the client or clients affected, but only after a full disclosure to them.[14]

---

10. *See* ABA CANON 37; *cf.* ABA Canon 6.

11. §6068 . . . It is the duty of an attorney: . . .

"(e) To maintain inviolate the confidence, and at every peril to himself to preserve the secrets, of his client." CAL. BUSINESS AND PROFESSIONS CODE §6068 (West 1962). Virtually the same provision is found in the Oregon statutes. ORE. REV. STATS. ch. 9 §9.460(5).

"Communications between lawyer and client are privileged (WIGMORE ON EVIDENCE, 3d Ed., Vol. 8 §§2290-2329). The modern theory underlying the privilege is subjective and is to give the client freedom of apprehension in consulting his legal adviser (*ibid.*, §2290, p. 548). The privilege applies to communications made in seeking legal advice for any purpose (*ibid.*, §2294, p. 563). The mere circumstance that the advice is given without charge therefor does not nullify the privilege (*ibid.*, §2303)." *ABA Opinion* 216 (1941).

"It is the duty of an attorney to maintain the confidence and preserve inviolate the secrets of his client. . . ." *ABA Opinion* 155 (1936).

12. *See* ABA CANON 11.

"The provision respecting employment is in accord with the general rule announced in the adjudicated cases that a lawyer may not make use of knowledge or information acquired by him through his professional relations with his client, or in the conduct of his client's business, to his own advantage or profit (7 C.J.S., §125, p. 958; Healy v. Gray, 184 Iowa 111, 168 N.W. 222; Baumgardner v. Hudson, D.C. App., 277 F. 552; Goodrum v. Clement, D.C. App., 277 F. 586)." *ABA Opinion* 250 (1943).

13. *See ABA Opinion* 177 (1938).

14. "[A lawyer] may not divulge confidential communications, information, and secrets imparted to him by the client or acquired during their professional relations, unless he is authorized to do so by the client (People v. Gerold, 265 Ill. 448, 107 N.E. 165, 178; Murphy v. Riggs 238 Mich. 151, 213 N.W. 110, 112; Opinion of this Committee, No. 91)." *ABA Opinion* 202 (1940).

Cf. ABA Opinion 91 (1933).

(2)   Confidences or secrets when permitted under Disciplinary Rules or required by law or court order.[15]

(3)   The intention of his client to commit a crime[16] and the information necessary to prevent the crime.[17]

(4)   Confidences or secrets necessary to estabish or collect his fee[18] or to defend himself or his employees or associates against an accusation of wrongful conduct.[19]

15. "A defendent in a criminal case when admitted to bail is not only regarded as in the custody of his bail, but he is also in the custody of the law, and admission to bail does not deprive the court of its inherent power to deal with the person of the prisoner. Being in lawful custody, the defendent is guilty of an escape when he gains his liberty before he is delivered in due process of law, and is guilty of a separate offense for which he may be punished. In failing to disclose his client's whereabouts as a fugitive under these circumstances the attorney would not only be aiding his client to escape trial on the charge for which he was indicted, but would likewise be aiding him in evading prosecution for the additional offense of escape.

"It is the opinion of the committee that under such circumstances the attorney's knowledge of his client's whereabouts is not privileged, and that he may be disciplined for failing to disclose that information to the proper authorities. . . ." *ABA Opinion* 155 (1936).

"We held in *Opinion* 155 that a communication by a client to his attorney in respect to the future commission of an unlawful act or to a continuing wrong is not privileged from disclosure. Public policy forbids that the relation of attorney and client should be used to conceal wrongdoing on the part of the client. . . .

"When an attorney representing a defendant in a criminal case applies on his behalf for probation or suspension of sentence, he represents to the court, by implication at least, that his client will abide by the terms and conditions of the court's order. When that attorney is later advised of a violation of that order, it is his duty to advise his client of the consequences of his act, and endeavor to prevent a continuance of the wrongdoing. If his client thereafter persists in violating the terms and conditions of his probation, it is the duty of the attorney as an officer of the court to advise the proper authorities concerning his client's conduct. Such information, even though coming to the attorney from the client in the course of his professional relations with respect to other matters in which he represents the defendant, is not privileged from disclosure. . . ."

See ABA Opinion 156 (1936).

16. *ABA Opinion* 314 (1965) indicates that a lawyer must disclose even the confidences of his clients if "the facts in the attorney's possession indicate beyond reasonable doubt that a crime will be committed."

See ABA Opinion 155 (1936).

17. *See* ABA CANON 37 and *ABA Opinion* 202 (1940).

18. *Cf. ABA Opinion* 250 (1943).

19. *See* ABA CANON 37 and *ABA Opinions* 202 (1940) and 19 (1930).

"[T]he adjudicated cases recognize an exception to the rule [that a lawyer shall not reveal the confidences of his client], where disclosure is necessary to protect the attorney's interests arising out of the relation of attorney and client in which disclosure was made.

"The exception is stated in MECHEM ON AGENCY, 2d Ed., Vo. 2, §2313, as follows: 'But the attorney may disclose information received from the client when it becomes necessary for his own protection, as if the client should bring an action against the attorney for negligence or misconduct, and it became necessary for the attorney to show what his instructions were, or what was the nature of the duty which the client expected him to perform. So if it became necessary for the attorney to bring an action against the client, the client's privilege could not prevent the attorney from disclosing what was essential as a means of obtaining or defending his own rights.'

"Mr. Jones, in his COMMENTARIES ON EVIDENCE, 2d Ed., Vol. 5, §2165, states the exception thus: 'It has frequently been held that the rule as to privileged communications does not apply when litigation arises between attorney and client to the extent that their communications are relevant to the issue. In such cases, if the disclosure of privileged communications becomes necessary to protect the attorney's rights, he is released from those obligations of

(D)   A lawyer shall exercise reasonable care to prevent his employees, associates, and others whose services are utilized by him from disclosing or
using confidences or secrets of a client, except that a lawyer may reveal
the information allowed by DR 4-101 (C) through an employee.

CANON 5
A LAWYER SHOULD EXERCISE
INDEPENDENT PROFESSIONAL
JUDGMENT ON BEHALF OF A CLIENT

Ethical Considerations

EC 5-1   The professional judgment of a lawyer should be exercised, within
the bounds of the law, solely for the benefit of his client and free of compro-
mising influences and loyalties.[1] Neither his personal interests, the interests
of other clients, nor the desires of third persons should be permitted to dilute his loyalty to his client.

---

secrecy which the law places upon him. He should not, however, disclose more than is necessary
for his own protection. It would be a manifest injustice to allow the client to take advantage of
the rule of exclusion as to professional confidence to the prejudice of his attorney, or that it
should be carried to the extent of depriving the attorney of the means of obtaining or defending his own rights. In such cases the attorney is exempted from the obligations of secrecy.' "
ABA Opinion 250 (1943).
    1. *Cf.* ABA CANON 35.
    "[A lawyer's] fiduciary duty is of the highest order and he must not represent interests ad-
verse to those of the client. It is true that because of his professional responsibility and the
confidence and trust which his client may legitimately repose in him, he must adhere to a high
standard of honesty, integrity and good faith in dealing with his client. He is not permitted to
take advantage of his position or superior knowledge to impose upon the client; nor to conceal
facts or law, nor in any way deceive him without being held responsible therefor." Smoot v.
Lund, 13 Utah 2d 168, 172, 369 P.2d 933, 936 (1962).
    "When a client engages the services of a lawyer in a given piece of business he is entitled to
feel that, until that business is finally disposed of in some manner, he has the undivided loyalty
of the one upon whom he looks as his advocate and champion. If, as in this case, he is sued and
his home attached by his own attorney, who is representing him in another matter, all feeling of
loyalty is necessarily destroyed, and the profession is exposed to the charge that it is interested
only in money." Grievance Comm. v. Rattner, 152 Conn. 59, 65, 203 A.2d 82, 84 (1964).
    "One of the cardinal principles confronting every attorney in the representation of a client is
the requirement of complete loyalty and service in good faith to the best of his ability. In a
criminal case the client is entitled to a fair trial, but not a perfect one. These are fundamental
requirements of due process under the Fourteenth Amendment.... The same principles are
applicable in Sixth Amendment cases (not pertinent herein) and suggest that an attorney
should have no conflict of interest and that he must devote his full and faithful efforts toward
the defense of his client." Johns v. Smyth, 176 F. Supp. 949, 952 (E.D. Va. 1959), *modified,*
United States ex rel. Wilkins v. Banmiller, 205 F. Supp. 123, 128 n. 5 (E.D. Pa. 1962), *aff'd,* 325
F.2d 514 (3d Cir. 1963), *cert. denied,* 379 U.S. 847, 13 L.Ed. 2d 51, 85 S.Ct. 87 (1964).

Interests of a Lawyer That May Affect His Judgment

EC 5-2   A lawyer should not accept proffered employment if his personal interests or desires will, or there is a reasonable probability that they will, affect adversely the advice to be given or services to be rendered the prospective client.[2] After accepting employment, a lawyer carefully should refrain from acquiring a property right or assuming a position that would tend to make his judgment less protective of the interests of his client.

EC 5-3   The self-interest of a lawyer resulting from his ownership of property in which his client also has an interest or which may affect property of his client may interfere with the exercise of free judgment on behalf of his client. If such interference would occur with respect to a prospective client, a lawyer should decline employment proffered by him. After accepting employment, a lawyer should not acquire property rights that would adversely affect his professional judgment in the representation of his client. Even if the property interests of a lawyer do not presently interfere with the exercise of his independent judgment, but the likelihood of interference can reasonably be foreseen by him, a lawyer should explain the situation to his client and should decline employment or withdraw unless the client consents to the continuance of the relationship after full disclosure. A lawyer should not seek to persuade his client to permit him to invest in an undertaking of his client nor make improper use of his professional relationship to influence his client to invest in an enterprise in which the lawyer is interested.

EC 5-4   If, in the course of his representation of a client, a lawyer is permitted to receive from his client a beneficial ownership in publication rights relating to the subject matter of the employment, he may be tempted to subordinate the interests of his client to his own anticipated pecuniary gain. For example, a lawyer in a criminal case who obtains from his client television, radio, motion picture, newspaper, magazine, book, or other publication rights with respect to the case may be influenced, consciously or unconsciously, to a course of conduct that will enhance the value of his publication rights to the prejudice of his client. To prevent these potentially differing interests, such arrangements should be scrupulously avoided prior

2. "Attorneys must not allow their private interests to conflict with those of their clients. . . . They owe their entire devotion to the interests of their clients." United States v. Anonymous, 215 F. Supp. 111, 113 (E.D. Tenn. 1963).

"[T]he court [below] concluded that a firm may not accept any action against a person whom they are presently representing even though there is no relationship between the two cases. In arriving at this conclusion, the court cites an opinion of the Committee on Professional Ethics of the New York County Lawyers' Association which stated in part: 'While under the circumstances . . . there may be no actual conflict of interest . . . "maintenance of public confidence in the Bar requires an attorney who has accepted representation of a client to decline, while representing such client, any employment from an adverse party in any matter even though wholly unrelated to the original retainer." See Question and Answer No. 350, N.Y. County L. Ass'n, Questions and Answer No. 450 (June 21, 1956).' " Grievance Comm. v. Rattner, 152 Conn. 59, 65, 203 A.2d 82, 84 (1964).

to the termination of all aspects of the matter giving rise to the employment, even though his employment has previously ended.

EC 5-5   A lawyer should not suggest to his client that a gift be made to himself or for his benefit. If a lawyer accepts a gift from his client, he is peculiarly susceptible to the charge that he unduly influenced or over-reached the client. If a client voluntarily offers to make a gift to his lawyer, the lawyer may accept the gift, but before doing so, he should urge that his client secure disinterested advice from an independent, competent person who is cognizant of all the circumstances.[3] Other than in exceptional circumstances, a lawyer should insist that an instrument in which his client desires to name him beneficially be prepared by another lawyer selected by the client.[4]

EC 5-6   A lawyer should not consciously influence a client to name him as executor, trustee, or lawyer in an instrument. In those cases where a client wishes to name his lawyer as such, care should be taken by the lawyer to avoid even the appearance of impropriety.[5]

EC 5-7   The possibility of an adverse effect upon the exercise of free judgment by a lawyer on behalf of his client during litigation generally makes it undesirable for the lawyer to acquire a proprietary interest in the cause of his client or otherwise to become financially interested in the outcome of the litigation.[6] However, it is not improper for a lawyer to protect his right to collect a fee for his services by the assertion of legally permissible liens, even though by doing so he may acquire an interest in the outcome of litigation. Although a contingent fee arrangement[7] gives a lawyer a financial interest in the outcome of litigation, a reasonable contingent fee is permissible in civil cases because it may be the only means by which a layman can obtain the services of a lawyer of his choice. But a lawyer, because he is in a better position to evaluate a cause of action, should enter into a contingent

---

3. "Courts of equity will scrutinize with jealous vigilance transactions between parties occupying fiduciary relations toward each other.... A deed will not be held invalid, however, if made by the grantor with full knowledge of its nature and effect, and because of the deliberate, voluntary and intelligent desire of the grantor.... Where a fiduciary relation exists, the burden of proof is on the grantee or beneficiary of an instrument executed during the existence of such relationship to show the fairness of the transaction, that it was equitable and just and that it did not proceed from undue influence.... The same rule has application where an attorney engages in a transaction with a client during the existence of the relation and is benefited thereby.... Conversely, an attorney is not prohibited from dealing with his client or buying his property, and such contracts, if open, fair and honest, when deliberately made, are as valid as contracts between other parties.... [I]mportant factors in determining whether a transaction is fair include a showing by the fiduciary (1) that he made a full and frank disclosure of all the relevant information that he had; (2) that the consideration was adequate; and (3) that the principal had independent advice before completing the transaction." McFail v. Braden, 19 Ill. 2d 108, 117-18, 166 N.E. 2d 46, 52 (1960).

4. See State ex rel. Nebraska State Bar Ass'n v. Richards, 165 Neb. 80, 94-95, 84 N.W. 2d 136, 146 (1957).

5. See ABA CANON 9.

6. See ABA CANON 10.

7. See CODE OF PROFESSIONAL RESPONSIBILITY, EC 2-20.

fee arrangement only in those instances where the arrangement will be beneficial to the client.

EC 5-8 A financial interest in the outcome of litigation also results if monetary advances are made by the lawyer to his client.[8] Although this assistance generally is not encouraged, there are instances when it is not improper to make loans to a client. For example, the advancing or guaranteeing of payment of the costs and expenses of litigation by a lawyer may be the only way a client can enforce his cause of action,[9] but the ultimate liability for such costs and expenses must be that of the client.

EC 5-9 Occasionally a lawyer is called upon to decide in a particular case whether he will be a witness or an advocate. If a lawyer is both counsel and witness, he becomes more easily impeachable for interest and thus may be a less effective witness. Conversely, the opposing counsel may be handicapped in challenging the credibility of the lawyer when the lawyer also appears as an advocate in the case. An advocate who becomes a witness is in the unseemly and ineffective position of arguing his own credibility. The roles of an advocate and of a witness are inconsistent; the function of an advocate is to advance or argue the cause of another, while that of a witness is to state facts objectively.

EC 5-10 Problems incident to the lawyer-witness relationship arise at different stages; they relate either to whether a lawyer should accept employment or should withdraw from employment.[10] Regardless of when the problem arises, his decision is to be governed by the same basic considerations. It is not objectionable for a lawyer who is a potential witness to be an advocate if it is unlikely that he will be called as a witness because his testimony would be merely cumulative or if his testimony will relate only to an

---

8. *See* ABA CANON 42.

9. *"Rule 3a. . . .* A member of the State Bar shall not directly or indirectly pay or agree to pay, or represent or sanction the representation that he will pay, medical, hospital or nursing bills or other personal expenses incurred by or for a client, prospective or existing; provided this rule shall not prohibit a member:

"(1) with the consent of the client, from paying or agreeing to pay to third persons such expenses from funds collected or to be collected for the client; or

(2) after he has been employed, from lending money to his client upon the client's promise in writing to repay such loan; or

(3) from advancing the costs of prosecuting or defending a claim or action. Such costs within the meaning of this subparagraph (3) include all taxable costs or disbursements, costs or investigation and costs of obtaining and presenting evidence." CAL. BUSINESS AND PROFESSIONS CODE §6076 (West Supp. 1967).

10. "When a lawyer knows, prior to trial, that he will be a necessary witness, except as to merely formal matters such as identification or custody of a document or the like, neither he nor his firm or associates should conduct the trial. If, during the trial, he discovers that the ends of justice require his testimony, he should, from that point on, if feasible and not prejudicial to his client's case, leave further conduct of the trial to other counsel. If circumstances do not permit withdrawal from the conduct of the trial, the lawyer should not argue the credibility of his own testimony." *A Code of Trial Conduct: Promulgated by the American College of Trial Lawyers,* 43 A.B.A.J. 223, 224-25 (1957).

uncontested issue.[11] In the exceptional situation where it will be manifestly unfair to the client for the lawyer to refuse employment or to withdraw when he will likely be a witness on a contested issue, he may serve as advocate even though he may be a witness.[12] In making such decision, he should determine the personal or financial sacrifice of the client that may result from his refusal of employment or withdrawal therefrom, the materiality of his testimony, and the effectiveness of his representation in view of his personal involvement. In weighing these factors, it should be clear that refusal or withdrawal will impose an unreasonable hardship upon the client before the lawyer accepts or continues the employment.[13] Where the question arises, doubts should be resolved in favor of the lawyer testifying and against his becoming or continuing as an advocate.[14]

EC 5-11   A lawyer should not permit his personal interests to influence his advice relative to a suggestion by his client that additional counsel be employed.[15] In like manner, his personal interests should not deter him from suggesting that additional counsel be employed; on the contrary, he should be alert to the desirability of recommending additional counsel when, in his judgment, the proper representation of his client requires it. However, a lawyer should advise his client not to employ additional counsel suggested by the client if the lawyer believes that such employment would be a disservice to the client, and he should disclose the reasons for his belief.

EC 5-12   Inability of co-counsel to agree on a matter vital to the representation of their client requires that their disagreement be submitted by them jointly to their client for his resolution, and the decision of the client shall control the action to be taken.[16]

---

11. *Cf.* CANON 19: "When a lawyer is a witness for his client, except as to merely formal matters, such as the attestation or custody of an instrument and the like, he should leave the trial of the case to other counsel."

12. "It is the general rule that a lawyer may not testify in litigation in which he is an advocate unless circumstances arise which could not be anticipated and it is necessary to prevent a miscarriage of justice. In those rare cases where the testimony of an attorney is needed to protect his client's interests, it is not only proper but mandatory that it be forthcoming." Schwartz v. Wenger, 267 Minn. 40, 43-44, 124 N.W. 2d 489, 492 (1963).

13. "The great weight of authority in this country holds that the attorney who acts as counsel and witness, in behalf of his client, in the same cause on a material matter, not of a merely formal character, and not in an emergency, but having knowledge that he would be required to be a witness in ample time to have secured other counsel and given up his service in the case, violates a highly important provision of the Code of Ethics and a rule of professional conduct, but does not commit a legal error in so testifying, as a result of which a new trial will be granted." Erwin M. Jennings Co. v. DiGenova, 107 Conn. 491, 499, 141A. 866, 869 (1928).

14. "[C]ases may arise, and in practice often do arise, in which there would be a failure of justice should the attorney withhold his testimony. In such a case it would be a vicious professional sentiment which would deprive the client of the benefit of his attorney's testimony." Connolly v. Straw, 53 Wis. 645, 649, 11 N.W. 17, 19 (1881).

But see CANON 19: "Except when essential to the ends of justice, a lawyer should avoid testifying in court in behalf of his client."

15. *Cf.* ABA CANON 7.

16. *See* ABA CANON 7.

EC 5-13   A lawyer should not maintain membership in or be influenced by any organization of employees that undertakes to prescribe, direct, or suggest when or how he should fulfill his professional obligations to a person or organization that employs him as a lawyer. Although it is not necessarily improper for a lawyer employed by a corporation or similar entity to be a member of an organization of employees, he should be vigilant to safeguard his fidelity as a lawyer to his employer, free from outside influences.

Interests of Multiple Clients

EC 5-14   Maintaining the independence of professional judgment required of a lawyer precludes his acceptance or continuation of employment that will adversely affect his judgment on behalf of or dilute his loyalty to a client.[17] This problem arises whenever a lawyer is asked to represent two or more clients who may have differing interests, whether such interests be conflicting, inconsistent, diverse, or otherwise discordant.[18]

EC 5-15   If a lawyer is requested to undertake or to continue representation of multiple clients having potentially differing interests, he must weigh carefully the possibility that his judgment may be impaired or his loyalty divided if he accepts or continues the employment. He should resolve all doubts against the propriety of the representation. A lawyer should never represent in litigation multiple clients with differing interests;[19] and there are few situations in which he would be justified in representing in litigation multiple clients with potentially differing interests. If a lawyer accepted such employment and the interests did become actually differing, he would have to withdraw from employment with likelihood of resulting hardship on the clients; and for this reason it is preferable that he refuse the employ-

---

17. *See* ABA CANON 6; *cf. ABA Opinions* 261 (1944), 242 (1942), 142 (1935), and 30 (1931).

18. The ABA Canons speak of "conflicting interests" rather than "differing interests" but make no attempt to define such other than the statement in Canon 6: "Within the meaning of this canon, a lawyer represents conflicting interests when, in behalf of one client, it is his duty to contend for that which duty to another client requires him to oppose."

19. "Canon 6 of the Canons of Professional Ethics, adopted by the American Bar Association on September 30, 1937, and by the Pennsylvania Bar Association on January 7, 1938, provides in part that 'It is unprofessional to represent conflicting interests, except by express consent of all concerned given after a full disclosure of the facts. Within the meaning of this Canon, a lawyer represents conflicting interests when, in behalf of one client, it is his duty to contend for that which duty to another client requires him to oppose.' The full disclosure required by this canon contemplates that the possibly adverse effect of the conflict be fully explained by the attorney to the client to be affected and by him thoroughly understood. . . .

"The foregoing canon applies to cases where the circumstances are such that possibly conflicting interests may permissibly be represented by the same attorney. But manifestly, there are instances where the conflicts of interest are so critically adverse as not to admit of one attorney's representing both sides. Such is the situation which this record presents. No one could conscionably contend that the same attorney may represent both the plaintiff and defendant in an adversary action. Yet, that is what is being done in this case." Jedwabny v. Philadelphia Transportation Co., 390 Pa. 231, 235, 135 A.2d 252, 254 (1957), *cert. denied*, 355 U.S. 966, 2 L. Ed. 2d 541, 78 S. Ct. 557 (1958).

ment initially. On the other hand, there are many instances in which a lawyer may properly serve multiple clients having potentially differing interests in matters not involving litigation. If the interests vary only slightly, it is generally likely that the lawyer will not be subjected to an adverse influence and that he can retain his independent judgment on behalf of each client; and if the interests become differing, withdrawal is less likely to have a disruptive effect upon the causes of his clients.

EC 5-16   In those instances in which a lawyer is justified in representing two or more clients having differing interests, it is nevertheless essential that each client be given the opportunity to evaluate his need for representation free of any potential conflict and to obtain other counsel if he so desires.[20] Thus before a lawyer may represent multiple clients, he should explain fully to each client the implications of the common representation and should accept or continue employment only if the clients consent.[21] If there are present other circumstances that might cause any of the multiple clients to question the undivided loyalty of the lawyer, he should also advise all of the clients of those circumstances.[22]

EC 5-17   Typically recurring situations involving potentially differing interests are those in which a lawyer is asked to represent co-defendants in a criminal case, co-plaintiffs in a personal injury case, an insured and his insurer,[23] and beneficiaries of the estate of a decedent. Whether a lawyer can

20. "Glasser wished the benefit of the undivided assistance of counsel of his own choice. We think that such a desire on the part of an accused should be respected. Irrespective of any conflict of interest, the additional burden of representing another party may conceivably impair counsel's effectiveness.

"To determine the precise degree of prejudice sustained by Glasser as a result of the court's appointment of Stewart as counsel for Kretske is at once difficult and unnecessary. The right to have the assistance of counsel is too fundamental and absolute to allow courts to indulge in nice calculations as to the amount of prejudice arising from its denial." Glasser v. United States, 315 U.S. 60, 75-76, 86 L. Ed. 680, 702 S. Ct. 457, 467 (1942).

21. *See* ABA CANON 6.

22. *Id.*

23. *Cf. ABA Opinion* 282 (1950).

"When counsel, although paid by the casualty company, undertakes to represent the policyholder and files his notice of appearance, he owes to his client, the assured, an undeviating and single allegiance. His fealty embraces the requirement to produce in court all witnesses, fact and expert, who are available and necessary for the proper protection of the rights of his client....

"... The Canons of Professional Ethics make it pellucid that there are not two standards, one applying to counsel privately retained by a client, and the other to counsel paid by an insurance carrier." American Employers Ins. Co. v. Goble Aircraft Specialties, 205 Misc. 1066, 1075, 131 N.Y.S.2d 393, 401 (1954), *motion to withdraw appeal granted*, 1 App. Div. 2d 1008, 154 N.Y.S.2d 835 (1956).

"[C]ounsel, selected by State Farm to defend Dorothy Walker's suit for $50,000 damages, was apprised by Walker that his earlier version of the accident was untrue and that actually the accident occurred because he lost control of his car in passing a Cadillac just ahead. At that point, Walker's counsel should have refused to participate further in view of the conflict of interest between Walker and State Farm.... Instead he participated in the ensuing deposition of the Walkers, even took an *ex parte* sworn statement from Mr. Walker in order to advise State Farm what action it should take, and later used the statement against Walker in the District Court. This action appears to contravene an Indiana attorney's duty 'at every peril to

fairly and adequately protect the interests of multiple clients in these and similar situations depends upon an analysis of each case. In certain circumstances, there may exist little chance of the judgment of the lawyer being adversely affected by the slight possibility that the interests will become actually differing; in other circumstances, the chance of adverse effect upon his judgment is not unlikely.

EC 5-18   A lawyer employed or retained by a corporation or similar entity owes his allegiance to the entity and not to a stockholder, director, officer, employee, representative, or other person connected with the entity. In advising the entity, a lawyer should keep paramount its interests and his professional judgment should not be influenced by the personal desires of any person or organization. Occasionally a lawyer for an entity is requested by a stockholder, director, officer, employee, representative, or other person connected with the entity to represent him in an individual capacity; in such case the lawyer may serve the individual only if the lawyer is convinced that differing interests are not present.

EC 5-19   A lawyer may represent several clients whose interests are not actually or potentially differing. Nevertheless, he should explain any circumstances that might cause a client to question his undivided loyalty.[24] Regardless of the belief of a lawyer that he may properly represent multiple clients, he must defer to a client who holds the contrary belief and withdraw from representation of that client.

EC 5-20   A lawyer is often asked to serve as an impartial arbitrator or mediator in matters which involve present or former clients. He may serve in either capacity if he first discloses such present of former relationships. After a lawyer has undertaken to act as an impartial arbitrator or mediator, he should not thereafter represent in the dispute any of the parties involved.

Desires of Third Persons

EC 5-21   The obligation of a lawyer to exercise professional judgment solely on behalf of his client requires that he disregard the desires of others that might impair his free judgment.[25] The desires of a third person will seldom adversely affect a lawyer unless that person is in a position to exert

---

himself, to preserve the secrets of his client'. . . ." State Farm Mut. Auto Ins. Co. v. Walker, 382 F.2d 548, 552 (1967), *cert. denied*, 389 U.S. 1045, 19 L. Ed. 2d 837, 88 S. Ct. 789 (1968).

24. *See* ABA CANON 6.

25. *See* ABA CANON 35.

"Objection to the intervention of a lay intermediary, who may control litigation or otherwise interfere with the rendering of legal services in a confidential relationship, . . . derives from the element of pecuniary gain. Fearful of dangers thought to arise from that element, the courts of several States have sustained regulations aimed at these activities. We intimate no view one way or the other as to the merits of those decisions with respect to the particular arrangements against which they are directed. It is enough that the superficial resemblance in form between those arrangements and that at bar cannot obscure the vital fact that here the entire arrangement employs constitutionally privileged means of expression to secure constitutionally guaran-

strong economic, political, or social pressures upon the lawyer. These influences are often subtle, and a lawyer must be alert to their existence. A lawyer subjected to outside pressures should make full disclosure of them to his client,[26] and if he or his client believes that the effectiveness of his representation has been or will be impaired thereby, the lawyer should take proper steps to withdraw from representation of his client.

EC 5-22 Economic, political, or social pressures by third persons are less likely to impinge upon the independent judgment of a lawyer in a matter in which he is compensated directly by his client and his professional work is exclusively with his client. On the other hand, if a lawyer is compensated from a source other than his client, he may feel a sense of responsibility to someone other than his client.

EC 5-23 A person or organization that pays or furnishes lawyers to represent others possesses a potential power to exert strong pressures against the independent judgment of those lawyers. Some employers may be interested in furthering their own economic, political, or social goals without regard to the professional responsibility of the lawyer to his individual client. Others may be far more concerned with establishment or extension of legal principles than in the immediate protection of the rights of the lawyer's individual client. On some occasions, decisions on priority of work may be made by the employer rather than the lawyer with the result that prosecution of work already undertaken for clients is postponed to their detriment. Similarly, an employer may seek, consciously or unconsciously, to further its own economic interests through the action of the lawyers employed by it. Since a lawyer must always be free to exercise his professional judgment without regard to the interests or motives of a third person, the lawyer who is employed by one to represent another must constantly guard against erosion of his professional freedom.[27]

EC 5-24 To assist a lawyer in preserving his professional independence, a number of courses are available to him. For example, a lawyer should not practice with or in the form of a professional legal corporation, even though the corporate form is permitted by law,[28] if any director, officer, or stock-

---

teed civil rights." NAACP v. Button, 371 U.S. 415, 441-42, 9 L. Ed. 2d 405, 423-24, 83 S. Ct. 328, 342-43 (1963).

26. *Cf.* ABA CANON 38.

27. "Certainly it is true that 'the professional relationship between an attorney and his client is highly personal, involving an intimate appreciation of each individual client's particular problem.' And this Committee does not condone practices which interfere with that relationship. However, the mere fact the lawyer is actually paid by some entity other than the client does not affect that relationship, so long as the lawyer is selected by and is directly responsible to the client. See Informal Opinions 469 and 679. Of course, as the latter decision points out, there must be full disclosure of the arrangement by the attorney to the client...." *ABA Opinion* 320 (1968).

"[A] third party may pay the cost of legal services as long as control remains in the client and the responsibility of the lawyer is solely to the client. Informal Opinions 469 ad [*sic*] 679. *See also Opinion* 237." *Id.*

28. *ABA Opinion* 303 (1961) recognized that "[s]tatutory provisions now exist in several states which are designed to make [the practice of law in a form that will be classified as a

holder of it is a non-lawyer. Although a lawyer may be employed by a business corporation with non-lawyers serving as directors or officers, and they necessarily have the right to make decisions of business policy, a lawyer must decline to accept direction of his professional judgment from any layman. Various types of legal aid offices are administered by boards of directors composed of lawyers and laymen. A lawyer should not accept employment from such an organization unless the board sets only broad policies and there is no interference in the relationship of the lawyer and the individual client he serves. Where a lawyer is employed by an organization, a written agreement that defines the relationship between him and the organization and provides for his independence is desirable since it may serve to prevent misunderstanding as to their respective roles. Although other innovations in the means of supplying legal counsel may develop, the responsibility of the lawyer to maintain his professional independence remains constant, and the legal profession must insure that changing circumstances do not result in loss of the professional independence of the lawyer.

Disciplinary Rules

DR 5-101   Refusing Employment When the Interests of the Lawyer May Impair His Independent Professional Judgment

(A)   Except with the consent of his client after full disclosure, a lawyer shall not accept employment if the exercise of his professional judgment on behalf of his client will be or reasonably may be affected by his own financial, business, property, or personal interests.[29]

(B)   A lawyer shall not accept employment in contemplated or pending litigation if he knows or it is obvious that he or a lawyer in his firm

---

corporation for federal income tax purposes] legally possible, either as a result of lawyers incorporating or forming associations with various corporate characteristics."

29. *Cf.* ABA CANON 6 and *ABA Opinions* 181 (1938), 104 (1934), 103 (1933), 72 (1932), 50 (1931), 49 (1931), and 33 (1931).

"New York County [Opinion] 203.... [A lawyer] should not advise a client to employ an investment company in which he is interested, without informing him of this." DRINKER, LEGAL ETHICS 956 (1953).

"In *Opinions* 72 and 49 this Committee held: The relations of partners in a law firm are such that neither the firm nor any member or associate thereof, may accept any professional employment which any member of the firm cannot properly accept.

"In *Opinion* 16 this Committee held that a member of a law firm could not represent a defendant in a criminal case which was being prosecuted by another member of the firm who was public prosecuting attorney. The Opinion stated that it was clearly unethical for one member of the firm to oppose the interest of the state while another member represented those interests.... Since the prosecutor himself could not represent both the public and the defendant, no member of his law firm could either." *ABA Opinion* 296 (1959).

ought to be called as a witness, except that he may undertake the employment and he or a lawyer in his firm may testify:

(1) If the testimony will relate solely to an uncontested matter.

(2) If the testimony will relate solely to a matter of formality and there is no reason to believe that substantial evidence will be offered in opposition to the testimony.

(3) If the testimony will relate solely to the nature and value of legal services rendered in the case by the lawyer or his firm to the client.

(4) As to any matter, if refusal would work a substantial hardship on the client because of the distinctive value of the lawyer or his firm as counsel in the particular case.

DR 5-102 Withdrawal as Counsel When the Lawyer Becomes a Witness[30]

(A) If, after undertaking employment in contemplated or pending litigation, a lawyer learns or it is obvious that he or a lawyer in his firm ought to be called as a witness on behalf of his client, he shall withdraw from the conduct of the trial and his firm, if any, shall not continue representation in the trial, except that he may continue the representation and he or a lawyer in his firm may testify in the circumstances enumerated in DR 5-101(B) (1) through (4).

(B) If, after undertaking employment in contemplated or pending litigation, a lawyer learns or it is obvious that he or a lawyer in his firm may be called as a witness other than on behalf of his client, he may continue the representation until it is apparent that his testimony is or may be prejudicial to his client.[31]

DR 5-103 Avoiding Acquisition of Interest in Litigation

(A) A lawyer shall not acquire a proprietary interest in the cause of action or subject matter of litigation he is conducting for a client,[32] except that he may:

(1) Acquire a lien granted by law to secure his fee or expenses.

---

30. *Cf.* ABA CANON 19 and *ABA Opinions* 220 (1941), 185 (1938), 50 (1931), and 33 (1931); *but cf.* Erwin M. Jennings Co. v. DiGenova, 107 Conn. 491, 498-99, 141 A. 866, 868 (1928).

31. "This *Canon* [19] *of Ethics* needs no elaboration to be applied to the facts here. Apparently, the object of this precept is to avoid putting a lawyer in the obviously embarrassing predicament of testifying and then having to argue the credibility and effect of his own testimony. It was not designed to permit a lawyer to call opposing counsel as a witness and thereby disqualify him as counsel." Galarowicz v. Ward, 119 Utah 611, 620, 230 P.2d 576, 580 (1951).

32. ABA CANON 10 and *ABA Opinions* 279 (1949), 246 (1942), and 176 (1938).

(2)   Contract with a client for a reasonable contingent fee in a civil
       case.[33]

(B)   While representing a client in connection with contemplated or pend-
       ing litigation, a lawyer shall not advance or guarantee financial assist-
       ance to his client,[34] except that a lawyer may advance or guarantee the
       expenses of litigation, including court costs, expenses of investigation, ex-
       penses of medical examination, and costs of obtaining and presenting
       evidence, provided the client remains ultimately liable for such expenses.

DR 5-104   Limiting Business Relations with a Client

(A)   A lawyer shall not enter into a business transaction with a client if they
       have differing interests therein and if the client expects the lawyer to
       exercise his professional judgment therein for the protection of the client,
       unless the client has consented after full disclosure.

(B)   Prior to conclusion of all aspects of the matter giving rise to his employ-
       ment, a lawyer shall not enter into any arrangement or understanding
       with a client or a prospective client by which he acquires an interest in
       publication rights with respect to the subject matter of his employment
       or proposed employment.

DR 5-105   Refusing to Accept or Continue Employment
if the Interests of Another Client May Impair
the Independent Professional Judgment of the
Lawyer

(A)   A lawyer shall decline proffered employment if the exercise of his inde-
       pendent professional judgment in behalf of a client will be or is likely to
       be adversely affected by the acceptence of the proffered employment,[35]
       or if it would be likely to involve him in representing differing interests,
       except to the extent permitted under DR 5-105(C).[36]

(B)   A lawyer shall not continue multiple employment if the exercise of his
       independent professional judgment in behalf of a client will be or is likely
       to be adversely affected by his representation of another client, or if it

33. *See* CODE OF PROFESSIONAL RESPONSIBILITY, DR 2-106(C).

34. *See* ABA CANON 42; *cf. ABA Opinion* 288 (1954).

35. *See* ABA CANON 6; *cf. ABA Opinions* 167 (1937), 60 (1931), and 40 (1931).

36. *ABA Opinion* 247 (1942) held that an attorney could not investigate a nightclub shooting
on behalf of one of the owner's liability insurers, obtaining the cooperation of the owner, and
later represent the injured patron in an action against the owner and a different insurance
company unless the attorney obtain the "express consent of all concerned given after a full
disclosure of the facts," since to do so would be to represent conflicting interests.

See ABA Opinions 247 (1942), 224 (1941), 222 (1941), 218 (1941), 112 (1934), 86 (1932), and 83
(1932).

would be likely to involve him in representing differing interests, except to the extent permitted under DR 5-105(C).[37]

(C)   In the situations covered by DR 5-105 (A) and (B), a lawyer may represent multiple clients if it is obvious that he can adequately represent the interest of each and if each consents to the representation after full disclosure of the possible effect of such representation on the exercise of his independent professional judgment on behalf of each.

(D)   If a lawyer is required to decline employment or to withdraw from employment under a Disciplinary Rule, no partner, or associate, or any other lawyer affiliated with him or his firm, may accept or continue such employment.

DR 5-106   Settling Similar Claims of Clients[38]

(A)   A lawyer who represents two or more clients shall not make or participate in the making of an aggregate settlement of the claims of or against his clients, unless each client has consented to the settlement after being advised of the existence and nature of all the claims involved in the proposed settlement, of the total amount of the settlement, and of the participation of each person in the settlement.

DR 5-107   Avoiding Influence by Others Than the Client

(A)   Except with the consent of his client after full disclosure, a lawyer shall not:

    (1)   Accept compensation for his legal services from one other than his client.

    (2)   Accept from one other than his client any thing of value related to his representation of or his employment by his client.[39]

(B)   A lawyer shall not permit a person who recommends, employs, or pays him to render legal services for another to direct or regulate his professional judgment in rendering such legal services.[40]

37. *Cf. ABA Opinions 231 (1941) and 160 (1936).*
38. *See ABA Opinion 235 (1941).*
39. *See* ABA CANON 38.
"A lawyer who receives a commission (whether delayed or not) from a title insurance company or guaranty fund for recommending or selling the insurance to his client, or for work done for the client or the company, without either fully disclosing to the client his financial interest in the transaction, or crediting the client's bill with the amount thus received, is guilty of unethical conduct." *ABA Opinion* 304 (1962).
40. *See* ABA CANON 35; *cf. ABA Opinion 237 (1941).*
"When the lay forwarder, as agent for the creditor, forwards a claim to an attorney, the direct relationship of attorney and client shall then exist between the attorney and the creditor, and the forwarder shall not interpose itself as an intermediary to control the activities of the attorney." *ABA Opinion* 294 (1958).

(C)   A lawyer shall not practice with or in the form of a professional corpora-
       tion or association authorized to practice law for a profit, if:
       (1)   A non-lawyer owns any interest therein,[41] except that a fiduciary
             representative of the estate of a lawyer may hold the stock or interest
             of the lawyer for a reasonable time during administration;
       (2)   A non-lawyer is a corporate director or officer thereof;[42] or
       (3)   A non-lawyer has the right to direct or control the professional
             judgment of a lawyer.[43]

CANON 6
A LAWYER SHOULD REPRESENT A
CLIENT COMPETENTLY

Ethical Considerations

EC 6-1   Because of his vital role in the legal process, a lawyer should act
with competence and proper care in representing clients. He should strive
to become and remain proficient in his practice[1] and should accept em-

41. "Permanent beneficial and voting rights in the organization set up to practice law, whatever its form, must be restricted to lawyers while the organization is engaged in the practice of
law." *ABA Opinion* 303 (1961).
42. "*Canon 33* . . . promulgates underlying principles that must be observed no matter in
what form of organization lawyers practice law. Its requirements that no person shall be admitted or held out as a practitioner or member who is not a member of the legal profession duly
authorized to practice, and amenable to professional discipline, makes it clear that any centralized management must be in lawyers to avoid a violation of this Canon." *ABA Opinion* 303
(1961).
43. "There is no intervention of any lay agency between lawyer and client when centralized
management provided only by lawyers may give guidance or direction to the services being
rendered by a lawyer-member of the organization to a client. The language in *Canon 35* that a
lawyer should avoid all relations which direct the performance of his duties by or in the interest
of an intermediary refers to lay intermediaries and not lawyer intermediaries with whom he is
associated in the practice of law." *ABA Opinion* 303 (1961).
1. "[W]hen a citizen is faced with the need for a lawyer, he wants, and is entitled to, the
best informed counsel he can obtain. Changing times produce changes in our law and legal
procedures. The natural complexities of law require continuing intensive study by a lawyer
if he is to render his clients a maximum of efficient service. And, in so doing, he maintains
the high standards of the legal profession; and he also increases respect and confidence by
the general public." Rochelle & Payne, *The Struggle for Public Understanding*, 25 TEXAS
B.J. 109, 160 (1962).
"We have undergone enormous changes in the last fifty years within the lives of most of
the adults living today who may be seeking advice. Most of these changes have been accompanied by changes and developments in the law. . . . Every practicing lawyer encounters
these problems and is often perplexed with his own inability to keep up, not only with
changes in the law, but also with changes in the lives of his clients and their legal problems.
"To be sure, no client has a right to expect that his lawyer will have all of the answers at
the end of his tongue or even in the back of his head at all times. But the client does have
the right to expect that the lawyer will have devoted his time and energies to maintaining
and improving his competence to know where to look for the answers, to know how to deal
with the problems, and to know how to advise to the best of his legal talents and abilities."

ployment only in matters which he is or intends to become competent to handle.

EC 6-2 A lawyer is aided in attaining and maintaining his competence by keeping abreast of current legal literature and developments, participating in continuing legal education programs,[2] concentrating in particular areas of the law, and by utilizing other available means. He has the additional ethical obligation to assist in improving the legal profession, and he may do so by participating in bar activities intended to advance the quality and standards of members of the profession. Of particular importance is the careful training of his younger associates and the giving of sound guidance to all lawyers who consult him. In short, a lawyer should strive at all levels to aid the legal profession in advancing the highest possible standards of integrity and competence and to meet those standards himself.

EC 6-3 While the licensing of a lawyer is evidence that he has met the standards then prevailing for admission to the bar, a lawyer generally should not accept employment in any area of the law in which he is not qualified.[3] However, he may accept such employment if in good faith he expects to become qualified through study and investigation, as long as such preparation would not result in unreasonable delay or expense to his client. Proper preparation and representation may require the association by the lawyer of professionals in other disciplines. A lawyer offered employment in a matter in which he is not and does not expect to become so qualified should either decline the employment or, with the consent of his client, accept the employment and associate a lawyer who is competent in the matter.

EC 6-4 Having undertaken representation, a lawyer should use proper care to safeguard the interests of his client. If a lawyer has accepted employment in a matter beyond his competence but in which he expected to become competent, he should diligently undertake the work and study necessary to qualify himself. In addition to being qualified to handle a particular matter, his obligation to his client requires him to prepare adequately for and give appropriate attention to his legal work.

Levy & Sprague, *Accounting and Law: Is Dual Practice in the Public Interest?*, 52 A.B.A.J. 1110, 1112 (1966).

2. "The whole purpose of continuing legal education, so enthusiastically supported by the ABA, is to make it possible for lawyers to make themselves better lawyers. But there are no nostrums for proficiency in the law; it must come through the hard work of the lawyer himself. To the extent that that work, whether it be in attending institutes or lecture courses, in studying after hours or in the actual day in and day out practice of his profession, can be concentrated within a limited field, the greater the proficiency and expertness that can be developed." *Report to the Special Committee on Specialization and Specialized Legal Education*, 79 A.B.A. REP. 582, 588 (1954).

3. "If the attorney is not competent to skillfully and properly perform the work, he should not undertake the service." Degen v. Steinbrink, 202 App. Div. 477, 481, 195 N. Y. S. 810, 814 (1922), *aff'd mem.*, 236 N. Y. 669 142 N. E. 328 (1923).

EC 6-5   A lawyer should have pride in his professional endeavors. His obligation to act competently calls for higher motivation than that arising from fear of civil liability or disciplinary penalty.

EC 6-6   A lawyer should not seek, by contract or other means, to limit his individual liability to his client for his malpractice. A lawyer who handles the affairs of his client properly has no need to attempt to limit his liability for his professional activities and one who does not handle the affairs of his client properly should not be permitted to do so. A lawyer who is a stockholder in or is associated with a professional legal corporation may, however, limit his liability for malpractice of his associates in the corporation, but only to the extent permitted by law.[4]

Disciplinary Rules

DR 6-101   Failing to Act Competently

(A)   A lawyer shall not:
    (1)   Handle a legal matter which he knows or should know that he is not competent to handle, without associating with him a lawyer who is competent to handle it.
    (2)   Handle a legal matter without preparation adequate in the circumstances.
    (3)   Neglect a legal matter entrusted to him.[5]

DR 6-102   Limiting Liability to Client

(A)   A lawyer shall not attempt to exonerate himself from or limit his liability to his client for his personal malpractice.

---

4. See ABA Opinion 303 (1961); cf. CODE OF PROFESSIONAL RESPONSIBILITY, EC 2-11.

5. The annual report for 1967-1968 of the Committee on Grievances of the Association of the Bar of the City of New York showed a receipt of 2,232 complaints; of the 828 offenses against clients, 76 involved conversion, 49 involved "overreaching," and 452, or more than half of all such offenses, involved neglect. Annual Report of the Committee on Grievances of the Association of the Bar of the City of New York, N.Y.L.J., Sept. 12, 1968, at 4, col. 5.

CANON 7
A LAWYER SHOULD REPRESENT A
CLIENT ZEALOUSLY WITHIN THE
BOUNDS OF THE LAW

Ethical Considerations

EC 7-1   The duty of a lawyer, both to his client[1] and to the legal system, is to represent his client zealously[2] within the bounds of the law,[3] which in-

1. "The right to be heard would be, in many cases, of little avail if it did not comprehend the right to be heard by counsel. Even the intelligent and educated layman has small and sometimes no skill in the science of law." Powell v. Alabama, 287 U.S. 45, 68-69, 77 L. Ed. 158, 170, 53 S. Ct. 55, 64 (1932).
   2. *Cf.* ABA CANON 4.
   "At times . . . [the tax lawyer] will be wise to discard some arguments and he should exercise discretion to emphasize the arguments which in his judgment are most likely to be persuasive. But this process involves legal judgment rather than moral attitudes. The tax lawyer should put aside private disagreements with Congressional and Treasury policies. His own notions of policy, and his personal view of what the law should be, are irrelevant. The job entrusted to him by his client is to use all his learning and ability to protect his client's rights, not to help in the process of promoting a better tax system. The tax lawyer need not accept his client's economic and social opinions, but the client is paying for technical attention and undivided concentration upon his affairs. He is equally entitled to performance unfettered by his attorney's economic and social predilections." Paul, *The Lawyer as a Tax Adviser*, 25 ROCKY MT. L. REV. 412, 418 (1953).
   3. *See* ABA CANONS 15 and 32.
   ABA Canon 5, although only speaking of one accused of crime, imposes a similar obligation on the lawyer: "[T]he lawyer is bound, by all fair and honorable means, to present every defense that the law of the land permits, to the end that no person may be deprived of life or liberty, but by due process of law."
   "Any persuasion or pressure on the advocate which deters him from planning and carrying out the litigation on the basis of 'what, within the framework of the law, is best for my client's interest?' interferes with the obligation to represent the client fully within the law.
   "This obligation, in its fullest sense, is the heart of the adversary process. Each attorney, as an advocate, acts for and seeks that which in his judgment is best for his client, within the bounds authoritatively established. The advocate does not *decide* what is just in this case — he would be usurping the function of the judge and jury — he acts for and seeks for his client that which he is entitled to under the law. He can do no less and properly represent the client." Thode, *The Ethical Standard for the Advocate*, 39 TEXAS L. REV. 575, 584 (1961).
   "The [Texas public opinion] survey indicates that distrust of the lawyer can be traced directly to certain factors. Foremost of these is a basic misunderstanding of the function of the lawyer as an advocate in an adversary system.
   "Lawyers are accused of taking advantage of 'loopholes' and 'technicalities' to win. Persons who make this charge are unaware, or do not understand, that the lawyer is hired to win, and if he does not exercise every legitimate effort in his client's behalf, then he is betraying a sacred trust." Rochelle and Payne, *The Struggle for Public Understanding*, 25 TEXAS B.J. 109, 159 (1962).
   "The importance of the attorney's undivided allegiance and faithful service to one accused of crime, irrespective of the attorney's personal opinion as to the guilt of his client, lies in Canon 5 of the American Bar Association Canon of Ethics.
   "The difficulty lies, of course, in ascertaining whether the attorney has been guilty of an error of judgment, such as an election with respect to trial tactics, or has otherwise been actuated by his conscience or belief that his client should be convicted in any event. All too frequently courts are called upon to review actions of defense counsel which are, at the most,

cludes Disciplinary Rules and enforceable professional regulations.[4] The professional responsibility of a lawyer derives from his membership in a profession which has the duty of assisting members of the public to secure and protect available legal rights and benefits. In our government of laws and not of men, each member of our society is entitled to have his conduct judged and regulated in accordance with the law,[5] to seek any lawful objective[6] through legally permissible means,[7] and to present for adjudication any lawful claim, issue, or defense.

---

errors of judgment, not properly reviewable on habeas corpus unless the trial is a farce and a mockery of justice which requires the court to intervene. . . . But when defense counsel in a truly adverse proceeding, admits that his conscience would not permit him to adopt certain customary trial procedures, this extends beyond the realm of judgment and strongly suggests an invasion of constitutional rights." Johns v. Smyth, 176 F. Supp. 949, 92 (E.D. Va. 1959), *modified*, United States ex rel. Wilkins v. Banmiller, 205 F. Supp. 123, 128, n. 5 (E.D. Pa. 1962), *aff'd*, 325 F. 2d 514 (3d Cir. 1963), *cert. denied*, 379 U.S. 847, 13 L. Ed. 2d 51, 85 S. Ct. 87 (1964).

"The adversary system in law administration bears a striking resemblance to the competitive economic system. In each we assume that the individual through partisanship or through self-interest will strive mightily for his side, and that kind of striving we must have. But neither system would be tolerable without restraints and modifications, and at times without outright departures from the system itself. Since the legal profession is entrusted with the system of law administration, a part of its task is to develop in its members appropriate restraints without impairing the values of partisan striving. An accompanying task is to aid in the modification of the adversary system or departure from it in areas to which the system is unsuited." Cheatham, *The Lawyer's Role and Surroundings*, 25 ROCKY MT. L. REV. 405, 410 (1953).

4. "Rule 4.15 prohibits, in the pursuit of a client's cause, 'any manner of fraud or chicane'; Rule 4.22 requires 'candor and fairness' in the conduct of the lawyer, and forbids the making of knowing misquotations; Rule 4.47 provides that a lawyer 'should always maintain his integrity,' and generally forbids all misconduct injurious to the interests of the public, the courts, or his clients, and acts contrary to 'justice, honesty, modesty or good morals.' Our Commissioner has accurately paraphrased these rules as follows: 'An attorney does not have the duty to do all and whatever he can that may enable him to win his client's cause or to further his client's interest. His duty and efforts in these respects, although they should be prompted by his "entire devotion" to the interest of his client, must be within and not without the bounds of the law.' " In re Wines, 370 S.W.2d 328, 333 (Mo. 1963).

See Note, 38 TEXAS L. REV. 107, 110 (1959).

5. "Under our system of government the process of adjudication is surrounded by safeguards evolved from centuries of experience. These safeguards are not designed merely to lend formality and decorum to the trial of causes. They are predicated on the assumption that to secure for any controversy a truly informed and dispassionate decision is a difficult thing, requiring for its achievement a special summoning and organization of human effort and the adoption of measures to exclude the biases and prejudgments that have free play outside the courtroom. All of this goes for naught if the man with an unpopular cause is unable to find a competent lawyer courageous enough to represent him. His chance to have his day in court loses much of its meaning if his case is handicapped from the outset by the very kind of prejudgment our rules of evidence and procedure are intended to prevent." *Professional Responsibility: Report of the Joint Conference*, 44 A.B.A.J. 1159, 1216 (1958).

6. "[I]t is . . . [the tax lawyer's] positive duty to show the client how to avail himself to the full of what the law permits. He is not the keeper of the Congressional conscience." Paul, *The Lawyer as a Tax Adviser*, 25 ROCKY MT. L. REV. 412, 418 (1953).

7. *See* ABA CANONS 15 and 30.

EC 7-2   The bounds of the law in a given case are often difficult to ascertain.[8] The language of legislative enactments and judicial opinions may be uncertain as applied to varying factual situations. The limits and specific meaning of apparently relevant law may be made doubtful by changing or developing constitutional interpretations, inadequately expressed statutes or judicial opinions, and changing public and judicial attitudes. Certainty of law ranges from well-settled rules through areas of conflicting authority to areas without precedent.

EC 7-3   Where the bounds of law are uncertain, the action of a lawyer may depend on whether he is serving as advocate or adviser. A lawyer may serve simultaneously as both advocate and adviser, but the two roles are essentially different.[9] In asserting a position on behalf of his client, an advocate for the most part deals with past conduct and must take the facts as he finds them. By contrast, a lawyer serving as adviser primarily assists his client in determining the course of future conduct and relationships. While serving as advocate, a lawyer should resolve in favor of his client doubts as to the bounds of the law.[10] In serving a client as adviser, a lawyer in appropriate circumstances should give his professional opinion as to what the ultimate decisions of the courts would likely be as to the applicable law.

---

8. "The fact that it desired to evade the law, as it is called, is immaterial, because the very meaning of a line in the law is that you intentionally may go as close to it as you can if you do not pass it. . . . It is a matter of proximity and degree as to which minds will differ. . . ." Justice Holmes, in Superior Oil Co. v. Mississippi, 280 U.S. 390, 395-96, 74 L. Ed 504, 508, 50 S. Ct. 169, 170 (1939).

9. "Today's lawyers perform two distinct types of functions, and our ethical standards should, but in the main do not, recognize these two functions. Judge Philbrick McCoy recently reported to the American Bar Association the need for a reappraisal of the Canons in light of the new and distinct function of counselor, as distinguished from advocate, which today predominates in the legal profession. . . .

". . . In the first place, any revision of the canons must take into account and speak to this new and now predominant function of the lawyer. . . . It is beyond the scope of this paper to discuss the ethical standards to be applied to the counselor except to state that in my opinion such standards should require a greater recognition and protection for the interest of the public generally than is presently expressed in the canons. Also, the counselor's obligation should extend to requiring him to inform and to impress upon the client a just solution of the problem, considering all interests involved." Thode, *The Ethical Standard for the Advocate*, 39 TEXAS L. REV. 575, 578-79 (1961).

"The man who has been called into court to answer for his own actions is entitled to fair hearing. Partisan advocacy plays its essential part in such a hearing, and the lawyer pleading his client's case may properly present it in the most favorable light. A similar resolution of doubts in one direction becomes inappropriate when the lawyer acts as counselor. The reasons that justify and even require partisan advocacy in the trial of a cause do not grant any license to the lawyer to participate as legal advisor in a line of conduct that is immoral, unfair, or of doubtful legality. In saving himself from this unworthy involvement, the lawyer cannot be guided solely by an unreflective inner sense of good faith; he must be at pains to preserve a sufficient detachment from his client's interests so that he remains capable of a sound and objective appraisal of the propriety of what his client proposes to do." *Professional Responsibility: Report of the Joint Conference*, 44 A.B.A.J. 1159, 1161 (1958).

10. "[A] lawyer who is asked to advise his client . . . may freely urge the statement of positions most favorable to the client just as long as there is reasonable basis for those positions." *ABA Opinion* 314 (1965).

Duty of the Lawyer to a Client

EC 7-4   The advocate may urge any permissible construction of the law favorable to his client, without regard to his professional opinion as to the likelihood that the construction will ultimately prevail.[11] His conduct is within the bounds of the law, and therefore permissible, if the position taken is supported by the law or is supportable by a good faith argument for an extension, modification, or reversal of the law. However, a lawyer is not justified in asserting a position in litigation that is frivolous.[12]

EC 7-5   A lawyer as adviser furthers the interest of his client by giving his professional opinion as to what he believes would likely be the ultimate decision of the courts on the matter at hand and by informing his client of the practical effect of such decision.[13] He may continue in the representation of his client even though his client has elected to pursue a course of conduct contrary to the advice of the lawyer so long as he does not thereby knowingly assist the client to engage in illegal conduct or to take a frivolous

---

11. "The lawyer . . . is not an umpire, but an advocate. He is under no duty to refrain from making every proper argument in support of any legal point because he is not convinced of its inherent soundness. . . . His personal belief in the soundness of his cause or of the authorities supporting it, is irrelevant." *ABA Opinion* 280 (1949).

"Counsel apparently misconceived his role. It was his duty to honorably present his client's contentions in the light most favorable to his client. Instead he presumed to advise the court as to the validity and sufficiency of prisoner's motion, by letter. We therefore conclude that prisoner had no effective assistance of counsel and remand this case to the District Court with instructions to set aside the Judgment, appoint new counsel to represent the prisoner if he makes no objection thereto, and proceed anew." McCartney v. United States, 343 F. 2d 471, 472 (9th Cir. 1965).

12. "Here the court-appointed counsel had the transcript but refused to proceed with the appeal because he found no merit in it. . . . We cannot say that there was a finding of frivolity by either of the California courts or that counsel acted in any greater capacity than merely as *amicus curiae* which was condemned in *Ellis, supra*. Hence California's procedure did not furnish petitioner with counsel acting in the role of an advocate nor did it provide that full consideration and resolution of the matter as is obtained when counsel is acting in that capacity. . . .

"The constitutional requirement of substantial equality and fair process can only be attained where counsel acts in the role of an active advocate in behalf of his client, as opposed to that of *amicus curiae*. The no-merit letter and the procedure it triggers do not reach that dignity. Counsel should, and can with honor and without conflict, be of more assistance to his client and to the court. His role as advocate requires that he support his client's appeal to the best of his ability. Of course, if counsel finds his case to be wholly frivolous, after a conscientious examination of it, he should so advise the court and request permission to withdraw. That request must, however, be accompanied by a brief referring to anything in the record that might arguably support the appeal. A copy of counsel's brief should be furnished the indigent and time allowed him to raise any points that he chooses; the court — not counsel — then proceeds, after a full examination of all the proceedings, to decide whether the case is wholly frivolous. If it so finds it may grant counsel's request to withdraw and dismiss the appeal insofar as federal requirements are concerned, or proceed to a decision on the merits, if state law so requires. On the other hand, if it finds any of the legal points arguable on their merits (and therefore not frivolous) it must, prior to decision, afford the indigent the assistance of counsel to argue the appeal." Anders v. California, 386 U.S. 738, 744, 18 L. Ed. 2d 493, 498, 87 S. Ct. 1396, 1399-1400 (1967), *rehearing denied*, 388 U.S. 924, 18 L. Ed. 2d 1377, 87 S. Ct. 2094 (1967).

See Paul, *The Lawyer As a Tax Adviser*, 25 ROCKY MT. L. REV. 412, 432 (1953).

13. *See* ABA CANON 32.

legal position. A lawyer should never encourage or aid his client to commit criminal acts or counsel his client on how to violate the law and avoid punishment therefor.[14]

EC 7-6 Whether the proposed action of a lawyer is within the bounds of the law may be a perplexing question when his client is contemplating a course of conduct having legal consequences that vary according to the client's intent, motive, or desires at the time of the action. Often a lawyer is asked to assist his client in developing evidence relevant to the state of mind of the client at a particular time. He may properly assist his client in the development and preservation of evidence of existing motive, intent, or desire; obviously, he may not do anything furthering the creation or preservation of false evidence. In many cases a lawyer may not be certain as to the state of mind of his client, and in those situations he should resolve reasonable doubts in favor of his client.

EC 7-7 In certain areas of legal representation not affecting the merits of the cause or substantially prejudicing the rights of a client, a lawyer is entitled to make decisions on his own. But otherwise the authority to make decisions is exclusively that of the client and, if made within the framework of the law, such decisions are binding on his lawyer. As typical examples in civil cases, it is for the client to decide whether he will accept a settlement offer or whether he will waive his right to plead an affirmative defense. A defense lawyer in a criminal case has the duty to advise his client fully on whether a particular plea to a charge appears to be desirable and as to the prospects of success on appeal, but it is for the client to decide what plea should be entered and whether an appeal should be taken.[15]

EC 7-8 A lawyer should exert his best efforts to insure that decisions of his client are made only after the client has been informed of relevant considerations. A lawyer ought to initiate this decision-making process if the client does not do so. Advice of a lawyer to his client need not be confined to purely legal considerations.[16] A lawyer should advise his client of the possi-

---

14. "For a lawyer to represent a syndicate notoriously engaged in the violation of the law for the purpose of advising the members how to break the law and at the same time escape it, is manifestly improper. While a lawyer may see to it that anyone accused of crime, no matter how serious and flagrant, has a fair trial, and present all available defenses, he may not cooperate in planning violations of the law. There is a sharp distinction, of course, between advising what can lawfully be done and advising how unlawful acts can be done in a way to avoid conviction. Where a lawyer accepts a retainer from an organization, known to be unlawful, and agrees in advance to defend its members when from time to time they are accused of crime arising out of its unlawful activities, this is equally improper."
"See also *Opinion 155.*" *ABA Opinion* 281 (1952).

15. *See* ABA Special Committee on Minimum Standards for the Administration of Criminal Justice, *Standards Relating to Pleas of Guilty*, pp. 69-70 (1968).

16. "First of all, a truly great lawyer is a wise counselor to all manner of men in the varied crises of their lives when they most need disinterested advice. Effective counseling necessarily involves a thoroughgoing knowledge of the principles of the law not merely as they appear in the books but as they actually operate in action." Vanderbilt, *The Five Functions of the Lawyer: Service to Clients and the Public*, 40 A.B.A.J. 31 (1954).

ble effect of each legal alternative.[17] A lawyer should bring to bear upon this decision-making process the fullness of his experience as well as his objective viewpoint.[18] In assisting his client to reach a proper decision, it is often desirable for a lawyer to point out those factors which may lead to a decision that is morally just as well as legally permissible.[19] He may emphasize the possibility of harsh consequences that might result from assertion of legally permissible positions. In the final analysis, however, the lawyer should always remember that the decision whether to forego legally available objectives or methods because of non-legal factors is ultimately for the client and not for himself. In the event that the client in a non-adjudicatory matter insists upon a course of conduct that is contrary to the judgment and advice of the lawyer but not prohibited by Disciplinary Rules, the lawyer may withdraw from the employment.[20]

EC 7-9   In the exercise of his professional judgment on those decisions which are for his determination in the handling of a legal matter,[21] a lawyer should always act in a manner consistent with the best interests of his client.[22] However, when an action in the best interest of his client seems to him to be unjust, he may ask his client for permission to forego such action.

EC 7-10   The duty of a lawyer to represent his client with zeal does not militate against his concurrent obligation to treat with consideration all

---

17. "A lawyer should endeavor to obtain full knowlege of his client's cause before advising thereon. . . ." ABA CANON 8.

18. "[I]n devising charters of collaborative effort the lawyer often acts where all of the affected parties are present as participants. But the lawyer also performs a similar function in situations where this is not so, as, for example, in planning estates and drafting wills. Here the instrument defining the terms of collaboration may affect persons not present and often not born. Yet here, too, the good lawyer does not serve merely as a legal conduit for his client's desires, but as a wise counselor, experienced in the art of devising arrangements that will put in workable order the entangled affairs and interests of human beings." *Professional Responsibility: Report of the Joint Conference*, 44 A.B.A.J. 1149, 1162 (1958).

19. *See* ABA CANON 8.
"Vital as is the lawyer's role in adjudication, it should not be thought that it is only as an advocate pleading in open court that he contributes to the administration of the law. The most effective realization of the law's aims often takes place in the attorney's office, where litigation is forestalled by anticipating its outcome, where the lawyer's quiet counsel takes the place of public force. Contrary to popular belief, the compliance with the law thus brought about is not generally lip-serving and narrow, for by reminding him of its long-run costs the lawyer often deters his client from a course of conduct technically permissible under existing law, though inconsistent with its underlying spirit and purpose." *Professional Responsibility: Report of the Joint Conference*, 44 A.B.A.J. 1159, 1161 (1958).

20. "My summation of Judge Sharswood's view of the advocate's duty to the client is that he owes to the client the duty to use all legal means in support of the client's case. However, at the same time Judge Sharswood recognized that many advocates would find this obligation unbearable if applicable without exception. Therefore, the individual lawyer is given the choice of representing his client fully within the bounds set by the law *or of telling his client that he cannot do so,* so that the client may obtain another attorney if he wishes." Thode, *The Ethical Standard for the Advocate,* 39 TEXAS L. REV. 575, 582 (1961).
Cf. CODE OF PROFESSIONAL RESPONSIBILITY, DR 2-110 (C).

21. *See* ABA CANON 24.

22. Thode, *The Ethical Standard for the Advocate,* 39 TEXAS L. REV. 575, 592 (1961).

persons involved in the legal process and to avoid the infliction of needless harm.

EC 7-11 The responsibilities of a lawyer may vary according to the intelligence, experience, mental condition or age of a client, the obligation of a public officer, or the nature of a particular proceeding. Examples include the representation of an illiterate or an incompetent, service as a public prosecutor or other government lawyer, and appearances before administrative and legislative bodies.

EC 7-12 Any mental or physical condition of a client that renders him incapable of making a considered judgment on his own behalf casts additional responsibilities upon his lawyer. Where an incompetent is acting through a guardian or other legal representative, a lawyer must look to such representative for those decisions which are normally the prerogative of the client to make. If a client under disability has no legal representative, his lawyer may be compelled in court proceedings to make decisions on behalf of the client. If the client is capable of understanding the matter in question or of contributing to the advancement of his interests, regardless of whether he is legally disqualified from performing certain acts, the lawyer should obtain from him all possible aid. If the disability of a client and the lack of a legal representative compel the lawyer to make decisions for his client, the lawyer should consider all circumstances then prevailing and act with care to safeguard and advance the interests of his client. But obviously a lawyer cannot perform any act or make any decision which the law requires his client to perform or make, either acting for himself if competent, or by a duly constituted representative if legally incompetent.

EC 7-13 The responsibility of a public prosecutor differs from that of the usual advocate; his duty is to seek justice, not merely to convict.[24] This special duty exists because: (1) the prosecutor represents the sovereign and therefore should use restraint in the discretionary exercise of governmental powers, such as in the selection of cases to prosecute; (2) during trial the prosecutor is not only an advocate but he also may

---

24. *See* ABA CANON 5 and Berger v. United States, 295 U.S. 78, 79 L. Ed. 1314, 55 S. Ct. 629 (1935).

"The public prosecutor cannot take as a guide for the conduct of his office the standards of an attorney appearing on behalf of an individual client. The freedom elsewhere wisely granted to a partisan advocate must be severely curtailed if the prosecutor's duties are to be properly discharged. The public prosecutor must recall that he occupies a dual role, being obligated, on the one hand, to furnish that adversary element essential to the informed decision of any controversy, but being possessed, on the other, of important governmental powers that are pledged to the accomplishment of one objective only, that of impartial justice. When the prosecutor is recreant to the trust implicit in his office, he undermines confidence, not only in his profession, but in government and the very ideal of justice itself." *Professional Responsibility: Report of the Joint Conference,* 44 A.B.A.J. 1159, 1218 (1958).

"The prosecuting attorney is the attorney for the state, and it is his primary duty not to convict but to see that justice is done." *ABA Opinion* 150 (1936).

make decisions normally made by an individual client, and those affecting the public interest should be fair to all; and (3) in our system of criminal justice the accused is to be given the benefit of all reasonable doubts. With respect to evidence and witnesses, the prosecutor has responsibilities different from those of a lawyer in private practice: the prosecutor should make timely disclosure to the defense of available evidence, known to him, that tends to negate the guilt of the accused, mitigate the degree of the offense, or reduce the punishment. Further, a prosecutor should not intentionally avoid pursuit of evidence merely because he believes it will damage the prosecutor's case or aid the accused.

EC 7-14   A governmental lawyer who has discretionary power relative to litigation should refrain from instituting or continuing litigation that is obviously unfair. A government lawyer not having such discretionary power who believes there is lack of merit in a controversy submitted to him should so advise his superiors and recommend the avoidance of unfair litigation. A government lawyer in a civil action or administrative proceeding has the responsibility to seek justice and to develop a full and fair record, and he should not use his position or the economic power of the government to harass parties or to bring about unjust settlements or results.

EC 7-15   The nature and purpose of proceedings before administrative agencies vary widely. The proceedings may be legislative or quasi-judicial, or a combination of both. They may be *ex parte* in character, in which event they may originate either at the instance of the agency or upon motion of an interested party. The scope of an inquiry may be purely investigative or it may be truly adversary looking toward the adjudication of specific rights of a party or of classes of parties. The foregoing are but examples of some of the types of proceedings conducted by administrative agencies. A lawyer appearing before an administrative agency,[25] regardless of the nature of the proceeding it is conducting, has the continuing duty to advance the cause of his client within the bounds of the law.[26] Where the applicable rules of the agency impose specific obligations upon a lawyer, it is his duty to comply therewith, unless the lawyer has a legitimate basis for challenging the validity thereof. In all appearances before administrative agencies, a lawyer should

25. As to appearances before a department of government, Canon 26 provides: "A lawyer openly ... may render professional services ... in advocacy of claims before departments of government, upon the same principles of ethics which justify his appearance before the Courts ...."

26. "But as an advocate before a service which itself represents the adversary point of view, where his client's case is fairly arguable, a lawyer is under no duty to disclose its weakness, any more than he would be to make such a disclosure to a brother lawyer. The limitations within which he must operate are best expressed in Canon 22 ...." *ABA Opinion* 314 (1965).

identify himself, his client if identity of his client is not privileged,[27] and the representative nature of his appearance. It is not improper, however, for a lawyer to seek from an agency information available to the public without identifying his client.

EC 7-16   The primary business of a legislative body is to enact laws rather than to adjudicate controversies, although on occasion the activities of a legislative body may take on the characteristics of an adversary proceeding, particularly in investigative and impeachment matters. The role of a lawyer supporting or opposing proposed legislation normally is quite different from his role in representing a person under investigation or on trial by a legislative body. When a lawyer appears in connection with proposed legislation, he seeks to affect the lawmaking process, but when he appears on behalf of a client in investigatory or impeachment proceedings, he is concerned with the protection of the rights of his client. In either event, he should identify himself and his client, if identity of his client is not privileged, and should comply with applicable laws and legislative rules.[28]

EC 7-17   The obligation of loyalty to his client applies only to a lawyer in the discharge of his professional duties and implies no obligation to adopt a personal viewpoint favorable to the interests or desires of his client.[29] While a lawyer must act always with circumspection in order that his conduct will not adversely affect the rights of a client in a matter he is then handling, he may take positions on public issues and espouse legal reforms he favors without regard to the individual views of any client.

EC 7-18   The legal system in its broadest sense functions best when persons in need of legal advice or assistance are represented by their own counsel. For this reason a lawyer should not communicate on the subject matter of the representation of his client with a person he knows to be represented in the matter by a lawyer, unless pursuant to law or rule of

---

27. See Baird v. Koerner, 279 F.2d 623 (9th Cir. 1960).

28. *See* ABA CANON 26.

29. "Law should be so practiced that the lawyer remains free to make up his own mind how he will vote, what causes he will support, what economic and political philosophy he will espouse. It is one of the glories of the profession that it admits of this freedom. Distinguished examples can be cited of lawyers whose views were at variance from those of their clients, lawyers whose skill and wisdom make them valued advisers to those who had little sympathy with their views as citizens." *Professional Responsibility: Report of the Joint Conference*, 44 A.B.A.J. 1159, 1217 (1958).

"No doubt some tax lawyers feel constrained to abstain from activities on behalf of a better tax system because they think that their clients may object. Clients have no right to object if the tax adviser handles their affairs competently and faithfully and independently of his private views as to tax policy. They buy his expert services, not his private opinions or his silence on issues that gravely affect the public interest." Paul, *The Lawyer as a Tax Adviser*, 25 ROCKY MT. L. REV. 412, 434 (1953).

court or unless he has the consent of the lawyer for that person.[30] If one is not represented by counsel, a lawyer representing another may have to deal directly with the unrepresented person; in such an instance, a lawyer should not undertake to give advice to the person who is attempting to represent himself,[31] except that he may advise him to obtain a lawyer.

Duty of the Lawyer to the Adversary System of Justice

EC 7-19 Our legal system provides for the adjudication of disputes governed by the rules of substantive, evidentiary, and procedural law. An adversary presentation counters the natural human tendency to judge too swiftly in terms of the familiar that which is not yet fully known,[32] the advocate, by his zealous preparation and presentation of facts and law, enables the tribunal to come to the hearing with an open and neutral mind and to render impartial judgments.[33] The duty of a lawyer to his client and his duty to the legal system are the same: to represent his client zealously within the bounds of the law.[34]

EC 7-20 In order to function properly, our adjudicative process requires an informed, impartial tribunal capable of administering justice promptly and efficiently[35] according to procedures that command public confidence and respect.[36] Not only must there be competent, adverse presentation of evidence and issues, but a tribunal must be aided by rules appropriate to an effective and dignified process. The procedures under which tribunals operate in our adversary system have been prescribed largely by legislative enactments, court rules and decisions, and administrative rules. Through the years certain concepts of proper professional conduct have become rules of law applicable to the adversary

30. *See* ABA CANON 9.

31. *Id.*

32. *See Professional Responsibility: Report of the Joint Conference*, 44 A.B.A.J. 1159, 1160 (1958).

33. "Without the participation of someone who can act responsibly for each of the parties, this essential narrowing of the issues [by exchange of written pleadings or stipulations of counsel] becomes impossible. But here again the true significance of partisan advocacy lies deeper, touching once more the integrity of the adjudicative process itself. It is only through the advocate's participation that the hearing may remain in fact what it purports to be in theory: a public trial of the facts and issues. Each advocate comes to the hearing prepared to present his proofs and arguments, knowing at the same time that his arguments may fail to persuade and that his proof may be rejected as inadequate. . . . The deciding tribunal, on the other hand, comes to the hearing uncommitted. It has not represented to the public that any fact can be proved, that any argument is sound, or that any particular way of stating a litigant's case is the most effective expression of its merits." *Professional Responsibility: Report of the Joint Conference*, 44 A.B.A.J. 1159, 1160-61 (1958).

34. *Cf.* ABA CANONS 15 and 32.

35. *Cf.* ABA CANON 21.

36. See *Professional Responsibility: Report of the Joint Conference*, 44 A.B.A.J. 1159, 1216 (1958).

adjudicative process. Many of these concepts are the bases for standards of professional conduct set forth in the Disciplinary Rules.

EC 7-21   The civil adjudicative process is primarily designed for the settlement of disputes between parties, while the criminal process is designed for the protection of society as a whole. Threatening to use, or using, the criminal process to coerce adjustment of private civil claims or controversies is a subversion of that process;[37] further, the person against whom the criminal process is so misused may be deterred from asserting his legal rights and thus the usefulness of the civil process in settling private disputes is impaired. As in all cases of abuse of judicial process, the improper use of criminal process tends to diminish public confidence in our legal system.

EC 7-22   Respect for judicial rulings is essential to the proper administration of justice; however, a litigant or his lawyer may, in good faith and within the framework of the law, take steps to test the correctness of a ruling of a tribunal.[38]

EC 7-23   The complexity of law often makes it difficult for a tribunal to be fully informed unless the pertinent law is presented by the lawyers in the cause. A tribunal that is fully informed on the applicable law is better able to make a fair and accurate determination of the matter before it. The adversary system contemplates that each lawyer will present and argue the existing law in the light most favorable to his client.[39] Where a lawyer knows of legal authority in the controlling jurisdiction directly adverse to the position of his client, he should inform the tribunal of its existence unless his adversary has done so; but, having made such disclosure, he may challenge its soundness in whole or in part.[40]

---

37. "We are of the opinion that the letter in question was improper, and that in writing and sending it respondent was guilty of unprofessional conduct. This court has heretofore expressed its disapproval of using threats of criminal prosecution as a means of forcing settlement of civil claims. . . .

"Respondent has been guilty of a violation of a principle which condemns any confusion of threats of criminal prosecution with the enforcement of civil claims. For this misconduct he should be severely censured." Matter of Gelman, 230 App. Div. 524, 527, N. Y. S. 416, 419 (1930).

38. "An attorney has the duty to protect the interests of his client. He has a right to press legitimate argument and to protest an erroneous ruling." Gallagher v. Municipal Court, 31 Cal. 2d 784, 796, 192 P.2d 905, 913 (1948).

"There must be protection, however, in the far more frequent case of the attorney who stands on his rights and combats the order in good faith and without disrespect believing with good cause that it is void, for it is here that the independence of the bar becomes valuable." Note, 39 COLUM. L. REV. 433, 438 (1939).

39. "Too many do not understand that accomplishment of the layman's abstract ideas of justice is the function of the judge and jury, and that it is the lawyer's sworn duty to portray his client's case in its most favorable light." Rochelle and Payne, *The Struggle for Public Understanding*, 25 TEXAS B.J. 109, 159 (1962).

40. "We are of the opinion that this Canon requires the lawyer to disclose such decisions [that are adverse to his client's contentions] to the court. He may, of course, after doing so, challenge the soundness of the decisions or present reasons which he believes would warrant the court in not following them in the pending case." *ABA Opinion* 146 (1935).

EC 7-24 In order to bring about just and informed decisions, evidentiary and procedural rules have been established by tribunals to permit the inclusion of relevant evidence and argument and the exclusion of all other considerations. The expression by a lawyer of his personal opinion as to the justness of a cause, as to the credibility of a witness, as to the culpability of a civil litigant, or as to the guilt or innocence of an accused is not a proper subject for argument to the trier of fact.[41] It is improper as to factual matters because admissible evidence possessed by a lawyer should be presented only as sworn testimony. It is improper as to all other matters because, were the rule otherwise, the silence of a lawyer on a given occasion could be construed unfavorably to his client. However, a lawyer may argue, on his analysis of the evidence, for any position or conclusion with respect to any of the foregoing matters.

EC 7-25 Rules of evidence and procedures are designed to lead to just decisions and are part of the framework of the law. Thus while a lawyer may take steps in good faith and within the framework of the law to test the validity of rules, he is not justified in consciously violating such rules and he should be diligent in his efforts to guard against his unintentional violation of them.[42] As examples, a lawyer should subscribe to or verify only those pleadings that he believes are in compliance with applicable law and rules; a lawyer should not make any prefatory statement before a tribunal in regard to the purported facts of the case on trial unless he believes that his statement will be supported by admissible evidence; a lawyer should not ask a witness a question solely for the purpose of harassing or embarrassing him; and a lawyer should not by subterfuge put before a jury matters which it cannot properly consider.

EC 7-26 The law and Disciplinary Rules prohibit the use of fraudulent, false, or perjured testimony or evidence.[43] A lawyer who knowingly[44] participates in introduction of such testimony or evidence is subject to discipline. A lawyer should, however, present any admissible evidence his client desires to have presented unless he knows, or from facts within his knowledge should know, that such testimony or evidence is false, fraudulent, or perjured.[45]

Cf. ABA Opinion 280 (1949) and Thode, *The Ethical Standard for the Advocate,* 39 TEXAS L. REV. 575, 585-86 (1961).

41. *See* ABA CANON 15.

"The traditional duty of an advocate is that he honorably uphold the contentions of his client. He should not voluntarily undermine them." Harders v. State of California, 373 F.2d 839, 842 (9th Cir. 1967).

42. *See* ABA CANON 22.

43. *Id.; cf.* ABA CANON 41.

44. *See generally ABA Opinion* 287 (1953) as to a lawyer's duty when he unknowingly participates in introducing perjured testimony.

45. "Under any standard of proper ethical conduct an attorney should not sit by silently and permit his client to commit what may have been perjury, and which certainly would mislead the court and the opposing party on a matter vital to the issue under consideration. . . .

EC 7-27 Because it interferes with the proper administration of justice, a lawyer should not suppress evidence that he or his client has a legal obligation to reveal or produce. In like manner, a lawyer should not advise or cause a person to secrete himself or to leave the jurisdiction of a tribunal for the purpose of making him unavailable as a witness therein.[46]

EC 7-28 Witnesses should always testify truthfully[47] and should be free from any financial inducements that might tempt them to do otherwise.[48] A lawyer should not pay or agree to pay a non-expert witness an amount in excess of reimbursement for expenses and financial loss incident to his being a witness; however, a lawyer may pay or agree to pay an expert witness a reasonable fee for his services as an expert. But in no event should a lawyer pay or agree to pay a contingent fee to any witness. A lawyer should exercise reasonable diligence to see that his client and lay associates conform to these standards.[49]

EC 7-29 To safeguard the impartiality that is essential to the judicial process, veniremen and jurors should be protected against extraneous influences.[50] When impartiality is present, public confidence in the judicial system is enhanced. There should be no extrajudicial communication with veniremen prior to trial or with jurors during trial by or on behalf of a lawyer connected with the case. Furthermore, a lawyer who is not connected with the case should not communicate with or cause another to communicate with a venireman or a juror about the case. After the trial, communication by a lawyer with jurors is permitted so long as he refrains from asking questions or making comments that tend to harass or embarrass the juror[51] or to influence actions of the juror in future cases. Were a lawyer to be prohibited from communicating af-

---

"Respondent next urges that it was his duty to observe the utmost good faith toward his client, and therefore he could not divulge any confidential information. This duty to the client of course does not extend to the point of authorizing collaboration with him in the commission of fraud." In re Carroll, 244 S.W.2d 474, 474-75 (Ky. 1951).

46. See ABA CANON 5; cf. ABA Opinion 131 (1935).

47. Cf. ABA CANON 39.

48. "The prevalence of perjury is a serious menace to the administration of justice, to prevent which no means have as yet been satisfactorily devised. But there certainly can be no greater incentive to perjury than to allow a party to make payments to its opponents witnesses under any guise or on any excuse, and at least attorneys who are officers of the court to aid it in the administration of justice, must keep themselves clear of any connection which in the slightest degree tends to induce witnesses to testify in favor of their clients." In re Robinson, 151 App. Div. 589, 600, 136 N.Y.S. 548, 556-57 (1912), aff'd, 209 N.Y. 354, 103 N.E. 160 (1913).

49. "It will not do for an attorney who seeks to justify himself against charges of this kind to show that he has escaped criminal responsibility under the Penal Law, nor can he blindly shut his eyes to a system which tends to suborn witnesses, to produce perjured testimony, and to suppress the truth. He has an active affirmative duty to protect the administration of justice from perjury and fraud, and that duty is not performed by allowing his subordinates and assistants to attempt to subvert justice and procure results for his clients based upon false testimony and perjured witnesses." Id., 151 App. Div. at 592, 136 N.Y.S. at 551.

50. See ABA CANON 23.

51. "[I]t is unfair to jurors to permit a disappointed litigant to pick over their private associations in search of something to discredit them and their verdict. And it would be unfair to the public too if jurors should understand that they cannot convict a man of means without risking

ter trial with a juror, he could not ascertain if the verdict might be subject to legal challenge, in which event the invalidity of a verdict might go undetected.[52] When an extrajudicial communication by a lawyer with a juror is permitted by law, it should be made considerately and with deference to the personal feelings of the juror.

EC 7-30 Vexatious or harassing investigations of veniremen or jurors seriously impair the effectiveness of our jury system. For this reason, a lawyer or anyone on his behalf who conducts an investigation of veniremen or jurors should act with circumspection and restraint.

EC 7-31 Communications with or investigations of members of families of veniremen or jurors by a lawyer or by anyone on his behalf are subject to the restrictions imposed upon the lawyer with respect to his communications with or investigations of veniremen and jurors.

EC 7-32 Because of his duty to aid in preserving the integrity of the jury system, a lawyer who learns of improper conduct by or towards a venireman, a juror, or a member of the family of either should make a prompt report to the court regarding such conduct.

EC 7-33 A goal of our legal system is that each party shall have his case, criminal or civil, adjudicated by an impartial tribunal. The attainment of this goal may be defeated by dissemination of news or comments which tend to influence judge or jury.[53] Such news or comments may prevent pro-

---

an inquiry of that kind by paid investigators, with, to boot, the distortions an inquiry of that kind can produce." State v. LaFera, 42 N.J. 97, 107, 199 A.2d 630, 636 (1946).

52. *ABA Opinion* 319 (1968) points out that "[m]any courts today, and the trend is in this direction, allow the testimony of jurors as to all irregularities in and out of the courtroom except those irregularities whose existence can be determined only by exploring the consciousness of a single particular juror, New Jesey v. Kociolek, 20 N.J. 92, 118 A.2d 812 (1955). Model Code of Evidence Rule 301. Certainly as to states in which the testimony and affidavits of jurors may be received in support of or against a motion for new trial, a lawyer, in his obligation to protect his client, must have the tools for ascertaining whether or not grounds for a new trial exist and it is not unethical for him to talk to and question jurors."

53. *Generally see* ABA ADVISORY COMMITTEE ON FAIR TRIAL AND FREE PRESS, STANDARDS RELATING TO FAIR TRIAL AND FREE PRESS (1966).

"[T]he trial court might well have proscribed extrajudicial statements by any lawyer, party, witness, or court official which divulged prejudicial matters .... See State v. Van Dwyne, 43 N.J. 369, 389, 204 A.2d 841, 852 (1964), in which the court interpreted Canon 20 of the American Bar Association's Canons of Professional Ethics to prohibit such statements. Being advised of the great public interest in the case, the mass coverage of the press, and the potential prejudicial impact of publicity, the court could also have requested the appropriate city and county officials to promulgate a regulation with respect to dissemination of information about the case by their employees. In addition, reporters who wrote or broadcast prejudicial stories, could have been warned as to the impropriety of publishing material not introduced in the proceedings. ... In this manner, Sheppard's right to a trial free from outside interference would have been given added protection without corresponding curtailment of the news media. Had the judge, the other officers of the court, and the police placed the interest of justice first, the news media would have soon learned to be content with the task of reporting the case as it unfolded in the courtroom — not pieced together from extrajudicial statements." Sheppard v. Maxwell, 384 U.S. 333, 361-62, 16 L. Ed. 2d 600, 619-20, 86 S. Ct. 1507, 1521-22 (1966).

"Court proceedings are held for the solemn purpose of endeavoring to ascertain the truth which is the *sine qua non* of a fair trial. Over the centuries Anglo-American courts have devised careful safeguards by rule and otherwise to protect and facilitate the performance of this high

spective jurors from being impartial at the outset of the trial[54] and may also interfere with the obligation of jurors to base their verdict solely upon the evidence admitted in the trial.[55] The release by a lawyer of out-of-court statements regarding an anticipated or pending trial may improperly affect the impartiality of the tribunal.[56] For these reasons, standards for permissible and prohibited conduct of a lawyer with respect to trial publicity have been established.

---

function. As a result, at this time those safeguards do not permit the televising and photographing of a criminal trial, save in two States and there only under restrictions. The federal courts prohibit it by specific rule. This is weighty evidence that our concepts of a fair trial do not tolerate such an indulgence. We have always held that the atmosphere essential to the preservation of a fair trial — the most fundamental of all freedoms — must be maintained at all costs." Estes v. State of Texas, 381 U.S. 532, 540, 14 L. Ed. 2d 543, 549, 85 S. Ct. 1628, 1631-32 (1965), *rehearing denied*, 382 U.S. 875, 15 L. Ed. 2d 118, 86 S. Ct. 18 (1965).

54. "Pretrial can create a major problem for the defendant in a criminal case. Indeed, it may be more harmful than publicity during the trial for it may well set the community opinion as to guilt or innocence. . . . The trial witnesses present at the hearing, as well as the original jury panel, were undoubtedly made aware of the peculiar public importance of the case by the press and television coverage being provided, and by the fact that they themselves were televised live and their pictures rebroadcast on the evening show." *Id.*, 381 U.S. at 536-37, 14 L. Ed. 2d at 546-47, 85 S. Ct. at 1629-30.

55. "The undeviating rule of this Court was expressed by Mr. Justice Holmes over half a century ago in Patterson v. Colorado, 205 U.S. 454, 462 (1907):
    The theory of our system is that the conclusions to be reached in a case will be induced only by evidence and argument in open court, and not by any outside influence, whether of private talk or public print."
Sheppard v. Maxwell, 384 U.S. 333, 351, 16 L. Ed. 2d 600, 614, 86 S. Ct. 1507, 1516 (1966).

"The trial judge has a large discretion in ruling on the issue of prejudice resulting from the reading by jurors of news articles concerning the trial. . . . Generalizations beyond that statement are not profitable, because each case must turn on its special facts. We have here the exposure of jurors to information of a character which the trial judge ruled was so prejudicial it could not be directly offered as evidence. The prejudice to the defendant is almost certain to be as great when that evidence reaches the jury through news accounts as when it is a part of the prosecution's evidence. . . . It may indeed be greater for it is then not tempered by protective procedures." Marshall v. United States, 360 U.S. 310, 312-13, 3 L. Ed. 2d 1250, 1252, 79 S. Ct. 1171, 1173 (1959).

"The experienced trial lawyer knows that an adverse public opinion is a tremendous disadvantage to the defense of his client. Although grand jurors conduct their deliberations in secret, they are selected from the body of the public. They are likely to know what the general public knows and to reflect the public attitude. Trials are open to the public, and aroused public opinion respecting the merits of a legal controversy creates a court room atmosphere which, without any vocal expression in the presence of the petit jury, makes itself felt and has its effect upon the action of the petit jury. Our fundamental concepts of justice and our American sense of fair play require that the petit jury shall be composed of persons with fair and impartial minds and without preconceived views as to the merits of the controversy, and that it shall determine the issues presented to it solely upon the evidence adduced at the trial and according to the law given in the instructions of the trial judge.

"While we may doubt that the effect of public opinion would sway or bias the judgment of the trial judge in an equity proceeding, the defendant should not be called upon to run that risk and the trial court should not have his work made more difficult by any dissemination of statements to the public that would be calculated to create a public demand for a particular judgment in a prospective or pending case." *ABA Opinion* 199 (1940).

Cf. Estes v. State of Texas, 381 U.S. 532, 544-45, 144 L. Ed. 2d 543, 551, 85 S. Ct. 1628, 1634 (1965), *rehearing denied*, 381 U.S. 875, 15 L. Ed. 2d 118, 86 S. Ct. 18 (1965).

56. *See* ABA CANON 20.

EC 7-34   The impartiality of a public servant in our legal system may be impaired by the receipt of gifts or loans. A lawyer,[57] therefore, is never justified in making a gift or a loan to a judge, a hearing officer, or an official or employee of a tribunal except as permitted by Section C(4) of Canon 5 of the Code of Judicial Conduct, but a lawyer may make a contribution to the campaign fund of a candidate for judicial office in conformity with Section B(2) under Canon 7 of the Code of Judicial Conduct.[58]

EC 7-35   All litigants and lawyers should have access to tribunals on an equal basis. Generally, in adversary proceedings a lawyer should not communicate with a judge relative to a matter pending before, or which is to be brought before, a tribunal over which he presides in circumstances which might have the effect or give the appearance of granting undue advantage to one party.[59] For example, a lawyer should not communicate with a tribunal by a writing unless a copy thereof is promptly delivered to opposing counsel or to the adverse party if he is not represented by a lawyer. Ordinarily an oral communication by a lawyer with a judge or hearing officer should be made only upon adequate notice to opposing counsel, or, if there is none, to the opposing party. A lawyer should not condone or lend himself to private importunities by another with a judge or hearing officer on behalf of himself or his client.

EC 7-36   Judicial hearings ought to be conducted through dignified and orderly procedures designed to protect the rights of all parties. Although a lawyer has the duty to represent his client zealously, he should not engage in any conduct that offends the dignity and decorum of proceedings.[60] While maintaining his independence, a lawyer should be respectful, courteous, and above-board in his relations with a judge or hearing officer before whom he appears.[61] He should avoid undue solicitude for the comfort or convenience of judge or jury and should avoid any other conduct calculated to gain special consideration.

---

57. Canon 3 observes that a lawyer "deserves rebuke and denunciation for any device or attempt to gain from a Judge special personal consideration or favor."
See ABA CANON 32.
58. "*Judicial Canon* 32 provides:
A judge should not accept any presents or favors from litigants, or form lawyers practicing before him or from others whose interests are likely to be submitted to him for judgment.
The language of this Canon is perhaps broad enough to prohibit campaign contributions by lawyers, practicing before the court upon which the candidate hopes to sit. However, we do not think it was intended to prohibit such contributions when the candidate is obligated, by force of circumstances over which he has no control, to conduct a campaign, the expense of which exceeds that which he should reasonably be expected to personally bear!"
ABA Opinion 226 (1941).
59. *See* ABA CANONS 3 and 32.
60. *Cf.* ABA CANON 18.
61. *See* ABA CANONS 1 and 3.

EC 7-37   In adversary proceedings, clients are litigants and though ill feeling may exist between clients, such ill feeling should not influence a lawyer in his conduct, attitude, and demeanor towards opposing lawyers.[62] A lawyer should not make unfair or derogatory personal reference to opposing counsel. Haranguing and offensive tactics by lawyers interfere with the orderly administration of justice and have no proper place in our legal system.

EC 7-38   A lawyer should be courteous to opposing counsel and should accede to reasonable requests regarding court proceedings, settings, continuances, waiver of procedural formalities, and similar matters which do not prejudice the rights of his client.[63] He should follow local customs of courtesy or practice, unless he gives timely notice to opposing counsel of his intention not to do so.[64] A lawyer should be punctual in fulfilling all professional commitments.[65]

EC 7-39   In the final analysis, proper functioning of the adversary system depends upon cooperation between lawyers and tribunals in utilizing procedures which will preserve the impartiality of tribunals and make their decisional processes prompt and just, without impinging upon the obligation of lawyers to represent their clients zealously within the framework of the law.

Disciplinary Rules

DR 7-101   Representing a Client Zealously

(A)   A lawyer shall not intentionally:[66]

(1)   Fail to seek the lawful objectives of his client through reasonably available means[67] permitted by law and the Disciplinary Rules, except as provided by DR 7-101 (B). A lawyer does not violate this Disciplinary Rule, however, by acceding to reasonable requests of opposing counsel which do not prejudice the rights of his client, by being punctual in fulfilling all professional commitments, by avoiding offensive tactics, or by treating with courtesy and consideration all persons involved in the legal process.

62. *See* ABA CANON 17.
63. *See* ABA CANON 24.
64. *See* ABA CANON 25.
65. *See* ABA CANON 21.
66. *See* ABA CANON 15.
67. *See* ABA CANONS 5 and 15; *cf.* ABA CANONS 4 and 32.

    (2)   Fail to carry out a contract of employment entered into with a client for professional services, but he may withdraw as permitted under DR 2-110, DR 5-102, and DR 5-105.

    (3)   Prejudice or damage his client during the course of the professional relationship,[68] except as required under DR 7-102 (B).

(B)   In his representation of a client, a lawyer may:

    (1)   Where permissible, exercise his professional judgment to waive or fail to assert a right or position of his client.

    (2)   Refuse to aid or participate in conduct that he believes to be unlawful, even though there is some support for an argument that the conduct is legal.

DR 7-102 Representing a Client Within the Bounds of the Law

(A)   In his representation of a client, a lawyer shall not:

    (1)   File a suit, assert a position, conduct a defense, delay a trial, or take other action on behalf of his client when he knows or when it is obvious that such action would serve merely to harass or maliciously injure another.[69]

    (2)   Knowingly advance a claim or defense that is unwarranted under existing law, except that he may advance such claim or defense if it can be supported by good faith argument for an extension, modification, or reversal of existing law.

    (3)   Conceal or knowingly fail to disclose that which he is required by law to reveal.

    (4)   Knowingly use perjured testimony or false evidence.[70]

    (5)   Knowingly make a false statement of law or fact.

    (6)   Participate in the creation or preservation of evidence when he knows or it is obvious that the evidence is false.

    (7)   Counsel or assist his client in conduct that the lawyer knows to be illegal or fraudulent.

    (8)   Knowingly engage in other illegal conduct or conduct contrary to a Disciplinary Rule.

(B)   A lawyer who receives information clearly establishing that:

    (1)   His client has, in the course of the representation, perpetrated a fraud upon a person or tribunal shall promptly call upon his client to rectify the same, and if his client refuses or is unable to do so, he shall reveal the fraud to the affected person or tribu-

---

68. *Cf.* ABA CANON 24.
69. *See* ABA CANON 30.
70. *Cf.* ABA CANONS 22 and 29.

nal, except when the information is protected as a privileged communication.[71]

(2) A person other than his client has perpetrated a fraud upon a tribunal shall promptly reveal the fraud to the tribunal.[72]

DR 7-103 Performing the Duty of Public Prosecutor or Other Government Lawyer[73]

(A) A public prosecutor or other government lawyer shall not institute or cause to be instituted criminal charges when he knows or it is obvious that the charges are not supported by probable cause.

(B) A public prosecutor or other government lawyer in criminal litigation shall make timely disclosure to counsel for the defendant, or to the defendant if he has no counsel, of the existence of evidence, known to the prosecutor or other government lawyer, that tends to negate the guilt of the accused, mitigate the degree of the offense, or reduce the punishment.

DR 7-104 Communicating With One of Adverse Interest[74]

(A) During the course of his representation of a client a lawyer shall not:

(1) Communicate or cause another to communicate on the subject of the representation with a party he knows to be represented by a lawyer in that matter unless he has the prior consent of the lawyer representing such other party[75] or is authorized by law to do so.

(2) Give advice to a person who is not represented by a lawyer, other than the advice to secure counsel,[76] if the interests of such

71. *See* ABA CANON 41; *cf.* Hinds v. State Bar, 19 Cal. 2d 87, 92-93, 119 P.2d 134, 137 (1941); *but see ABA Opinion* 287 (1953) and TEXAS CANON 38. *Also see* CODE OF PROFESSIONAL RESPONSIBILITY, DR 4-101(C) (2).

72. *See* Precision Inst. Mfg. Co. v. Automotive M.M. Co., 324 U.S. 806, 89 L. Ed. 1381, 65 S. Ct. 993 (1945).

73. *Cf.* ABA CANON 5.

74. "*Rule 12* .... A member of the State Bar shall not communicate with a party represented by counsel upon a subject of controversy, in the absence and without the consent of such counsel. This rule shall not apply to communications with a public officer, board, committee or body." CAL. BUSINESS AND PROFESSIONS CODE §6076 (West 1962).

75. *See* ABA CANON 9; *cf. ABA Opinions* 124 (1934), 108 (1934), 95 (1933), and 75 (1932); *also see* In re Schwabe, 242 Or. 169, 174-75, 408 P.2d 922, 924 (1965).

"It is clear from the earlier opinions of this committee that *Canon 9* is to be construed literally and does not allow a communication with an opposing party, without the consent of his counsel, though the purpose merely be to investigate the facts. *Opinions 117, 55, 66,*" *ABA Opinion* 187 (1938).

76. *Cf. ABA Opinion* 102 (1933).

person are or have a reasonable possibility of being in conflict with the interests of his client.[77]

DR 7-105 Threatening Criminal Prosecution

(A)   A lawyer shall not present, participate in presenting, or threaten to present criminal charges solely to obtain an advantage in a civil matter.

DR 7-106 Trial Conduct

(A)   A lawyer shall not disregard or advise his client to disregard a standing rule of a tribunal or a ruling of a tribunal made in the course of a proceeding, but he may take appropriate steps in good faith to test the validity of such rule or ruling.

(B)   In presenting a matter to a tribunal, a lawyer shall disclose:[78]
   (1)   Legal authority in the controlling jurisdiction known to him to be directly adverse to the position of his client and which is not disclosed by opposing counsel.[79]
   (2)   Unless privileged or irrelevant, the identities of the clients he represents and of the persons who employed him.[80]

77. *Cf.* ABA CANON 9 and *ABA Opinion* 58 (1931).
78. *Cf.* Note, 38 TEXAS L. REV. 107, 108-09 (1959).
79. "In the brief summary in the 1947 edition of the Committee's decisions (p. 17), *Opinion 146* was thus summarized: *Opinion 146* — A lawyer should disclose to the court a decision directly adverse to his client's case that is unknown to his adversary. . . .
"We would not confine the Opinion to 'controlling authorities' — i.e., those decisive of the pending case — but, in accordance with the tests hereafter suggested, would apply it to a decision directly adverse to any proposition of law on which the lawyer expressly relies, which would reasonably be considered important by the judge sitting on the case. . . .
". . . The test in every case should be: Is the decision which opposing counsel has overlooked one which the court should clearly consider in deciding the case? Would a reasonable judge properly feel that a lawyer who advanced, as the law, a proposition adverse to the undisclosed decision, was lacking in candor and fairness to him? Might the judge consider himself misled by an implied representation that the lawyer knew of no adverse authority?" *ABA Opinion* 280 (1949).
80. "The authorities are substantially uniform against any privilege as applied to the fact of retainer or identity of the client. The privilege is limited to confidential communications, and a retainer is not a confidential communication, although it cannot come into existence without some communication between the attorney and the — at that stage prospective — client." United States v. Pape, 144 F.2d 778, 782 (2d Cir. 1944), *cert. denied*, 323 U.S. 752, 89 L. Ed. 2d 602, 65 S. Ct. 86 (1944).
"To be sure, there may be circumstances under which the identification of a client may amount to the prejudicial disclosure of a confidential communication, as where the substance of a disclosure has already been revealed but not its source." Colton v. United States, 306 F.2d 633, 637 (2d Cir. 1962).

(C) In appearing in his professional capacity before a tribunal, a lawyer shall not:

   (1) State or allude to any matter that he has no reasonable basis to believe is relevant to the case or that will not be supported by admissible evidence.[81]

   (2) Ask any question that he has no reasonable basis to believe is relevant to the case and that is intended to degrade a witness or other person.[82]

   (3) Assert his personal knowledge of the facts in issue, except when testifying as a witness.

   (4) Assert his personal opinion as to the justness of a cause, as to the credibility of a witness, as to the culpability of a civil litigant, or as to the guilt or innocence of an accused;[83] but he may argue, on his analysis of the evidence, for any position or conclusion with respect to the matters stated herein.

   (5) Fail to comply with known local customs of courtesy or practice of the bar or a particular tribunal without giving to opposing counsel timely notice of his intent not to comply.[84]

   (6) Engage in undignified or discourteous conduct which is degrading to a tribunal.

---

81. *See* ABA CANON 22; *cf.* ABA CANON 17.

"The rule allowing counsel when addressing the jury the widest latitude in discussing the evidence and presenting the client's theories falls far short of authorizing the statement by counsel of matter not in evidence, or indulging in argument founded on no proof, or demanding verdicts for purposes other than the just settlement of the matters at issue between the litigants, or appealing to prejudice or passion. The rule confining counsel to legitimate argument is not based on etiquette, but on justice. Its violation is not merely an overstepping of the bounds of propriety, but a violation of a party's rights. The jurors must determine the issues upon the evidence. Counsel's address should help them do this, not tend to lead them astray." Cherry Creek Nat. Bank v. Fidelity & Cas. Co., 207 App. Div. 787, 790-91, 202 N.Y.S. 611, 614 (1924).

82. *Cf.* ABA CANON 18.

§6068. . . . It is the duty of an attorney: . . .

"(f) To abstain from all offensive personality, and to advance no fact prejudicial to the honor or reputation of a party or witness, unless required by the justice of the cause with which he is charged." CAL. BUSINESS AND PROFESSIONS CODE §6068 (West 1962).

83. "The record in the case at bar was silent concerning the qualities and character of the deceased. It is especially improper, in addressing the jury in a murder case, for the prosecuting attorney to make reference to his knowledge of the good qualities of the deceased where there is no evidence in the record bearing upon his character. . . . A prosecutor should never inject into his argument evidence not introduced at the trial." People v. Dukes, 12 Ill. 2d 334, 341, 146 N.E.2d 14, 17-18 (1957).

84. "A lawyer should not ignore known customs or practice of the Bar or of a particular Court, even when the law permits, without giving timely notice to the opposing counsel." ABA CANON 25.

(7)   Intentionally or habitually violate any established rule of procedure or of evidence.

DR 7-107   Trial Publicity[85]

(A)   A lawyer participating in or associated with the investigation of a criminal matter shall not make or participate in making an extrajudicial statement that a reasonable person would expect to be disseminated by means of public communication and that does more than state without elaboration:

    (1)   Information contained in a public record.

    (2)   That the investigation is in progress.

    (3)   The general scope of the investigation including a description of the offense and, if permitted by law, the identity of the victim.

    (4)   A request for assistance in apprehending a suspect or assistance in other matters and the information necessary thereto.

    (5)   A warning to the public of any dangers.

(B)   A lawyer or law firm associated with the prosecution or defense of a criminal matter shall not, from the time of the filing of a complaint, information, or indictment, the issuance of an arrest warrant, or arrest until the commencement of the trial or disposition without trial,

---

85. The provisions of Section (A), (B), (C), and (D) of this Disciplinary Rule incorporate the fair trial-free press standards which apply to lawyers as adopted by the ABA House of Delegates, Feb. 19, 1968, upon the recommendation of the Fair Trial and Free Press Advisory Committee of the ABA Special Committee on Minimum Standards for the Administration of Criminal Justice.

Cf. ABA CANON 20; *see generally* ABA ADVISORY COMMITTEE ON FAIR TRIAL AND FREE PRESS, STANDARDS RELATING TO FAIR TRIAL AND FREE PRESS (1966).

"From the cases coming here we note that unfair and prejudicial news comment on pending trials has become increasingly prevalent. Due process requires that the accused receive a trial by an impractical jury free from outside influences. Given the pervasiveness of modern communications and the difficulty of effacing prejudicial publicity from the minds of the jurors, the trial courts must take strong measures to ensure that the balance is never weighed against the accused. And appellate tribunals have the duty to make an independent evaluation of the circumstances. Of course, there is nothing that proscribes the press from reporting events that transpire in the courtroom. But where there is a reasonable likelihood that prejudicial news prior to trial will prevent a fair trial, the judge should continue the case until the threat abates, or transfer it to another county not so permeated with publicity. . . . The courts must take such steps by rule and regulation that will protect their processes from prejudicial outside interferences. Neither prosecutors, counsel for defense, the accused, witnesses, court staff nor enforcement officers coming under the jurisdiction of the court should be permitted to frustrate its function. Collaboration between counsel and the press as to information affecting the fairness of a criminal trial is not only subject to regulation, but is highly censurable and worthy of disciplinary measures." Sheppard v. Maxwell, 384 U.S. 333, 362-63, 16 L. Ed. 2d 600, 620, 86 S. Ct. 1507, 1522 (1966).

make or participate in making an extrajudicial statement that a reasonable person would expect to be disseminated by means of public communication and that relates to:

   (1)   The character, reputation, or prior criminal record (including arrests, indictments, or other charges of crime) of the accused.
   (2)   The possibility of a plea of guilty to the offense charged or to a lesser offense.
   (3)   The existence or contents of any confession, admission, or statement given by the accused or his refusal or failure to make a statement.
   (4)   The performance or results of any examinations or tests or the refusal or failure of the accused to submit to examinations or tests.
   (5)   The identity, testimony, or credibility of a prospective witness.
   (6)   Any opinion as to the guilt or innocence of the accused, the evidence, or the merits of the case.
(C) DR 7-107 (B) does not preclude a lawyer during such period from announcing:
   (1)   The name, age, residence, occupation, and family status of the accused.
   (2)   If the accused has not been apprehended, any information necessary to aid in his apprehension or to warn the public of any dangers he may present.
   (3)   A request for assistance in obtaining evidence.
   (4)   The identity of the victim of the crime.
   (5)   The fact, time, and place of arrest, resistance, pursuit, and use of weapons.
   (6)   The identity of investigating and arresting officers or agencies and the length of the investigation.
   (7)   At the time of seizure, a description of the physical evidence seized, other than a confession, admission, or statement.
   (8)   The nature, substance, or text of the charge.
   (9)   Quotations from or references to public records of the court in the case.
   (10) The scheduling or result of any step in the judicial proceedings.
   (11) That the accused denies the charges made against him.
(D) During the selection of a jury or the trial of a criminal matter, a lawyer or law firm associated with the prosecution or defense of a criminal matter shall not make or participate in making an extrajudicial statement that a reasonable person would expect to be disseminated by means of public communication and that relates to the trial, parties, or issues in the trial or other matters that are reasonably likely to interfere with a fair trial, except that he may quote from or refer without comment to public records of the court in the case.

(E)   After the completion of a trial or disposition without trial of a criminal matter and prior to the imposition of sentence, a lawyer or law firm associated with the prosecution or defense shall not make or participate in making an extrajudicial statement that a reasonable person would expect to be disseminated by public communication and that is reasonably likely to affect the imposition of sentence.

(F)   The foregoing provisions of DR 7-107 also apply to professional disciplinary proceedings and juvenile disciplinary proceedings when pertinent and consistent with other law applicable to such proceedings.

(G)   A lawyer or law firm associated with a civil action shall not during its investigation or litigation make or participate in making an extrajudicial statement, other than a quotation from or reference to public records, that a reasonable person would expect to be disseminated by means of public communication and that relates to:

(1)   Evidence regarding the occurrence or transaction involved.

(2)   The character, credibility, or criminal record of a party, witness, or prospective witness.

(3)   The performance or results of any examinations or tests or the refusal or failure of a party to submit to such.

(4)   His opinion as to the merits of the claims or defenses of a party, except as required by law or administrative rule.

(5)   Any other matter reasonably likely to interfere with a fair trial of the action.

(H)   During the pendency of an administrative proceeding, a lawyer or law firm associated therewith shall not make or participate in making a statement, other than a quotation from or reference to public records, that a reasonable person would expect to be disseminated by means of public communication if it is made outside the official course of the proceeding and relates to:

(1)   Evidence regarding the occurences or transaction involved.

(2)   The character, credibility, or criminal record of a party, witness, or prospective witness.

(3)   Physical evidence or the performance or results of any examinations or tests or the refusal or failure of a party to submit to such.

(4)   His opinion as to the merits of the claims, defenses, or positions of an interested person.

(5)   Any other matter reasonably likely to interfere with a fair hearing.

(I)   The foregoing provisions of DR 7-107 do not preclude a lawyer from replying to charges of misconduct publicly made against him or from participating in the proceedings of legislative, administrative, or other investigative bodies.

(J)   A lawyer shall exercise reasonable care to prevent his employees and associates from making an extrajudicial statement that he would be prohibited from making under DR 7-107.

DR 7-108   Communication with or Investigation of Jurors

(A)   Before the trial of a case a lawyer connected therewith shall not communicate with or cause another to communicate with anyone he knows to be a member of the venire from which the jury will be selected for the trial of the case.

(B)   During the trial of a case:
   (1)   A lawyer connected therewith shall not communicate with or cause another to communicate with any member of the jury.[86]
   (2)   A lawyer who is not connected therewith shall not communicate with or cause another to communicate with a juror concerning the case.

(C)   DR 7-108 (A) and (B) do not prohibit a lawyer from communicating with veniremen or jurors in the course of official proceedings.

(D)   After discharge of the jury from further consideration of a case with which the lawyer was connected, the lawyer shall not ask questions of or make comments to a member of that jury that are calculated merely to harass or embarrass the juror or to influence his actions in the future jury service.[87]

(E)   A lawyer shall not conduct or cause, by financial support or otherwise, another to conduct a vexatious or harassing investigation of either a venireman or a juror.

(F)   All restrictions imposed by DR 7-108 upon a lawyer also apply to communications with or investigations of members of a family of a venireman or a juror.

(G)   A lawyer shall reveal promptly to the court improper conduct by a venireman or a juror, or by another toward a venireman or a juror or a member of his family, of which the lawyer has knowledge.

DR 7-109   Contact with Witnesses

(A)   A lawyer shall not suppress any evidence that he or his client has a legal obligation to reveal or produce.[88]

---

86. *See* ABA CANON 23.
87. "[I]t would be unethical for a lawyer to harass, entice, induce or exert influence on a juror to obtain his testimony." *ABA Opinion* 319 (1968).
88. *See* ABA CANON 5.

(B) A lawyer shall not advise or cause a person to secrete himself or to leave the jurisdiction of a tribunal for the purpose of making him unavailable as a witness therein.[89]

(C) A lawyer shall not pay, offer to pay, or acquiesce in the payment of compensation to a witness contingent upon the content of his testimony or the outcome of the case.[90] But a lawyer may advance, guarantee, or acquiesce in the payment of:

  (1) Expenses reasonably incurred by a witness in attending or testifying.

  (2) Reasonable compensation to a witness for his loss of time in attending or testifying.

  (3) A reasonable fee for the professional services of an expert witness.

DR 7-110 Contact with Officials[91]

(A) A lawyer shall not give or lend any thing of value to a judge, official, or employee of a tribunal except as permitted by Section C(4) of Canon 5 of the Code of Judicial Conduct, but a lawyer may make a contribution to the campaign fund of a candidate for judicial office in conformity with Section B(2) under Canon 7 of the Code of Judicial Conduct.

(B) In an adversary proceeding, a lawyer shall not communicate, or cause another to communicate, as to the merits of the cause with a judge or an official before whom the proceeding is pending, except:

  (1) In the course of official proceedings in the cause.

  (2) In writing if he promptly delivers a copy of the writing to opposing counsel or to the adverse party if he is not represented by a lawyer.

  (3) Orally upon adequate notice to opposing counsel or to the adverse party if he is not represented by a lawyer.

  (4) As otherwise authorized by law, or by Section A(4) under Canon 3 of the Code of Judicial Conduct.[92]

---

89. *Cf.* ABA CANON 5.

"*Rule 15....* A member of the State Bar shall not advise a person, whose testimony could establish or tend to establish a material fact, to avoid service of process, or secrete himself, or otherwise to make his testimony unavailable." CAL. BUSINESS AND PROFESSIONS CODE §6076 (West 1962).

90. *See* In re O'Keefe, 49 Mont. 369, 142 P. 638 (1914).

91. *Cf.* ABA CANON 3.

92. "*Rule 16....* A member of the State Bar shall not, in the absence of opposing counsel, communicate with or argue to a judge or judicial officer except in open court upon the merits of a contested matter pending before such judge or judicial officer; nor shall he, without furnishing opposing counsel with a copy thereof, address a written communication to a judge or judicial officer concerning the merits of a contested matter pending before such judge or judi-

CANON 8
A LAWYER SHOULD ASSIST IN
IMPROVING THE LEGAL SYSTEM

Ethical Considerations

EC 8-1   Changes in human affairs and imperfections in human institutions make necessary constant efforts to maintain and improve our legal system.[1] This system should function in a manner that commands public respect and fosters the use of legal remedies to achieve redress of grievances. By reason of education and experience, lawyers are especially qualified to recognize deficiencies in the legal system and to initiate corrective measures therein. Thus they should participate in proposing and supporting legislation and programs to improve the system,[2] without regard to the general interests or desires of clients or former clients.[3]

EC 8-2   Rules of law are deficient if they are not just, understandable, and responsive to the needs of society. If a lawyer believes that the existence or absence of a rule of law, substantive or procedural, causes or contributes to an unjust result, he should endeavor by lawful means to obtain appropriate changes in the law. He should encourage the simplification of laws and the repeal or amendment of laws that are outmoded.[4] Likewise, legal procedures should be improved whenever experience indicates a change is needed.

---

cial officer. This rule shall not apply to ex parte matters." CAL. BUSINESS AND PROFESSIONS CODE §6076 (West 1962).

1. ". . . [Another] task of the great lawyer is to do his part individually and as a member of the organized bar to improve his profession, the courts, and the law. As President Theodore Roosevelt aptly put it, 'Every man owes some of his time to the upbuilding of the profession to which he belongs.' Indeed, this obligation is one of the great things which distinguishes a profession from a business. The soundness and the necessity of President Roosevelt's admonition insofar as it relates to the legal profession cannot be doubted. The advances in natural science and technology are so startling and the velocity of change in business and in social life is so great that the law along with the other social sciences, and even human life itself, is in grave danger of being extinguished by new gods of its own invention if it does not awake from its lethargy. Vanderbilt, *The Five Functions of the Lawyer: Service to Clients and the Public*, 40 A.B.A.J. 31, 31-32 (1954).

2. *See* ABA CANON 29; *Cf.* Cheatham, *The Lawyer's Role and Surroundings*, 25 ROCKY MT. L. REV. 405, 406-07 (1953).

"The lawyer tempted by repose should recall the heavy costs paid by his profession when needed legal reform has to be accomplished through the initiative of public-spirited laymen. Where change must be thrust from without upon an unwilling Bar, the public's least flattering picture of the lawyer seems confirmed. The lawyer concerned for the standing of his profession will, therefore, interest himself actively in the improvement of the law. In doing so he will not only help to maintain confidence in the Bar, but will have the satisfaction of meeting a responsibility inhering in the nature of his calling." *Professional Responsibility: Report of the Joint Conference*, 44 A.B.A.J. 1159, 1217 (1958).

3. *See* Stayton, *Cum Honore Officium*, 19 TEX. B.J. 765, 766 (1956); *Professional Responsibility: Report of the Joint Conference*, 44 A.B.A.J. 1159, 1162 (1958); and Paul, *The Lawyer as a Tax Adviser*, 25 ROCKY MT. L. REV. 412, 433-34 (1953).

4. "There are few great figures in the history of the Bar who have not concerned themselves with the reform and improvement of the law. The special obligation of the profession with

EC 8-3   The fair administration of justice requires the availability of competent lawyers. Members of the public should be educated to recognize the existence of legal problems and the resultant need for legal services, and should be provided methods for intelligent selection of counsel. Those persons unable to pay for legal services should be provided needed services. Clients and lawyers should not be penalized by undue geographical restraints upon representation in legal matters, and the bar should address itself to improvements in licensing, reciprocity, and admission procedures consistent with the needs of modern commerce.

EC 8-4   Whenever a lawyer seeks legislative or administrative changes, he should identify the capacity in which he appears, whether on behalf of himself, a client, or the public.[5] A lawyer may advocate such changes on behalf of a client even though he does not agree with them. But when a lawyer purports to act on behalf of the public, he should espouse only those changes which he conscientiously believes to be in the public interest.

EC 8-5   Fraudulent, deceptive, or otherwise illegal conduct by a participant in a proceeding before a tribunal or legislative body is inconsistent with fair administration of justice, and it should never be participated in or condoned by lawyers. Unless constrained by his obligation to preserve the confidences and secrets of his client, a lawyer should reveal to appropriate authorities any knowledge he may have of such improper conduct.

EC 8-6   Judges and administrative officials having adjudicatory powers ought to be persons of integrity, competence, and suitable temperament. Generally, lawyers are qualified, by personal observation or investigation, to evaluate the qualifications of persons seeking or being considered for such public offices, and for this reason they have a special responsibility to aid in the selection of only those who are qualified.[6] It is the duty of lawyers to endeavor to prevent political considerations from outweighing judicial fitness in the selection of judges. Lawyers should protest earnestly

---

respect to legal reform rests on considerations too obvious to require enumeration. Certainly it is the lawyer who has both the best chance to know when the law is working badly and the special competence to put it in order." *Professional Responsibililty: Report of the Joint Conference,* 44 A.B.A.J. 1159, 1217 (1958).

5. "*Rule 14.* . . . A member of the State Bar shall not communicate with, or appear before, a public officer, board, committee or body, in his professional capacity, without first disclosing that he is an attorney representing interests that may be affected by action of such officer, board, committee or body." CAL. BUSINESS AND PROFESSIONS CODE §6076 (West 1962).

6. *See* ABA CANON 2.

"Lawyers are better able than laymen to appraise accurately the qualifications of candidates for judicial office. It is proper that they should make that appraisal known to the voters in a proper and dignified manner. A lawyer may with propriety endorse a candidate for judicial office and seek like endorsement from other lawyers. But the lawyer who endorses a judicial candidate or seeks that endorsement from other lawyers should be actuated by a sincere belief in the superior qualifications of the candidate for judicial service and not by personal or selfish motives; and a lawyer should not use or attempt to use the power or prestige of the judicial office to secure such endorsement. On the other hand, the lawyer whose endorsement is sought, if he believes the candidate lacks the essential qualifications for the office or believes the opposing candidate is better qualified, should have the courage and moral stamina to refuse the request for endorsement." *ABA Opinion* 189 (1938).

against the appointment or election of those who are unsuited for the bench and should strive to have elected[7] or appointed thereto only those who are willing to forego pursuits, whether of a business, political, or other nature, that may interfer with the free and fair consideration of questions presented for adjudication. Adjudicatory officials, not being wholly free to defend themselves, are entitled to receive the support of the bar against unjust criticism.[8] While a lawyer as a citizen has a right to criticize such officials publicly,[9] he should be certain of the merit of his complaint, use appropriate language, and avoid petty criticisms, for unrestrained and intemperate statements tend to lessen public confidence in our legal system.[10] Criticisms motivated by reasons other than a desire to improve the legal system are not justified.

EC 8-7 Since lawyers are a vital part of the legal system, they should be persons of integrity, of professional skill, and of dedication to the improvement of the system. Thus a lawyer should aid in establishing, as well as enforcing, standards of conduct adequate to protect the public by insuring that those who practice law are qualified to do so.

EC 8-8 Lawyers often serve as legislators or as holders of other public offices. This is highly desirable, as lawyers are uniquely qualified to make significant contributions to the improvement of the legal system. A lawyer who is a public officer, whether full or part-time, should not engage in activities in which his personal or professional interests are or foreseeably may be in conflict with his official duties.[11]

---

7. "[W]e are of the opinion that, whenever a candidate for judicial office merits the endorsement and support of lawyers, the lawyers may make financial contributions toward the campaign if its cost, when reasonably conducted, exceeds that which the candidate would be expected to bear personally." *ABA Opinion* 226 (1941).

8. *See* ABA CANON 1.

9. "Citizens have a right under our constitutional system to criticize governmental officials and agencies, Courts are not, and should not be, immune to such criticism." Konigsberg v. State Bar of California, 353 U.S. 252, 269 (1957).

10. "[E]very lawyer, worthy of respect, realizes that public confidence in our courts is the cornerstone of our governmental structure, and will refrain from unjustified attack on the character of the judge, while recognizing the duty to denounce and expose a corrupt or dishonest judge." Kentucky State Bar Ass'n. v. Lewis, 287 S.W. 2d 321, 326 (Ky. 1955).

"We should be the last to deny that Mr. Meeker has the right to uphold the honor of the profession and to expose without fear or favor corrupt or dishonest conduct in the profession, whether the conduct be that of a judge or not . . . However, this Canon [29] does not permit one to make charges which are false and untrue and unfounded in fact. When one's fancy leads him to make false charges, attacking the character and integrity of others, he does so at his peril. He should not do so without adequate proof of his charges and he is certainly not authorized to make careless, untruthful and vile charges against his professional brethren." In re Meeker, 76 N. M. 354, 364-65, 414 P.2d 862, 869 (1966), *appeal dismissed*, 385 U.S. 449, 17 L. Ed. 2d 510, 87 S. Ct. 613 (1967).

11. "*Opinins 16, 30, 34, 77, 118* and *134* relate to *Canon 6*, and pass on questions concerning the propriety of the conduct of an attorney who is a public officer, in representing private interests adverse to those of the public body which he represents. The principle applied in those opinions is that an attorney holding public office should avoid all conduct which might lead the layman to conclude that the attorney is utilizing his public position to further his professional success or personal interests." *ABA Opinion* 192 (1939).

EC 8-9 The advancement of our legal system is of vital importance in maintaining the rule of law and in facilitating orderly changes; therefore, lawyers should encourage, and should aid in making, needed changes and improvements.

Disciplinary Rules

DR 8-101 Action as a Public Official

(A) A lawyer who holds public office shall not:
(1) Use his public position to obtain, or attempt to obtain, a special advantage in legislative matters for himself or for a client under circumstances where he knows or it is obvious that such action is not in the public interest.
(2) Use his public position to influence, or attempt to influence, a tribunal to act in favor of himself or of a client.
(3) Accept any thing of value from any person when the lawyer knows or it is obvious that the offer is for the purpose of influencing his action as a public official.

DR 8-102 Statements Concerning Judges and Other Adjudicatory Officers[12]

(A) A lawyer shall not knowingly make false statements of fact concerning the qualifications of a candidate for election or appointment to a judicial office.
(B) A lawyer shall not knowingly make false accusations against a judge or other adjudicatory officer.

"The next question is whether a lawyer-member of a legislative body may appear as counsel or co-counsel at hearings before a zoning board of appeals, or similar tribunal, created by the legislative group of which he is a member. We are of the opinion that he may practice before fact-finding officers, hearing bodies and comissioners, since under our views he may appear as counsel in the courts where his municipality is a party. Decisions made at such hearings are usually subject to administrative review by the courts upon the record there made. It would be inconsistent to say that a lawyer-member of a legislative body could not participate in a hearing at which the record is made, but could appear thereafter when the cause is heard by the courts on administrative review. This is subject to an important exception. He should not appear as counsel where the matter is subjet to review by the legislative body of which he is a member. . . . We are of the opinion that where a lawyer does so appear there would be conflict of interests between his duty as an advocate for his client on the one hand and the obligation to his governmental unit on the other." In re Becker, 16 Ill. 2d 488, 494-95, 158 N. E. 2d 753, 756-57 (1959).

Cf. ABA Opinions 186 (1938), 136 (1935), 118 (1934), and 77 (1932).

12. *Cf.* ABA CANONS 1 and 2.

DR 8-103   Lawyer Candidate for Judicial Office

(A)   A lawyer who is a candidate for judicial office shall comply with the applicable provisions of Canon 7 of the Code of Judicial Conduct.

CANON 9
A LAWYER SHOULD AVOID EVEN THE APPEARANCE OF PROFESSIONAL IMPROPRIETY

Ethical Considerations

EC 9-1   Continuation of the American concept that we are to be governed by rules of law requires that the peope have faith that justice can be obtained through our legal system.[1] A lawyer should promote public confidence in our system and in the legal profession.[2]

EC 9-2   Public confidence in law and lawyers may be eroded by irresponsible or improper conduct of a lawyer. On occasion, ethical conduct of a lawyer may appear to laymen to be unethical. In order to avoid misunderstandings and hence to maintain confidence, a lawyer should fully and promptly inform his client of material developments in the matters being handled for the client. While the lawyer should guard against otherwise proper conduct that has a tendency to diminish public confidences in the legal system or in the legal profession, his duty to clients or to the public should never be subordinate merely because the full discharge of his obligation may be misunderstood or may tend to subject him or the legal profession to criticism. When explicit ethical guidance does not exist, a lawyer should determine his conduct by acting in a manner that promotes public confidence in the integrity and efficiency of the legal system and the legal profession.[3]

EC 9-3   After a lawyer leaves judicial office or other public employment, he should not accept employment in connection with any matter in which he had substantial responsibility prior to his leaving, since to accept employment would give the appearance of impropriety even if none exists.[4]

EC 9-4   Because the very essence of the legal system is to provide procedures by which matters can be presented in an impartial manner so that

---

1. "Integrity is the very breath of justice. Confidence in our law, our courts, and in the administration of justice is our supreme interest. No practice must be permitted to prevail which invites towards the administration of justice a doubt or distrust of its integrity." Erwin M. Jennings Co. v. DiGenova, 107 Conn. 491, 499, 141 A. 866, 868 (1928).

2. "A lawyer should never be reluctant or too proud to answer unjustified criticism of his profession, of himself, or of his brother lawyer. He should guard the reputation of his profession and of his brothers as zealously as he guards his own." Rochelle and Payne, *The Struggle for Public Understanding*, 25 TEXAS B. J. 109, 162 (1962).

3. *See* ABA CANON 29.

4. *See* ABA CANON 36.

they may be decided solely upon the merits, any statement or suggestion by a lawyer that he can or would attempt to circumvent those procedures is detrimental to the legal system and tends to undermine public confidence in it.

EC 9-5 Separation of the funds of a client from those of his lawyer not only serves to protect the client but also avoids even the appearance of impropriety, and therefore commingling of such funds should be avoided.

EC 9-6 Every lawyer owes a solemn duty to uphold the integrity and honor of his profession; to encourage respect for the law and for the courts and the judges thereof; to observe the Code of Professional Responsibility; to act as a member of a learned profession, one dedicated to public service; to cooperate with his brother lawyers in supporting the organized bar through the devoting of his time, efforts, and financial support as his professional standing and ability reasonably permit; to conduct himself so as to reflect credit on the legal profession and to inspire the confidence, respect, and trust of his clients and of the public; and to strive to avoid not only professional impropriety but also the appearance of impropriety.[5]

EC 9-7 A lawyer has an obligation to the public to participate in collective efforts of the bar to reimburse persons who have lost money or property as a result of the misappropriation or defalcation of another lawyer, and contribution to a clients' security fund is an acceptable method of meeting this obligation.

Disciplinary Rules

DR 9-101   Avoiding Even the Appearance of Impropriety[6]

(A)   A lawyer shall not accept private employment in a matter upon the merits of which he has acted in a judicial capacity.[7]

---

5. "As said in Opinion 49, of the Committee on Professional Ethics and Grievances of the American Bar Association, page 134: 'An attorney should not only avoid impropriety but should avoid the appearance of impropriety.' " State ex rel. Nebraska State Bar Ass'n v. Richards, 165 Neb. 80, 93, 84 N.W.2d 136, 145 (1957).

"It would also be preferable that such contribution [to the campaign of a candidate for judicial office] be made to campaign committee rather than to the candidate personally. In so doing, possible appearances of impropriety would be reduced to a minimum." ABA Opinion 226 (1941).

"The lawyer assumes high duties, and has imposed upon him grave responsibilities. He may be the means of much good or much mischief. Interests of vast magnitude are entrusted to him; confidence is reposed in him; life, liberty, character and property should be protected by him. He should guard, with jealous watchfulness, his own reputation, as well as that of his profession." People ex rel. Cutler v. Ford, 54 Ill. 520, 522 (1870), and also quoted in State Board of Law Examiners v. Sheldon, 43 Wyo. 522, 526, 7 P.2d 226, 227 (1932).

See ABA *Opinion* 150 (1936).

6. *Cf.* CODE OF PROFESSIONAL RESPONSIBILITY, EC 5-6.

7. *See* ABA CANON 36.

(B)   A lawyer shall not accept private employment in a matter in which he had substantial responsibility while he was a public employee.[8]

(C)   A lawyer shall not state or imply that he is able to influence improperly or upon irrelevant grounds any tribunal, legislative body,[9] or public official.

DR 9-102   Preserving Identity of Funds and Property of a Client[10]

(A)   All funds of clients paid to a lawyer or law firm, other than advances for costs and expenses, shall be deposited in one or more identifiable

---

"It is the duty of the judge to rule on questions of law and evidence in misdemeanor cases and examinations in felony cases. That duty calls for impartial and uninfluenced judgment, regardless of the effect on those immediately involved or others who may, directly or indirectly, be affected. Discharge of that duty might be greatly interfered with if the judge, in another capacity, were permitted to hold himself out to employment by those who are to be, or who may be, brought to trial in felony cases, even though he did not conduct the examination. His private interests as a lawyer in building up his clientele, his duty as such zealously to espouse the cause of his private clients and to defend against charges of crime brought by law-enforcement agencies of which he is a part, might prevent, or even destroy, that unbiased judicial judgment which is so essential in the administration of justice.

"In our opinion, acceptance of a judgeship with the duties of conducting misdemeanor trials, and examinations in felony cases to determine whether those accused should be bound over for trial in a higher court, ethically bars the judge from acting as attorney for the defendants upon such trial, whether they were examined by him or by some other judge. Such a practice would not only diminish public confidence in the administration of justice in both courts, but would produce serious conflict between the private interests of the judge, as a lawyer, and of his clients, and his duties as a judge in adjudicating important phases of criminal processes in other cases. The public and private duties would be incompatible. The prestige of the judicial office would be diverted to private benefit, and the judicial office would be demeaned thereby." *ABA Opinion* 242 (1942).

"A lawyer, who has previously occupied a judicial position or acted in a judicial capacity, shoud refrain from accepting employment in any matter involving the same facts as were involved in any specific question which he acted upon in a judicial capacity and, for the same reasons, should also refrain from accepting any employment which might reasonably appear to involve the same facts." *ABA Opinion* 49 (1931).

See *ABA Opinion* 110 (1934).

8. See *ABA Opinions* 135 (1935) and 134 (1935); *cf.* ABA CANON 36 and *ABA Opinions* 39 (1931) and 26 (1930). *But see ABA Opinion* 37 (1931).

9. "[A statement by a governmental department or agency with regard to a lawyer resigning from its staff that includes a laudation of his legal ability] carries implications, probably not founded in fact, that the lawyer's acquaintance and previous relations with the personnel of the administrative agencies of the government place him in an advantageous position in practicing before such agencies. So to imply would not only represent what probably is untrue, but would be highly reprehensible." *ABA Opinion* 184 (1938).

10. See ABA CANON 11.

"*Rule 9.* . . . A member of the State Bar shall not commingle the money or other property of a client with his own; and he shall promptly report to the client the receipt by him of all money and other property belonging to such client. Unless the client otherwise directs in writing, he shall promptly deposit his client's funds in a bank or trust company . . . in a bank account separate from his own account and clearly designated as 'Clients' Funds Account' or 'Trust Funds Account' or words of similar import. Unless the client otherwise directs in writing, securities of a client in bearer form shall be kept by the attorney in a safe deposit box at a bank or bank accounts maintained in the state in which the law office is situated and no funds belonging to the lawyer or law firm shall be deposited therein except as follows:

   (1)   Funds reasonably sufficient to pay bank charges may be deposited therein.

   (2)   Funds belonging in part to a client and in part presently or potentially to the lawyer or law firm must be deposited therein, but the portion belonging to the lawyer or law firm may be withdrawn when due unless the right of the lawyer or law firm to receive it is disputed by the client, in which event the disputed portion shall not be withdrawn until the dispute is finally resolved.

(B)   A lawyer shall:

   (1)   Promptly notify a client of the receipt of his funds, securities, or other properties.

   (2)   Identify and label securities and properties of a client promptly upon receipt and place them in a safe deposit box or other place of safekeeping as soon as practicable.

   (3)   Maintain complete records of all funds, securities, and other properties of a client coming into the possession of the lawyer and render appropriate accounts to his client regarding them.

   (4)   Promptly pay or deliver to the client as requested by a client the funds, securities, or other properties in the possession of the lawyer which the client is entitled to receive.

DEFINITIONS*

As used in the Disciplinary Rules of the Model Code of Professional Responsibililty:

   (1)   "Differing interests" include every interest that will adversely affect either the judgment or the loyalty of a lawyer to a client, whether it be a conflicting, inconsistent, diverse, or other interest.

   (2)   "Law firm" includes a professional legal corporation.

   (3)   "Person" includes a corporation, an association, a trust, a partnership, and any other organization or legal entity.

---

trust company, . . . which safe deposit box shall be clearly designated as 'Clients' Account' or 'Trust Account' or words of similar import, and be separate from the attorney's own safe deposit box." CAL. BUSINESS AND PROFESSIONS CODE §6076 (West 1962).

   "[C]ommingling is committed when a client's money is intermingled with that of hs attorney and its separate identity lost so that it may be used for the attorney's personal expenses or subjected to claims of his creditors. . . . The rule against commingling was adopted to provide against the probability in some cases, the possibility in many cases, and the danger in all cases that such commingling will result in the loss of clients' money." Black v. State Bar, 57 Cal. 2d 219, 225-26, 368 P.2d 118, 122, 18 Cal. Rptr. 518, 522 (1962).

   * "Confidence" and "secret" are defined in DR 4-101(A).

(4) "Professional legal corporation" means a corporation, or an association treated as a corporation, authorized by law to practice law for profit.

(5) "State" includes the District of Columbia, Puerto Rico, and other federal territories and possessions.

(6) "Tribunal" includes all courts and all other adjudicatory bodies.

(7) "A Bar association" includes a bar association of specialists as referred to in DR 2-105 (A) (1) or (4).

(8) "Qualified legal assistance organization" means an office or organization of one of the four types listed in DR 2-103(D) (1)-(4), inclusive that meets all the requirements thereof.

A.B.A. MODEL RULES OF PROFESSIONAL CONDUCT*

PREAMBLE: A LAWYER'S RESPONSIBILITIES

A lawyer is a representative of clients, an officer of the legal system and a public citizen having special responsibility for the quality of justice.

As a representative of clients, a lawyer performs various functions. As advisor, a lawyer provides a client with an informed understanding of the client's legal rights and obligations and explains their practical implications. As advocate, a lawyer zealously asserts the client's position under the rules of the adversary system. As negotiator, a lawyer seeks a result advantageous to the client but consistent with requirements of honest dealing with others. As intermediary between clients, a lawyer seeks to reconcile their divergent interests as an advisor and, to a limited extent, as a spokesman for each client. A lawyer acts as evaluator by examining a client's legal affairs and reporting about them to the client or to others.

In all professional functions a lawyer should be competent, prompt and diligent. A lawyer should maintain communication with a client concerning the representation. A lawyer should keep in confidence information relating to representation of a client except so far as disclosure is required or permitted by the Rules of Professional Conduct or other law.

A lawyer's conduct should conform to the requirements of the law, both in professional service to clients and in the lawyer's business and personal affairs. A lawyer should use the law's procedures only for legitimate purposes and not to harass or intimidate others. A lawyer should demonstrate respect for the legal system and for those who serve it, including judges, other lawyers and public officials. While it is a lawyer's duty, when necessary, to challenge the rectitude of official action, it is also a lawyer's duty to uphold legal process.

As a public citizen, a lawyer should seek improvement of the law, the administration of justice and the quality of service rendered by the legal profession. As a member of a learned profession, a lawyer should cultivate knowledge of the law beyond its use for clients, employ that knowledge in reform of the law and work to strengthen legal education. A lawyer should

---

*The Model Rules of Professional Conduct were adopted by the House of Delegates of the American Bar Association on August 2, 1983. Copyright © 1983 by the American Bar Association. All rights reserved. Reprinted with permission of the American Bar Association.

be mindful of deficiencies in the administration of justice and of the fact that the poor, and sometimes persons who are not poor, cannot afford adequate legal assistance, and should therefore devote professional time and civic influence in their behalf. A lawyer should aid the legal profession in pursuing these objectives and should help the bar regulate itself in the public interest.

Many of a lawyer's professional responsibilities are prescribed in the Rules of Professional Conduct, as well as substantive and procedural law. However, a lawyer is also guided by personal conscience and the approbation of professional peers. A lawyer should strive to attain the highest level of skill, to improve the law and the legal profession and to exemplify the legal profession's ideals of public service.

A lawyer's responsibilities as a representative of clients, an officer of the legal system and a public citizen are usually harmonious. Thus, when an opposing party is well represented, a lawyer can be a zealous advocate on behalf of a client and at the same time assume that justice is being done. So also, a lawyer can be sure that preserving client confidences ordinarily serves the public interest because people are more likely to seek legal advice, and thereby heed their legal obligations, when they know their communications will be private.

In the nature of law practice, however, conflicting responsibilities are encountered. Virtually all difficult ethical problems arise from conflict between a lawyer's responsibilities to clients, to the legal system and to the lawyer's own interest in remaining an upright person while earning a satisfactory living. The Rules of Professional Conduct prescribe terms for resolving such conflicts. Within the framework of these Rules many difficult issues of professional discretion can arise. Such issues must be resolved through the exercise of sensitive professional and moral judgment guided by the basic principles underlying the Rules.

The legal profession is largely self-governing. Although other professions also have been granted powers of self-government, the legal profession is unique in this respect because of the close relationship between the profession and the processes of government and law enforcement. This connection is manifested in the fact that ultimate authority over the legal profession is vested largely in the courts.

To the extent that lawyers meet the obligations of their professional calling, the occasion for government regulation is obviated. Self-regulation also helps maintain the legal profession's independence from government domination. An independent legal profession is an important force in preserving government under law, for abuse of legal authority is more readily challenged by a profession whose members are not dependent on government for the right to practice.

The legal profession's relative autonomy carries with it special responsibilities of self-government. The profession has a responsibility to assure that its regulations are conceived in the public interest and not in furtherance of parochial or self-interested concerns of the bar. Every lawyer is responsible for observance of the Rules of Professional Conduct. A lawyer should also aid in securing their observance by other lawyers. Neglect of these responsibilities compromises the independence of the profession and the public interest which it serves.

Lawyers play a vital role in the preservation of society. The fulfillment of this role requires an understanding by lawyers of their relationship to our legal system. The Rules of Professional Conduct, when properly applied, serve to define that relationship.

SCOPE

The Rules of Professional Conduct are rules of reason. They should be interpreted with reference to the purposes of legal representation and of the law itself. Some of the Rules are imperatives, cast in the terms "shall" or "shall not." These define proper conduct for purposes of professional discipline. Others, generally cast in the term "may," are permissive and define areas under the Rules in which the lawyer has professional discretion. No disciplinary action should be taken when the lawyer chooses not to act or acts within the bounds of such discretion. Other Rules define the nature of relationships between the lawyer and others. The Rules are thus partly obligatory and disciplinary and partly constitutive and descriptive in that they define a lawyer's professional role. Many of the Comments use the term "should." Comments do not add obligations to the Rules but provide guidance for practicing in compliance with the Rules.

The Rules presuppose a larger legal context shaping the lawyer's role. That context includes court rules and statutes relating to matters of licensure, laws defining specific obligations of lawyers and substantive and procedural law in general. Compliance with the Rules, as with all law in an open society, depends primarily upon understanding and voluntary compliance, secondarily upon reinforcement by peer and public opinion and finally, when necessary, upon enforcement through disciplinary proceedings. The Rules do not, however, exhaust the moral and ethical considerations that should inform a lawyer, for no worthwhile human activity can be completely defined by legal rules. The Rules simply provide a framework for the ethical practice of law.

Furthermore, for purposes of determining the lawyer's authority and responsibility, principles of substantive law external to these Rules determine whether a client-lawyer relationship exists. Most of the duties flowing from the client-lawyer relationship attach only after the client has requested the lawyer to render legal services and the lawyer has agreed to do so. But there are some duties, such as that of confidentiality under Rule 1.6, that may attach when the lawyer agrees to consider whether a client-lawyer relationship shall be established. Whether a client-lawyer relationship exists for any specific purpose can depend on the circumstances and may be a question of fact.

Under various legal provisions, including constitutional, statutory and common law, the responsibilities of government lawyers may include authority concerning legal matters that ordinarily reposes in the client in private client-lawyer relationships. For example, a lawyer for a government agency may have authority on behalf of the government to decide upon settlement or whether to appeal from an adverse judgment. Such authority in various respects is generally vested in the attorney general and the state's attorney in state government, and their federal counterparts, and the same may be true of other government law officers. Also, lawyers under the supervision of these officers may be authorized to represent several government agencies in intragovernmental legal controversies in circumstances where a private lawyer could not represent multiple private clients. They also may have authority to represent the "public interest" in circumstances where a private lawyer would not be authorized to do so. These Rules do not abrogate any such authority.

Failure to comply with an obligation or prohibition imposed by a Rule is a basis for invoking the disciplinary process. The Rules presuppose that disciplinary assessment of a lawyer's conduct will be made on the basis of the facts and circumstances as they existed at the time of the conduct in question and in recognition of the fact that a lawyer often has to act upon uncertain or incomplete evidence of the situation. Moreover, the Rules presuppose that whether or not discipline should be imposed for a violation, and the severity of a sanction, depend on all the circumstances, such as the willfulness and seriousness of the violation, extenuating factors and whether there have been previous violations.

Violation of a Rule should not give rise to a cause of action nor should it create any presumption that a legal duty has been breached. The Rules are designed to provide guidance to lawyers and to provide a structure for regulating conduct through disciplinary agencies. They are not designed to be a basis for civil liability. Furthermore, the purpose of the Rules can be subverted when they are invoked by opposing parties as procedural weapons. The fact that a Rule is a just basis for a lawyer's self-assessment, or for sanctioning a lawyer under the administration of a disciplinary authority, does not imply that an antagonist in a collateral proceeding or transaction has standing to seek enforcement of the Rule. Accordingly, nothing in the Rules should be deemed to augment any substantive legal duty of lawyers or the extra-disciplinary consequences of violating such a duty.

Moreover, these Rules are not intended to govern or affect judicial application of either the attorney-client or work product privilege. Those privileges were developed to promote compliance with law and fairness in litigation. In reliance on the attorney-client privilege, clients are entitled to expect that communications within the scope of the privilege will be protected against compelled disclosure. The attorney-client privilege is that of the client and not of the lawyer. The fact that in exceptional situations the lawyer under the Rules has a limited discretion to disclose a client confidence does not vitiate the proposition that, as a general matter, the client has a reasonable expectation that information relating to the client will not be voluntarily disclosed and that disclosure of such information may be judicially compelled only in accordance with recognized exceptions to the attorney-client and work product privileges.

The lawyer's exercise of discretion not to disclose information under Rule 1.6 should not be subject to reexamination. Permitting such reexamination would be incompatible with the general policy of promoting compliance with law through assurances that communications will be protected against disclosure.

The Comment accompanying each Rule explains and illustrates the meaning and purpose of the Rule. The Preamble and this note on Scope provide general orientation. The Comments are intended as guides to interpretation, but the text of each Rule is authoritative. Research notes were prepared to compare counterparts in the ABA Model Code of Professional Responsibility (adopted 1969, as amended) and to provide selected references to other authorities. The notes have not been adopted, do not constitute part of the Model Rules, and are not intended to affect the application or interpretation of the Rules and Comments.

TERMINOLOGY

"Belief" or "Believes" denotes that the person involved actually supposed the fact in question to be true. A person's belief may be inferred from circumstances.

"Consult" or "Consultation" denotes communication of information reasonably sufficient to permit the client to appreciate the significance of the matter in question.

"Firm" or "Law firm" denotes a lawyer or lawyers in a private firm, lawyers employed in the legal department of a corporation or other organization and lawyers employed in a legal services organization. See Comment, Rule 1.10.

"Fraud" or "Fraudulent" denotes conduct having a purpose to deceive and not merely negligent misrepresentation or failure to apprise another of relevant information.

"Knowingly," "Known," or "Knows" denotes actual knowledge of the fact in question. A person's knowledge may be inferred from circumstances.

"Partner" denotes a member of a partnership and a shareholder in a law firm organized as a professional corporation.

"Reasonable" or "Reasonably" when used in relation to conduct by a lawyer denotes the conduct of a reasonably prudent and competent lawyer.

"Reasonable belief" or "Reasonably believes" when used in reference to a lawyer denotes that the lawyer believes the matter in question and that the circumstances are such that the belief is reasonable.

"Reasonably should know" when used in reference to a lawyer denotes that a lawyer of reasonable prudence and competence would ascertain the matter in question.

"Substantial" when used in reference to degree or extent denotes a material matter of clear and weighty importance.

CLIENT-LAWYER RELATIONSHIP

Rule 1.1   Competence

A lawyer shall provide competent representation to a client. Competent representation requires the legal knowledge, skill, thoroughness and preparation reasonably necessary for the representation.

COMMENT:

Legal Knowledge and Skill

In determining whether a lawyer employs the requisite knowledge and skill in a particular matter, relevant factors include the relative complexity and specialized nature of the matter, the lawyer's general experience, the lawyer's training and experience in the field in question, the preparation and study the lawyer is able to give the matter and whether it is feasible to refer the matter to, or associate or consult with, a lawyer of established competence in the field in question. In many instances, the required proficiency is that of a general practitioner. Expertise in a particular field of law may be required in some circumstances.

A lawyer need not necessarily have special training or prior experience to handle legal problems of a type with which the lawyer is unfamiliar. A newly admitted lawyer can be as competent as a practitioner with long experience. Some important legal skills, such as the analysis of precedent, the evaluation of evidence and legal drafting, are required in all legal problems. Perhaps the most fundamental legal skill consists of determining what kind of legal problems a situation may involve, a skill that necessarily transcends any particular specialized knowledge. A lawyer can provide adequate representation in a wholly novel field through necessary study. Competent representation can also be provided through the association of a lawyer of established competence in the field in question.

In an emergency a lawyer may give advice or assistance in a matter in which the lawyer does not have the skill ordinarily required where referral to or consultation or association with another lawyer would be impractical. Even in an emergency, however, assistance should be limited to that reasonably necessary in the circumstances, for ill considered action under emergency conditions can jeopardize the client's interest.

A lawyer may accept representation where the requisite level of competence can be achieved by reasonable preparation. This applies as well to a lawyer who is appointed as counsel for an unrepresented person. See also Rule 6.2.

Thoroughness and Preparation

Competent handling of a particular matter includes inquiry into and analysis of the factual and legal elements of the problem, and use of methods and procedures meeting the standards of competent practitioners. It also includes adequate preparation. The required attention and preparation are determined in part by what is at stake; major litigation and complex transactions ordinarily require more elaborate treatment than matters of lesser consequence.

Maintaining Competence

To maintain the requisite knowledge and skill, a lawyer should engage in continuing study and education. If a system of peer review has been established, the lawyer should consider making use of it in appropriate circumstances.

Rule 1.2   Scope of representation

(a) A lawyer shall abide by a client's decisions concerning the objectives of representation, subject to paragraphs (c), (d) and (e), and shall consult with the client as to the means by which they are to be pursued. A lawyer shall abide by a client's decision whether to accept an offer of settlement of a matter. In a criminal case, the lawyer shall abide by the client's decision, after consultation with the lawyer, as to a plea to be entered, whether to waive jury trial and whether the client will testify.

(b) A lawyer's representation of a client, including representation by appointment, does not constitute an endorsement of the client's political, economic, social or moral views or activities.

(c)   A lawyer may limit the objectives of the representation if the client consents after consultation.

(d)   A lawyer shall not counsel a client to engage, or assist a client, in conduct that the lawyer knows is criminal or fraudulent, but a lawyer may discuss the legal consequences of any proposed course of conduct with a client and may counsel or assist a client to make a good faith effort to determine the validity, scope, meaning or application of the law.

(e)   When a lawyer knows that a client expects assistance not permitted by the rules of professional conduct or other law, the lawyer shall consult with the client regarding the relevant limitations on the lawyer's conduct.

COMMENT:

Scope of Representation

Both lawyer and client have authority and responsibility in the objectives and means of representation. The client has ultimate authority to determine the purposes to be served by legal representation, within the limits imposed by law and the lawyer's professional obligations. Within those limits, a client also has a right to consult with the lawyer about the means to be used in pursuing those objectives. At the same time, a lawyer is not required to pursue objectives or employ means simply because a client may wish that the lawyer do so. A clear distinction between objectives and means sometimes cannot be drawn, and in many cases the client-lawyer relationship partakes of a joint undertaking. In questions of means, the lawyer should assume responsibility for technical and legal tactical issues, but should defer to the client regarding such questions as the expense to be incurred and concern for third persons who might be adversely affected. Law defining the lawyer's scope of authority in litigation varies among jurisdictions.

In a case in which the client appears to be suffering mental disability, the lawyer's duty to abide by the client's decisions is to be guided by reference to Rule 1.14.

Independence From Client's Views or Activities

Legal representation should not be denied to people who are unable to afford legal services, or whose cause is controversial or the subject of popular disapproval. By the same token, representing a client does not constitute approval of the client's views or activities.

Services Limited in Objectives or Means

The objectives or scope of services provided by a lawyer may be limited by agreement with the client or by the terms under which the lawyer's services are made available to the client. For example, a retainer may be for a specifically defined purpose. Representation provided through a legal aid agency may be subject to limitations on the types of cases the agency handles. When a lawyer has been retained by an insurer to represent an insured, the representation may be limited to matters related to the insurance coverage. The terms upon which representation is undertaken may exclude specific objectives or means. Such limitations may exclude objectives or means that the lawyer regards as repugnant or imprudent.

An agreement concerning the scope of representation must accord with the Rules of Professional Conduct and other law. Thus, the client may not be asked to agree to representation so limited in scope as to violate Rule 1.1, or to surrender the right to terminate the lawyer's services or the right to settle litigation that the lawyer might wish to continue.

Criminal, Fraudulent and Prohibited Transactions

A lawyer is required to give an honest opinion about the actual consequences that appear likely to result from a client's conduct. The fact that a client uses advice in a course of action that is criminal or fraudulent does not, of itself, make a lawyer a party to the course of action. However, a lawyer may not knowingly assist a client in criminal or fraudulent conduct. There is a critical distinction between presenting an analysis of legal aspects of questionable conduct and recommending the means by which a crime or fraud might be committed with impunity.

When the client's course of action has already begun and is continuing, the lawyer's responsibility is especially delicate. The lawyer is not permitted to reveal the client's wrongdoing, except where permitted by Rule 1.6. However, the lawyer is required to avoid furthering the purpose, for example, by suggesting how it might be concealed. A lawyer may not continue assisting a client in conduct that the lawyer originally supposes is legally proper but then discovers is criminal or fraudulent. Withdrawal from the representation, therefore, may be required.

Where the client is a fiduciary, the lawyer may be charged with special obligations in dealings with a beneficiary.

Paragraph (d) applies whether or not the defrauded party is a party to the transaction. Hence, a lawyer should not participate in a sham transaction; for example, a transaction to effectuate criminal or fraudulent escape of tax liability. Paragraph (d) does not preclude undertaking a criminal defense incident to a general retainer for legal services to a lawful enterprise. The last clause of paragraph (d) recognizes that determining the validity or interpretation of a statute or regulation may require a course of action involving disobedience of the statute or regulation or of the interpretation placed upon it by governmental authorities.

Rule 1.3   Diligence

A lawyer shall act with reasonable diligence and promptness in representing a client.

COMMENT:

A lawyer should pursue a matter on behalf of a client despite opposition, obstruction or personal inconvenience to the lawyer, and may take whatever lawful and ethical measures are required to vindicate a client's cause or endeavor. A lawyer should act with commitment and dedication to the interests of the client and with zeal in advocacy upon the client's behalf. However, a lawyer is not bound to press for every advantage that might be realized for a client. A lawyer has professional discretion in determining the means by which a matter should be pursued. See Rule 1.2. A lawyer's workload should be controlled so that each matter can be handled adequately.

Perhaps no professional shortcoming is more widely resented than procrastination. A client's interests often can be adversely affected by the passage of time or the change of conditions; in extreme instances, as when a lawyer overlooks a statute of limitations, the client's legal position may be destroyed. Even when the client's interests are not affected in substance, however, unreasonable delay can cause a client needless anxiety and undermine confidence in the lawyer's trustworthiness.

Unless the relationship is terminated as provided in Rule 1.16, a lawyer should carry through to conclusion all matters undertaken for a client. If a lawyer's employment is limited to a specific matter, the relationship terminates when the matter has been resolved. If a lawyer has served a client over a substantial period in a variety of matters, the client sometimes may assume that the lawyer will continue to serve on a continuing basis unless the lawyer gives notice of withdrawl. Doubt about whether a client-lawyer relationship still exists should be clarified by the lawyer, preferably in writing, so that the client will not mistakenly suppose the lawyer is looking after the client's affairs when the lawyer has ceased to do so. For example, if a lawyer has handled a judicial or administrative proceeding that produced a result adverse to the client but has not been specifically instructed concerning pursuit of an appeal, the lawyer should advise the client of the possibility of appeal before relinquishing responsibility for the matter.

Rule 1.4   Communication

(a) A lawyer shall keep a client reasonably informed about the status of a matter and promptly comply with reasonable requests for information.
(b) A lawyer shall explain a matter to the extent reasonably necessary to permit the client to make informed decisions regarding the representation.

COMMENT:

The client should have sufficient information to participate intelligently in decisions concerning the objectives of the representation and the means by which they are to be pursued, to the extent the client is willing and able to do so. For example, a lawyer negotiating on behalf of a client should provide the client with facts relevant to the matter, inform the client of communications from another party and take other reasonable steps that permit the client to make a decision regarding a serious offer from another party. A lawyer who receives from opposing counsel an offer of settlement in a civil controversy or a proffered plea bargain in a criminal case should promptly inform the client of its substance unless prior discussions with the client have left it clear that the proposal will be unacceptable. See Rule 1.2(a). Even when a client delegates authority to the lawyer, the client should be kept advised of the status of the matter.

Adequacy of communcation depends in part on the kind of advice or assistance involved. For example, in negotiations where there is time to explain a proposal, the lawyer should review all important provisions with the client before proceeding to an agreement. In litigation a lawyer should explain the general strategy and prospects of success and ordinarily should consult the client on tactics that might injure or coerce others. On the other hand, a lawyer ordinarily cannot be expected to describe trial or negotiation strategy in detail. The guiding principle is that the lawyer should fulfill reasonable client expectations for information consistent with the duty to act in the client's best interests, and the client's overall requirements as to the character of representation.

Ordinarily, the information to be provided is that appropriate for a client who is a comprehending and responsible adult. However, fully informing the client according to this standard may be impracticable, for example, where the client is a child or suffers from mental disability. See Rule 1.14. When the client is an organization or group, it is often impossible or inappropriate to inform everyone of its members about its legal affairs; ordinarily, the lawyer should address communications to the appropriate officials of the organization. See Rule 1.13. Where many routine matters are involved, a system of limited or occasional reporting may be arranged with the client. Practical exigency may also require a lawyer to act for a client without prior consultation.

Withholding Information

In some circumstances, a lawyer may be justified in delaying transmission of information when the client would be likely to react imprudently to an immediate communication. Thus, a lawyer might withhold a psychiatric diagnosis of a client when the examining psychiatrist indicates that disclosure would harm the client. A lawyer may not withhold information to serve the lawyer's own interest or convenience. Rules or court orders governing litigation may provide that information supplied to a lawyer may not be disclosed to the client. Rule 3.4(c) directs compliance with such rules or orders.

Rule 1.5   Fees

(a) A lawyer's fee shall be reasonable. The factors to be considered in determining the reasonableness of a fee include the following:

    (1) the time and labor required, the novelty and difficulty of the questions involved, and the skill requisite to perform the legal service properly;

    (2) the likelihood, if apparent to the client, that the acceptance of the particular employment will preclude other employment by the lawyer;

    (3) the fee customarily charged in the locality for similar legal services;

    (4) the amount involved and the results obtained;

    (5) the time limitations imposed by the client or by the circumstances;

    (6) the nature and length of the professional relationship with the client;

    (7) the experience, reputation, and ability of the lawyer or lawyers performing the services; and

    (8) whether the fee is fixed or contingent.

(b) When the lawyer has not regularly represented the client, the basis or rate of the fee shall be communicated to the client, preferably in writing, before or within a reasonable time after commencing the representation.

(c) A fee may be contingent on the outcome of the matter for which the service is rendered, except in a matter in which a contingent fee is prohibited by paragraph (d) or other law. A contingent fee agreement shall be in writing and shall state the method by which the fee is to be determined, including the percentage or percentages that shall accrue to the lawyer in the event of settlement, trial or appeal, litigation and other expenses to be deducted from the recovery, and whether such expenses are to be deducted before or after the contingent fee is calculated. Upon conclusion of a contingent fee matter, the lawyer shall provide the client with a written statement stating the outcome of the matter and, if there is a recovery, showing the remittance to the client and the method of its determination.

(d)   A lawyer shall not enter into an arrangement for, charge, or collect:

    (1)   any fee in a domestic relations matter, the payment or amount of which is contingent upon the securing of a divorce or upon the amount of alimony or support, or property settlement in lieu thereof; or

    (2)   a contingent fee for representing a defendant in a criminal case.

(e)   A division of fee between lawyers who are not in the same firm may be made only if:

    (1)   the division is in proportion to the services performed by each lawyer or, by written agreement with the client, each lawyer assumes joint responsibility for the representation;

    (2)   the client is advised of and does not object to the participation of all the lawyers involved; and

    (3)   the total fee is reasonable.

COMMENT:

Basis or Rate of Fee

When the lawyer has regularly represented a client, they ordinarily will have evolved an understanding concerning the basis or rate of the fee. In a new client-lawyer relationship, however, an understanding as to the fee should be promptly established. It is not necessary to recite all the factors that underlie the basis of the fee, but only those that are directly involved in its computation. It is sufficient, for example, to state that the basic rate is an hourly charge or a fixed amount or an estimated amount, or to identify the factors that may be taken into account in finally fixing the fee. When developments occur during the representation that render an earlier estimate substantially inaccurate, a revised estimate should be provided to the client. A written statement concerning the fee reduces the possibility of misunderstanding. Furnishing the client with a simple memorandum or a copy of the lawyer's customary fee schedule is sufficient if the basis or rate of the fee is set forth.

Terms of Payment

A lawyer may require advance payment of a fee, but is obliged to return any unearned portion. See Rule 1.16(d). A lawyer may accept property in payment for services, such as an ownership interest in an enterprise, providing this does not involve acquisition of a proprietary interest in the cause of action or subject matter of the litigation contrary to Rule 1.8(j). However, a fee paid in property instead of money may be subject to special scrutiny because it involves questions concerning both the value of the services and the lawyer's special knowledge of the value of the property.

An agreement may not be made whose terms might induce the lawyer improperly to curtail services for the client or perform them in a way contrary to the client's interest. For example, a lawyer should not enter into an agreement whereby services are to be provided only up to a stated amount when it is foreseeable that more extensive services probably will be required, unless the situation is adequately explained to the client. Otherwise, the client might have to bargain for further assistance in the midst of a proceeding or transaction. However, it is proper to define the extent of services in light of the client's ability to pay. A lawyer should not exploit a fee arrangement based primarily on hourly charges by using wasteful procedures. When there is doubt whether a contingent fee is consistent with the client's best interest, the lawyer should offer the client alternative bases for the fee and explain their implications. Applicable law may impose limitations on contingent fees, such as a ceiling on the percentage.

Division of Fee

A division of fee is a single billing to a client covering the fee of two or more lawyers who are not in the same firm. A division of fee facilitates association of more than one lawyer in a matter in which neither alone could serve the client as well, and most often is used when the fee is contingent and the division is between a referring lawyer and a trial specialist. Paragraph (e) permits the lawyers to divide a fee on either the basis of the proportion of services they render or by agreement between the participating lawyers if all assume responsibility for the representation as a whole and the client is advised and does not object. It does not require disclosure to the client of the share that each lawyer is to receive. Joint responsibility for the representation entails the obligations stated in Rule 5.1 for purposes of the matter involved.

Disputes over Fees

If a procedure has been established for resolution of fee disputes, such as an arbitration or mediation procedure established by the bar, the lawyer should conscientiously consider submitting to it. Law may prescribe a procedure for determining a lawyer's fee, for example, in representation of an executor or administrator, a class or a person entitled to a reasonable fee as part of the measure of damages. The lawyer entitled to such a fee and a lawyer representing another party concerned with the fee should comply with the prescribed procedure.

Rule 1.6   Confidentiality of information

(a)   A lawyer shall not reveal information relating to representation of a client unless the client consents after consultation, except for disclosures that are impliedly authorized in order to carry out the representation, and except as stated in paragraph (b).

(b)   A lawyer may reveal such information to the extent the lawyer reasonably believes necessary:

(1)   to prevent the client from committing a criminal act that the lawyer believes is likely to result in imminent death or substantial bodily harm; or

(2)   to establish a claim or defense on behalf of the lawyer in a controversy between the lawyer and the client, to establish a defense to a criminal charge or civil claim against the lawyer based upon conduct in which the client was involved, or to respond to allegations in any proceeding concerning the lawyer's representation of the client.

COMMENT:

The lawyer is part of a judicial system charged with upholding the law. One of the lawyer's functions is to advise clients so that they avoid any violation of the law in the proper exercise of their rights.

The observance of the ethical obligation of a lawyer to hold inviolate confidential information of the client not only facilitates the full development of facts essential to proper representation of the client but also encourages people to seek early legal assistance.

Almost without exception, clients come to lawyers in order to determine what their rights are and what is, in the maze of laws and regulations, deemed to be legal and correct. The common law recognizes that the client's confidences must be protected from disclosure. Based upon experience, lawyers know that almost all clients follow the advice given, and the law is upheld.

A fundamental principle in the client-lawyer relationship is that the lawyer maintain confidentiality of information relating to the representation.

The client is thereby encouraged to communicate fully and frankly with the lawyer even as to embarrassing or legally damaging subject matter.

The principle of confidentiality is given effect in two related bodies of law, the attorney-client privilege (which includes the work product doctrine) in the law of evidence and the rule of confidentiality established in professional ethics. The attorney-client privilege applies in judicial and other proceedings in which a lawyer may be called as a witness or otherwise required to produce evidence concerning a client. The rule of client-lawyer confidentiality applies in situations other than those where evidence is sought from the lawyer through compulsion of law. The confidentiality rule applies not merely to matters communicated in confidence by the client but also to all information relating to the representation, whatever its source. A lawyer may not disclose such information except as authorized or required by the Rules of Professional Conduct or other law. See also Scope.

The requirement of maintaining confidentiality of information relating to representation applies to government lawyers who may disagree with the policy goals that their representation is designed to advance.

Authorized Disclosure

A lawyer is impliedly authorized to make disclosures about a client when appropriate in carrying out the representation, except to the extent that the client's instructions or special circumstances limit that authority. In litigation, for example, a lawyer may disclose information by admitting a fact that cannot properly be disputed, or in negotiation by making a disclosure that facilitates a satisfactory conclusion.

Lawyers in a firm may, in the course of the firm's practice, disclose to each other information relating to a client of the firm, unless the client has instructed that particular information be confined to specified lawyers.

Disclosure Adverse to Client

The confidentiality rule is subject to limited exceptions. In becoming privy to information about a client, a lawyer may foresee that the client intends serious harm to another person. However, to the extent a lawyer is required or permitted to disclose a client's purposes, the client will be inhibited from revealing facts which would enable the lawyer to counsel against a wrongful course of action. The public is better protected if full and open communication by the client is encouraged than if it is inhibited.

Several situations must be distinguished.

First, the lawyer may not counsel or assist a client in conduct that is criminal or fraudulent. See Rule 1.2(d). Similarly, a lawyer has a duty under Rule 3.3(a)(4) not to use false evidence. This duty is essentially a special instance of the duty prescribed in Rule 1.2(d) to avoid assisting a client in criminal or fraudulent conduct.

Second, the lawyer may have been innocently involved in past conduct by the client that was criminal or fraudulent. In such a situation the lawyer has not violated Rule 1.2(d), because to "counsel or assist" criminal or fraudulent conduct requires knowing that the conduct is of that character.

Third, the lawyer may learn that a client intends prospective conduct that is criminal and likely to result in immiment death or substantial bodily harm. As stated in paragraph (b) (1), the lawyer has professional discretion to reveal information in order to prevent such consequences. The lawyer may make a disclosure in order to prevent homicide or serious bodily injury which the lawyer reasonably believes is intended by a client. It is very difficult for a lawyer to "know" when such a heinous purpose will actually be carried out, for the client may have a change of mind.

The lawyer's exercise of discretion requires consideration of such factors as the nature of the lawyer's relationship with the client and with those who might be injured by the client, the lawyer's own involvement in the transaction and factors that may extenuate the conduct in question. Where practical, the lawyer should seek to persuade the client to take suitable action. In any case, a disclosure adverse to the client's interest should be no greater than the lawyer reasonably believes necessary to the purpose. A lawyer's decision not to take preventive action permitted by paragraph (b) (1) does not violate this Rule.

Withdrawal

If the lawyer's services will be used by the client in materially furthering a course of criminal or fraudulent conduct, the lawyer must withdraw, as stated in Rule 1.16(a) (1).

After withdrawl the lawyer is required to refrain from making disclosure of the clients' confidences, except as otherwise provided in Rule 1.6. Neither this rule nor Rule 1.8(b) nor Rule 1.16(d) prevents the lawyer from giving notice of the fact of withdrawal, and the lawyer may also withdraw or disaffirm any opinion, document, affirmation, or the like.

Where the client is an organization, the lawyer may be in doubt whether contemplated conduct will actually be carried out by the organization. Where necessary to guide conduct in connection with this Rule, the lawyer may make inquiry within the organization as indicated in Rule 1.13(b).

Dispute Concerning Lawyer's Conduct

Where a legal claim or disciplinary charge alleges complicity of the lawyer in a client's conduct or other misconduct of the lawyer involving representation of the client, the lawyer may respond to the extent the lawyer reasonably believes necessary to establish a defense. The same is true with respect to a claim involving the conduct or representation of a former client. The lawyer's right to respond arises when an assertion of such complicity has been made. Paragraph (b) (2) does not require the lawyer to await the commencement of an action or proceeding that charges such complicity, so that the defense may be established by responding directly to a third party who has made such an assertion. The right to defend, of course, applies where a proceeding has been commenced. Where practicable and not prejudicial to the lawyer's ability to establish the defense, the lawyer should advise the client of the third party's assertion and request that the client respond appropriately. In any event, disclosure should be no greater than the lawyer reasonably believes is necessary to vindicate innocence, the disclosure should be made in a manner which limits access to the information to the tribunal or other persons having a need to know it, and appropriate protective orders or other arrangements should be sought by the lawyer to the fullest extent practicable.

If the lawyer is charged with wrongdoing in which the client's conduct is implicated, the rule of confidentiality should not prevent the lawyer from defending against the charge. Such a charge can arise in a civil, criminal or professional disciplinary proceeding, and can be based on a wrong allegedly committed by the lawyer against the client, or on a wrong alleged by a third person; for example, a person claiming to have been defrauded by the lawyer and client acting together. A lawyer entitled to a fee is permitted by paragraph (b) (2) to prove the services rendered in an action to collect it. This aspect of the rule expresses the principle that the beneficiary of a fiduciary relationship may not exploit it to the detriment of the fiduciary. As stated above, the lawyer must make every effort practicable to avoid unnecessary disclosure of information relating to a representation, to limit disclosure to those having the need to know it, and to obtain protective orders or make other arrangements minimizing the risk of disclosure.

Disclosures Otherwise Required or Authorized

The attorney-client privilege is differently defined in various jurisdictions. If a lawyer is called as a witness to give testimony concerning a client, absent waiver by the client, Rule 1.6(a) requires the lawyer to invoke the privilege when it is applicable. The lawyer must comply with the final orders of a court or other tribunal of competent jurisdiction requiring the lawyer to give information about the client.

The Rules of Professional Conduct in various circumstances permit or require a lawyer to disclose information relating to the representation. See Rules 2.2, 2.3, 3.3 and 4.1. In addition to these provisions, a lawyer may be obligated or permitted by other provisions of law to give information about a client. Whether another provision of law supersedes Rule 1.6 is a matter of interpretation beyond the scope of these Rules, but a presumption should exist against such a supersession.

Former Client

The duty of confidentiality continues after the client-lawyer relationship has terminated.

Rule 1.7   Conflict of interest: general rule

(a) A lawyer shall not represent a client if the representation of that client will be directly adverse to another client, unless:
  (1) the lawyer reasonably believes the representation will not adversely affect the relationship with the other client; and
  (2) each client consents after consultation.
(b) A lawyer shall not represent a client if the representation of that client may be materially limited by the lawyer's responsibilities to another client or to a third person, or by the lawyer's own interests, unless:
  (1) the lawyer reasonably believes the representation will not be adversely affected; and
  (2) the client consents after consultation. When representation of multiple clients in a single matter is undertaken, the consultation shall include explanation of the implications of the common representation and the advantages and risks involved.

COMMENT:

Loyalty to a Client

Loyalty is an essential element in the lawyer's relationship to a client. An impermissible conflict of interest may exist before representation is undertaken, in which event the representation should be declined. If such a conflict arises after representation has been undertaken, the lawyer should withdraw from the representation. See Rule 1.16. Where more than one client is involved and the lawyer withdraws because a conflict arises after representation, whether the lawyer may continue to represent any of the clients is determined by Rule 1.9. See also Rule 2.2(c). As to whether a client-lawyer relationship exists or, having once been established, is continuing, see Comment to Rule 1.3 and Scope.

As a general proposition, loyalty to a client prohibits undertaking representation directly adverse to that client without that client's consent. Paragraph (a) expresses that general rule. Thus, a lawyer ordinarily may not act as advocate against a person the lawyer represents in some other matter, even if it is wholly unrelated. On the other hand, simultaneous representation in unrelated matters of clients whose interests are only generally adverse, such as competing economic enterprises, does not require consent of the respective clients. Paragraph (a) applies only when the representation of one client would be directly adverse to the other.

Loyalty to a client is also impaired when a lawyer cannot consider, recommend or carry out an appropriate course of action for the client because of the lawyer's other responsibilities or interests. The conflict in effect forecloses alternatives that would otherwise be available to the client. Paragraph (b) addresses such situations. A possible conflict does not itself preclude the representation. The critical questions are the likelihood that a conflict will eventuate and, if it does, whether it will materially interfere with the lawyer's independent professional judgment in considering alternatives or foreclose courses of action that reasonably should be pursued on behalf of the client. Consideration should be given to whether the client wishes to accommodate the other interest involved.

Consultation and Consent

A client may consent to representation notwithstanding a conflict. However, as indicated in paragraph (a) (1) with respect to representation directly adverse to a client, and paragraph (b) (1) with respect to material limitations on representation of a client, when a disinterested lawyer would conclude that the client should not agree to the representation under the circumstances, the lawyer involved cannot properly ask for such agreement or provide representation on the basis of the client's consent. When more than one client is involved, the question of conflict must be resolved as to each client. Moreover, there may be circumstances where it is impossible to make the disclosure necessary to obtain consent. For example, when the lawyer represents different clients in related matters and one of the clients refuses to consent to the disclosure necessary to permit the other client to make an informed decision, the lawyer cannot properly ask the latter to consent.

Lawyer's Interests

The lawyer's own interests should not be permitted to have adverse effect on representation of a client. For example, a lawyer's need for income should not lead the lawyer to undertake matters that cannot be handled competently and at a reasonable fee. See Rules 1.1 and 1.5. If the probity of a lawyer's own conduct in a transaction is in serious question, it may be difficult or impossible for the lawyer to give a client detached advice. A lawyer may not allow related business interests to affect representation, for example, by referring clients to an enterprise in which the lawyer has an undisclosed interest.

Conflicts in Litigation

Paragraph (a) prohibits representation of opposing parties in litigation. Simultaneous representation of parties whose interests in litigation may conflict, such as co-plaintiffs or co-defendants, is governed by paragraph (b). An impermissible conflict may exist by reason of substantial discrepancy in the parties' testimony, incompatibility in positions in relation to an opposing party or the fact that there are substantially different possibilities of settlement of the claims or liabilities in question. Such conflicts can arise in criminal cases as well as civil. The potential for conflict of interest in representing multiple defendants in a criminal case is so grave that ordinarily a lawyer should decline to represent more than one co-defendant. On the other hand, common representation of persons having similar interests is proper if the risk of adverse effect is minimal and the requirements of paragraph (b) are met. Compare Rule 2.2 involving intermediation between clients.

Ordinarily, a lawyer may not act as advocate against a client the lawyer represents in some other matter, even if the other matter is wholly unrelated. However, there are circumstances in which a lawyer may act as advocate against a client. For example, a lawyer representing an enterprise with diverse operations may accept employment as an advocate against the enterprise in an unrelated matter if doing so will not adversely affect the lawyer's relationship with the enterprise or conduct of the suit and if both clients consent upon consultation. By the same token, government lawyers in some circumstances may represent government employees in proceedings in which a government agency is the opposing party. The propriety of concurrent representation can depend on the nature of the litigation. For example, a suit charging fraud entails conflict to a degree not involved in a suit for a declaratory judgment concerning statutory interpretation.

A lawyer may represent parties having antagonistic positions on a legal question that has arisen in different cases, unless representation of either client would be adversely affected. Thus, it is ordinarily not improper to assert such positions in cases pending in different trial courts, but it may be improper to do so in cases pending at the same time in an appellate court.

Interest of Person Paying for a Lawyer's Service

A lawyer may be paid from a source other than the client, if the client is informed of that fact and consents and the arrangement does not compromise the lawyer's duty of loyalty to the client. See Rule 1.8(f). For example, when an insurer and its insured have conflicting interests in a matter arising from a liability insurance agreement, and the insurer is required to provide special counsel for the insured, the arrangement should assure the special counsel's professional independence. So also, when a corporation and its directors or employees are involved in a controversy in which they have conflicting interests, the corporation may provide funds for separate legal representation of the directors or employees, if the clients consent after consultation and the arrangement ensures the lawyer's professional independence.

Other Conflict Situations

Conflicts of interest in contexts other than litigation sometimes may be difficult to assess. Relevant factors in determining whether there is potential for adverse effect include the duration and intimacy of the lawyer's relationship with the client or clients involved, the functions being performed by the lawyer, the likelihood that actual conflict will arise and the likely prejudice to the client from the conflict if it does arise. The question is often one of proximity and degree.

For example, a lawyer may not represent multiple parties to a negotiation whose interests are fundamentally antagonistic to each other, but common representation is permissible where the clients are generally aligned in interest even though there is some difference of interest among them.

Conflict questions may also arise in estate planning and estate administration. A lawyer may be called upon to prepare wills for several family members, such as husband and wife, and, depending upon circumstances, a conflict of interest may arise. In estate administration the identity of the client may be unclear under the law of a particular jurisdiction. Under one view, the client is the fiduciary; under another view the client is the estate or trust, including its beneficiaries. The lawyer should make clear the relationship to the parties involved.

A lawyer for a corporation or other organization who is also a member of its board of directors should determine whether the responsibilities of the two roles may conflict. The lawyer may be called on to advise the corporation in matters involving actions of the directors. Consideration should be given to the frequency with which such situations may arise, the potential intensity of the conflict, the effect of the lawyers resignation from the board and the possibility of the corporation's obtaining legal advice from another lawyer in such situations. If there is material risk that the dual role will compromise the lawyer's independence of professional judgment, the lawyer should not serve as a director.

Conflict Charged by an Opposing Party

Resolving questions of conflict of interest is primarily the responsibility of the lawyer undertaking the representation. In litigation, a court may raise the question when there is reason to infer that the lawyer has neglected the responsibility. In a criminal case, inquiry by the court is generally required when a lawyer represents multiple defendants. Where the conflict is such as clearly to call in question the fair or efficient administration of justice, opposing counsel may properly raise the question. Such an objection should be viewed with caution, however, for it can be misused as a technique of harassment. See Scope.

Rule 1.8   Conflict of interest: prohibited transactions

(a)   A lawyer shall not enter into a business transaction with a client or knowingly acquire an ownership, possessory, security or other pecuniary interest adverse to a client unless:
   (1)   the transaction and terms on which the lawyer acquires the interest are fair and reasonable to the client and are fully disclosed and transmitted in writing to the client in a manner which can be reasonably understood by the client;
   (2)   the client is given a reasonable opportunity to seek the advice of independent counsel in the transaction; and
   (3)   the client consents in writing thereto.
(b)   A lawyer shall not use information relating to representation of a client to the disadvantage of the client unless the client consents after consultation.
(c)   A lawyer shall not prepare an instrument giving the lawyer or a person related to the lawyer as parent, child, sibling, or spouse any substantial gift from a client, including a testamentary gift, except where the client is related to the donee.
(d)   Prior to the conclusion of representation of a client, a lawyer shall not make or negotiate an agreement giving the lawyer literary or media rights to a portrayal or account based in substantial part on information relating to the representation.
(e)   A lawyer shall not provide financial assistance to a client in connection with pending or contemplated litigation, except that:
   (1)   a lawyer may advance court costs and expenses of litigation, the repayment of which may be contingent on the outcome of the matter; and

       (2)   a lawyer representing an indigent client may pay court costs and expenses of litigation on behalf of the client.

(f)   A lawyer shall not accept compensation for representing a client from one other than the client unless:

       (1)   the client consents after consultation;

       (2)   there is no interference with the lawyer's independence of professional judgment or with the client-lawyer relationship; and

       (3)   information relating to representation of a client is protected as required by Rule 1.6.

(g)   A lawyer who represents two or more clients shall not participate in making an aggregate settlement of the claims of or against the clients, or in a criminal case an aggregated agreement as to guilty or nolo contendere pleas, unless each client consents after consultation, including disclosure of the existence and nature of all the claims or pleas involved and of the participation of each person in the settlement.

(h)   A lawyer shall not make an agreement prospectively limiting the lawyer's liability to a client for malpractice unless permitted by law and the client is independently represented in making the agreement, or settle a claim for such liability with an unrepresented client or former client without first advising that person in writing that independent representation is appropriate in connection therewith.

(i)   A lawyer related to another lawyer as parent, child, sibling or spouse shall not represent a client in a representation directly adverse to a person who the lawyer knows is represented by the other lawyer except upon the consent by the client after consultation regarding the relationship.

(j)   A lawyer shall not acquire a proprietary interest in the cause of action or subject matter of litigation the lawyer is conducting for a client, except that the lawyer may:

       (1)   acquire a lien granted by law to secure the lawyer's fee or expenses; and

       (2)   contract with a client for a reasonable contingent fee in a civil case.

COMMENT:

Transactions Between Client and Lawyer

As a general principle, all transactions between client and lawyer should be fair and reasonable to the client. In such transactions a review by independent counsel on behalf of the client is often advisable. Furthermore, a lawyer may not exploit information relating to the representation to the client's disadvantage. For example, a lawyer who has learned that the client is investing in specific real estate may not, without the client's consent, seek to acquire nearby property where doing so would adversely affect the client's plan for investment. Paragraph (a) does not, however, apply to standard commercial transactions between the lawyer and the client for products or services that the client generally markets to others, for example, banking or brokerage services, medical services, products manufactured or distributed by the client, and utilities services. In such transactions, the lawyer has no advantage in dealing with the client, and the restrictions in paragraph (a) are unnecessary and impracticable.

A lawyer may accept a gift from a client, if the transaction meets general standards of fairness. For example, a simple gift such as a present given at a holiday or as a token of appreciation is permitted. If effectuation of a substantial gift requires preparing a legal instrument such as a will or conveyance, however, the client should have the detached advice that another lawyer can provide. Paragraph (c) recognizes an exception where the client is a relative of the donee or the gift is not substantial.

Literary Rights

An agreement by which a lawyer acquires literary or media rights concerning the conduct of the representation creates a conflict between the interests of the client and the personal interests of the lawyer. Measures suitable in the representation of the client may detract from the publication value of an account of the representation. Paragraph (d) does not prohibit a lawyer representing a client in a transaction concerning literary property from agreeing that the lawyer's fee shall consist of a share in ownership in the property, if the arrangement conforms to Rule 1.5 and paragraph (j).

Person Paying for Lawyer's Services

Rule 1.8(f) requires disclosure of the fact that the lawyer's services are being paid for by a third party. Such an arrangement must also conform to the requirements of Rule 1.6 concerning confidentiality and Rule 1.7 concerning conflict of interest. Where the client is a class, consent may be obtained on behalf of the class by court-supervised procedure.

Family Relationships Between Lawyers

Rule 1.8(i) applies to related lawyers who are in different firms. Related lawyers in the same firm are governed by Rules 1.7, 1.9, and 1.10. The disqualification stated in Rule 1.8(i) is personal and is not imputed to members of firms with whom the lawyers are associated.

Acquisition of Interest in Litigation

Paragraph (j) states the traditional general rule that lawyers are prohibited from acquiring a proprietary interest in litigation. This general rule, which has its basis in common law champerty and maintenance, is subject to specific exceptions developed in decisional law and continued in these Rules, such as the exception for reasonable contingent fees set forth in Rule 1.5 and the exception for certain advances of the costs of litigation set forth in paragraph (e).

This Rule is not intended to apply to customary qualification and limitations in legal opinions and memoranda.

Rule 1.9   Conflict of interest: former client

A lawyer who has formerly represented a client in a matter shall not thereafter:
  (a)   represent another person in the same or a substantially related matter in which that person's interests are materially adverse to the interests of the former client unless the former client consents after consultation; or
  (b)   use information relating to the representation to the disadvantage of the former client except as Rule 1.6 would permit with respect to a client or when the information has become generally known.

COMMENT:

After termination of a client-lawyer relationship, a lawyer may not represent another client except in conformity with this Rule. The principles in Rule 1.7 determine whether the interests of the present and former client are adverse. Thus, a lawyer could not properly seek to rescind on behalf of a new client a contract drafted on behalf of the former client. So also a lawyer who has prosecuted an accused person could not properly represent the accused in a subsequent civil action against the government concerning the same transaction.

The scope of a "matter" for purposes of Rule 1.9(a) may depend on the facts of a particular situation or transaction. The lawyer's involvement in a matter can also be a question of degree. When a lawyer has been directly involved in a specific transaction, subsequent representation of other clients with materially adverse interests clearly is prohibited. On the other hand, a lawyer who recurrently handled a type of problem for a former client is not precluded from later representing another client in a wholly distinct problem of that type even though the subsequent representation involves a position adverse to the prior client. Similar considerations can apply to the reassignment of military lawyers between defense and prosecution functions within the same military jurisdiction. The underlying question is whether the lawyer was so involved in the matter that the subsequent representation can be justly regarded as a changing of sides in the matter in question.

Information acquired by the lawyer in the course of representing a client may not subsequently be used by the lawyer to the disadvantage of the client. However, the fact that a lawyer has once served a client does not preclude the lawyer from using generally known information about that client when later representing another client.

Disqualification from subsequent representation is for the protection of clients and can be waived by them. A waiver is effective only if there is disclosure of the circumstances, including the lawyer's intended role in behalf of the new client.

With regard to an opposing party's raising a question of conflict of interest, see Comment to Rule 1.7. With regard to disqualification of a firm with which a lawyer is associated, see Rule 1.10.

Rule 1.10   Imputed disqualification: general rule

(a)   While lawyers are associated in a firm, none of them shall knowingly represent a client when any one of them practicing alone would be prohibited from doing so by Rules 1.7, 1.8(c), 1.9 or 2.2.

(b)   When a lawyer becomes associated with a firm, the firm may not knowingly represent a person in the same or a substantially related matter in which that lawyer, or a firm with which the lawyer was associated, had previously represented a client whose interests are materially adverse to that person and about whom the lawyer had acquired information protected by Rules 1.6 and 1.9(b) that is material to the matter.

(c)   When a lawyer has terminated an association with a firm, the firm is not prohibited from thereafter representing a person with interests materially adverse to those of a client represented by the formerly associated lawyer unless:

   (1)   the matter is the same or substantially related to that in which the formerly associated lawyer represented the client; and

   (2)   any lawyer remaining in the firm has information protected by Rules 1.6 and 1.9(b) that is material to the matter.

(d)   A disqualification prescribed by this rule may be waived by the affected client under the conditions stated in Rule 1.7.

COMMENT:

Definition of "Firm"

For purposes of the Rules of Professional Conduct, the term "firm" includes lawyers in a private firm, and lawyers employed in the legal department of a corporation or other organization, or in a legal services organization. Whether two or more lawyers constitute a firm within this definition can depend on the specific facts. For example, two practitioners who share office space and occasionally consult or assist each other ordinarily would not be regarded as constituting a firm. However, if they present themselves to the public in a way suggesting that they are a firm or conduct themselves as a firm, they should be regarded as a firm for purposes of the Rules. The terms of any formal agreement between associated lawyers are relevant in determining whether they are a firm, as is the fact that they have mutual access to confidential information concerning the clients they serve. Furthermore, it is relevant in doubtful cases to consider the underlying purpose of the rule that is involved. A group of lawyers could be regarded as a firm for purposes of the rule that the same lawyer should not represent opposing parties in litigation, while it might not be so regarded for purposes of the rule that information acquired by one lawyer is attributed to another.

With respect to the law department of an organization, there is ordinarily no question that the members of the department constitute a firm within the meaning of the Rules of Professional Conduct. However, there can be uncertainty as to the identity of the client. For example, it may not be clear whether the law department of a corporation represents a subsidiary or an affiliated corporation, as well as the corporation by which the members of the department are directly employed. A similar question can arise concerning an unincorporated association and its local affiliates.

Similar questions can also arise with respect to lawyers in legal aid. Lawyers employed in the same unit of a legal service organization constitute a firm, but not necessarily those employed in separate units. As in the case of independent practitioners, whether the lawyers should be treated as associated with each other can depend on the particular rule that is involved, and on the specific facts of the situation.

Where a lawyer has joined a private firm after having represented the government, the situation is governed by Rule 1.11(a) and (b); where a lawyer represents the government after having served private clients, the situation is governed by Rule 1.11(c)(1). The individual lawyer involved is bound by the Rules generally, including Rules 1.6, 1.7, and 1.9.

Different provisions are thus made for movement of a lawyer from one private firm to another and for movement of a lawyer between a private firm and the government. The government is entitled to protection of its client confidences, and therefore to the protections provided in Rules 1.6, 1.9, and 1.11. However, if the more extensive disqualification in Rule 1.10 were applied to former government lawyers, the potential effect on the government would be unduly burdensome. The government deals with all private citizens and organizations, and thus has a much wider circle of adverse legal interests than does any private law firm. In these circumstances, the government's recruitment of lawyers would be seriously impaired if Rule 1.10 were applied to the government. On balance, therefore, the government is better served in the long run by the protections stated in Rule 1.11.

Principles of Imputed Disqualification

The rule of imputed disqualification stated in paragraph (a) gives effect to the principle of loyalty to the client as it applies to lawyers who practice in a law firm. Such situations can be considered from the premise that a firm of lawyers is essentially one lawyer for purposes of the rules governing loyalty to the client, or from the premise that each lawyer is vicariously bound by the obligation of loyalty owed by each lawyer with whom the lawyer is associated. Paragraph (a) operates only among the lawyers currently associated in a firm. When a lawyer moves from one firm to another, the situation is governed by paragraphs (b) and (c).

Lawyers Moving Between Firms

When lawyers have been associated in a firm but then end their association, however, the problem is more complicated. The fiction that the law firm is the same as a single lawyer is no longer wholly realistic. There are several competing considerations. First, the client previously represented must be reasonably assured that the principle of loyalty to the client is not compromised. Second, the rule of disqualification should not be so broadly cast as to preclude other persons from having reasonable choice of legal counsel. Third, the rule of disqualification should not unreasonably hamper lawyers from forming new associations and taking on new clients after having left a previous association. In this connection, it should be recognized that today many lawyers practice in firms, that many to some degree limit their practice to one field or another, and that many move from one association to another several times in their careers. If the concept of imputed disqualification were defined with unqualified rigor, the result would be radical curtailment of the opportunity of lawyers to move from one practice setting to another and of the opportunity of clients to change counsel.

Reconciliation of these competing principles in the past has been attempted under two rubrics. One approach has been to seek per se rules of disqualification. For example, it has been held that a partner in a law firm is conclusively presumed to have access to all confidences concerning all clients of the firm. Under this analysis, if a lawyer has been a partner in one law firm and then becomes a partner in another law firm, there is a presumption that all confidences known by a partner in the first firm are known to all partners in the second firm. This presumption might properly be applied in some circumstances, especially where the client has been extensively represented, but may be unrealistic where the client was represented only for limited purposes. Furthermore, such a rigid rule exaggerates the difference between a partner and an associate in modern law firms.

The other rubric formerly used for dealing with vicarious disqualification is the appearance of impropriety proscribed in Canon 9 of the ABA Model Code of Professional Responsibility. This rubric has a twofold problem. First, the appearance of impropriety can be taken to include any new client-lawyer relationship that might make a former client feel anxious. If that meaning were adopted, disqualification would become little more than a question of subjective judgment by the former client. Second, since "impropriety" is undefined, the term "appearance of impropriety" is question-begging. It therefore has to be recognized that the problem of imputed disqualification cannot be properly resolved either by simple analogy to a lawyer practicing alone or by the very general concept of appearance of impropriety.

A rule based on a functional analysis is more appropriate for determining the question of vicarious disqualification. Two functions are involved: preserving confidentiality and avoiding positions adverse to a client.

Confidentiality

Preserving confidentiality is a question of access to information. Access to information, in turn, is essentially a question of fact in particular circumstances, aided by inferences, deductions or working presumptions that reasonably may be made about the way in which lawyers work together. A lawyer may have general access to files of all clients of a law firm and may regularly participate in discussions of their affairs; it should be inferred that such a lawyer in fact is privy to all information about all the firm's clients. In contrast, another lawyer may have access to the files of only a limited number of clients and participate in discussion of the affairs of no other clients; in the absence of information to the contrary, it should be inferred that such a lawyer in fact is privy to information about the clients actually served but not those of other clients.

Application of paragraphs (b) and (c) depends on a situation's particular facts. In any such inquiry, the burden of proof should rest upon the firm whose disqualification is sought.

Paragraph (b) and (c) operate to disqualify the firm only when the lawyer involved has actual knowledge of information protected by Rules 1.6 and 1.9(b). Thus, if a lawyer while with one firm acquired no knowledge of information relating to a particular client of the firm, and that lawyer later joined another firm, neither the lawyer individually nor the second firm is disqualified from representing another client in the same or a related matter even though the interests of the two clients conflict.

Independent of the question of disqualification of a firm, a lawyer changing professional association has a continuing duty to preserve confidentiality of information about a client formerly represented. See Rules 1.6 and 1.9.

Adverse Positions

The second aspect of loyalty to client is the lawyer's obligation to decline subsequent representations involving positions adverse to a former client arising in substantially related matters. This obligation requires abstention from adverse representation by the individual lawyer involved, but does not properly entail abstention of other lawyers through imputed disqualification. Hence, this aspect of the problem is governed by Rule 1.9(a). Thus, if a lawyer left one firm for another, the new affiliation would not preclude the firms involved from continuing to represent clients with adverse interests in the same or related matters, so long as the conditions of Rule 1.10(b) and (c) concerning confidentiality have been met.

Rule 1.11   Successive government and private employment

(a)   Except as law may otherwise expressly permit, a lawyer shall not represent a private client in connection with a matter in which the lawyer participated personally and substantially as a public officer or employee, unless the appropriate government agency consents after consultation. No lawyer in a firm with which that lawyer is associated may knowingly undertake or continue representation in such a matter unless:

(1)   the disqualified lawyer is screened from any participation in the matter and is apportioned no part of the fee therefrom; and

(2)   written notice is promptly given to the appropriate government agency to enable it to ascertain compliance with the provisions of this rule.

(b) Except as law may otherwise expressly permit, a lawyer having information that the lawyer knows is confidential government information about a person acquired when the lawyer was a public officer or employee, may not represent a private client whose interests are adverse to that person in a matter in which the information could be used to the material disadvantage of that person. A firm with which that lawyer is associated may undertake or continue representation in the matter only if the disqualified lawyer is screened from any participation in the matter and is apportioned no part of the fee therefrom.

(c) Except as law may otherwise expressly permit, a lawyer serving as a public officer or employee shall not:

    (1) participate in a matter in which the lawyer participated personally and substantially while in private practice or nongovernmental employment, unless under applicable law no one is, or by lawful delegation may be, authorized to act in the lawyer's stead in the matter; or

    (2) negotiate for private employment with any person who is involved as a party or as attorney for a party in a matter in which the lawyer is participating personally and substantially.

(d) As used in this rule, the term "matter" includes:

    (1) any judicial or other proceeding, application, request for a ruling or other determination, contract, claim, controversy, investigation, charge, accusation, arrest or other particular matter involving a specific party or parties; and

    (2) any other matter covered by the conflict of interest rules of the appropriate government agency.

(e) As used in this rule, the term "confidential government information" means information which has been obtained under governmental authority and which, at the time this rule is applied, the government is prohibited by law from disclosing to the public or has a legal privilege not to disclose, and which is not otherwise available to the public.

COMMENT:

This Rule prevents a lawyer from exploiting public office for the advantage of a private client. It is a counterpart of Rule 1.10(b), which applies to lawyers moving from one firm to another.

A lawyer representing a government agency, whether employed or specially retained by the government, is subject to the Rules of Professional Conduct, including the prohibition against representing adverse interests stated in Rule 1.7 and the protections afforded former clients in Rule 1.9. In addition, such a lawyer is subject to Rule 1.11 and to statutes and government regulations regarding conflict of interest. Such statutes and regulations may circumscribe the extent to which the government agency may give consent under this Rule.

Where the successive clients are a public agency and a private client, the risk exists that power or discretion vested in public authority might be used for the special benefit of a private client. A lawyer should not be in a position where benefit to a private client might affect performance of the lawyer's professional functions on behalf of public authority. Also, unfair advantage could accrue to the private client by reason of access to confidential government information about the client's adversary obtainable only through the lawyer's government service. However, the rules governing lawyers presently or formerly employed by a government agency should not be so restrictive as to inhibit transfer of employment to and from the government. The government has a legitimate need to attract qualified lawyers as well as to maintain high ethical standards. The provisions for screening and waiver are necessary to prevent the disqualification rule from imposing too severe a deterrent against entering public service.

When the client is an agency of one government, that agency should be treated as a private client for purposes of this Rule if the lawyer thereafter represents an agency of another government, as when a lawyer represents a city and subsequently is employed by a federal agency.

Paragraphs (a) (1) and (b) (1) do not prohibit a lawyer from receiving a salary or partnership share established by prior independent agreement. They prohibit directly relating the attorney's compensation to the fee in the matter in which the lawyer is disqualified.

Paragraph (a) (2) does not require that a lawyer give notice to the government agency at a time when premature disclosure would injure the client; a requirement for premature disclosure might preclude engagement of the lawyer. Such notice is, however, required to be given as soon as practicable in order that the government agency or affected person will have a reasonable opportunity to ascertain that the lawyer is complying with Rule 1.11 and to take appropriate action if they believe the lawyer is not complying.

Paragraph (b) operates only when the lawyer in question has knowledge of the information, which means actual knowledge; it does not operate with respect to information that merely could be imputed to the lawyer.

Paragraphs (a) and (c) do not prohibit a lawyer from jointly representing a private party and a government agency when doing so is permitted by Rule 1.7 and is not otherwise prohibited by law.

Paragraph (c) does not disqualify other lawyers in the agency with which the lawyer in question has become associated.

Rule 1.12   Former judge or arbitrator

(a)   Except as stated in paragraph (d), a lawyer shall not represent anyone in connection with a matter in which the lawyer participated personally and substantially as a judge or other adjudicative officer, arbitrator or law clerk to such a person, unless all parties to the proceeding consent after disclosure.

(b) A lawyer shall not negotiate for employment with any person who is involved as a party or as attorney for a party in a matter in which the lawyer is participating personally and substantially as a judge or other adjudicative officer, or arbitrator. A lawyer serving as a law clerk to a judge, other adjudicative officer or arbitrator may negotiate for employment with a party or attorney involved in a matter in which the clerk is participating personally and substantially, but only after the lawyer has notified the judge, other adjudicative officer or arbitrator.

(c) If a lawyer is disqualified by paragraph (a), no lawyer in a firm with which that lawyer is associated may knowingly undertake or continue representation in the matter unless:

  (1) the disqualified lawyer is screened from any participation in the matter and is apportioned no part of the fee therefrom; and

  (2) written notice is promptly given to the appropriate tribunal to enable it to ascertain compliance with the provisions of this rule.

(d) An arbitrator selected as a partisan of a party in a multi-member arbitration panel is not prohibited from subsequently representing that party.

COMMENT:

This Rule generally parallels Rule 1.11. The term "personally and substantially" signifies that a judge who was a member of a multimember court, and thereafter left judicial office to practice law, is not prohibited from representing a client in a matter pending in the court, but in which the former judge did not participate. So also the fact that a former judge exercised administrative responsibility in a court does not prevent the former judge from acting as a lawyer in a matter where the judge had previously exercised remote or incidental administrative responsibility that did not affect the merits. Compare the Comment to Rule 1.11. The term "adjudicative officer" includes such officials as judges pro tempore, referees, special masters, hearing officers and other parajudicial officers, and also lawyers who serve as part-time judges. Compliance Canons A (2), B (2) and C of the Model Code of Judicial Conduct provide that a part-time judge, judge pro tempore or retired judge recalled to active service, may not "act as a lawyer in any proceeding in which he served as a judge or in any other proceeding related thereto." Although phrased differently from this Rule, those rules correspond in meaning.

Rule 1.13   Organization as client

(a)   A lawyer employed or retained by an organization represents the organization acting through its duly authorized constitutents.

(b)   If a lawyer for an organization knows that an officer, employee or other person associated with the organization is engaged in action, intends to act or refuses to act in a matter related to the representation that is a violation of a legal obligation to the organization, or a violation of law which reasonably might be imputed to the organization, and is likely to result in substantial injury to the organization, the lawyer shall proceed as is reasonably necessary in the best interest of the organization. In determining how to proceed, the lawyer shall give due consideration to the seriousness of the violation and its consequences, the scope and nature of the lawyer's representation, the responsibility in the organization and the apparent motivation of the person involved, the policies of the organization concerning such matters and any other relevant considerations. Any measures taken shall be designed to minimize disruption of the organization and the risk of revealing information relating to the representation to persons outside the organization. Such measures may include among others:

  (1)   asking reconsideration of the matter;

  (2)   advising that a separate legal opinion on the matter be sought for presentation to appropriate authority in the organization; and

  (3)   referring the matter to higher authority in the organization, including, if warranted by the seriousness of the matter, referral to the highest authority that can act in behalf of the organization as determined by applicable law.

(c)   If despite the lawyer's efforts in accordance with paragraph (b), the highest authority that can act on behalf of the organization insists upon action, or a refusal to act, that is clearly a violation of law and is likely to result in substantial injury to the organization, the lawyer may resign in accordance with Rule 1.16.

(d)   In dealing with an organization's directors, officers, employees, members, shareholders or other constitutents, a lawyer shall explain the identity of the client when it is apparent that the organization's interests are adverse to those of the constitutents with whom the lawyer is dealing.

(e)   A lawyer representing an organization may also represent any of its directors, officers, employees, members, shareholders or other constituents, subject to the provisions of Rule 1.7. If the organization's consent to the dual representation is required by Rule 1.7, the consent shall be given by an appropriate official of the organization other than the individual who is to be represented, or by the shareholders.

COMMENT:

The Entity as the Client

An organizational client is a legal entity, but it cannot act except through its officers, directors, employees, shareholders and other constituents.

Officers, directors, employees and shareholders are the constituents of the corporate organizational client. The duties defined in this Comment apply equally to unincorporated associations. "Other constituents" as used in this Comment means the positions equivalent to officers, directors, employees and shareholders held by persons acting for organizational clients that are not corporations.

When one of the constituents of an organizational client communicates with the organization's lawyer in that person's organizational capacity, the communication is protected by Rule 1.6. Thus, by way of example, if an organizational client requests its lawyer to investigate allegations of wrongdoing, interviews made in the course of that investigation between the lawyer and the client's employees or other constituents are covered by Rule 1.6. This does not mean, however, that constituents of an organizational client are the clients of the lawyer. The lawyer may not disclose to such constituents information relating to the representation except for disclosures explicitly or impliedly authorized by the organizational client in order to carry out the representation or as otherwise permitted by Rule 1.6.

When constituents of the organization make decisions for it, the decisions ordinarily must be accepted by the lawyer even if their utility or prudence is doubtful. Decisions concerning policy and operations, including ones entailing serious risk, are not as such in the lawyer's province. However, different considerations arise when the lawyer knows that the organization may be substantially injured by action of constituent that is in violation of law. In such a circumstance, it may be reasonably necessary for the lawyer to ask the constituent to reconsider the matter. If that fails, or if the matter is of sufficient seriousness and importance to the organization, it may be reasonably necessary for the lawyer to take steps to have the matter reviewed by a higher authority in the organization. Clear justification should exist for seeking review over the head of the constituent normally responsible for it. The stated policy of the organization may define circumstances and prescribe channels for such review, and a lawyer should encourage the formulation of such a policy. Even in the absence of organization policy, however, the lawyer may have an obligation to refer a matter to higher authority, depending on the seriousness of the matter and whether the constituent in question has apparent motives to act at variance with the organization's interest. Review by the chief executive officer or by the board of directors may be required when the matter is of importance commensurate with their authority. At some point it may be useful or essential to obtain an independent legal opinion.

In an extreme case, it may be reasonably necessary for the lawyer to refer the matter to the organization's highest authority. Ordinarily, that is the board of directors or similar governing body. However, applicable law may prescribe that under certain conditions highest authority reposes elsewhere; for example, in the independent directors of a corporation.

Relation to Other Rules

The authority and responsibility provided in paragraph (b) are concurrent with the authority and responsibility provided in other Rules. In particular, this Rule does not limit or expand the lawyer's responsibility under Rules 1.6, 1.8, and 1.16, 3.3, or 4.1. If the lawyer's services are being used by an organization to further a crime or fraud by the organization, Rule 1.2(d) can be applicable.

Government Agency

The duty defined in this Rule applies to governmental organizations. However, when the client is a governmental organization, a different balance may be appropriate between maintaining confidentiality and assuring that the wrongful official act is prevented or rectified, for public business is involved. In addition, duties of lawyers employed by the government or lawyers in military service may be defined by statutes and regulation. Therefore, defining precisely the identity of the client and prescribing the resulting obligations of such lawyers may be more difficult in the government context. Although in some circumstances the client may be a specific agency, it is generally the government as a whole. For example, if the action or failure to act involves the head of a bureau, either the department of which the bureau is a part or the government as a whole may be the client for purpose of this Rule. Moreover, in a matter involving the conduct of government officials, a government lawyer may have authority to question such conduct more extensively than that of a lawyer for a private organization in similar circumstances. This Rule does not limit that authority. See note on Scope.

Clarifying the Lawyer's Role

There are times when the organization's interest may be or become adverse to those of one or more of its constituents. In such circumstances the lawyer should advise any constituent, whose interest he finds adverse to that of the organization of the conflict or potential conflict of interest, that the lawyer cannot represent such constituent, and that such person may wish to obtain independent representation. Care must be taken to assure that the individual understands that, when there is such adversity of interest, the lawyer for the organization cannot provide legal representation for that constituent individual, and that discussions between the lawyer for the organization and the individual may not be privileged.

Whether such a warning should be given by the lawyer for the organization to any constituent individual may turn on the facts of each case.

Dual Representation

Paragraph (e) recognizes that a lawyer for an organization may also represent a principal officer or major shareholder.

Derivative Actions

Under generally prevailing law, the shareholders or members of a corporation may bring suit to compel the directors to perform their legal obligations in the supervision of the organization. Members of unincorporated associations have essentially the same right. Such an action may be brought nominally by the organization, but usually is, in fact, a legal controversy over management of the organization.

The question can arise whether counsel for the organization may defend such an action. The proposition that the organization is the lawyer's client does not alone resolve the issue. Most derivative actions are a normal incident of an organization's affairs, to be defended by the organization's lawyer like any other suit. However, if the claim involves serious charges of wrongdoing by those in control of the organization, a conflict may arise between the lawyer's duty to the organization and the lawyer's relationship with the board. In those circumstances, Rule 1.7 governs who should represent the directors and the organization.

Rule 1.14   Client under a disability

(a)   **When a client's ability to make adequately considered decisions in connection with the representation is impaired, whether because of minority, mental disability or for some other reason, the lawyer shall, as far as reasonably possible, maintain a normal client-lawyer relationship with the client.**

(b) A lawyer may seek the appointment of a guardian or take other protective action with respect to a client, only when the lawyer reasonably believes that the client cannot adequately act in the client's own interest.

COMMENT:

The normal client-lawyer relationship is based on the assumption that the client, when properly advised and assisted, is capable of making decisions about important matters. When the client is a minor or suffers from a mental disorder or disability, however, maintaining the ordinary client-lawyer relationship may not be possible in all respects. In particular, an incapacitated person may have no power to make legally binding decisions. Nevertheless, a client lacking legal competence often has the ability to understand, deliberate upon, and reach conclusions about matters affecting the client's own well-being. Furthermore, to an increasing extent the law recognizes intermediate degrees of competence. For example, children as young as five or six years of age, and certainly those of ten or twelve, are regarded as having opinions that are entitled to weight in legal proceedings concerning their custody. So also, it is recognized that some persons of advanced age can be quite capable of handling routine financial matters while needing special legal protection concerning major transactions.

The fact that a client suffers a disability does not diminish the lawyer's obligation to treat the client with attention and respect. If the person has no guardian or legal representative, the lawyer often must act as de facto guardian. Even if the person does have a legal representative, the lawyer should as far as possible accord the represented person the status of client, particularly in maintaining comunication.

If a legal representative has already been appointed for the client, the lawyer should ordinarily look to the representative for decisions on behalf of the client. If a legal representative has not been appointed, the lawyer should see to such an appointment where it would serve the client's best interests. Thus, if a disabled client has substantial property that should be sold for the client's benefit, effective completion of the transaction ordinarily requires appointment of a legal representative. In many circumstances, however, appointment of a legal representative may be expensive or traumatic for the client. Evaluation of these considerations is a matter of professional judgment on the lawyer's part.

If the lawyer represents the guardian as distinct from the ward, and is aware that the guardian is acting adversely to the ward's interest, the lawyer may have an obligation to prevent or rectify the guardian's misconduct. See Rule 1.2(d).

Disclosure of the Client's Condition

Rules of procedure in litigation generally provide that minors or persons suffering mental disability shall be represented by a guardian or next friend if they do not have a general guardian. However, disclosure of the client's disability can adversely affect the client's interests. For example, raising the question of disability could, in some circumstances, lead to proceedings for involuntary commitment. The lawyer's position in such cases is an unavoidably difficult one. The lawyer may seek guidance from an appropriate diagnostician.

Rule 1.15   Safekeeping property

(a)   A lawyer shall hold property of clients or third persons that is in a lawyer's possession in connection with a representation separate from the lawyer's own property. Funds shall be kept in a separate account maintained in the state where the lawyer's office is situated, or elsewhere with the consent of the client or third person. Other property shall be identified as such and appropriately safeguarded. Complete records of such account funds and other property shall be kept by the lawyer and shall be preserved for a period of [five years] after termination of the representation.

(b)   Upon receiving funds or other property in which a client or third person has an interest, a lawyer shall promptly notify the client or third person. Except as stated in this rule or otherwise permitted by law or by agreement with the client, a lawyer shall promptly deliver to the client or third person any funds or other property that the client or third person is entitled to receive and, upon request by the client or third person, shall promptly render a full accounting regarding such property.

(c)   When in the course of representation a lawyer is in possession of property in which both the lawyer and another person claim interests, the property shall be kept separate by the lawyer until there is an accounting and severance of their interests. If a dispute arises concerning their respective interests, the portion in dispute shall be kept separate by the lawyer until the dispute is resolved.

COMMENT:

A lawyer should hold property of others with the care required of a professional fiduciary. Securities should be kept in a safe deposit box, except when some other form of safekeeping is warranted by special circumstances. All property which is the property of clients or third persons should be kept separate from the lawyer's business and personal property and, if monies, in one or more trust accounts. Separate trust accounts may be warranted when administering estate monies or acting in similar fiduciary capacities.

Lawyers often receive funds from third parties from which the lawyer's fee will be paid. If there is risk that the client may divert the funds without paying the fee, the lawyer is not required to remit the portion from which the fee is to be paid. However, a lawyer may not hold funds to coerce a client into accepting the lawyer's contention. The disputed portion of the funds should be kept in trust and the lawyer should suggest means for prompt resolution of the dispute, such as arbitration. The undisputed portion of the funds shall be promptly distributed.

Third parties, such as a client's creditors, may have just claims against funds or other property in a lawyer's custody. A lawyer may have a duty under applicable law to protect such third-party claims against wrongful interference by the client, and accordingly may refuse to surrender the property to the client. However, a lawyer should not unilaterally assume to arbitrate a dispute between the client and the third party.

The obligations of a lawyer under this Rule are independent of those arising from activity other than rendering legal services. For example, a lawyer who serves as an escrow agent is governed by the applicable law relating to fiduciaries even though the lawyer does not render legal services in the transaction.

A "client's security fund" provides a means through the collective efforts of the bar to reimburse persons who have lost money or property as a result of dishonest conduct of a lawyer. Where such a fund has been established, a lawyer should participate.

Rule 1.16   Declining or terminating representation

(a)   Except as stated in paragraph (c), a lawyer shall not represent a client or, where representation has commenced, shall withdraw from the representation of a client if:
   (1)   the representation will result in violation of the rules of professional conduct or other law;
   (2)   the lawyer's physical or mental condition materially impairs the lawyer's ability to represent the client; or
   (3)   the lawyer is discharged.
(b)   Except as stated in paragraph (c), a lawyer may withdraw from representing a client if withdrawal can be accomplished without material adverse effect on the interests of the client, or if:

(1) the client persists in a course of action involving the lawyer's services that the lawyer reasonably believes is criminal or fraudulent;

(2) the client has used the lawyer's services to perpetrate a crime or fraud;

(3) a client insists upon pursuing an objective that the lawyer considers repugnant or imprudent;

(4) the client fails substantially to fulfill an obligation to the lawyer regarding the lawyer's services and has been given reasonable warning that the lawyer will withdraw unless the obligation is fulfilled;

(5) the representation will result in an unreasonable financial burden on the lawyer or has been rendered unreasonably difficult by the client; or

(6) other good cause for withdrawal exists.

(c) When ordered to do so by a tribunal, a lawyer shall continue representation notwithstanding good cause for terminating the representation.

(d) Upon termination of representation, a lawyer shall take steps to the extent reasonably practicable to protect a client's interests, such as giving reasonable notice to the client, allowing time for employment of other counsel, surrendering papers and property to which the client is entitled and refunding any advance payment of fee that has not been earned. The lawyer may retain papers relating to the client to the extent permitted by other law.

COMMENT:

A lawyer should not accept representation in a matter unless it can be performed competently, promptly, without improper conflict of interest and to completion.

Mandatory Withdrawal

A lawyer ordinarily must decline or withdraw from representation if the client demands that the lawyer engage in conduct that is illegal or violates the Rules of Professional Conduct or other law. The lawyer is not obliged to decline or withdraw simply becaue the client suggests such a course of conduct; a client may make such a suggestion in the hope that a lawyer will not be constrained by a professional obligation.

When a lawyer has been appointed to represent a client, withdrawal ordinarily requires approval of the appointing authority. See also Rule 6.2. Difficulty may be encountered if withdrawal is based on the client's demand that the lawyer engage in unprofessional conduct. The court may wish an explanation for the withdrawal, while the lawyer may be bound to keep confidential the facts that would constitute such an explanation. The lawyer's statement that professional considerations require termination of the representation ordinarily should be accepted as sufficient.

Discharge

A client has a right to discharge a lawyer at any time, with or without cause, subject to liability for payment for the lawyer's services. Where future dispute about the withdrawal may be anticipated, it may be advisable to prepare a written statement reciting the circumstances.

Whether a client can discharge appointed counsel may depend on applicable law. A client seeking to do so should be given a full explanation of the consequences. These consequences may include a decision by the appointing authority that appointment of successor counsel is unjustified, thus requiring the client to represent himself.

If the client is mentally incompetent, the client may lack the legal capacity to discharge the lawyer, and in any event the discharge may be seriously adverse to the client's interests. The lawyer should make special effort to help the client consider the consequences and, in an extreme case, may initiate proceedings for a conservatorship or similar protection of the client. See Rule 1.14.

Optional Withdrawal

A lawyer may withdraw from the representation in some circumstances. The lawyer has the option to withdraw if it can be accomplished without material adverse effect on the client's interests. Withdrawal is also justified if the client persists in a course of action that the lawyer reasonably believes is criminal or fraudulent, for a lawyer is not required to be associated with such conduct even if the lawyer does not further it. Withdrawal is also permitted if the lawyer's services were misused in the past even if that would materially prejudice the client. The lawyer also may withdraw where the client insists on a repugnant or imprudent objective.

A lawyer may withdraw if the client refuses to abide by the terms of an agreement relating to the representation, such as an agreement concerning fees or court costs or an agreement limiting the objectives of the representation.

Assisting the Client Upon Withdrawal

Even if the lawyer has been unfairly discharged by the client, a lawyer must take all reasonable steps to mitigate the consequences to the client.

The lawyer may retain papers as security for a fee only to the extent permitted by law.

Whether or not a lawyer for an organization may under certain unusual circumstances have a legal obligation to the organization after withdrawing or being discharged by the organization's highest authority is beyond the scope of these Rules.

COUNSELOR

Rule 2.1   Advisor

In representing a client, a lawyer shall exercise independent professional judgment and render candid advice. In rendering advice, a lawyer may refer not only to law but to other considerations such as moral, economic, social and political factors, that may be relevant to the client's situation.

COMMENT:

Scope of Advice

A client is entitled to straightforward advice expressing the lawyer's honest assessment. Legal advice often involves unpleasant facts and alternatives that a client may be disinclined to confront. In presenting advice, a lawyer endeavors to sustain the client's morale and may put advice in as acceptable a form as honesty permits. However, a lawyer should not be deterred from giving candid advice by the prospect that the advice will be unpalatable to the client.

Advice couched in narrowly legal terms may be of little value to a client, especially where practical considerations, such as cost or effects on other people, are predominant. Purely technical legal advice, therefore, can sometimes be inadequate. It is proper for a lawyer to refer to relevant moral and ethical considerations in giving advice. Although a lawyer is not a moral advisor as such, moral and ethical considerations impinge upon most legal questions and may decisively influence how the law will be applied.

A client may expressly or impliedly ask the lawyer for purely technical advice. When such a request is made by a client experienced in legal matters, the lawyer may accept it at face value. When such a request is made by a client inexperienced in legal matters, however, the lawyer's responsibility as advisor may include indicating that more may be involved than strictly legal considerations.

Matters that go beyond strictly legal questions may also be in the domain of another profession. Family matters can involve problems within the professional competence of psychiatry, clinical psychology or social work; business matters can involve problems within the competence of the accounting profession or of financial specialists. Where consultation with a professional in another field is itself something a competent lawyer would recommend, the lawyer should make such a recommendation. At the same time, a lawyer's advice at its best often consists of recommending a course of action in the face of conflicting recommendations of experts.

Offering Advice

In general, a lawyer is not expected to give advice until asked by the client. However, when a lawyer knows that a client proposes a course of action that is likely to result in substantial adverse legal consequences to the client, duty to the client under Rule 1.4 may require that the lawyer act if the client's course of action is related to the representation. A lawyer ordinarily has no duty to initiate investigation of a client's affairs or to give advice that the client has indicated is unwanted, but a lawyer may initiate advice to a client when doing so appears to be in the client's interest.

Rule 2.2   Intermediary

(a)   A lawyer may act as intermediary between clients if:
 (1)   the lawyer consults with each client concerning the implications of the common representation, including the advantages and risks involved, and the effect on the attorney-client privileges, and obtains each client's consent to the common representation;
 (2)   the lawyer reasonably believes that the matter can be resolved on terms compatible with the clients' best interests, that each client will be able to make adequately informed decisions in the matter and that there is little risk of material prejudice to the interests of any of the clients if the contemplated resolution is unsuccessful; and
 (3)   the lawyer reasonably believes that the common representation can be undertaken impartially and without improper effect on other responsibilities the lawyer has to any of the clients.
(b)   While acting as intermediary, the lawyer shall consult with each client concerning the decisions to be made and the considerations relevant in making them, so that each client can make adequately informed decisions.

(c)   A lawyer shall withdraw as intermediary if any of the clients so requests, or if any of the conditions stated in paragraph (a) is no longer satisfied. Upon withdrawal, the lawyer shall not continue to represent any of the clients in the matter that was the subject of the intermediation.

COMMENT:

A lawyer acts as intermediary under this Rule when the lawyer represents two or more parties with potentially conflicting interests. A key factor in defining the relationship is whether the parties share responsibility for the lawyer's fee, but the common representation may be inferred from other circumstances. Because confusion can arise as to the lawyer's role where each party is not separately represented, it is important that the lawyer make clear the relationship.

The Rule does not apply to a lawyer acting as arbitrator or mediator between or among parties who are not clients of the lawyer, even where the lawyer has been appointed with the concurrence of the parties. In performing such a role the lawyer may be subject to applicable codes of ethics, such as the Code of Ethics for Arbitration in Commercial Disputes prepared by a joint Committee of the American Bar Association and the American Arbitration Association.

A lawyer acts as intermediary in seeking to establish or adjust a relationship between clients on an amicable and mutually advantageous basis; for example, in helping to organize a business in which two or more clients are entrepreneurs, working out the financial reorganization of an enterprise in which two or more clients have an interest, arranging a property distribution in settlement of an estate or mediating a dispute between clients. The lawyer seeks to resolve potentially conflicting interests by developing the parties' mutual interests. The alternative can be that each party may have to obtain separate representation, with the possibility in some situations of incurring additional cost, complication or even litigation. Given these and other relevant factors, all the clients may prefer that the lawyer act as intermediary.

In considering whether to act as intermediary between clients, a lawyer should be mindful that if the intermediation fails the result can be additional cost, embarrassment and recrimination. In some situations the risk of failure is so great that intermediation is plainly impossible. For example, a lawyer cannot undertake common representation of clients between whom contentious litigation is imminent or who contemplate contentious negotiations. More generally, if the relationship between the parties has already assumed definite antagonism, the possibility that the clients' interests can be adjusted by intermediation ordinarily is not very good.

The appropriateness of intermediation can depend on its form. Forms of intermediation range from informal arbitration, where each client's case is presented by the respective client and the lawyer decides the outcome, to mediation, to common representation where the clients' interests are substantially though not entirely compatible. One form may be appropriate in circumstances where another would not. Other relevant factors are whether the lawyer subsequently will represent both parties on a continuing basis and whether the situation involves creating a relationship between the parties or terminating one.

Confidentiality and Privilege

A particularly important factor in determining the appropriateness of intermediation is the effect on client-lawyer confidentiality and the attorney-client privilege. In a common representation, the lawyer is still required both to keep each client adequately informed and to maintain confidentiality of information relating to the representation. See Rules 1.4 and 1.6. Complying with both requirements while acting as intermediary requires a delicate balance. If the balance cannot be maintained, the common representation is improper. With regard to the attorney-client privilege, the prevailing rule is that as between commonly represented clients the privilege does not attach. Hence, it must be assumed that if litigation eventuates between the clients, the privilege will not protect any such communications, and the clients should be so advised.

Since the lawyer is required to be impartial between commonly represented clients, intermediation is improper when that impartiality cannot be maintained. For example, a lawyer who has represented one of the clients for a long period and in a variety of matters might have difficulty being impartial between that client and one to whom the lawyer has only recently been introduced.

Consultation

In acting as intermediary between clients, the lawyer is required to consult with the clients on the implications of doing so, and proceed only upon consent based on such a consultation. The consultation should make clear that the lawyer's role is not that of partisanship normally expected in other circumstances.

Paragraph (b) is an application of the principle expressed in Rule 1.4. Where the lawyer is intermediary, the clients ordinarily must assume greater responsibility for decisions than when each client is independently represented.

Withdrawal

Common representation does not diminish the rights of each client in the client-lawyer relationship. Each has the right to loyal and diligent representation, the right to discharge the lawyer as stated in Rule 1.16, and the protection of Rule 1.9 concerning obligations to a former client.

Rule 2.3   Evaluation for use by third persons

(a) A lawyer may undertake an evaluation of a matter affecting a client for the use of someone other than the client if:

    (1) the lawyer reasonably believes that making the evaluation is compatible with other aspects of the lawyer's relationship with the client; and

    (2) the client consents after consultation.

(b) Except as disclosure is required in connection with a report of an evaluation, information relating to the evaluation is otherwise protected by Rule 1.6.

COMMENT:

Definition

An evaluation may be performed at the client's direction but for the primary purpose of establishing information for the benefit of third parties; for example, an opinion concerning the title of property rendered at the behest of a vendor for the information of a prospective purchaser, or at the behest of a borrower for the information of a prospective lender. In some situations, the evaluation may be required by a government agency; for example, an opinion concerning the legality of the securities registered for sale under the securities laws. In other instances, the evaluation may be required by a third person, such as a purchaser of a business.

Lawyers for the government may be called upon to give a formal opinion on the legality of contemplated government agency action. In making such an evaluation, the government lawyer acts at the behest of the government as the client but for the purpose of establishing the limits of the agency's authorized activity. Such an opinion is to be distinguished from confidential legal advice given agency officials. The critical question is whether the opinion is to be made public.

A legal evaluation should be distinguished from an investigation of a person with whom the lawyer does not have a client-lawyer relationship. For example, a lawyer retained by a purchaser to analyze a vendor's title to property does not have a client-lawyer relationship with the vendor. So also, an investigation into a person's affairs by a government lawyer, or by special counsel employed by the government, is not an evaluation as that term is used in this Rule. The question is whether the lawyer is retained by the person whose affairs are being examined. When the lawyer is retained by that person, the general rules concerning loyalty to client and preservation of confidences apply, which is not the case if the lawyer is retained by someone else. For this reason, it is essential to identify the person by whom the lawyer is retained. This should be made clear not only to the person under examination, but also to others to whom the results are to be made available.

Duty to Third Person

When the evaluation is intended for the information or use of a third person, a legal duty to that person may or may not arise. That legal question is beyond the scope of this Rule. However, since such an evaluation involves a departure from the normal client-lawyer relationship, careful analysis of the situation is required. The lawyer must be satisfied as a matter of professional judgment that making the evaluation is compatible with other functions undertaken in behalf of the client. For example, if the lawyer is acting as advocate in defending the client against charges of fraud, it would normally be incompatible with that responsibility for the lawyer to perform an evaluation for others concerning the same or a related transaction. Assuming no such impediment is apparent, however, the lawyer should advise the client of the implications of the evaluation, particularly the lawyer's responsibilities to third persons and the duty to disseminate the findings.

Access to and Disclosure of Information

The quality of an evaluation depends on the freedom and extent of the investigation upon which it is based. Ordinarily a lawyer should have whatever latitude of investigation seems necessary as a matter of professional judgment. Under some circumstances, however, the terms of the evaluation may be limited. For example, certain issues or sources may be categorically excluded, or the scope of search may be limited by time constraints or the noncooperation of persons having relevant information. Any such limitations which are material to the evaluation should be described in the report. If after a lawyer has commenced an evaluation, the client refuses to comply with the terms upon which it was understood the evaluation was to have been made, the lawyer's obligations are determined by law, having reference to the terms of the client's agreement and the surrounding circumstances.

Financial Auditors' Requests for Information

When a question concerning the legal situation of a client arises at the instance of the client's financial auditor and the question is referred to the lawyer, the lawyer's response may be made in accordance with procedures recognized in the legal profession. Such a procedure is set forth in the American Bar Association Statement of Policy Regarding Lawyers' Responses to Auditors' Requests for Information, adopted in 1975.

ADVOCATE

Rule 3.1   Meritorious claims and contentions

A lawyer shall not bring or defend a proceeding, or assert or controvert an issue therein, unless there is a basis for doing so that is not frivolous, which includes a good faith argument for an extension, modification or reversal of existing law. A lawyer for the defendant in a criminal proceeding, or the respondent in a proceeding that could result in incarceration, may nevertheless so defend the proceeding as to require that every element of the case be established.

COMMENT:

The advocate has a duty to use legal procedure for the fullest benefit of the client's cause, but also a duty not to abuse legal procedure. The law, both procedural and substantive, establishes the limits within which an advocate may proceed. However, the law is not always clear and never is static. Accordingly, in determining the proper scope of advocacy, account must be taken of the law's ambiguities and potential for change.

The filing of an action or defense or similar action taken for a client is not frivolous merely because the facts have not first been fully substantiated or because the lawyer expects to develop vital evidence only by discovery. Such action is not frivolous even though the lawyer believes that the client's position ultimately will not prevail. The action is frivolous, however, if the client desires to have the action taken primarily for the purpose of harassing or maliciously injuring a person or if the lawyer is unable either to make a good faith argument on the merits of the action taken or to support the action taken by a good faith argument for an extension, modification or reversal of existing law.

Rule 3.2   Expediting litigation

A lawyer shall make reasonable efforts to expedite litigation consistent with the interests of the client.

COMMENT:

Dilatory practices bring the administration of justice into disrepute. Delay should not be indulged merely for the convenience of the advocates, or for the purpose of frustrating an opposing party's attempt to obtain rightful redress or repose. It is not a justification that similar conduct is often tolerated by the bench and bar. The question is whether a competent lawyer acting in good faith would regard the course of action as having some substantial purpose other than delay. Realizing financial or other benefit from otherwise improper delay in litigation is not a legitimate interest of the client.

Rule 3.3   Candor toward the tribunal

(a)   A lawyer shall not knowingly:
  (1)   make a false statement of material fact or law to a tribunal;
  (2)   fail to disclose a material fact to a tribunal when disclosure is necessary to avoid assisting a criminal or fraudulent act by the client;
  (3)   fail to disclose to the tribunal legal authority in the controlling jurisdiction known to the lawyer to be directly adverse to the position of the client and not disclosed by opposing counsel; or
  (4)   offer evidence that the lawyer knows to be false. If a lawyer has offered material evidence and comes to know of its falsity, the lawyer shall take reasonable remedial measures.
(b)   The duties stated in paragraph (a) continue to the conclusion of the proceeding, and apply even if compliance requires disclosure of information otherwise protected by Rule 1.6.
(c)   A lawyer may refuse to offer evidence that the lawyer reasonably believes is false.
(d)   In an ex parte proceeding, a lawyer shall inform the tribunal of all material facts known to the lawyer which will enable the tribunal to make an informed decision, whether or not the facts are adverse.

COMMENT:

The advocate's task is to present the client's case with persuasive force. Performance of that duty while maintaining confidences of the client is qualified by the advocate's duty of candor to the tribunal. However, an advocate does not vouch for the evidence submitted in a cause; the tribunal is responsible for assessing its probative value.

Representations by a Lawyer

An advocate is responsible for pleadings and other documents prepared for litigation, but is usually not required to have personal knowledge of matters asserted therein, for litigation documents ordinarily present assertions by the client, or by someone on the client's behalf, and not assertions by the lawyer. Compare Rule 3.1. However, an assertion purporting to be on the lawyer's own knowledge, as in an affidavit by the lawyer or in a statement in open court, may properly be made only when the lawyer knows the assertion is true or believes it to be true on the basis of a reasonably diligent inquiry. There are circumstances where failure to make a disclosure is the equivalent of an affirmative misrepresentation. The obligation prescribed in Rule 1.2(d) not to counsel a client to commit or assist the client in committing a fraud applies in litigation. Regarding compliance with Rule 1.2(d), see the Comment to that Rule. See also the Comment to Rule 8.4(b).

Misleading Legal Argument

Legal argument based on a knowingly false representation of law constitutes dishonesty toward the tribunal. A lawyer is not required to make a disinterested exposition of the law, but must recognize the existence of pertinent legal authorities. Furthermore, as stated in paragraph (a) (3), an advocate has a duty to disclose directly adverse authority in the controlling jurisdiction which has not been disclosed by the opposing party. The underlying concept is that the legal argument is a discussion seeking to determine the legal premises properly applicable to the case.

False Evidence

When evidence that a lawyer knows to be false is provided by a person who is not the client, the lawyer must refuse to offer it regardless of the client's wishes.

When false evidence is offered by the client, however, a conflict may arise between the lawyer's duty to keep the client's revelations confidential and the duty of candor to the court. Upon ascertaining that material evidence is false, the lawyer should seek to persuade the client that the evidence should not be offered or, if it has been offered, that its false character should immediately be disclosed. If the persuasion is ineffective, the lawyer must take reasonable remedial measures.

Except in the defense of a criminal accused, the rule generally recognized is that, if necessary to rectify the situation, an advocate must disclose the existence of the client's deception to the court or to the other party. Such a disclosure can result in grave consequences to the client, including not only a sense of betrayal but also loss of the case and perhaps a prosecution for perjury. But the alternative is that the lawyer cooperate in deceiving the court, thereby subverting the truth-finding process which the adversary system is designed to implement. See Rule 1.2(d). Furthermore, unless it is clearly understood that the lawyer will act upon the duty to disclose the existence of false evidence, the client can simply reject the lawyer's advice to reveal the false evidence and insist that the lawyer keep silent. Thus the client could in effect coerce the lawyer into being a party to fraud on the court.

Perjury by a Criminal Defendant

Whether an advocate for a criminally accused has the same duty of disclosure has been intensely debated. While it is agreed that the lawyer should seek to persuade the client to refrain from perjurious testimony, there has been dispute concerning the lawyer's duty when that persuasion fails. If the confrontation with the client occurs before trial, the lawyer ordinarily can withdraw. Withdrawal before trial may not be possible, however, either because trial is imminent, or because the confrontation with the client does not take place until the trial itself, or because no other counsel is available.

The most difficult situation, therefore, arises in a criminal case where the accused insists on testifying when the lawyer knows that the testimony is perjurious. The lawyer's effort to rectify the situation can increase the likelihood of the client's being convicted as well as opening the possibility of a prosecution for perjury. On the other hand, if the lawyer does not exercise control over the proof, the lawyer participates, although in a merely passive way, in deception of the court.

Three resolutions of this dilemma have been proposed. One is to permit the accused to testify by a narrative without guidance through the lawyer's questioning. This compromises both contending principles; it exempts the lawyer from the duty to disclose false evidence but subjects the client to an implicit disclosure of information imparted to counsel. Another suggested resolution, of relatively recent origin, is that the advocate be entirely excused from the duty to reveal perjury if the perjury is that of the client. This is a coherent solution but makes the advocate a knowing instrument of perjury.

The other resolution of the dilemma is that the lawyer must reveal the client's perjury if necessary to rectify the situation. A criminal accused has a right to the assistance of an advocate, a right to testify and a right of confidential communication with counsel. However, an accused should not have a right to assistance of counsel in committing perjury. Furthermore, an advocate has an obligation, not only in professional ethics but under the law as well, to avoid implication in the commission of perjury or other falsification of evidence. See Rule 1.2(d).

Remedial Measures

If perjured testimony or false evidence has been offered, the advocate's proper course ordinarily is to remonstrate with the client confidentially. If that fails, the advocate should seek to withdraw if that will remedy the situation. If withdrawal will not remedy the situation or is impossible, the advocate should make disclosure to the court. It is for the court then to determine what should be done — making a statement about the matter to the trier of fact, ordering a mistrial or perhaps nothing. If the false testimony was that of the client, the client may controvert the lawyer's version of their communication when the lawyer discloses the situation to the court. If there is an issue whether the client has committed perjury, the lawyer cannot represent the client in resolution of the issue, and a mistrial may be unavoidable. An unscrupulous client might in this way attempt to produce a series of mistrials and thus escape prosecution. However, a second such encounter could be construed as a deliberate abuse of the right to counsel and as such a waiver of the right to further representation.

Constitutional Requirements

The general rule — that an advocate must disclose the existence of perjury with respect to a material fact, even that of a client — applies to defense counsel in criminal cases, as well as in other instances. However, the definition of the lawyer's ethical duty in such a situation may be qualified by constitutional provisions for due process and the right to counsel in criminal cases. In some jurisdictions these provisions have been construed to require that counsel present an accused as a witness if the accused wishes to testify, even if counsel knows the testimony will be false. The obligation of the advocate under these Rules is subordinate to such a constitutional requirement.

Duration of Obligation

A practical time limit on the obligation to rectify the presentation of false evidence has to be established. The conclusion of the proceeding is a reasonably definite point for the termination of the obligation.

Refusing to Offer Proof Believed to Be False

Generally speaking, a lawyer has authority to refuse to offer testimony or other proof that the lawyer believes is untrustworthy. Offering such proof may reflect adversely on the lawyer's ability to discriminate in the quality of evidence and thus impair the lawyer's effectiveness as an advocate. In criminal cases, however, a lawyer may, in some jurisdictions, be denied this authority by constitutional requirements governing the right to counsel.

Ex Parte Proceedings

Ordinarily, an advocate has the limited responsibility of presenting one side of the matters that a tribunal should consider in reaching a decision; the conflicting position is expected to be presented by the opposing party. However, in an ex parte proceeding, such as an application for a temporary restraining order, there is no balance of presentation by opposing advocates. The object of an ex parte proceeding is nevertheless to yield a substantially just result. The judge has an affirmative responsibility to accord the absent party just consideration. The lawyer for the represented party has the correlative duty to make disclosures of material facts known to the lawyer and that the lawyer reasonably believes are necessary to an informed decision.

Rule 3.4   Fairness to opposing party and counsel

A Lawyer shall not:
(a) unlawfully obstruct another party's access to evidence or unlawfully alter, destroy or conceal a document or other material having potential evidentiary value. A lawyer shall not counsel or assist another person to do any such act;
(b) falsify evidence, counsel or assist a witness to testify falsely, or offer an inducement to a witness that is prohibited by law;
(c) knowingly disobey an obligation under the rules of a tribunal except for an open refusal based on an assertion that no valid obligation exists;
(d) in pretrial procedure, make a frivolous discovery request or fail to make reasonably diligent effort to comply with a legally proper discovery request by an opposing party;

153

(e) in trial, allude to any matter that the lawyer does not reasonably believe is relevant or that will not be supported by admissible evidence, assert personal knowledge of facts in issue except when testifying as a witness, or state a personal opinion as to the justness of a cause, the credibility of a witness, the culpability of a civil litigant or the guilt or innocence of an accused; or

(f) request a person other than a client to refrain from voluntarily giving relevant information to another party unless:

   (1) the person is a relative or an employee or other agent of a client; and

   (2) the lawyer reasonably believes that the person's interests will not be adversely affected by refraining from giving such information.

COMMENT:

The procedure of the adversary system contemplates that the evidence in a case is to be marshalled competitively by the contending parties. Fair competition in the adversary system is secured by prohibitions against destruction or concealment of evidence, improperly influencing witnesses, obstructive tactics in discovery procedure, and the like.

Documents and other items of evidence are often essential to establish a claim or defense. Subject to evidentiary privileges, the right of an opposing party, including the government, to obtain evidence through discovery or subpoena is an important procedural right. The exercise of that right can be frustrated if relevant material is altered, concealed or destroyed. Applicable law in many jurisdictions makes it an offense to destroy material for purpose of impairing its availability in a pending proceeding or one whose commencement can be foreseen. Falsifying evidence is also generally a criminal offense. Paragraph (a) applies to evidentiary material generally, including computerized information.

With regard to paragraph (b), it is not improper to pay a witness's expenses or to compensate an expert witness on terms permitted by law. The common law rule in most jurisdictions is that it is improper to pay an occurrence witness any fee for testifying and that it is improper to pay an expert witness a contingent fee.

Paragraph (f) permits a lawyer to advise employees of a client to refrain from giving information to another party, for the employees may identify their interests with those of the client. See also Rule 4.2.

Rule 3.5   Impartiality and decorum of the tribunal

A lawyer shall not:

(a) seek to influence a judge, juror, prospective juror or other official by means prohibited by law;

(b) communicate ex parte with such a person except as permitted by law; or

(c) engage in conduct intended to disrupt a tribunal.

COMMENT:

Many forms of improper influence upon a tribunal are proscribed by criminal law. Others are specified in the ABA Model Code of Judicial Conduct, with which an advocate should be familiar. A lawyer is required to avoid contributing to a violation of such provisions.

The advocate's function is to present evidence and argument so that the cause may be decided according to law. Refraining from abusive or obstreperous conduct is a corollary of the advocate's right to speak on behalf of litigants. A lawyer may stand firm against abuse by a judge but should avoid reciprocation; the judge's default is no justification for similar dereliction by an advocate. An advocate can present the cause, protect the record for subsequent review and preserve professional integrity by patient firmness no less effectively than by belligerence or theatrics.

Rule 3.6   Trial publicity

(a) A lawyer shall not make an extrajudicial statement that a reasonable person would expect to be disseminated by means of public communication if the lawyer knows or reasonably should know that it will have a substantial likelihood of materially prejudicing an adjudicative proceeding.

(b) A statement referred to in paragraph (a) ordinarily is likely to have such an effect when it refers to a civil matter triable to a jury, a criminal matter, or any other proceeding that could result in incarceration, and the statement relates to:

(1) the character, credibility, reputation or criminal record of a party, suspect in a criminal investigation or witness, or the identity of a witness, or the expected testimony of a party or witness;

(2) a criminal case or proceeding that could result in incarceration, the possibility of a plea of guilty to the offense or the existence or contents of any confession, admission, or statement given by a defendant or suspect of that person's refusal or failure to make a statement;

(3) the performance or results of any examination or test or the refusal or failure of a person to submit to an examination or

test, or the identity or nature of physical evidence expected to be presented;

(4)   any opinion as to the guilt or innocence of a defendant or suspect in a criminal case or proceeding that could result in incarceration;

(5)   information the lawyer knows or reasonably should know is likely to be inadmissible as evidence in a trial and would if disclosed create a substantial risk of prejudicing an impartial trial; or

(6)   the fact that a defendant has been charged with a crime, unless there is included therein a statement explaining that the charge is merely an accusation and that the defendant is presumed innocent until and unless proven guilty.

(c)   Notwithstanding paragraph (a) and (b) (1-5), a lawyer involved in the investigation or litigation of a matter may state without elaboration:

(1)   the general nature of the claim or defense;

(2)   the information contained in a public record;

(3)   that an investigation of the matter is in progress, including the general scope of the investigation, the offense or claim or defense involved and, except when prohibited by law, the identity of the persons involved;

(4)   the scheduling or result of any step in litigation;

(5)   a request for assistance in obtaining evidence and information necessary thereto;

(6)   a warning of danger concerning the behavior of a person involved, when there is reason to believe that there exists the likelihood of substantial harm to an individual or to the public interest; and

(7)   in a criminal case:

(i)   the identity, residence, occupation and family status of the accused;

(ii)   if the accused has not been apprehended, information necessary to aid in apprehension of that person;

(iii) the fact, time and place of arrest; and

(iv)   the identity of investigating and arresting officers or agencies and the length of the investigation.

COMMENT:

It is difficult to strike a balance between protecting the right to a fair trial and safeguarding the right of free expression. Preserving the right to a fair trial necessarily entails some curtailment of the information that may be disseminated about a party prior to trial, particularly where trial by jury is involved. If there were no such limits, the result would be the practical nulli-fication of the protective effect of the rules of forensic decorum and the exclusionary rules of evidence. On the other hand, there are vital social in-terests served by the free dissemination of information about events having legal consequences and about legal proceedings themselves. The public has a right to know about threats to its safety and measures aimed at assuring its security. It also has a legitimate interest in the conduct of judicial proceed-ings, particularly in matters of general public concern. Furthermore, the sub-ject matter of legal proceedings is often of direct significance in debate and deliberation over questions of public policy.

No body of rules can simultaneously satisfy all interests of fair trial and all those of free expression. The formula in this Rule is based upon the ABA Model Code of Professional Responsibility and the ABA Standards Relat-ing to Fair Trial and Free Press, as amended in 1978.

Special rules of confidentiality may validly govern proceedings in juvenile, domestic relations and mental disability proceedings, and perhaps other types of litigation. Rule 3.4(c) requires compliance with such Rules.

Rule 3.7   Lawyer as witness

(a)   A lawyer shall not act as advocate at a trial in which the lawyer is likely to be a necessary witness except where:
   (1)   the testimony relates to an uncontested issue;
   (2)   the testimony relates to the nature and value of legal services rendered in the case; or
   (3)   disqualification of the lawyer would work substantial hardship on the client.

(b)   A lawyer may act as advocate in a trial in which another lawyer in the lawyer's firm is likely to be called as a witness unless precluded from doing so by Rule 1.7 or Rule 1.9.

COMMENT:

Combining the roles of advocate and witness can prejudice the opposing party and can involve a conflict of interest between the lawyer and client.

The opposing party has proper objection where the combination of roles may prejudice that party's rights in the litigation. A witness is required to testify on the basis of personal knowledge, while an advocate is expected to explain and comment on evidence given by others. It may not be clear whether a statement by an advocate-witness should be taken as proof or as an analysis of the proof.

Paragraph (a) (1) recognizes that if the testimony will be uncontested, the ambiguities in the dual role are purely theoretical. Paragraph (a) (2) recognizes that where the testimony concerns the extent and value of legal services rendered in the action in which the testimony is offered, permitting the lawyers to testify avoids the need for a second trial with new counsel to resolve that issue. Moreover, in such a situation the judge has first hand knowledge of the matter in issue; hence, there is less dependence on the adversary process to test the credibility of the testimony.

Apart from these two exceptions, paragraph (a) (3) recognizes that a balancing is required between the interests of the client and those of the opposing party. Whether the opposing party is likely to suffer prejudice depends on the nature of the case, the importance and probable tenor of the lawyer's testimony, and the probability that the lawyer's testimony will conflict with that of other witnesses. Even if there is risk of such prejudice, in determining whether the lawyer should be disqualified due regard must be given to the effect of disqualification on the lawyer's client. It is relevant that one or both parties could reasonably foresee that the lawyer would probably be a witness. The principle of imputed disqualification stated in Rule 1.10 has no application to this aspect of the problem.

Whether the combination of roles involves an improper conflict of interest with respect to the client is determined by Rule 1.7 or 1.9. For example, if there is likely to be substantial conflict between the testimony of the client and that of the lawyer or a member of the lawyer's firm, the representation is improper. The problem can arise whether the lawyer is called as a witness on behalf of the client or is called by the opposing party. Determining whether or not such a conflict exists is primarily the responsibility of the lawyer involved. See Comment to Rule 1.7. If a lawyer who is a member of a firm may not act as both advocate and witness by reason of conflict of interest, Rule 1.10 disqualifies the firm also.

Rule 3.8   Special responsibilities of a prosecutor

The prosecutor in a criminal case shall:
  (a) refrain from prosecuting a charge that the prosecutor knows is not supported by probable cause;
  (b) make reasonable efforts to assure that the accused has been advised of the right to, and the procedure for obtaining, counsel and has been given reasonable opportunity to obtain counsel;
  (c) not seek to obtain from an unrepresented accused a waiver of important pretrial rights, such as the right to a preliminary hearing;
  (d) make timely disclosure to the defense of all evidence or information known to the prosecutor that tends to negate the guilt of the accused or mitigates the offense, and, in connection with sentencing, disclose to the defense and to the tribunal all unprivileged mitigating information known to the prosecutor, except when the prosecu-

tor is relieved of this responsibility by a protective order of the tribunal; and

(e) exercise reasonable care to prevent investigators, law enforcement personnel, employees or other persons assisting or associated with the prosecutor in a criminal case from making an extrajudicial statement that the prosecutor would be prohibited from making under Rule 3.6.

COMMENT:

A prosecutor has the responsibility of a minister of justice and not simply that of an advocate. This responsibility carries with it specific obligations to see that the defendant is accorded procedural justice and that guilt is decided upon the basis of sufficient evidence. Precisely how far the prosecutor is required to go in this direction is a matter of debate and varies in different jurisdictions. Many jurisdictions have adopted the ABA Standards of Criminal Justice Relating to Prosecution Function, which in turn are the product of prolonged and careful deliberation by lawyers experienced in both criminal prosecution and defense. See also Rule 3.3(d), governing ex parte proceedings, among which grand jury proceedings are included. Applicable law may require other measures by the prosecutor and knowing disregard of those obligations or a systematic abuse of prosecutorial discretion could constitute a violation of Rule 8.4.

Paragraph (c) does not apply to an accused representing himself with the approval of the tribunal. Nor does it forbid the lawful questioning of a suspect who has knowingly waived his rights to counsel and silence.

The exception in paragraph (d) recognizes that a prosecutor may seek an appropriate protective order from the tribunal if disclosure of information to the defense could result in substantial harm to an individual or to the public interest.

Rule 3.9   Advocate in nonadjudicative proceedings

A lawyer representing a client before a legislative or administrative tribunal in a nonadjudicative proceeding shall disclose that the appearance is in a representative capacity and shall conform to the provisions of Rules 3.3(a) through (c), 3.4(a) through (c), and 3.5.

COMMENT:

In representation before bodies such as legislatures, municipal councils, and executive and administrative agencies acting in a rule-making or policy-making capacity, lawyers present facts, formulate issues and advance argument in the matters under consideration. The decision-making body, like a court, should be able to rely on the integrity of the submissions made to it. A lawyer appearing before such a body should deal with the tribunal honestly and in conformity with applicable rules of procedure.

Lawyers have no exclusive right to appear before nonadjudicative bodies, as they do before a court. The requirements of this Rule therefore may subject lawyers to regulations inapplicable to advocates who are not lawyers. However, legislatures and administrative agencies have a right to expect lawyers to deal with them as they deal with courts.

This Rule does not apply to representation of a client in a negotiation or other bilateral transaction with a governmental agency; representation in such a transaction is governed by Rules 4.1 through 4.4.

TRANSACTIONS WITH PERSONS OTHER THAN CLIENTS

Rule 4.1   Truthfulness in statements to others

In the course of representing a client a lawyer shall not knowingly:
(a) make a false statement of material fact or law to a third person; or
(b) fail to disclose a material fact to a third person when disclosure is necessary to avoid assisting a criminal or fraudulent act by a client, unless disclosure is prohibited by Rule 1.6.

COMMENT:

Misrepresentation

A lawyer is required to be truthful when dealing with others on a client's behalf, but generally has no affirmative duty to inform an opposing party of relevant facts. A misrepresentation can occur if the lawyer incorporates or affirms a statement of another person that the lawyer knows is false. Misrepresentations can also occur by failure to act.

Statements of Fact

This Rule refers to statements of fact. Whether a particular statement should be regarded as one of fact can depend on the circumstances. Under

160

generally accepted conventions in negotiation, certain types of statements ordinarily are not taken as statements of material fact. Estimates of price or value placed on the subject of a transaction and a party's intentions as to an acceptable settlement of a claim are in this category, and so is the existence of an undisclosed principal except where nondisclosure of the principal would constitute fraud.

Fraud by Client

Paragraph (b) recognizes that substantive law may require a lawyer to disclose certain information to avoid being deemed to have assisted the client's crime or fraud. The requirement of disclosure created by this paragraph is, however, subject to the obligations created by Rule 1.6.

Rule 4.2   Communication with person represented by counsel

In representing a client, a lawyer shall not communicate about the subject of the representation with a party the lawyer knows to be represented by another lawyer in the matter, unless the lawyer has the consent of the other lawyer or is authorized by law to do so.

COMMENT:

This Rule does not prohibit communication with a party, or an employee or agent of a party, concerning matters outside the representation. For example, the existence of a controversy between a government agency and a private party, or between two organizations, does not prohibit a lawyer for either from communicating with nonlawyer representatives of the other regarding a separate matter. Also, parties to a matter may communicate directly with each other and a lawyer having independent justification for communicating with the other party is permitted to do so. Communications authorized by law include, for example, the right of a party to a controversy with a government agency to speak with government officials about the matter.

In the case of an organization, this Rule prohibits communications by a lawyer for one party concerning the matter in representation with persons having a managerial responsibility on behalf of the organization, and with any other person whose act or omission in connection with that matter may be imputed to the organization for purposes of civil or criminal liability or whose statement may constitute an admission on the part of the organization. If an agent or employee of the organization is represented in the matter by his or her own counsel, the consent by that counsel to a communication will be sufficient for purposes of this Rule. Compare Rule 3.4(f).

This rule also covers any person, whether or not a party to a formal proceeding, who is represented by counsel concerning the matter in question.

Rule 4.3   Dealing with unrepresented person

In dealing on behalf of a client with a person who is not represented by counsel, a lawyer shall not state or imply that the lawyer is disinterested. When the lawyer knows or reasonably should know that the unrepresented person misunderstands the lawyer's role in the matter, the lawyer shall make reasonable efforts to correct the misunderstanding.

COMMENT:

An unrepresented person, particularly one not experienced in dealing with legal matters, might assume that a lawyer is disinterested in loyalties or is a disinterested authority on the law even when the lawyer represents a client. During the course of a lawyer's representation of a client, the lawyer should not give advice to an unrepresented person other than the advice to obtain counsel.

Rule 4.4   Respect for rights of third persons

In representing a client, a lawyer shall not use means that have no substantial purpose other than to embarrass, delay, or burden a third person, or use methods of obtaining evidence that violate the legal rights of such a person.

COMMENT:

Responsibility to a client requires a lawyer to subordinate the interests of others to those of the client, but that responsibility does not imply that a lawyer may disregard the rights of third persons. It is impractical to catalogue all such rights, but they include legal restrictions on methods of obtaining evidence from third persons.

LAW FIRMS AND ASSOCIATIONS

Rule 5.1   Responsibilities of a partner or supervisory lawyer

(a)   A partner in a law firm shall make reasonable efforts to ensure that the firm has in effect measures giving reasonable assurance that all lawyers in the firm conform to the rules of professional conduct.

(b)   A lawyer having direct supervisory authority over another lawyer shall make reasonable efforts to ensure that the other lawyer conforms to the rules of professional conduct.

(c)   A lawyer shall be responsible for another lawyer's violation of the rules of professional conduct if:

    (1)   the lawyer orders or, with knowledge of the specific conduct, ratifies the conduct involved; or

    (2)   the lawyer is a partner in the law firm in which the other lawyer practices, or has direct supervisory authority over the other lawyer, and knows of the conduct at a time when its consequences can be avoided or mitigated but fails to take reasonable remedial action.

COMMENT:

Paragraphs (a) and (b) refer to lawyers who have supervisory authority over the professional work of a firm or legal department of a government agency. This includes members of a partnership and the shareholders in a law firm organized as a professional corporation; lawyers having supervisory authority in the law department of an enterprise or government agency; and lawyers who have intermediate managerial responsibilities in a firm.

The measures required to fulfill the responsibility prescribed in paragraphs (a) and (b) can depend on the firm's structure and the nature of its practice. In a small firm, informal supervision and occasional admonition ordinarily might be sufficient. In a large firm, or in practice situations in which intensely difficult ethical problems frequently arise, more elaborate procedures may be necessary. Some firms, for example, have a procedure whereby junior lawyers can make confidential referral of ethical problems directly to a designated senior partner or special committee. See Rule 5.2. Firms, whether large or small, may also rely on continuing legal education in professional ethics. In any event, the ethical atmosphere of a firm can influence the conduct of all its members and a lawyer having authority over the work of another may not assume that the subordinate lawyer will inevitably conform to the Rules.

Paragraph (c)(1) expresses a general principle of responsibility for acts of another. See also Rule 8.4(a).

Paragraph (c)(2) defines the duty of a lawyer having direct supervisory authority over performance of specific legal work by another lawyer. Whether a lawyer has such supervisory authority in particular circumstances is a question of fact. Partners of a private firm have at least indirect responsibility for all work being done by the firm, while a partner in charge of a particular matter ordinarily has direct authority over other firm lawyers engaged in the matter. Appropriate remedial action by a partner would depend on the immediacy of the partner's involvement and the seriousness of the misconduct. The supervisor is required to intervene to prevent avoidable consequences of misconduct if the supervisor knows that the misconduct occurred. Thus, if a supervising lawyer knows that a subordinate misrepresented a matter to an opposing party in negotiation, the supervisor as well as the subordinate has a duty to correct the resulting misapprehension.

Professional misconduct by a lawyer under supervision could reveal a violation of paragraph (b) on the part of the supervisory lawyer even though it does not entail a violation of paragraph (c) because there was no direction, ratification or knowledge of the violation.

Apart from this Rule and Rule 8.4(a), a lawyer does not have disciplinary liability for the conduct of a partner, associate or subordinate. Whether a lawyer may be liable civilly or criminally for another lawyer's conduct is a question of law beyond the scope of these Rules.

Rule 5.2 Responsibilities of a subordinate lawyer

(a) A lawyer is bound by the rules of professional conduct notwithstanding that the lawyer acted at the direction of another person.

(b) A subordinate lawyer does not violate the rules of professional conduct if that lawyer acts in accordance with a supervisory lawyer's reasonable resolution of an arguable question of professional duty.

COMMENT:

Although a lawyer is not relieved of responsibility for a violation by the fact that the lawyer acted at the direction of a supervisor, that fact may be relevant in determining whether a lawyer had the knowledge required to render conduct a violation of the Rules. For example, if a subordinate filed a frivolous pleading at the direction of a supervisor, the subordinate would not be guilty of a professional violation unless the subordinate knew of the document's frivolous character.

When lawyers in a supervisor-subordinate relationship encounter a matter involving professional judgment as to ethical duty, the supervisor may assume responsibility for making the judgment. Otherwise a consistent course of action or position could not be taken. If the question can reasonably be answered only one way, the duty of both lawyers is clear and they are equally responsible for fulfilling it. However, if the question is reasonably arguable, someone has to decide upon the course of action. That authority ordinarily reposes in the supervisor, and a subordinate may be guided accordingly. For example, if a question arises whether the interests of two clients conflict under Rule 1.7, the supervisor's reasonable resolution of the question should protect the subordinate professionally if the resolution is subsequently challenged.

Rule 5.3   Responsibilities Regarding Nonlawyer Assistants

With respect to a nonlawyer employed or retained by or associated with a lawyer:

(a) a partner in a law firm shall make reasonable efforts to ensure that the firm has in effect measures giving reasonable assurance that the person's conduct is compatible with the professional obligations of the lawyer;

(b) a lawyer having direct supervisory authority over the nonlawyer shall make reasonable efforts to ensure that the person's conduct is compatible with the professional obligations of the lawyer; and

(c) a lawyer shall be responsible for conduct of such a person that would be a violation of the rules of professional conduct if engaged in by a lawyer if:

(1) the lawyer orders or, with the knowledge of the specific conduct, ratifies the conduct involved; or

(2) the lawyer is a partner in the law firm in which the person is employed, or has direct supervisory authority over the person, and knows of the conduct at a time when its consequences can be avoided or mitigated but fails to take reasonable remedial action.

COMMENT:

Lawyers generally employ assistants in their practice, including secretaries, investigators, law student interns, and paraprofessionals. Such assistants, whether employees or independent contractors, act for the lawyer in rendition of the lawyer's professional services. A lawyer should give such assistants appropriate instruction and supervision concerning the ethical aspects of their employment, particularly regarding the obligation not to disclose information relating to representation of the client, and should be responsible for their work product. The measures employed in supervising nonlawyers should take account of the fact that they do not have legal training and are not subject to professional discipline.

Rule 5.4   Professional independence of a lawyer

(a) A lawyer or law firm shall not share legal fees with a nonlawyer, except that:
  (1) an agreement by a lawyer with his firm, partner, or associate may provide for the payment of money, over a reasonable period of time after his death, to his estate or to one or more specified persons;
  (2) a lawyer who undertakes to complete unfinished legal business of a deceased lawyer may pay to the estate of the deceased lawyer that proportion of the total compensation which fairly represents the services rendered by the deceased lawyer; and
  (3) a lawyer or law firm may include nonlawyer employees in a compensation or retirement plan, even though the plan is based in whole or in part on a profit-sharing arrangement.

(b) A lawyer shall not form a partnership with a nonlawyer if any of the activities of the partnership consist of the practice of law.

(c) A lawyer shall not permit a person who recommends, employs, or pays him to render legal services for another to direct or regulate his professional judgment in rendering such legal services.

(d) A lawyer shall not practice with or in the form of a professional corporation or association authorized to practice law for a profit, if:
  (1) a nonlawyer owns any interest therein, except that a fiduciary representative of the estate of a lawyer may hold the stock or interest of the lawyer for a reasonable time during administration;
  (2) a nonlawyer is a corporate director or officer thereof; or
  (3) a nonlawyer has the right to direct or control the professional judgment of a lawyer.

COMMENT:

The provisions of this Rule express traditional limitations on sharing fees. These limitations are to protect the lawyer's professional independence of judgment. Where someone other than the client pays the lawyer's fee or salary, or recommends employment of the lawyer, that arrangement does not modify the lawyer's obligation to the client. As stated in paragraph (c), such arrangements should not interfere with the lawyer's professional judgment.

Rule 5.5   Unauthorized practice of law

A lawyer shall not:
  (a)   practice law in a jurisdiction where doing so violates the regulation of the legal profession in that jurisdiction; or
  (b)   assist a person who is not a member of the bar in the performance of activity that constitutes the unauthorized practice of law.

COMMENT:

The definition of the practice of law is established by law and varies from one jurisdiction to another. Whatever the definition, limiting the practice of law to members of the bar protects the public against rendition of legal services by unqualified persons. Paragraph (b) does not prohibit a lawyer from employing the services of paraprofessionals and delegating functions to them, so long as the lawyer supervises the delegated work and retains responsibility for their work. See Rule 5.3. Likewise, it does not prohibit lawyers from providing professional advice and instruction to nonlawyers whose employment requires knowledge of law; for example, claims adjusters, employees of financial or commercial institutions, social workers, accountants and persons employed in government agencies. In addition, a lawyer may counsel nonlawyers who wish to proceed pro se.

Rule 5.6   Restrictions on right to practice

A lawyer shall not participate in offering or making:
  (a)   a partnership or employment agreement that restricts the rights of a lawyer to practice after termination of the relationship, except an agreement concerning benefits upon retirement; or
  (b)   an agreement in which a restriction on the lawyer's right to practice is part of the settlement of a controversy between private parties.

COMMENT:

An agreement restricting the right of partners or associates to practice after leaving a firm not only limits their professional autonomy but also limits the freedom of clients to choose a lawyer. Paragraph (a) prohibits such agreements except for restrictions incident to provisions concerning retirement benefits for service with the firm.

Paragraph (b) prohibits a lawyer from agreeing not to represent other persons in connection with settling a claim on behalf of a client.

PUBLIC SERVICE

Rule 6.1   Pro bono publico service

A lawyer should render public interest legal service. A lawyer may discharge this responsibility by providing professional services at no fee or a reduced fee to persons of limited means or to public service or charitable groups or organizations, by service in activities for improving the law, the legal system or the legal profession, and by financial support for organizations that provide legal services to persons of limited means.

COMMENT:

The ABA House of Delegates has formally acknowledged "the basic responsibility of each lawyer engaged in the practice of law to provide public interest legal services" without fee, or at a substantially reduced fee, in one or more of the following areas: poverty law, civil rights law, public rights law, charitable organization representation and the administration of justice. This Rule expresses that policy but is not intended to be enforced through disciplinary process.

The rights and responsibilities of individuals and organizations in the United States are increasingly defined in legal terms. As a consequence, legal assistance in coping with the web of statutes, rules and regulations is imperative for persons of modest and limited means, as well as for the relatively well-to-do.

The basic responsibility for providing legal services for those unable to pay ultimately rests upon the individual lawyer, and personal involvement in the problems of the disadvantaged can be one of the most rewarding experiences in the life of a lawyer. Every lawyer, regardless of professional prominence or professional workload, should find time to participate in or otherwise support the provision of legal services to the disadvantaged. The provision of free legal services to those unable to pay reasonable fees continues to be an obligation of each lawyer as well as the profession generally, but the efforts of individual lawyers are often not enough to meet the need. Thus, it has been necessary for the profession and government to institute additional programs to provide legal services. Accordingly, legal aid offices, lawyer referral services and other related programs have been developed, and others will be developed by the profession and government. Every lawyer should support all proper efforts to meet this need for legal services.

Rule 6.2   Accepting appointments

A lawyer shall not seek to avoid appointment by a tribunal to represent a person except for good cause, such as:

  (a)   representing the client is likely to result in violation of the rules of professional conduct or other law;

  (b)   representing the client is likely to result in an unreasonable financial burden on the lawyer; or

  (c)   the client or the cause is so repugnant to the lawyer as to be likely to impair the client-lawyer relationship or the lawyer's ability to represent the client.

COMMENT:

A lawyer ordinarily is not obliged to accept a client whose character or cause the lawyer regards as repugnant. The lawyer's freedom to select clients is, however, qualified. All lawyers have a responsibility to assist in providing pro bono publico service. See Rule 6.1. An individual lawyer fulfills this responsibility by accepting a fair share of unpopular matters or indigent or unpopular clients. A lawyer may also be subject to appointment by a court to serve unpopular clients or persons unable to afford legal services.

Appointed Counsel

For good cause a lawyer may seek to decline an appointment to represent a person who cannot afford to retain counsel or whose cause is unpopular. Good cause exists if the lawyer could not handle the matter competently, see Rule 1.1, or if undertaking the representation would result in an improper conflict of interest, for example, when the client or the cause is so repugnant to the lawyer as to be likely to impair the client-lawyer relationship or the lawyer's ability to represent the client. A lawyer may also seek to decline an appointment if acceptance would be unreasonably burdensome, for example, when it would impose a financial sacrifice so great as to be unjust.

An appointed lawyer has the same obligations to the client as retained counsel, including the obligations of loyalty and confidentiality, and is subject to the same limitations on the client-lawyer relationship, such as the obligation to refrain from assisting the client in violation of the Rules.

Rule 6.3   Membership in legal services organization

A lawyer may serve as a director, officer or member of a legal services organization, apart from the law firm in which the lawyer practices, notwithstanding that the organization serves persons having interests adverse to a client of the lawyer. The lawyer shall not knowingly participate in a decision or action of the organization:

(a)   if participating in the decision would be incompatible with the lawyer's obligations to a client under Rule 1.7; or

(b)   where the decision could have a material adverse effect on the representation of a client of the organization whose interests are adverse to a client of the lawyer.

COMMENT:

Lawyers should be encouraged to support and participate in legal service organizations. A lawyer who is an officer or a member of such an organization does not thereby have a client-lawyer relationship with persons served by the organization. However, there is potential conflict between the interests of such persons and the interests of the lawyer's clients. If the possibility of such conflict disqualified a lawyer from serving on the board of a legal services organization, the profession's involvement in such organizations would be severely curtailed.

It may be necessary in appropriate cases to reassure a client of the organization that the representation will not be affected by conflicting loyalties of a member of a board. Established, written policies in this respect can enhance the credibility of such assurances.

Rule 6.4   Law reform activities affecting client interests

A lawyer may serve as a director, officer or member of an organization involved in reform of the law or its administration not withstanding that the reform may affect the interests of a client of the lawyer. When the lawyer knows that the interests of a client may be materially benefitted by a decision in which the lawyer participates, the lawyer shall disclose that fact but need not identify the client.

COMMENT:

Lawyers involved in organization seeking law reform generally do not have a client-lawyer relationship with the organization. Otherwise, it might follow that a lawyer could not be involved in a bar association law reform program that might indirectly affect a client. See also Rule 1.2(b). For example, a lawyer specializing in antitrust litigation might be regarded as disqualified from participating in drafting revisions of rules governing that subject. In determining the nature and scope of participation in such activities, a lawyer should be mindful of obligations to clients under other Rules, particularly Rule 1.7. A lawyer is professionally obligated to protect the integrity of the program by making an appropriate disclosure within the organization when the lawyer knows a private client might be materially benefitted.

INFORMATION ABOUT LEGAL SERVICES

Rule 7.1   Communications concerning a lawyer's services

A lawyer shall not make a false or misleading communication about the lawyer or the lawyer's services. A communication is false or misleading if it:
  (a)   contains a material misrepresentation of fact or law, or omits a fact necessary to make the statement considered as a whole not materially misleading;
  (b)   is likely to create an unjustified expectation about results the lawyer can achieve, or states or implies that the lawyer can achieve results by means that violate the rules of professional conduct or other law; or
  (c)   compares the lawyer's services with other lawyers services, unless the comparison can be factually substantiated.

COMMENT:

This Rule governs all communications about a lawyer's services, including advertising permitted by Rule 7.2. Whatever means are used to make known a lawyer's services, statements about them should be truthful. The prohibition in paragraph (b) of statements that may create "unjustified expectations" would ordinarily preclude advertisements about results obtained on behalf of a client, such as the amount of a damage award or the lawyer's record in obtaining favorable verdicts, and advertisements containing client endorsements. Such information may create the unjustified expectation that similar results can be obtained for others without reference to the specific factual and legal circumstances.

Rule 7.2   Advertising

  (a)   Subject to the requirements of Rule 7.1, a lawyer may advertise services through public media, such as a telephone directory, legal directory, newspaper or other periodical, outdoor, radio or television, or through written communication not involving solicitation as defined in Rule 7.3.

(b)   A copy or recording of an advertisement or written communication shall be kept for two years after its last dissemination along with a record of when and where it was used.

(c)   A lawyer shall not give anything of value to a person for recommending the lawyer's services, except that a lawyer may pay the reasonable cost of advertising or written communication permitted by this rule and may pay the usual charges of a not-for-profit lawyer referral service or other legal service organization.

(d)   Any communication made pursuant to this rule shall include the name of at least one lawyer responsible for its content.

COMMENT:

To assist the public in obtaining legal services, lawyers should be allowed to make known their services not only through reputation but also through organized information campaigns in the form of advertising. Advertising involves an active quest for clients, contrary to the tradition that a lawyer should not seek clientele. However, the public's need to know about legal services can be fulfilled in part through advertising. This need is particularly acute in the case of persons of moderate means who have not made extensive use of legal services. The interest in expanding public information about legal services ought to prevail over considerations of tradition. Nevertheless, advertising by lawyers entails the risk of practices that are misleading or overreaching.

This Rule permits public dissemination of information concerning a lawyer's name or firm name, address and telephone number; the kinds of services the lawyer will undertake; the basis on which the lawyer's fees are determined, including prices for specific services and payment and credit arrangements; a lawyer's foreign language ability; names of references and, with their consent, names of clients regularly represented; and other information that might invite the attention of those seeking legal assistance.

Questions of effectiveness and taste in advertising are matters of speculation and subjective judgment. Some jurisdictions have had extensive prohibitions against television advertising, against advertising going beyond specified facts about a lawyer, or against "undignified" advertising. Television is now one of the most powerful media for getting information to the public, particularly persons of low and moderate income; prohibiting television advertising, therefore, would impede the flow of information about legal services to many sectors of the public. Limiting the information that may be advertised has a similar effect and assumes that the bar can accurately forecast the kind of information that the public would regard as relevant.

Neither this Rule nor Rule 7.3 prohibits communications authorized by law, such as notice to members of a class in class action litigation.

Record of Advertising

Paragraph (b) requires that a record of the content and use of advertising be kept in order to facilitate enforcement of this Rule. It does not require that advertising be subject to review prior to dissemination. Such a requirement would be burdensome and expensive relative to its possible benefits, and may be of doubtful constitutionality.

Paying Others to Recommend a Lawyer

A lawyer is allowed to pay for advertising permitted by this Rule, but otherwise is not permitted to pay another person for channeling professional work. This restriction does not prevent an organization or person other than the lawyer from advertising or recommending the lawyer's services. Thus, a legal aid agency or prepaid legal services plan may pay to advertise legal services provided under its auspices. Likewise, a lawyer may participate in not-for-profit lawyer referral programs and pay the usual fees charged by such programs. Paragraph (c) does not prohibit paying regular compensation to an assistant, such as a secretary, to prepare communications permitted by this Rule.

Rule 7.3   Direct contact with prospective clients

A lawyer may not solicit professional employment from a prospective client with whom the lawyer has no family or prior professional relationship, by mail, in-person or otherwise, when a significant motive for the lawyer's doing so is the lawyer's pecuniary gain. The term "solicit" includes contact in person, by telephone or telegraph, by letter or other writing, or by other communication directed to a specific recipient, but does not include letters addressed or advertising circulars distributed generally to persons not known to need legal services of the kind provided by the lawyer in a particular matter, but who are so situated that they might in general find such services useful.

COMMENT:

The use of general advertising to transmit information from lawyer to prospective client, rather than direct private contact, will help to assure that the information flows cleanly as well as freely. Advertising is out in public view, thus subject to scrutiny by those who know the lawyer. This informal review is itself likely to help guard against statements and claims that might constitute false or misleading communications, in violation of Rule 7.1. Direct, private communications from a lawyer to a prospective client are not subject to such third-scrutiny and consequently are much more likely to approach (and occasionally cross) the dividing line between accurate representations and those that are false and misleading.

There is a potential for abuse inherent in direct solicitation by a lawyer of prospective clients known to need legal services. It subjects the lay person to the private importuning of a trained advocate, in a direct interpersonal encounter. A prospective client often feels overwhelmed by the situation giving rise to the need for legal services, and may have an impaired capacity or reason, judgment and protective self-interest. Furthermore, the lawyer seeking the retainer is faced with a conflict stemming from the lawyer's own interest, which may color the advice and representation offered the vulnerable prospect.

The situation is therefore fraught with the possibility of undue influence, intimidation, and over-reaching. This potential for abuse inherent in direct solicitation of prospective clients justifies its prohibition, particularly since lawyer advertising permitted under Rule 7.2 offers an alternative means of communicating necessary information to those who may be in need of legal services.

Advertising makes it possible for a prospective client to be informed about the need for legal services, and about the qualifications of available lawyers and law firms, without subjecting the prospective client to direct personal persuasion that may overwhelm the client's judgment.

The use of general advertising to transmit information from lawyer to prospective client, rather than direct private contact, will help to assure that the information flows clearly as well as freely. Advertising is out in public view, thus subject to scrutiny by those who know the lawyer. This informal review is itself likely to help guard against statements and claims that might constitute false or misleading communications, in violation of Rule 7.1. Direct, private communications from a lawyer to a prospective client are not subject to such third-scrutiny and consequently are much more likely to approach (and occasionally cross) the dividing line between accurate representations and those that are false and misleading.

These dangers attend direct solicitation whether in-person or by mail. Direct mail solicitation cannot be effectively regulated by means less drastic than outright prohibition. One proposed safeguard is to require that the designation "Advertising" be stamped on any envelope containing a solicitation letter. This would do nothing to assure the accuracy and reliability of the contents. Another suggestion is that solicitation letters be filed with a state regulatory agency. This would be ineffective as a practical matter. State lawyer discipline agencies struggle for resources to investigate specific complaints, much less for those necessary to screen lawyers' mail solicitation material. Even if they could examine such materials, agency staff members are unlikely to know anything about the lawyer or about the prospective client's underlying problem. Without such knowledge they cannot determine whether the lawyer's representations are misleading. In any event, such review would be after the fact, potentially too late to avert the undesirable consequences of disseminating false and misleading material.

General mailings not speaking to a specific matter do not pose the same danger of abuse as targeted mailings, and therefore are not prohibited by this Rule. The representations made in such mailings are necessarily general rather than tailored, less importuning than informative. They are addressed to recipients unlikely to be specially vulnerable at the time, hence who are likely to be more skeptical about unsubstantiated claims. General mailings not addressed to recipients involved in a specific legal matter or incident, therefore, more closely resemble permissible advertising rather than prohibited solicitation.

Similarly, this Rule would not prohibit a lawyer from contacting representatives of organizations or groups that may be interested in establishing a group or prepaid legal plan for its members, insureds, beneficiaries or other third parties for the purpose of informing such entities of the availability of and details concerning the plan or arrangement which he or his firm is willing to offer. This form of communication is not directed to a specific prospective client known to need legal services related to a particular matter. Rather, it is usually addressed to an individual acting in a fiduciary capacity seeking a supplier of legal services for others who may, if they choose, become prospective clients of the lawyer. Under these circumstances, the activity which the lawyer undertakes in communicating with such representatives and the type of information transmitted to the individual are functionally similar to and serve the same purpose as advertising permitted under Rule 7.2.

Rule 7.4   Communication of fields of practice

A lawyer may communicate the fact that the lawyer does or does not practice in particular fields of law. A lawyer shall not state or imply that the lawyer is a specialist except as follows:

   (a)   a lawyer admitted to engage in patent practice before the United States Patent and Trademark Office may use the designation "patent attorney" or a substantially similar designation;

   (b)   a lawyer engaged in admiralty practice may use the designation "admiralty," "proctor in admiralty" or a substantially similar designation; and

   (c)   (provisions on designation of specialization of the particular state).

COMMENT:

This Rule permits a lawyer to indicate areas of practice in communications about the lawyer's services; for example, in a telephone directory or other advertising. If a lawyer practices only in certain fields, or will not accept matters except in such fields, the lawyer is permitted so to indicate. However, stating that the lawyer is a "specialist" or that the lawyer's practice "is limited to" or "concentrated in" particular fields is not permitted. These terms have acquired a secondary meaning implying formal recognition as a specialist. Hence, use of these terms may be misleading unless the lawyer is certified or recognized in accordance with procedures in the state where the lawyer is licensed to practice.

Recognition of specialization in patent matters is a matter of long-established policy of the Patent and Trademark Office. Designation of admiralty practice has a long historical tradition associated with maritime commerce and the federal courts.

Rule 7.5   Firm names and letterheads

  (a) A lawyer shall not use a firm name, letterhead or other professional designation that violates Rule 7.1. A trade name may be used by a lawyer in private practice if it does not imply a connection with a government agency or with a public or charitable legal services organization and is not otherwise in violation of Rule 7.1.

  (b) A law firm with offices in more than one jurisdiction may use the same name in each jurisdiction, but identification of the lawyers in an office of the firm shall indicate the jurisdictional limitations on those not licensed to practice in the jurisdiction where the office is located.

  (c) The name of a lawyer holding a public office shall not be used in the name of a law firm, or in communications on its behalf, during any substantial period in which the lawyer is not actively and regularly practicing with the firm.

  (d) Lawyers may state or imply that they practice in a partnership or other organization only when that is the fact.

COMMENT:

A firm may be designated by the names of all or some of its members, by the names of deceased members where there has been a continuing succession in the firm's indentity or by a trade name such as the "ABC Legal Clinic." Although the United States Supreme Court has held that legislation may prohibit the use of trade names in professional practice, use of such names in law practice is acceptable so long as it is not misleading. If a private firm uses a trade name that includes a geographical name such as "Springfield Legal Clinic," an express disclaimer that it is a public legal aid agency may be required to avoid a misleading implication. It may be observed that any firm name including the name of a deceased partner is, strictly speaking, a trade name. The use of such names to designate law firms has proven a useful means of identification. However, it is misleading to use the name of a lawyer not associated with the firm or a predecessor of the firm.

With regard to paragraph (d), lawyers sharing office facilities, but who are not in fact partners, may not denominate themselves as, for example, "Smith and Jones," for that title suggests partnership in the practice of law.

MAINTAINING THE INTEGRITY OF THE PROFESSION

Rule 8.1   Bar admission and disciplinary matters

An applicant for admission to the bar, or a lawyer in connection with a bar admission application or in connection with a disciplinary matter, shall not:
 (a)   knowingly make a false statement of material fact; or
 (b)   fail to disclose a fact necessary to correct a misapprehension known by the person to have arisen in the matter, or knowingly fail to respond to a lawful demand for information from an admissions or disciplinary authority, except that this Rule does not require disclosure of information otherwise protected by Rule 1.6.

COMMENT:

The duty imposed by this Rule extends to persons seeking admission to the bar as well as to lawyers. Hence, if a person makes a material false statement in connection with an application for admission, it may be the basis for subsequent disciplinary action if the person is admitted, and in any event may be relevant in a subsequent admission application. The duty imposed by this Rule applies to a lawyer's own admission or discipline as well as that of others. Thus, it is a separate professional offense for a lawyer to knowingly make a misrepresentation or omission in connection with a disciplinary investigation of the lawyer's own conduct. This Rule also requires affirmative clarification of any misunderstanding on the part of the admissions or disciplinary authority of which the person involved becomes aware.

This Rule is subject to the provisions of the Fifth Amendment of the United States Constitution and corresponding provisions of state constitutions. A person relying on such a provision in reponse to a question, how-

177

ever, should do so openly and not use the right of nondisclosure as a justification for failure to comply with this Rule.

A lawyer representing an applicant for admission to the bar, or representing a lawyer who is the subject of a disciplinary inquiry or proceeding, is governed by the rules applicable to the client-lawyer relationship.

Rule 8.2   Judicial and legal officials

(a)   A lawyer shall not make a statement that the lawyer knows to be false or with reckless disregard as to its truth or falsity concerning the qualifications or integrity of a judge, adjudicatory officer or public legal officer, or of a candidate for election or appointment to judicial or legal office.

(b)   A lawyer who is a candidate for judcial office shall comply with the applicable provisions of the code of judicial conduct.

COMMENT:

Assessments by lawyers are relied on in evaluating the professional or personal fitness of persons being considered for election or appointment to judicial office and to public legal offices, such as attorney general, prosecuting attorney and public defender. Expressing honest and candid opinions on such matters contributes to improving the administration of justice. Conversely, false statements by a lawyer can unfairly undermine public confidence in the administration of justice.

When a lawyer seeks judicial office, the lawyer should be bound by applicable limitations on political activity.

To maintain the fair and independent administration of justice, lawyers are encouraged to continue traditional efforts to defend judges and courts unjustly criticized.

Rule 8.3   Reporting professional misconduct

(a)   A lawyer having knowledge that another lawyer has committed a violation of the rules of professional conduct that raises a substantial question as to that lawyer's honesty, trustworthiness or fitness as a lawyer in other respects, shall inform the appropriate professional authority.

(b)   A lawyer having knowledge that a judge has committed a violation of applicable rules of judicial conduct that raises a substantial question as to the judge's fitness for office shall inform the appropriate authority.

(c) This rule does not require disclosure of information otherwise pro-
     tected by Rule 1.6.

COMMENT:

Self-regulation of the legal profession requires that members of the profession initiate diciplinary investigation when they know of a violation of
the Rules of Professional Conduct. Lawyers have a similar obligation with
respect to judicial misconduct. An apparently isolated violation may indicate a pattern of misconduct that only a disciplinary investigation can un-
cover. Reporting a violation is especially important where the vicitm is
unlikely to discover the offense.

A report about misconduct is not required where it would involve violation of Rule 1.6. However, a lawyer should encourage a client to consent to
disclosure where prosecution would not substantially prejudice the client's
interests.

If a lawyer were obliged to report every violation of the Rules, the failure
to report any violation would itself be a professional offense. Such a requirement existed in many jurisdictions but proved to be unenforceable. This
Rule limits the reporting obligation to those offenses that a self-regulating
profession must vigorously endeavor to prevent. A measure of judgment is,
therefore, required in complying with the provisions of this Rule. The term
"substantial" refers to the seriousness of the possible offense and not the
quantum of evidence of which the lawyer is aware. A report should be made
to the bar disciplinary agency unless some other agency, such as a peer review agency, is more appropriate in the circumstances. Similar considerations apply to the reporting of judicial misconduct.

The duty to report professional misconduct does not apply to a lawyer
retained to represent a lawyer whose professional conduct is in question.
Such a situation is governed by the rules applicable to the client-lawyer
relationship.

Rule 8.4   Misconduct

It is professional misconduct for a lawyer to:
  (a) violate or attempt to violate the rules of professional conduct, know-
       ingly assist or induce another to do so, or do so through the acts of
       another;
  (b) commit a criminal act that reflects adversely on the lawyer's honesty,
       trustworthiness or fitness as a lawyer in other respects;
  (c) engage in conduct involving dishonesty, fraud, deceit or
       misrepresentation;
  (d) engage in conduct that is prejudicial to the administration of justice;

    (e)   state or imply an ability to influence improperly a government agency or official; or

    (f)   knowingly assist a judge or judicial officer in conduct that is a violation of applicable rules of judicial conduct or other law.

COMMENT:

Many kinds of illegal conduct reflect adversely on fitness to practice law, such as offenses involving fraud and the offense of willful failure to file an income tax return. However, some kinds of offense carry no such implication. Traditionally, the distinction was drawn in terms of offenses involving "moral turpitude." That concept can be construed to include offenses concerning some matters of personal morality, such as adultery and comparable offenses, that have no specific connection to fitness for the practice of law. Although a lawyer is personally answerable to the entire criminal law, a lawyer should be professionally answerable only for offenses that indicate lack of those characteristics relevant to law practice. Offenses involving violence, dishonesty, or breach of trust, or serious interference with the administration of justice are in that category. A pattern of repeated offenses, even ones of minor significance when considered separately, can indicate indifference to legal obligation.

A lawyer may refuse to comply with an obligation imposed by law upon a good faith belief that no valid obligation exists. The provisions of Rule 1.2(d) concerning a good faith challenge to the validity, scope, meaning or application of the law apply to challenges of legal regulation of the practice of law.

Lawyers holding public office assume legal responsibilities going beyond those of other citizens. A lawyer's abuse of public office can suggest an inability to fulfill the professional role of attorney. The same is true of abuse of positions of private trust such as trustee, executor, administrator, guardian, agent and officer, director or manager of a corporation or other organization.

Rule 8.5   Jurisdiction

A lawyer admitted to practice in this jurisdiction is subject to the disciplinary authority of this jurisdiction although engaged in practice elsewhere.

COMMENT:

In modern practice lawyers frequently act outside the territorial limits of the jurisdiction in which they are licensed to practice, either in another state or outside the United States. In doing so, they remain subject to the governing authority of the jurisdiction in which they are licensed to practice. If their activity in another jurisdiction is substantial and continuous, it may constitute practice of law in that jurisdiction. See Rule 5.5.

If the rules of professional conduct in the two jurisdictions differ, principles of conflict of laws may apply. Similar problems can arise when a lawyer is licensed to practice in more than one jurisdiction.

Where the lawyer is licensed to practice law in two jurisdictions which impose conflicting obligations, applicable rules of choice of law may govern the situation. A related problem arises with respect to practice before a federal tribunal, where the general authority of the states to regulate the practice of law must be reconciled with such authority as federal tribunals may have to regulate practice before them.

A.B.A. STANDARDS FOR
CRIMINAL JUSTICE*

CHAPTER 3
THE PROSECUTION FUNCTION

Standard 3-1.1. The function of the prosecutor

(a) The office of prosecutor is charged with responsibility for prosecutions in its jurisdiction.

(b) The prosecutor is both an administrator of justice and an advocate. The prosecutor must exercise sound discretion in the performance of his or her functions.

(c) The duty of the prosecutor is to seek justice, not merely to convict.

(d) It is the duty of the prosecutor to know and be guided by the standards of professional conduct as defined in the codes and canons of the legal profession, and in this chapter. The prosecutor should make use of the guidance afforded by an advisory council of the kind described in standard 4-1.4.

(e) As used in this chapter, the term "unprofessional conduct" denotes conduct which, in either identical or similar language, is or should be made subject to disciplinary sanctions pursuant to codes of professional responsibility in force in each jurisdiction. Where other terms are used, the standard is intended as a guide to honorable professional conduct and performance. These standards are not intended as criteria for the judicial evaluation of alleged misconduct of the prosecutor to determine the validity of a conviction. They may or may not be relevant in such judicial evaluation, depending upon all the circumstances.

Standard 3-1.2. Conflicts of interest

A prosecutor should avoid the appearance or reality of a conflict of interest with respect to official duties. In some instances, as defined in codes of professional responsibility, failure to do so will constitute unprofessional conduct.

Standard 3-1.3.   Public statements

(a) The prosecutor should not exploit the office by means of personal publicity connected with a case before trial, during trial, or thereafter.

(b) The prosecutor should comply with the chapter on Fair Trial and Free Press in these standards. In some instances, as defined in codes of professional responsibility, failure to do so will constitute unprofessional conduct.

(c) In order to assure a fair trial for the accused, the prosecutor and police should cooperate in achieving compliance with the chapter on Fair Trial and Free Press of these standards and codes of professional responsibility.

Standard 3-1.4.   Duty to improve the law

It is an important function of the prosecutor to seek to reform and improve the administration of criminal justice. When inadequacies or injustices in the substantive or procedural law come to the prosecutor's attention, he or she should stimulate efforts for remedial action.

Standard 3-2.1.   Prosecution authority to be vested in a public official

The prosecution function should be performed by a public prosecutor who is a lawyer subject to the standards of professional conduct and discipline.

Standard 3-2.2.   Interrelationship of prosecution offices within a state

(a) Local authority and responsibility for prosecution is properly vested in a district, county, or city attorney. Wherever possible, a unit of prosecution should be designed on the basis of population, caseload, and other relevant factors sufficient to warrant at least one full-time prosecutor and the supporting staff necessary to effective prosecution.

(b) In some states, conditions such as geographical area and population may make it appropriate to create a statewide system of prosecution in which the state attorney general is the chief prosecutor and the local prosecutors are deputies.

(c) In all states, there should be coordination of the prosecution policies of local prosecution offices to improve the administration of justice and assure the maximum practicable uniformity in the enforcement of the criminal law throughout the state. A state council of prosecutors should be established in each state.

(d) In cases where questions of law of statewide interest or concern arise which may create important precedents, the prosecutor should consult and advise with the attorney general of the state.

(e) A central pool of supporting resources and manpower, including laboratories, investigators, accountants, special counsel, and other experts to the extent needed, should be maintained by the state government and should be available to all local prosecutors.

Standard 3-2.3. Assuring high standards of professional skill

(a) The function of public prosecution requires highly developed professional skills. This objective can best be achieved by promoting continuity of service and broad experience in all phases of the prosecution function.

(b) Wherever feasible, the offices of chief prosecutor and staff should be full-time occupations.

(c) Professional competence should be the only basis for selection for prosecutorial office. Prosecutors should select their staffs on the basis of professional competence without regard to partisan political influence.

(d) In order to achieve the objective of professionalism and to encourage competent lawyers to accept such offices, compensation for prosecutors and their staffs should be commensurate with the high responsibilities of the office and comparable to the compensation of their peers in the private sector.

Standard 3-2.4. Special assistants, investigative resources, experts

(a) Funds should be provided to enable a prosecutor to appoint special assistants from among the trial bar experienced in criminal cases, as needed for the prosecution of a particular case or to assist generally.

(b) Funds should be provided to the prosecutor for the employment of a regular staff of professional investigative personnel and other necessary supporting personnel, under the prosecutor's direct control, to the extent warranted by the responsibilities and scope of the office. The prosecutor should also be provided with funds for the employment of qualified experts as needed for particular cases.

Standard 3-2.5.   Prosecutor's handbook; policy guidelines and procedures

(a) Each prosecutor's office should develop a statement of:
   (i)   general policies to guide the exercise of prosecutorial discretion, and
   (ii) procedures of the office.
      The objectives of these policies as to discretion and procedures should be to achieve a fair, efficient, and effective enforcement of the criminal law.
(b) In the interest of continuity and clarity, such statement of policies and procedures should be maintained in an office handbook. This handbook should be available to the public, except for subject matters declared "confidential," when it is reasonably believed that public access to their contents would adversely affect the prosecution function.

Standard 3-2.6.   Training programs

Training programs should be established within the prosecutor's office for new personnel and for continuing education of the staff. Continuing education programs for prosecutors should be substantially expanded and public funds should be provided to enable prosecutors to attend such programs.

Standard 3-2.7.   Relations with police

(a) The prosecutor should provide legal advise to the police concerning police functions and duties in criminal matters.
(b) The prosecutor should cooperate with police in providing the services of the prosecutor's staff to aid in training police in the performance of their function in accordance with law.

Standard 3-2.8.   Relations with the courts and bar

(a) It is unprofessional conduct for a prosecutor intentionally to misrepresent matters of fact or law to the court.
(b) A prosecutor's duties necessarily involve frequent and regular official contacts with the judge or judges of the prosecutor's jurisdiction. In such contacts the prosecutor should carefully strive to preserve the appearance as well as the reality of the correct rela-

tionship which professional traditions and canons require between advocates and judges.

(c) It is unprofessional conduct for a prosecutor to engage in unauthorized ex parte discussions with or submission of material to a judge relating to a particular case which is or may come before the judge.

(d) In the prosecutor's necessarily frequent contacts with other members of the bar, the prosecutor should strive to avoid the appearance as well as the reality of any relationship which would tend to cast doubt on the independence and integrity of the office.

Standard 3-2.9. Prompt disposition of criminal charges

(a) A prosecutor should not intentionally use procedural devices for delay for which there is no legitimate basis.

(b) The prosecution function should be so organized and supported with staff and facilities as to enable it to dispose of all criminal charges promptly. The prosecutor should be punctual in attendance in court and in the submission of all motions, briefs, and other papers. The prosecutor should emphasize to all witnesses the importance of punctuality in attendance in court.

(c) It is unprofessional conduct intentionally to misrepresent facts or otherwise mislead the court in order to obtain a continuance.

Standard 3-2.10. Supersession and substitution of prosecutor

(a) Procedures should be established by appropriate legislation to the end that the governor or other elected state official is empowered by law to suspend and supersede a local prosecutor upon making a public finding, after reasonable notice and hearing, that the prosecutor is incapable of fulfilling the duties of office.

(b) The governor or other elected official should be empowered by law to substitute special counsel in the place of the local prosecutor in a particular case, or category of cases, upon making a public finding that this is required for the protection of the public interest.

Standard 3-3.1. Investigative function of prosecutor

(a) A prosecutor ordinarily relies on police and other investigative agencies for investigation of alleged criminal acts, but the prosecutor has an affirmative responsibility to investigate suspected illegal activity when it is not adequately dealt with by other agencies.

(b) It is unprofessional conduct for a prosecutor knowingly to use illegal means to obtain evidence or to employ or instruct or encourage others to use such means.

(c) A prosecutor should not discourage or obstruct communication between prospective witnesses and defense counsel. It is unprofessional conduct for the prosecutor to advise any person or cause any person to be advised to decline to give to the defense information which such person has the right to give.

(d) It is unprofessional conduct for a prosecutor to secure the attendance of persons for interviews by use of any communication which has the appearance or color of a subpoena or similar judicial process unless the prosecutor is authorized by law to do so.

(e) It is unprofessional conduct for a prosecutor to promise not to prosecute for prospective criminal activity, except where such activity is part of an officially supervised investigative and enforcement program.

(f) Unless a prosecutor is prepared to forgo impeachment of a witness by the prosecutor's own testimony as to what the witness stated in an interview or to seek leave to withdraw from the case in order to present the impeaching testimony, a prosecutor should avoid interviewing a prospective witness except in the presence of a third person.

Standard 3-3.2.   Relations with prospective witnesses

(a) It is unprofessional conduct to compensate a witness, other than an expert, for giving testimony, but it is not improper to reimburse an ordinary witness for the reasonable expenses of attendance upon court, attendance for depositions pursuant to statute or court rule, or attendance for pretrial interviews. Payments to a witness may be for transportation and loss of income, provided there is no attempt to conceal the fact of reimbursement.

(b) Whenever a prosecutor knows or has reason to believe that the conduct of a witness to be interviewed may be the subject of a criminal prosecution, the prosecutor or the prosecutor's investigator should advise the witness concerning possible self-incrimination and the possible need for counsel.

Standard 3-3.3.   Relations with expert witnesses

(a) A prosecutor who engages an expert for an opinion should respect the independence of the expert and should not seek to dictate the formation of the expert's opinion on the subject. To the extent necessary, the prosecutor should explain to the expert his or her role in the trial as an impartial expert called to aid the fact finders and the manner in which the examination of witnesses is conducted.

(b) It is unprofessional conduct for a prosecutor to pay an excessive fee for the purpose of influencing the expert's testimony or to fix the amount of the fee contingent upon the testimony the expert will give or the result in the case.

Standard 3-3.4. Decision to charge

(a) The decision to institute criminal proceedings should be initially and primarily the responsibility of the prosecutor.

(b) Absent exceptional circumstances, no arrest warrant or search warrant should issue without the approval of the prosecutor.

(c) The prosecutor should establish standards and procedures for evaluating complaints to determine whether criminal proceedings should be instituted.

(d) Where the law permits a citizen to complain directly to a judicial officer or the grand jury, the citizen complainant should be required to present the complaint for prior approval to the prosecutor, and the prosecutor's action or recommendation thereon should be communicated to the judicial officer or grand jury.

Standard 3-3.5. Relations with grand jury

(a) Where the prosecutor is authorized to act as legal adviser to the grand jury, the prosecutor may appropriately explain the law and express an opinion on the legal significance of the evidence but should give due deference to its status as an independent legal body.

(b) The prosecutor should not make statements or arguments in an effort to influence grand jury action in a manner which would be impermissible at trial before a petit jury.

(c) The prosecutor's communications and presentations to the grand jury should be on the record.

Standard 3-3.6. Quality and scope of evidence before grand jury

(a) A prosecutor should present to the grand jury only evidence which the prosecutor believes would be admissible at trial. However, in appropriate cases, the prosecutor may present witnesses to summarize admissible evidence available to the prosecutor which the prosecutor believes he or she will be able to present at trial.

(b) No prosecutor should knowingly fail to disclose to the grand jury evidence which will tend substantially to negate guilt.

(c) A prosecutor should recommend that the grand jury not indict if it is believed the evidence presented does not warrant an indictment under governing law.

(d) If the prosecutor believes that a witness is a potential defendant, the prosecutor should not seek to compel the witness's testimony before the grand jury without informing the witness that he or she may be charged and that the witness should seek independent legal advice concerning his or her rights.

(e) The prosecutor should not compel the appearance of a witness before the grand jury whose activities are the subject of the inquiry if the witness states in advance that if called he or she will exercise the constitutional privilege not to testify, unless the prosecutor intends to seek a grant of immunity according to the law.

Standard 3-3.7.   Quality and scope of evidence for information

Where the prosecutor is empowered to charge by information, the prosecutor's decisions should be governed by the principles embodied in standards 3-3.6 and 3-3.9.

Standard 3-3.8.   Discretion as to noncriminal disposition

(a) The prosecutor should explore the availability of noncriminal disposition, including programs of rehabilitation, formal or informal, in deciding whether to press criminal charges. Especially in the case of a first offender, the nature of the offense may warrant noncriminal disposition.

(b) Prosecutors should be familiar with the resources of social agencies which can assist in the evaluation of cases for diversion from the criminal process.

Standard 3-3.9.   Discretion in the charging decision

(a) It is unprofessional conduct for a prosecutor to institute, or cause to be instituted, or to permit the continued pendency of criminal charges when it is known that the charges are not supported by probable cause. A prosecutor should not institute, cause to be instituted, or permit the continued pendency of criminal charges in the absence of sufficient admissible evidence to support a conviction.

(b)   The prosecutor is not obliged to present all charges which the evidence might support. The prosecutor may in some circumstances and for good cause consistent with the public interest decline to prosecute, notwithstanding that sufficient evidence may exist which would support a conviction. Illustrative of the factors which the prosecutor may properly consider in exercising his or her discretion are:

    (i)   the prosecutor's reasonable doubt that the accused is in fact guilty;

    (ii)   the extent of the harm caused by the offense;

    (iii)   the disproportion of the authorized punishment in relation to the particular offense or the offender;

    (iv)   possible improper motives of a complainant;

    (v)   reluctance of the victim to testify;

    (vi)   cooperation of the accused in the apprehension or conviction of others; and

    (vii)   availability and likelihood of prosecution by another jurisdiction.

(c)   In making the decision to prosecute, the prosecutor should give no weight to the personal or political advantages or disadvantages which might be involved or to a desire to enhance his or her record of convictions.

(d)   In cases which involve a serious threat to the community, the prosecutor should not be deterred from prosecution by the fact that in the jurisdiction juries have tended to acquit persons accused of the particular kind of criminal act in question.

(e)   The prosecutor should not bring or seek charges greater in number or degree than can reasonably be supported with evidence at trial.

Standard 3-3.10.   Role in first appearance and preliminary hearing

(a)   A prosecutor who is present at the first appearance (however denominated) of the accused before a judicial officer should not communicate with the accused unless a waiver of counsel has been entered, except for the purpose of aiding in obtaining counsel or in arranging for the pretrial release of the accused.

(b)   The prosecutor should cooperate in good faith in arrangements for release under the prevailing system for pretrial release.

(c)   The prosecutor should not encourage an uncounseled accused to waive preliminary hearing.

(d)   The prosecutor should not seek a continuance solely for the purpose of mooting the preliminary hearing by securing an indictment.

(e)   Except for good cause, the prosecutor should not seek delay in the preliminary hearing after an arrest has been made if the accused is in custody.

(f)   The prosecutor should ordinarily be present at a preliminary hearing where such hearing is required by law.

Standard 3-3.11.   Disclosure of evidence by the prosecutor

(a)   It is unprofessional conduct for a prosecutor intentionally to fail to make disclosure to the defense, at the earliest feasible opportunity, of the existence of evidence which tends to negate the guilt of the accused as to the offense charged or which would tend to reduce the punishment of the accused.

(b)   The prosecutor should comply in good faith with discovery procedures under the applicable law.

(c)   It is unprofessional conduct for a prosecutor intentionally to avoid pursuit of evidence because he or she believes it will damage the prosecution's case or aid the accused.

Standard 3-4.1.   Availability for plea discussions

(a)   The prosecutor should make known a general policy of willingness to consult with defense counsel concerning disposition of charges by plea.

(b)   It is unprofessional conduct for a prosecutor to engage in plea discussions directly with an accused who is represented by counsel, except with counsel's approval. Where the defendant has properly waived counsel, the prosecuting attorney may engage in plea discussions with the defendant, although ordinarily a verbatim record of such discussions should be made and preserved.

(c)   It is unprofessional conduct for a prosecutor knowingly to make false statements or representations in the course of plea discussions with defense counsel or the accused.

Standard 3-4.2.   Fulfillment of plea discussions

(a)   It is unprofessional conduct for a prosecutor to make any promise or commitment concerning the sentence which will be imposed or concerning a suspension of sentence. A prosecutor may properly advise the defense what position will be taken concerning disposition.

(b) It is unprofessional conduct for a prosecutor to imply a greater power to influence the disposition of a case than is actually possessed.

(c) It is unprofessional conduct for a prosecutor to fail to comply with a plea agreement, unless a defendant fails to comply with a plea agreement or other extenuating circumstances are present.

Standard 3-4.3. Record of reasons for nolle prosequi disposition

Whenever felony criminal charges are dismissed by way of nolle prosequi (or its equivalent), the prosecutor should make a record of the reasons for the action.

Standard 3-5.1. Calendar control

Control over the trial calendar should be vested in the court. The prosecuting attorney should be required to file with the court as a public record periodic reports setting forth the reasons for delay as to each case for which the prosecuting attorney has not requested trial within a prescribed time following charging. The prosecuting attorney should also advise the court of facts relevant in determining the order of cases on the calendar.

Standard 3-5.2. Courtroom decorum

(a) The prosecutor should support the authority of the court and the dignity of the trial courtroom by strict adherence to the rules of decorum and by manifesting an attitude of professional respect toward the judge, opposing counsel, witnesses, defendants, jurors, and others in the courtroom.

(b) When court is in session the prosecutor should address the court, not opposing counsel, on all matters relating to the case.

(c) It is unprofessional conduct for a prosecutor to engage in behavior or tactics purposefully calculated to irritate or annoy the court or opposing counsel.

(d) A prosecutor should comply promptly with all orders and directives of the court, but the prosecutor has a duty to have the record reflect adverse rulings or judicial conduct which the prosecutor considers prejudicial. The prosecutor has a right to make respectful requests for reconsideration of adverse rulings.

(e) A prosecutor should be punctual in all court appearances and in the submission of all motions, briefs, and other papers.

(f)   Prosecutors should cooperate with courts and the organized bar in developing codes of decorum and professional etiquette for each jurisdiction.

Standard 3-5.3.   Selection of jurors

(a)   The prosecutor should prepare himself or herself prior to trial to discharge effectively the prosecution function in the selection of the jury and the exercise of challenges for cause and peremptory challenges.

(b)   In those cases where it appears necessary to conduct a pretrial investigation of the background of jurors, investigatory methods of the prosecutor should neither harass nor unduly embarrass potential jurors or invade their privacy and, whenever possible, should be restricted to an investigation of records and sources of information already in existence.

(c)   The opportunity to question jurors personally should be used solely to obtain information for the intelligent exercise of challenges. A prosecutor should not intentionally use the voir dire to present factual matter which the prosecutor knows will not be admissible at trial or to argue the prosecution's case to the jury.

Standard 3-5.4.   Relations with jury

(a)   It is unprofessional conduct for a prosecutor to communicate privately with persons summoned for jury duty or impaneled as jurors concerning a case prior to or during trial. The prosecutor should avoid the reality or appearance of any such improper communications.

(b)   The prosecutor should treat jurors with deference and respect, avoiding the reality or appearance of currying favor by a show of undue solicitude for their comfort or convenience.

(c)   After discharge of the jury from further consideration of a case, it is unprofessional conduct for the prosecutor to intentionally make comments to or ask questions of a juror for the purpose of harassing or embarrassing the juror in any way which will tend to influence judgment in future jury service.

Standard 3-5.5.   Opening statement

The prosecutor's opening statement should be confined to a brief statement of the issues in the case and to remarks on evidence the prosecutor intends to offer which the prosecutor believes in good faith will be available and admissible. It is unprofessional conduct to allude to any evidence unless there is a good faith and reasonable basis for believing that such evidence will be tendered and admitted in evidence.

Standard 3-5.6.   Presentation of evidence

(a)   It is unprofessional conduct for a prosecutor knowingly to offer false evidence, whether by documents, tangible evidence, or the testimony of witnesses, or fail to seek withdrawl thereof upon discovery of its falsity.

(b)   It is unprofessional conduct for a prosecutor knowingly and for the purpose of bringing inadmissible matter to the attention of the judge or jury to offer inadmissible evidence, ask legally objectionable questions, or make other impermissible comments or arguments in the presence of the judge or jury.

(c)   It is unprofessional conduct for a prosecutor to permit any tangible evidence to be displayed in the view of the judge or jury which would tend to prejudice fair consideration by the judge or jury until such time as a good faith tender of such evidence is made.

(d)   It is unprofessional conduct to tender tangible evidence in the view of the judge or jury if it would tend to prejudice fair consideration by the judge or jury unless there is a reasonable basis for its admission in evidence. When there is any substantial doubt about the admissibility of such evidence, it should be tendered by an offer of proof and a ruling obtained.

Standard 3-5.7.   Examination of witnesses

(a)   The interrogation of all witnesses should be conducted fairly, objectively, and with due regard for the dignity and legitimate privacy of the witness, and without seeking to intimidate or humiliate the witness unnecessarily. Proper cross-examination can be conducted without violating rules of decorum.

(b)   The prosecutor's belief that the witness is telling the truth does not preclude cross-examination, but may affect the method and scope of cross-examination. A prosecutor should not use the power of cross-examination to discredit or undermine a witness if the prosecutor knows the witness is testifying truthfully.

(c)   A prosecutor should not call a witness who the prosecutor knows will claim a valid privilege not to testify for the purpose of impressing upon the jury the fact of the claim of privilege. In some instances, as defined in codes of professional responsibility, doing so will constitute unprofessional conduct.

(d) It is unprofessional conduct for a prosecutor to ask a question which implies the existence of a factual predicate for which a good faith belief is lacking.

Standard 3-5.8.   Argument to the jury

(a) The prosecutor may argue all reasonable inferences from evidence in the record. It is unprofessional conduct for the prosecutor intentionally to misstate the evidence or mislead the jury as to the inferences it may draw.

(b) It is unprofessional conduct for the prosecutor to express his or her personal belief or opinion as to the truth or falsity of any testimony or evidence or the guilt of the defendant.

(c) The prosecutor should not use arguments calculated to inflame the passions or prejudices of the jury.

(d) The prosecutor should refrain from argument which would divert the jury from its duty to decide the case on the evidence, by injecting issues broader than the guilt or innocence of the accused under the controlling law, or by making predictions of the consequences of the jury's verdict.

(e) It is the responsibility of the court to ensure that final argument to the jury is kept within proper, accepted bounds.

Standard 3-5.9.   Facts outside the record

It is unprofessional conduct for the prosecutor intentionally to refer to or argue on the basis of facts outside the record whether at trial or on appeal, unless such facts are matters of common public knowledge based on ordinary human experience or matters of which the court may take judicial notice.

Standard 3-5.10.   Comments by prosecutor after verdict

The prosecutor should not make public comments critical of a verdict, whether rendered by judge or jury.

Standard 3-6.1.   Role in sentencing

(a) The prosecutor should not make the severity of sentences the index of his or her effectiveness. To the extent that the prosecutor be-

comes involved in the sentencing process, he or she should seek to
assure that a fair and informed judgment is made on the sentence
and to avoid unfair sentence disparities.

(b)   Where sentence is fixed by the court without jury participation, the
prosecutor should be afforded the opportunity to address the court
at sentencing and to offer a sentencing recommendation. When requested by the court to furnish a sentencing recommendation, the
prosecutor should have the obligation to do so.

(c)   Where sentence is fixed by the jury, the prosecutor should present
evidence on the issue within the limits permitted in the jurisdiction,
but the prosecutor should avoid introducing evidence bearing on
sentence which will prejudice the jury's determination of the issue of
guilt.

Standard 3-6.2.   Information relevant to sentencing

(a)   The prosecutor should assist the court in basing its sentence on
complete and accurate information for use in the presentence report. The prosecutor should disclose to the court any information
in the prosecutor's files relevant to the sentence. If incomplete-
ness or inaccurateness in the presentence report comes to the prosecutor's attention, the prosecutor should take steps to present the
complete and correct information to the court and to defense
counsel.

(b)   The prosecutor should disclose to the defense and to the court at or
prior to the sentencing proceeding all information in the prosecutor's files which is relevant to the sentencing issue.

CHAPTER 4
THE DEFENSE FUNCTION

Standard 4-1.1   Role of defense counsel

(a)   Counsel for the accused is an essential component of the administration of criminal justice. A court properly constituted to hear a criminal case must be viewed as a tripartite entity consisting of the judge
(and jury, where appropriate), counsel for the prosecution, and counsel for the accused.

(b)   The basic duty the lawyer for the accused owes to the administration of justice is to serve as the accused's counselor and advocate

with courage, devotion, and to the utmost of his or her learning and ability and according to law.

(c)   The defense lawyer, in common with all members of the bar, is subject to standards of conduct stated in statutes, rules, decisions of courts, and codes, canons, or other standards of professional conduct. The defense lawyer has no duty to execute any directive of the accused which does not comport with law or such standards. The defense lawyer is the professional representative of the accused, not the accused's alter ego.

(d)   It is unprofessional conduct for a lawyer intentionally to misrepresent matters of fact or law to the court.

(e)   It is the duty of every lawyer to know the standards of professional conduct as defined in codes and canons of the legal profession and in this chapter. The functions and duties of defense counsel are governed by such standards whether defense counsel is assigned or privately retained.

(f)   As used in this chapter, the term "unprofessional conduct" denotes conduct which, in either identical or similar language, is or should be made subject to disciplinary sanctions pursuant to codes of professional responsibility. Where other terms are used, the standard is intended as a guide to honorable professional conduct and performance. These standards are not intended as criteria for the judicial evaluation of alleged misconduct of counsel to determine the validity of a conviction. They may or may not be relevant in such judicial evaluation, depending upon all the circumstances.

Standard 4-1.2.   Delays; punctuality

(a)   Defense counsel should avoid unnecessary delay in the disposition of cases. Defense counsel should be punctual in attendance upon court and in the submission of all motions, briefs, and other papers. Defense counsel should emphasize to the client and all witnesses the importance of punctuality in attendance in court.

(b)   It is unprofessional conduct for defense counsel intentionally to misrepresent facts or otherwise mislead the court in order to obtain a continuance.

(c)   Defense counsel should not intentionally use procedural devices for delay for which there is no legitimate basis.

(d)   A lawyer should not accept more employment than the lawyer can discharge within the spirit of the constitutional mandate for speedy trial and the limits of the lawyer's capacity to give each client effective representation. It is unprofessional conduct to accept employment for the purpose of delaying trial.

Standard 4-1.3.   Public statements

   (a)   The lawyer representing an accused should avoid personal publicity connected with the case before trial, during trial, and thereafter.

   (b)   The lawyer should comply with the standards on Fair Trial and Free Press herein. In some instances, as defined in codes of professional responsibility, the lawyer's failure to do so will constitute unprofessional conduct.

Standard 4-1.4.   Advisory councils on professional conduct

   (a)   In every jurisdiction an advisory body of lawyers selected for their experience, integrity, and standing at the trial bar should be established as an advisory council on problems of professional conduct in criminal cases. This council should provide prompt and confidential guidance and advice to lawyers seeking assistance in the application of standards of professional conduct in criminal cases.

   (b)   Communications between a lawyer and such an advisory council should have the same privilege for protection of the client's confidences as exists between lawyer and client. The council should be bound by statute or rule of court in the same manner as a lawyer is bound not to reveal any disclosure of the client except

      (i)   if the client challenges the effectiveness of the lawyer's conduct of the case and the lawyer relies on the guidance received from the council, and

      (ii)   if the lawyer's conduct is called into question in an authoritative disciplinary inquiry or proceeding.

Standard 4-1.5.   Trial lawyer's duty to administration of justice

   (a)   The bar should encourage through every available means the widest possible participation in the defense of criminal cases by experienced trial lawyers. Lawyers active in general trial practice should be encouraged to qualify themselves for participation in criminal cases both by formal training and through experience as associate counsel.

   (b)   All qualified trial lawyers should stand ready to undertake the defense of an accused regardless of public hostility toward the accused or personal distaste for the offense charged or the person of the defendant.

199

(c)   Qualified trial lawyers should not assert or announce a general unwillingness to appear in criminal cases. Law firms should encourage partners and associates to appear in criminal cases.

Standard 4-1.6.   Client interests paramount

The duties of a lawyer to a client are to represent the client's legitimate interests, and considerations of personal and professional advantage should not influence the lawyer's advice or performance.

Standard 4-2.1.   Communication

Every jurisdiction should guarantee by statute or rule of court the right of an accused person to prompt and effective communication with a lawyer and should require that reasonable access to a telephone or other facilities be provided for that purpose.

Standard 4-2.2.   Referral service for criminal cases

(a)   To assist persons who wish to retain counsel privately and who do not know a lawyer or how to engage one, every jurisdiction should have a referral service for criminal cases. The referral service should maintain a list of lawyers willing and qualified to undertake the defense of a criminal case; it whould be so organized that it can provide prompt service at all times.

(b)   The availability of the referral service should be publicized. In addition, notices containing the essential information about the referral service and how to contact it should be posted conspicuously in police stations, jails, and wherever else it is likely to give effective notice.

Standard 4-2.3.   Prohibited referrals

(a)   It is unprofessional conduct for a lawyer to accept referrals by agreement or as a regular practice from law enforcement personnel, bondsmen, or court personnel.

(b)   Regulations and licensing requirements governing the conduct of law enforcement personnel, bondsmen, court personnel, and others in similar positions should prohibit their referring an accused to any particular lawyer and should require them, when asked to suggest the name of an attorney, to direct the accused to the referral service or to the local bar association if no referral service exists.

Standard 4-3.1.   Establishment of relationship

(a) Defense counsel should seek to establish a relationship of trust and confidence with the accused. The lawyer should explain the necessity of full disclosure of all facts known to the client for an effective defense, and the lawyer should explain the obligation of confidentiality which makes privileged the accused's disclosures relating to the case.

(b) The conduct of the defense of a criminal case requires trained professional skill and judgment. Therefore, the technical and professional decisions must rest with the lawyer without impinging on the right of the accused to make the ultimate decisions on certain specified matters, as delineated in chapter 5, part II.

(c) To ensure the privacy essential for confidential communication between lawyer and client, adequate facilities should be available for private discussions between counsel and accused in jails, prisons, courthouses, and other places where accused persons must confer with counsel.

(d) Personnel of jails, prisons, and custodial institutions should be prohibited by law or administrative regulations from examining or otherwise interfering with any communication or correspondence between client and lawyer relating to legal action arising out of charges or incarceration.

Standard 4-3.2.   Interviewing the client

(a) As soon as practicable the lawyer should seek to determine all relevant facts known to the accused. In so doing, the lawyer should probe for all legally relevant information without seeking to influence the direction of the client's responses.

(b) It is unprofessional conduct for the lawyer to instruct the client or to intimate to the client in any way that the client should not be candid in revealing facts so as to afford the lawyer free rein to take action which would be precluded by the lawyer's knowing of such facts.

Standard 4-3.3.   Fees

(a) In determining the amount of the fee in a criminal case, it is proper to consider the time and effort required, the responsibility assumed by counsel, the novelty and difficulty of the questions involved, the skill requisite to proper representation, the likelihood that other employment will be precluded, the fee customarily charged in the locality for similar services, the gravity of the charge, the experience, reputation, and ability of the lawyer, and the capacity of the client to pay the fee.

(b)   It is unprofessional conduct for a lawyer to imply that compensation of the lawyer is for anything other than professional services rendered by the lawyer or by others for the lawyer.

(c)   It is unprofessional conduct for a lawyer to enter into an agreement for, charge, or collect an illegal or clearly excessive fee.

(d)   It is unprofessional conduct for a lawyer to divide a fee with a non-lawyer, except as permitted by the Code of Professional Responsibility. A lawyer may share a fee with another lawyer only on the basis of their respective services and responsibility in a case, in accordance with the Code of Professional Responsibility.

(e)   It is unprofessional conduct for a lawyer to enter into an arrangement for, charge, or collect a contingent fee for representing a defendant in a criminal case.

Standard 4-3.4.   Obtaining publication rights from the accused

It is unprofessional conduct for a lawyer, prior to conclusion of all aspects of the matter giving rise to his or her employment, to enter into any agreement or understanding with a client or a prospective client by which the lawyer acquires an interest in publication rights with respect to the subject matter of the employment or proposed employment.

Standard 4-3.5.   Conflict of interest

(a)   At the earliest feasible opportunity defense counsel should disclose to the defendant any interest in or connection with the case or any other matter that might be relevant to the defendant's selection of a lawyer to represent him or her.

(b)   Except for preliminary matters such as initial hearings or applications for bail, a lawyer or lawyers who are associated in practice should not undertake to defend more than one defendant in the same criminal case if the duty to one of the defendants may conflict with the duty to another. The potential for conflict of interest in representing multiple defendants is so grave that ordinarily a lawyer should decline to act for more than one of several codefendants except in unusual situations when, after careful investigation, it is clear that:

(i)   no conflict is likely to develop;

(ii)   the several defendants give an informed consent to such multiple representation; and

(iii) the consent of the defendants is made a matter of judicial record. In determining the presence of consent by the defendants, the trial judge should make appropriate inquiries respecting actual or potential conflicts of interest of counsel and whether the defendants fully comprehend the difficulties that an attorney sometimes encounters in defending multiple clients.

In some instances, accepting or continuing employment by more than one defendant in the same criminal case is unprofessional conduct.

(c) In accepting payment of fees by one person for the defense of another, a lawyer should be careful to determine that he or she will not be confronted with a conflict of loyalty since the lawyer's entire loyalty is due the accused. It is unprofessional conduct for the lawyer to accept such compensation except with the consent of the accused after full disclosure. It is unprofessional conduct for a lawyer to permit a person who recommends, employs, or pays the lawyer to render legal services for another to direct or regulate the lawyer's professional judgment in rendering such legal services.

(d) It is unprofessional conduct for a lawyer to defend a criminal case in which the lawyer's partner or other professional associate is or has been the prosecutor.

Standard 4-3.6.   Prompt action to protect the accused

(a) Many important rights of the accused can be protected and preserved only by prompt legal action. The lawyer should inform the accused of his or her rights forthwith and take all necessary action to vindicate such rights. The lawyer should consider all procedural steps which in good faith may be taken, including, for example, motions seeking pretrial release of the accused, obtaining psychiatric examination of the accused when a need appears, moving for change of venue or continuance, moving to suppress illegally obtained evidence, moving for severance from jointly charged defendants, and seeking dismissal of the charges.

(b) A lawyer should not act as surety on a bail bond either for the accused or for others.

Standard 4-3.7.   Advice and service on anticipated un-
lawful conduct

(a) It is a lawyer's duty to advise a client to comply with the law, but the lawyer may advise concerning the meaning, scope, and validity of a law.

(b) It is unprofessional conduct for a lawyer to counsel a client in or knowingly assist a client to engage in conduct which the lawyer knows to be illegal or fraudulent.

(c) It is unprofessional conduct for a lawyer to agree in advance of the commission of a crime that the lawyer will serve as counsel for the defendant, except as part of a bona fide effort to determine the validity, scope, meaning, or application of the law, or where the defense is incident to a general retainer for legal services to a person or enterprise engaged in legitimate activity.

(d) A lawyer may reveal the expressed intention of a client to commit a crime and the information necessary to prevent the crime, and the lawyer must do so if the contemplated crime is one which would seriously endanger the life or safety of any person or corrupt the processes of the courts and the lawyer believes such action on his or her part is necessary to prevent it.

Standard 4-3.8. Duty to keep client informed

The lawyer has a duty to keep the client informed of the developments in the case and the progress of preparing the defense.

Standard 4-3.9. Obligations to client and duty to court

Once a lawyer has undertaken the representation of an accused, the duties and obligations are the same whether the lawyer is privately retained, appointed, or serving in a legal aid or defender program.

Standard 4-4.1. Duty to investigate

It is the duty of the lawyer to conduct a prompt investigation of the circumstances of the case and to explore all avenues leading to facts relevant to the merits of the case and the penalty in the event of conviction. The investigation should always include efforts to secure information in the possession of the prosecution and law enforcement authorities. The duty to investigate exists regardless of the accused's admissions or statments to the lawyer of facts constituting guilt or the accused's stated desire to plead guilty.

Standard 4-4.2. Illegal investigation

It is unprofessional conduct for a lawyer knowingly to use illegal means to obtain evidence or information or to employ, instruct, or encourage others to do so.

Standard 4-4.3.   Relations with prospective witnesses

(a) It is unprofessional conduct to compensate a witness, other than an expert, for giving testimony, but it is not improper to reimburse a witness for the reasonable expenses of attendance upon court, including transportation and loss of income, attendance for depositions pursuant to statute or court rule, or attendance for pretrial interviews, provided there is no attempt to conceal the fact of reimbursement.

(b) It is not necessary for the lawyer or the lawyer's investigator, in interviewing a prospective witness, to caution the witness concerning possible self-incrimination and the need for counsel.

(c) A lawyer should not discourage or obstruct communication between prospective witnesses and the prosecutor. It is unprofessional conduct to advise any person, other than a client, or cause such person to be advised to decline to give to the prosecutor or counsel for co-defendants information which such person has a right to give.

(d) Unless the lawyer for the accused is prepared to forgo impeachment of a witness by the lawyer's own testimony as to what the witness stated in an interview or to seek leave to withdraw from the case in order to present such impeaching testimony, the lawyer should avoid interviewing a prospective witness except in the presence of a third person.

Standard 4-4.4.   Relations with expert witnesses

(a) A lawyer who engages an expert for an opinion should respect the independence of the expert and should not seek to dictate the formation of the expert's opinion on the subject. To the extent necessary, the lawyer should explain to the expert his or her role in the trial as an impartial witness called to aid the fact finders and the manner in which the examination of witnesses is conducted.

(b) It is unprofessional conduct for a lawyer to pay an excessive fee for the purpose of influencing the expert's testimony or to fix the amount of the fee contingent upon the testimony the expert will give or the result in the case.

Standard 4-4.5.   Compliance with discovery procedure

The lawyer should comply in good faith with discovery procedures under the applicable law.

Standard 4-5.1.   Advising the defendant

(a)   After informing himself or herself fully on the facts and the law, the lawyer should advise the accused with complete candor concerning all aspects of the case, including a candid estimate of the probable outcome.

(b)   It is unprofessional conduct for the lawyer intentionally to understate or overstate the risks, hazards, or prospects of the case to exert undue influence on the accused's decision as to his or her plea.

(c)   The lawyer should caution the client to avoid communication about the case with witnesses, except with the approval of the lawyer, to avoid any contact with jurors or prospective jurors, and to avoid either the reality or the appearance of any other improper activity.

Standard 4-5.2.   Control and direction of the case

(a)   Certain decisions relating to the conduct of the case are ultimately for the accused and others are ultimately for defense counsel. The decisions which are to be made by the accused after full consultation with counsel are:
  (i)   what plea to enter;
  (ii)   whether to waive jury trial; and
  (iii) whether to testify in his or her own behalf.

(b)   The decisions on what witnesses to call, whether and how to conduct cross-examination, what jurors to accept or strike, what trial motions should be made, and all other strategic and tactical decisions are the exclusive province of the lawyer after consultation with the client.

(c)   If a disagreement on significant matters of tactics or strategy arises between the lawyer and the client, the lawyer should make a record of the circumstances, the lawyer's advice and reasons, and the conclusion reached. The record should be made in a manner which protects the confidentiality of the lawyer-client relationship.

Standard 4-6.1.   Duty to explore disposition without trial

(a)   Whenever the nature and circumstances of the case permit, the lawyer for the accused should explore the possibility of an early diversion of the case from the criminal process through the use of other community agencies.

(b)   A lawyer may engage in plea discussions with the prosecutor, al-
      though ordinarily the client's consent to engage in such discussions
      should be obtained in advance. Under no circumstances should a
      lawyer recommend to a defendant acceptance of a plea unless a full
      investigation and study of the case has been completed, including an
      analysis of controlling law and the evidence likely to be introduced
      at trial.

Standard 4-6.2.   Conduct of discussions

(a)   In conducting discussions with the prosecutor the lawyer should
      keep the accused advised of developments at all times and all pro-
      posals made by the prosecutor should be communicated promptly to
      the accused.
(b)   It is unprofessional conduct for a lawyer knowingly to make false
      statements concerning the evidence in the course of plea discussions
      with the prosecutor.
(c)   It is unprofessional conduct for a lawyer to seek or accept conces-
      sions favorable to one client by any agreement which is detrimental
      to the legitimate interests of any other client.

Standard 4-7.1.   Courtroom decorum

(a)   As an officer of the court the lawyer should support the authority of
      the court and the dignity of the trial courtroom by strict adherence
      to the rules of decorum and by manifesting an attitude of profes-
      sional respect toward the judge, opposing counsel witnesses, jurors,
      and others in the courtroom.
(b)   When court is in session defense counsel should address the court
      and should not address the prosecutor directly on any matter relat-
      ing to the case.
(c)   It is unprofessional conduct for a lawyer to engage in behavior or
      tactics purposefully calculated to irritate or annoy the court or the
      prosecutor.
(d)   The lawyer should comply promptly with all orders and directives of
      the court, but the lawyer has a duty to have the record reflect ad-
      verse rulings or judicial conduct which the lawyer considers prejudi-
      cial to his or her client's legitimate interests. The lawyer has a right
      to make respectful requests for reconsiderations of adverse rulings.
(e)   Lawyers should cooperate with courts and the organized bar in de-
      veloping codes of decorum and professional etiquette for each
      jurisdiction.

Standard 4-7.2. Selection of jurors

(a) The lawyer should prepare himself or herself prior to trial to discharge effectively his or her function in the selection of the jury,
including the raising of any appropriate issues concerning the
method by which the jury panel was selected and the exercise of
both challenges for cause and peremptory challenges.

(b) In those cases where it appears necessary to conduct a pretrial investigation of the background of jurors, investigatory methods of the
lawyer should neither harass nor unduly embarrass potential jurors
or invade their privacy and, whenever possible, should be restricted
to an investigation of records and sources of information already in
existence.

(c) The opportunity to question jurors personally should be used solely
to obtain information for the intelligent exercise of challenges. A
lawyer should not intentionally use the voir dire to present factual
matter which the lawyer knows will not be admissible at trial or to
argue the lawyer's case to the jury.

Standard 4-7.3. Relations with jury

(a) It is unprofessional conduct for the lawyer to communicate privately
with persons summoned for jury duty or impaneled as jurors concerning the case prior to or during the trial. The lawyer should avoid
the reality or appearance of any such improper communications.

(b) The lawyer should treat jurors with deference and respect, avoiding
the reality or appearance of currying favor by a show of undue solicitude for their comfort or convenience.

(c) After discharge of the jury from further consideration of a case, it is
unprofessional conduct for a lawyer to intentionally make comments
to or ask questions of a juror for the purpose of harassing or embarrassing the juror in any way which will tend to influence judgment in
future jury service. If the lawyer believes that the verdict may be
subject to legal challenge, the lawyer may properly, if no statute or
rule prohibits such course, communicate with jurors to determine
whether such challenge may be available.

Standard 4-7.4. Opening statement

The lawyer's opening statement should be confined to a brief statement
of the issues in the case and evidence the lawyer intends to offer which the
lawyer believes in good faith will be available and admissible. It is unprofessional conduct to allude to any evidence unless there is a good faith and

reasonable basis for believing such evidence will be tendered and admitted in evidence.

Standard 4-7.5.   Presentation of evidence

(a)   It is unprofessional conduct for a lawyer knowingly to offer false evidence, whether by documents, tangible evidence, or the testimony of witnesses, or fail to seek withdrawal thereof upon discovery of its falsity.

(b)   It is unprofessional conduct for a lawyer knowingly and for the purpose of bringing inadmissible matter to the attention of the judge or jury to offer inadmissible evidence, ask legally objectionable questions, or make other impermissible comments or arguments in the presence of the judge or jury.

(c)   It is unprofessional conduct to permit any tangible evidence to be displayed in the view of the judge or jury which would tend to prejudice fair consideration of the case by the judge or jury until such time as a good faith tender of such evidence is made.

(d)   It is unprofessional conduct to tender tangible evidence in the presence of the judge or jury if it would tend to prejudice fair consideration of the case unless there is a reasonable basis for its admission in evidence. When there is any substantial doubt about the admissibility of such evidence it should be tendered by an offer of proof and a ruling obtained.

Standard 4-7.6.   Examination of witnesses

(a)   The interrogation of all witnesses should be conducted fairly, objectively, and with due regard for the dignity and legitimate privacy of the witness, and without seeking to intimidate or humiliate the witness unnecessarily. Proper cross-examination can be conducted without violating rules of decorum.

(b)   A lawyer's belief or knowledge that the witness is telling the truth does not preclude cross-examination, but should, if possible, be taken into consideration by counsel in conducting the cross-examination.

(c)   A lawyer should not call a witness who the lawyer knows will claim a valid privilege not to testify, for the purpose of impressing upon the jury the fact of the claim of privilege. In some instances, doing so will constitute unprofessional conduct.

(d)   It is unprofessional conduct for a lawyer to ask a question which implies the existence of a factual predicate for which a good faith belief is lacking.

[Standard 4-7.7.   Testimony by the defendant]

[(a)   If the defendant has admitted to defense counsel facts which establish guilt and counsel's independent investigation established that
the admissions are true but the defendant insists on the right to
trial, counsel must strongly discourage the defendant against taking
the witness stand to testify perjuriously.

[(b)   If, in advance of trial, the defendant insists that he or she will take
the stand to testify perjuriously, the lawyer may withdraw from the
case, if that is feasible, seeking leave of the court if necessary, but
the court should not be advised of the lawyer's reason for seeking to
do so.

[(c)   If withdrawal from the case is not feasible or is not permitted by the
court, or if the situation arises immediately preceding trial or during
the trial and the defendant insists upon testifying perjuriously in his
or her own behalf, it is unprofessional conduct for the lawyer to lend
aid to the perjury or use the perjured testimony. Before the defendant takes the stand in these circumstances, the lawyer should make
a record of the fact that the defendant is taking the stand against
the advice of counsel in some appropriate manner without revealing
the fact to the court. The lawyer may identify the witness as the
defendant and may ask appropriate questions of the defendant
when it is believed that the defendant's answers will not be perjurious. As to matters for which it is believed the defendant will offer
perjurious testimony, the lawyer should seek to avoid direct examination of the defendant in the conventional manner; instead, the
lawyer should ask the defendant if he or she wishes to make any
additional statement concerning the case to the trier or triers of the
facts. A lawyer may not later argue the defendant's known false version of facts to the jury as worthy of belief, and may not recite or
rely upon the false testimony in his or her closing argument.]

Standard 4-7.8.   Argument to the jury

(a)   In closing argument to the jury the lawyer may argue all reasonable
inferences from the evidence in the record. It is unprofessional conduct for a lawyer intentionally to misstate the evidence or mislead
the jury as to the inferences it may draw.

(b)   It is unprofessional conduct for a lawyer to express a personal belief
or opinion in his or her client's innocence or personal belief or opinion in the truth or falsity of any testimony or evidence, or to attribute the crime to another person unless such an inference is
warranted by the evidence.

(c)   A lawyer should not make arguments calculated to inflame the passions or prejudices of the jury.

(d)   A lawyer should refrain from argument which would divert the jury from its duty to decide the case on the evidence by injecting issues broader than the guilt or innocence of the accused under the controlling law or by making predictions of the consequences of the jury's verdict.

(e)   It is the responsibility of the court to ensure that final argument to the jury is kept within proper, accepted bounds.

Standard 4-7.9.   Facts outside the record

It is unprofessional conduct for a lawyer intentionally to refer to or argue on the basis of facts outside the record, unless such facts are matters of common public knowledge based on ordinary human experience or matters of which the court can take judicial notice.

Standard 4-7.10.   Posttrial motions

The trial lawyer's responsibility includes presenting appropriate motions, after verdict and before sentence, to protect the defendant's rights.

Standard 4-8.1.   Sentencing

(a)   The lawyer for the accused should be familiar with the sentencing alternatives available to the court and should endeavor to learn its practices in exercising sentencing discretion. The consequences of the various dispositions available should be explained fully by the lawyer to the accused.

(b)   Defense counsel should present to the court any ground which will assist in reaching a proper disposition favorable to the accused. If a presentence report or summary is made available to the defense lawyer, he or she should seek to verify the information contained in it and should be prepared to supplement or challenge it if necessary. If there is no presentence report or if it is not disclosed, the lawyer should submit to the court and the prosecutor all favorable information relevant to sentencing and in an appropriate case be prepared to suggest a program of rehabilitation based on the lawyer's exploration of employment, educational, and other opportunities made available by community services.

(c)   Counsel should alert the accused to the right of allocution, if any, and to the possible dangers of making a judicial confession in the course of allocution which might tend to prejudice an appeal.

Standard 4-8.2.   Appeal

(a)   After conviction, the lawyer should explain to the defendant the meaning and consequences of the court's judgment and defendant's right of appeal. The lawyer should give the defendant his or her professional judgment as to whether there are meritorious grounds for appeal and as to the probable results of an appeal. The lawyer should also explain to the defendant the advantages and disadvantages of an appeal. The decision whether to appeal must be the defendant's own choice.
(b)   The lawyer should take whatever steps are necessary to protect the defendant's right of appeal.

Standard 4-8.3.   Counsel on appeal

Appellate counsel should not seek to withdraw from a case solely on the basis of his or her own determination that the appeal lacks merit.

Standard 4-8.4.   Conduct of appeal

(a)   Appellate counsel should be diligent in perfecting an appeal and expediting its prompt submission to the appellate court.
(b)   Appellate counsel should be scrupulously accurate in referring to the record and the authorities upon which counsel relies in the presentation to the court of briefs and oral argument.
(c)   It is unprofessional conduct for a lawyer intentionally to refer to or argue on the basis of facts outside the record on appeal, unless such facts are matters of common public knowledge based on ordinary human experience or matters of which the court may take judicial notice.

Standard 4-8.5.   Postconviction remedies

After a conviction is affirmed on appeal, appellate counsel should determine whether there is any ground for relief under other postconviction remedies. If there is a reasonable prospect of a favorable result counsel should explain to the defendant the advantages and disadvantages of taking such action. Appellate counsel is not obligated to represent the defendant in a postconviction proceeding unless counsel has agreed to do so. In other respects the responsibility of a lawyer in a postconviction proceeding should be guided generally by the standards governing the conduct of lawyers in criminal cases.

Standard 4-8.6.   Challenges to the effectiveness of counsel

(a) If a lawyer, after investigation, is satisfied that another lawyer who served in an earlier phase of the case did not provide effective assistance, he or she should not hesitate to seek relief for the defendant on that ground.

(b) If a lawyer, after investigation, is satisfied that another lawyer who served in an earlier phase of the case provided effective assistance, he or she should so advise the client and may decline to proceed further.

(c) A lawyer whose conduct of a criminal case is drawn into question is entitled to testify concerning the matters charged and is not precluded from disclosing the truth concerning the accusation, even though this involves revealing matters which were given in confidence.

NATIONAL CONFERENCE OF BAR EXAMINERS MULTISTATE PROFESSIONAL RESPONSIBILITY EXAMINATION

Sample Examination Questions and Answers*

Question 1.

Alpha is a member of the bar in State First and is also licensed as a stockbroker in State Second. In his application for renewal of his stockbroker's license in State Second, Alpha knowingly filed a false financial statement.

Is Alpha *subject to discipline* in State First for so doing?
A. Yes, if his actions are found to involve dishonesty.
B. Yes, but only if he is first convicted of a criminal offense in State Second.
C. No, because his action was not in his capacity as an attorney.
D. No, because his action was not in State First.

Question 2.

Attorney is the majority shareholder of a collection agency, incorporated as Collecto. If Collecto's efforts have not been successful, Attorney has authorized Collecto's manager, who is not a member of the bar, to write any needed collection letter to the debtor on Attorney's letterhead. The letter is to contain a statement that the matter has been referred to Attorney and that suit will be filed in five days if payment is not received. The manager is authorized to sign Attorney's name to the letter.

Is Attorney *subject to discipline*?

*See answers on page 225, based on A.B.A. Code of Professional Responsibility.

A. Yes, because the letter is a form of extortion.
B. Yes, because Collecto is thereby engaging in the unauthorized practice of law.
C. No, because Attorney does not manage Collecto.
D. No, because the manager is acting as Attorney's agent.

Question 3.

Buyer and Seller are about to close a transaction for the purchase and sale of a business. Broker suggests Broker's Attorney as escrow holder, advising Buyer and Seller that Attorney will charge less than a bank or escrow company. In fact, as Broker knows, Attorney charges more than a bank or escrow company and divides the overcharge with Broker.

Is Attorney *subject to discipline?*
A. Yes, because Attorney is party to a dishonest practice.
B. Yes, because as escrow holder, Attorney is acting for both Buyer and Seller.
C. No, because Attorney is not acting in a legal capacity for Buyer or Seller.
D. No, because Buyer and Seller did not deal directly with Attorney.

Question 4.

Attorney Alpha, representing Doctor, writes Attorney Beta, who represents Secretary. Secretary formerly worked for Doctor, who has accused Secretary of misappropriating $5,000. Alpha's letter states:
"I have personally investigated the matter and I am satisfied Secretary is at fault. However, Doctor is willing to forgive and forget if Secretary will acknowledge Secretary's fault and make arrangements for repayment in full within a reasonable period of time. If these arrangements are not satisfactorily concluded by next Monday, Doctor will present the matter to District Attorney."

Is Attorney Alpha *subject to discipline?*
A. Yes, because the letter threatened to present criminal charges to District Attorney if Secretary did not settle the claim.
B. Yes, because an attorney should not assert his own personal belief in the merits of the matter.
C. No, if in his judgment, sending the letter was in his client's best interests.
D. No, if he was instructed by his client to send the letter.

Question 5.

Attorney, who represented Plaintiff, received a check from Deft payable to Attorney's order in the sum of $10,000 in settlement of Plaintiff's claim against Deft.

Which of the following is(are) consistent with Attorney's *ethical obligation*?
I.   Endorse the check and send it to Plaintiff.
II. Deposit the check in Attorney's personal bank account and send Attorney's personal check for $10,000 to Plaintiff.
III. Deposit the check in a Client Trust Account, advise Plaintiff, and forward check drawn on that account to Plaintiff.
A. I only
B. III only
C. I and III, but not II
D. I, II, and III

Question 6.

Attorney prepared a will for Client and acted as one of the subscribing witnesses to Client's execution of the will. The will left all of Client's estate to Client's Son. Later, at Client's request, Attorney prepared a second will for Client and acted as one of the subscribing witnesses to Client's execution of the second will. The second will left one-half of Client's estate to Son and the other one-half to Client's Housekeeper. Client died and Housekeeper has offered the second will for probate.

If Son requests Attorney to represent him in opposing probate of the second will on the grounds of fraud and undue influence, is it *proper* for Attorney to do so?
A. Yes, because after Client's death Attorney may represent Son.
B. Yes, because Son is a beneficiary under both wills.
C. No, because an attorney guarantees the validity of a will that she prepares.
D. No, because Attorney would be taking a position adverse to a will she prepared and witnessed.

Questions 7-8 are based on the following fact situation.

Attorney was formerly employed by Insurance Company as a lawyer solely to handle fire insurance claims. While so employed she investigated a fire

217

loss claim of Claimant against Insurance Company. Attorney is now in private practice.

Question 7.

Assume the claim has not been settled and Claimant consults Attorney and asks Attorney either to represent him or refer him to another lawyer for suit on the claim.

Which of the following is(are) *proper?*
 I.   Attorney may refuse to discuss the matter with Claimant.
 II. Attorney may represent Claimant.
 III. Attorney may refer Claimant to an associate in her law firm, provided Attorney does not share in any fee.
 IV. Attorney may give Claimant a list of lawyers who Attorney knows are competent and specialize in such claims.
 A.   I only
 B.   I and II, but not III or IV
 C.   I and III, but not II or IV
 D.   I and IV, but not II or III

Question 8.

Assume that the original claim was settled. One year after Attorney left the employ of Insurance Company, Claimant slipped and fell in Insurance Company's office. Claimant now asks Attorney to represent him or refer him to another lawyer for suit on the "slip and fall" claim.

Which of the follwing is(are) *proper?*
 I.   Attorney may refuse to discuss the matter with Claimant.
 II. Attorney may represent Claimant.
 III. Attorney may give Claimant a list of lawyers who Attorney knows are competent and specialize in such claims.
 A.   I only
 B.   I and II, but not III
 C.   I and III, but not II
 D.   I, II, and III

Question 9.

The sale of a business by Seller to Buyer was negotiated by a broker. After the terms had been agreed upon, Buyer and Seller then consulted Attorney and told her that they were in full agreement, asked her to prepare the closing documents, asked her to act as escrow holder, and told her that they would each pay one-half of her charges and costs for so acting.

Is it *proper* for Attorney so to act and accept one-half from each of the parties?

A. Yes, because Attorney's activities are not the "practice of law."
B. Yes, if the interests of Buyer and Seller are fully protected.
C. No, because Attorney is representing both parties.
D. No, because Attorney is aiding an unlicensed person, the broker, to practice law.

Question 10.

Alpha, representing Plaintiff in an automobile collision suit, is aware that there is a possible defense arising out of the conduct of a person not a party to the lawsuit. Alpha realizes that Beta, representing Defendant and Defendant's Insurance Company, is unaware of the possible defense because of Beta's failure to investigate the circumstances.

Alpha's *ethical obligation* is to:

A. inform Beta so that the possible defense will be considered.
B. request from Plaintiff permission to inform Beta.
C. continue to represent Plaintiff without disclosing the possible defense.
D. inform the court so that Alpha cannot be charged with presenting a false claim.

Question 11.

Poe consults Attorney for advice about bringing an action to quiet Poe's title to Blackacre, a parcel of land. Poe does not disclose any of the facts on which his claim is based or the name of the potential defendant and holder of record title. Attorney informs Poe that she will consider the matter and then advise Poe whether she will represent him. Attorney then searches the records, which disclose that Client, a long-standing client of Attorney, is the holder of record title to Blackacre. Attorney immediately advises Poe that she will not represent him. Poe, through another lawyer, sues to quiet title.

Is it *proper* for Attorney to represent Client?

A. Yes, because Client was prior in time to Poe.
B. Yes, because Attorney acquired no disqualifying information from Poe.

C.   No, because after Poe had consulted Attorney on the matter, Attorney could not accept any case adverse to the interest of Poe in the same matter.

D.   No, because Attorney ascertained the name of the holder of title as a result of Poe's inquiry.

Questions 12-13 are based on the following fact situation.

Attorney represented Defendant in a breach of contract case tried before a court sitting with a jury. The verdict was for Plaintiff, and Attorney intends to move for a new trial on the grounds of insufficiency of the evidence and misconduct of the jury. Attorney believes that Witt, a witness for Plaintiff, testified falsely at the trial and that Juror, one of the jurors who voted for Plaintiff, was prejudiced against Defendant and concealed this prejudice when examined on *voir dire*.

Question 12.

Which of the following methods is(are) *proper* for Attorney in attempting to ascertain if Witt testified falsely?
  I.   Interview Witt himself
 II.   Hire a private detective to investigate Witt's background
III.   Promise to recommend Witt for a position if Witt will repudiate her testimony and testify for Defandant on a retrial
  A.   I only
  B.   II only
  C.   I and II, but not III
  D.   I, II, and III

Question 13.

Which of the following methods is(are) *proper* for Attorney in attempting to ascertain if Juror was in fact prejudiced?
  I.   Interview Juror himself
 II.   Hire a private detective to investigate Juror's background
III.   Inquire of the other jurors whether Juror said anything in the jury room that might indicate prejudice
  A.   I only
  B.   II only
  C.   I and III, but not II
  D.   I, II, and III

Questions 14-15 are based on the following fact situation.

Alpha represents Defendant in bitter and protracted litigation. Alpha, at Defendant's request, has made several offers of settlement to Plaintiff's lawyer, Beta, all of which have been rejected.

Question 14.

During a week's recess in the trial, Alpha and Plaintiff were both present at a cocktail party. Plaintiff went over to Alpha and said: "Why can't we settle that case for $50,000? This trial is costing both sides more than it's worth."

Which of the following is a *proper* response by Alpha?
  I.   "I can't discuss the matter with you."
  II. "If that's the way you feel, why don't you and Defendant get together."
  III. "I agree. We already have made several offers to settle this matter."
  A.   I only
  B.   I and II, but not III
  C.   II and III, but I
  D.   I, II, and III

Question 15.

The following day, Alpha telephoned Beta and told Beta of the meeting with Plaintiff and that Plaintiff was willing to settle the case for $50,000. Alpha further stated that Defendant had authorized a $50,000 settlement.

Is Alpha's conduct in telephoning Beta *proper*?
A.   Yes, because it is the duty of an attorney to seek to avoid litigation.
B.   Yes, because it is the duty of an attorney to use any lawful means to protect a client's proper interests.
C.   No, because the information came directly from an adverse party represented by counsel.
D.   No, because only Beta, the attorney of record for Plaintiff, has authority to make a settlement offer.

Questions 16-19 are based on the following fact situation.

Attorney was retained to represent Client in an effort to recover damages for Client arising out of an automobile collision in which Client sustained minor property damage. The other party to the collision was Utility Company, a corporation Client intensely disliked as a result of several utility bill disputes over a period of years. Client told Attorney, "I hate that outfit. I want you to take this case to court and wring every penny out of them that you can." Attorney filed suit against Utility Company.

Question 16.

Was Attorney's action in filing the suit *proper?*
A. No, if Client's primary motive was maliciously to injure Utility Company.
B. No, if one of Client's significant motives was hate of Utility Company.
C. Yes, because Client's motive is irrelevant.
D. Yes, unless Client's only motive was maliciously to injure Utility Company.

Question 17.

Utility Company's lawyer requested a meeting with Attorney to discuss settlement. Attorney refused and pushed the claim to early trial.

Was Attorney's action in refusing to discuss settlement with Utility Company's attorney *proper?*
A. No, because it was unreasonable to refuse to discuss settlement.
B. No, if the refusal to discuss settlement was solely to harass Utility Company.
C. Yes, because no insurance company was involved.
D. Yes, if Attorney followed Client's instructions.

Question 18.

During cross-examination, Client denied that she hated Utility Company and denied that she ever stated she wanted her Attorney to "wring every penny out of them that you can."

Attorney's *ethical obligation* is to:
A. withdraw immediately as counsel in the case and say nothing to anyone about the matter.
B. withdraw immediately as counsel in the case and inform the court that Client's statement was untrue.
C. proceed to final judgment and say nothing to anyone about the matter.

D.   attempt, at the first opportunity, to convince Client that she should set the record straight.

Question 19.

Verdict and judgment were for Client, but she was disappointed by the small amount of the damages awarded. Client then demanded that Attorney file a Motion for New Trial based on jury prejudice as evidenced by the small amount of the judgment. Attorney does not believe that a good faith argument can be made in support of Client's position.

Attorney's *ethical obligation* is to:
A.   do as Client demands.
B.   withdraw immediately from the case.
C.   withdraw from the case after taking reasonable steps to avoid prejudice to Client's rights.
D.   ignore Client's demand and accept payment of the judgment on Client's behalf.

Questions 20-21 are based on the following fact situation.

Insurance Company, as required by its liability insurance policy, provided a lawyer to represent Insured, the named defendant in a collision case brought by Nonresident. The lawyer is Alpha, who is often employed by Insurance Company to represent its insureds. Nonresident's suit seeks damages in an amount that is four times the maximum amount recoverable under the policy. Insured also suffered personal injury and property damage in the collision.

Question 20.

With regard to a possible counterclaim by Insured against Nonresident, Alpha's *ethical obligation* is to:
A.   withdraw from the case because of a possible conflict.
B.   not mention it to Insured because it would appear that Alpha is soliciting Insured's business.
C.   inform Insured that he has a possible counterclaim and that he should consult an attorney of his choice about it.
D.   file it for Insured without consulting him if Alpha believes that it will aid in the disposition of the claim against Insured.

Question 21.

Alpha, in the investigation of the claim against Insured, found that Nonresident was uninsured, thereby making likely a claim by Insured against Insurance Company under the Uninsured Motorist coverage of Insured's policy.

Alpha's *ethical obligation* is to:
A. take no action that will jeopardize Insured's claim under the Uninsured Motorist coverage.
B. seek information to establish that Insured cannot recover from Insurance Company.
C. bring to the attention of Insurance Company information already in Alpha's file establishing a defense to Insured's potential claim.
D. send copies of Alpha's entire file to Insurance Company and Insured.

Question 22.

Attorney is retained by Client to bring a quiet title action against Defendant. Greenacre, the land involved in the action, is worth $100,000. The agreed fee to be paid Attorney is a retainer of $10,000 and 15% of the value of any interest in Greenacre quieted in Client by judgment or settlement or of any amount paid in settlement. As security for the fee, Client conveyed to Attorney a 15% interest in Whiteacre, another parcel that Client owned.

Is Attorney *subject to discipline?*
A. No, unless the amount of the fee is found to be unconscionable.
B. No, because fee arrangements between lawyers and clients are not subject to review by the bar.
C. Yes, because a lawyer may not acquire an interest in a client's property.
D. Yes, because attorney's liens are forbidden as a matter of public policy.

Question 23.

Smith is a member of the bar. He does not practice law, but operates a licensed investment counseling business. Investor consults Smith, who persuades Investor to invest $10,000 in a business venture. Smith does not reveal to Investor that he, Smith, owns 100% of the business venture.

Is Smith *subject to discipline?*
A. Yes, because a lawyer cannot have an interest in a business.
B. Yes, because Smith's nondisclosure of his interest is a form of fraud.
C. No, because Investor did not consult Smith as an attorney.
D. No, because Smith does not practice law.

Question 24.

During the trial of a case by Attorney Alpha, Attorney Beta took shelter in a tavern from an unexpected rainstorm. While in the tavern, Attorney Beta saw Attorney Alpha having a drink with a juror on the case Attorney Alpha was trying.

The *ethical obligation* of Attorney Beta is to:
A. keep this knowledge confidential.
B. identify herself to Alpha and reprimand Alpha for drinking in a public place with a juror.
C. inform the judge trying the case of this incident.
D. caution Alpha and the juror not to talk further to each other.

Question 25.

Attorney represented Client in the trial of a lawsuit in which Client was defendant. Judgment was rendered against Client for $100,000. Client cannot now pay the judgment, but expects to have sufficient funds to pay it within six months. Client has directed Attorney to file an appeal in order to obtain a stay of execution until Client can pay the judgment.

Is it *proper* for Attorney to file the appeal?
A. Yes, because Client has requested it.
B. Yes, because it is in Client's best interests to do so.
C. No, unless Attorney can make a good faith argument for reversal on appeal.
D. No, if Client's motive is to delay collection of the judgment against Client.

Answer Key

1. A	6. D	11. B	16. D	21. A
2. B	7. D	12. C	17. B	22. A
3. A	8. D	13. D	18. D	23. B
4. A	9. B	14. A	19. C	24. C
5. C	10. C	15. B	20. C	25. C

SELECTED FEDERAL STATUTES AND RULES RELATING TO FEDERAL PUBLIC OFFICERS AND EMPLOYEES

BRIBERY, GRAFT, AND CONFLICTS OF INTEREST
18 U.S.C.A. §§201-218

§201. Bribery of public officials and witnesses

(a) For the purpose of this section:
"public official" means Member of Congress, the Delegate from the District of Columbia, or Resident Commissioner, either before or after he has qualified, or an officer or employee or person acting for or on behalf of the United States, or any department, agency or branch of Government thereof, including the District of Columbia, in any official function, under or by authority of any such department, agency, or branch of Government or a juror; and

"person who has been selected to be a public official" means any person who has been nominated or appointed to be a public official, or has been officially informed that he will be so nominated or appointed; and

"official act" means any decision or action on any question, matter, cause, suit, proceeding or controversy, which may at any time be pending, or which may by law be brought before any public official, in his official capacity, or in his place of trust or profit.

(b) Whoever, directly or indirectly, corruptly gives, offers or promises anything of value to any public official or person who has been selected to be a public official, or offers or promises any public official or any person who has been selected to be a public official to give anything of value to any other person or entity, with intent —

    (1) to influence any official act; or

    (2) to influence such public official or person who has been selected to be a public official to commit or aid in committing, or collude in, or allow, any fraud, or make opportunity for the commission of any fraud, on the United States; or

(3)   to induce such public official or such person who has been selected to be a public official to do or omit to do any act in
violation of his lawful duty, or

(c)   Whoever, being a public official or person selected to be a public
official, directly or indirectly, corruptly asks, demands, exacts, solicits, seeks, accepts, receives, or agrees to receive anything of value for
himself or for any other person or entity, in return for:
(1)   being influenced in his performance of any official act; or
(2)   being influenced to commit or aid in committing, or to collude
in, or allow, any fraud, or make opportunity for the commission
of any fraud, on the United States; or
(3)   being induced to do or omit to do any act in violation of his
official duty; or

(d)   Whoever, directly or indirectly, corruptly gives, offers, or promises
anything of value to any person, or offers or promises such person to
give anything of value to any other person or entity, with intent to
influence the testimony under oath or affirmation of such first-men-
tioned person as a witness upon a trial, hearing, or other proceeding,
before any court, any committee of either House or both Houses of
Congress, or any agency, commission, or officer authorized by the
laws of the United States to hear evidence or take testimony, or with
intent to influence such person to absent himself therefrom; or

(e)   Whoever, directly or indirectly, corruptly asks, demands, exacts, solicits, seeks, accepts, receives, or agrees to receive anything of value
for himself or for any other person or entity in return for being influenced in his testimony under oath or affirmation as a witness upon
any such trial, hearing, or other proceeding, or in return for absent-
ing himself therefrom —
Shall be fined not more than $20,000 or three times the monetary
equivalent of the thing of value, whichever is greater, or imprisoned
for not more than fifteen years, or both, and may be disqualified
from holding any office of honor, trust, or profit under the United
States.

(f)   Whoever, otherwise than as provided by law for the proper discharge of official duty, directly or indirectly gives, offers, or promises
anything of value to any public official, former public official, or
person selected to be a public official, for or because of any official
act performed or to be performed by such public official, former
public official, or person selected to be a public official; or

(g)   Whoever, being a public official, former public official, or person
selected to be a public official, otherwise than as provided by law for
the proper discharge of official duty, directly or indirectly asks, demands, exacts, solicits, seeks, accepts, receives, or agrees to receive
anything of value for himself for or because of any official act performed or to be performed by him; or

(h)   Whoever, directly or indirectly, gives, offers, or promises anything of value to any person, for or because of the testimony under oath or affirmation given or to be given by such person as a witness upon a trial, hearing, or other proceeding, before any court, any committee of either House or both Houses of Congress, or any agency, commission, or officer authorized by the laws of the United States to hear evidence or take testimony, or for or because of his absence therefrom; or

(i)   Whoever, directly or indirectly, asks, demands, exacts, solicits, seeks, accepts, receives, or agrees to receive anything of value for himself for or because of the testimony under oath or affirmation given or to be given by him as a witness upon any such trial, hearing, or other proceeding, or for or because of his absence therefrom —
       Shall be fined not more than $10,000 or imprisoned for not more than two years, or both.

(j)   Subsections (d), (e), (h), and (i) shall not be construed to prohibit the payment or receipt of witness fees provided by law, or the payment, by the party upon whose behalf a witness is called and receipt by a witness, of the reasonable cost of travel and subsistence incurred and the reasonable value of time lost in attendance at any such trial, hearing, or proceeding, or in the case of expert witnesses, involving a technical or professional opinion, a reasonable fee for time spent in the preparation of such opinion, and in appearing and testifying.

(k)   The offenses and penalties prescribed in this section are separate from and in addition to those prescribed in sections 1503, 1504, and 1505 of this title.

§202.   Definitions

(a)   For the purpose of sections 203, 205, 207, 208, and 209 of this title the term "special Government employee" shall mean an officer or employee of the executive or legislative branch of the United States Government, of any independent agency of the United States or of the District of Columbia, who is retained, designated, appointed, or employed to perform, with or without compensation, for not to exceed one hundred and thirty days during any period of three hundred and sixty-five consecutive days, temporary duties either on a full-time or intermittent basis, a part-time United States commissioner, or a part-time United States magistrate. Notwithstanding the next preceding sentence, every person serving as a part-time local representative of a Member of Congress in the Member's home district or State shall be classified as a special Government employee. . . .

(b)   For the purposes of sections 205 and 207 of this title, the term "offi-
      cial responsibility" means the direct administrative or operating au-
      thority, whether intermediate or final, and either exercisable alone
      or with others, and either personally or through subordinates, to ap-
      prove, disapprove, or otherwise direct Govenment action.

§203.   Compensation to Members of Congress, officers, and others in matters affecting the Government

(a)   Whoever, otherwise than as provided by law for the proper dis-
      charge of official duties, directly or indirectly receives or agrees to
      receive, or asks, demands, solicits, or seeks, any compensation for any
      services rendered or to be rendered either by himself or another —
      (1)   at a time when he is a Member of Congress, Member of Con-
            gress Elect, Delegate from the District of Columbia, Delegate
            Elect from the District of Columbia, Resident Commissioner,
            or Resident Commissioner Elect; or
      (2)   at a time when he is an officer or employee of the United
            States in the executive, legislative, or judicial branch of the
            Government, or in any agency of the United States, including
            the District of Columbia,
      in relation to any proceeding, application, request for a ruling or
      other determination, contract, claim, controversy, charge, accusa-
      tion, arrest, or other particular matter in which the United States is
      a party or has a direct and substantial interest, before any depart-
      ment, agency, courtmartial, officer, or any civil, military, or naval
      commission, or
(b)   Whoever, knowingly, otherwise than as provided by law for the
      proper discharge of official duties, directly or indirectly gives,
      promises, or offers any compensation for any such services rendered
      or to be rendered at a time when the person to whom the compensa-
      tion is given, promised, or offered, is or was such a Member, Dele-
      gate, Commissioner, officer, or employee —
      Shall be fined not more than $10,000 or imprisoned for not more
      than two years, or both; and shall be incapable of holding any office
      of honor, trust, or profit under the United States.
(c)   A special Government employee shall be subject to subsection (a)
      only in relation to a particular matter involving a specific party or
      parties (1) in which he has at any time participated personally and
      substantially as a Government employee or as a special Government
      employee through decision, approval, disapproval, recommendation,
      the rendering of advice, investigation or otherwise, or (2) which is
      pending in the department or agency of the Government in which
      he is serving: *Provided*, That clause (2) shall not apply in the case of

a special Government employee who has served in such department or agency no more than sixty days during the immediately preceding period of three hundred and sixty-five consecutive days.

§204. Practice in Court of Claims by Members of Congress [omitted]

§205. Activities of officers and employees in claims against and other matters affecting the Government

Whoever, being an officer or employee of the United States in the executive, legislative, or judicial branch of the Government or in any agency of the United States, including the District of Columbia, otherwise than in the proper discharge of his official duties —

(1) acts as agent or attorney for prosecuting any claim against the United States, or receives any gratuity, or any share of or interest in any such claim in consideration of assistance in the prosecution of such claim, or

(2) acts as agent or attorney for anyone before any department, agency, court, court-martial, officer, or any civil, military, or naval commission in connection with any proceeding, application, request for a ruling or other determination, contract claim, controversy, charge, accusation, arrest, or other particular matter in which the United States is a party or has a direct and substantial interest —

Shall be fined not more than $10,000 or imprisoned for not more than two years, or both.

A special Government employee shall be subject to the preceding paragraphs only in relation to a particular matter involving a specific party or parties (1) in which he has at any time participated personally and substantially as a Government employee or as a special Government employee through decision, approval, disapproval, recommendation, the rendering of advice, investigation or otherwise, or (2) which is pending in the department or agency of the Government in which he is serving: *Provided*, That clause (2) shall not apply in the case of a special Government employee who has served in such department or agency no more than sixty days during the immediately preceding period of three hundred and sixty-five consecutive days.

Nothing herein prevents an officer or employee, if not inconsistent with the faithful performance of his duties, from acting without compensation as agent or attorney for any person who is the subject of disciplinary, loyalty, or other personnel administration proceedings in connection with those proceedings.

Nothing herein or in section 203 prevents an officer or employee, including a special Government employee, from acting, with or without compensation, as agent or attorney for his parents, spouse, child, or any person for whom, or for any estate for which, he is serving as guardian, executor, administrator, trustee, or other personal fiduciary except in those matters in which he has participated personally and substantially as a Government employee, through decision, approval, disapproval, recommendation, the rendering of advice, investigation, or otherwise, or which are the subject of his official responsibility, provided that the Government official responsible for appointment to his position approves.

Nothing herein or in section 203 prevents a special Government employee from acting as agent or attorney for another person in the performance of work under a grant by, or a contract with or for the benefit of, the United States provided that the head of the department or agency concerned with the grant or contract shall certify in writing that the national interest so requires.

Such certification shall be published in the Federal Register.

Nothing herein prevents an officer or employee from giving testimony under oath or from making statements required to be made under penalty for perjury or contempt.

§206. Exemption of retired officers of the uniformed services [omitted]

§207. Disqualification of former officers and employees; disqualification of partners of current officers and employees

(a) Whoever, having been an officer or employee of the executive branch of the United States Government, of any independent agency of the United States, or of the District of Columbia, including a special Government employee, after his employment has ceased, knowingly acts as agent or attorney for, or otherwise represents, any other person (except the United States), in any formal or informal appearance before, or, with the intent to influence, makes any oral or written communication on behalf of any other person (except the United States) to —

   (1) any department, agency, court, court-martial, or any civil, military, or naval commission of the United States or the District of Columbia, or any officer or employee thereof, and

   (2) in connection with any judicial or other proceeding, application, request for a ruling or other determination, contract,

claim, controversy, investigation, charge, accusation, arrest, or other particular matter involving a specific party or parties in which the United States or the District of Columbia is a party or has a direct and substantial interest, and

(3) in which he participated personally and substantially as an officer or employee through decision, approval, disapproval, recommendation, the rendering of advice, investigation or otherwise, while so employed; or

(b) Whoever, (i) having been so employed, within two years after his employment has ceased, knowingly acts as agent or attorney for, or otherwise represents, any other person (except the United States), in any formal or informal appearance before, or, with the intent to influence, makes any oral or written communication on behalf of any other person (except the United States) to, or (ii) having been so employed and as specified in subsection (d) of this section, within two years after his employment has ceased, knowingly represents or aids, counsels, advises, consults, or assists in representing any other person (except the United States) by personal presence at any formal or informal appearance before —

(1) any department, agency, court, court-martial, or any civil, military or naval commission of the United States or the District of Columbia, or any officer or employee thereof, and

(2) in connection with any judicial or other proceeding, application, request for a ruling or other determination, contract, claim, controversy, investigation, charge, accusation, arrest or other particular matter involving a specific party or parties in which the United States or the District of Columbia is a party or has a direct and substantial interest, and

(3) as to (i), which was actually pending under his official responsibility as an officer or employee within a period of one year prior to the termination of such responsibility, or, as to (ii), in which he participated personally and substantially as an officer or employee; or

(c) Whoever, other than a special Government employee who serves for less than sixty days in a given calendar year, having been so employed as specified in subsection (d) of this section, within one year after such employment has ceased, knowingly acts as agent or attorney for, or otherwise represents, anyone other than the United States in any formal or informal appearance before, or, with the intent to influence, makes any oral or written communication on behalf of anyone other than the United States, to —

(1) the department or agency in which he served as an officer or employee, or any officer or employee thereof, and

(2) in connection with any judicial, rulemaking, or other proceeding, application, request for a ruling or other determination,

contract, claim, controversy, investigation, charge, accusation, arrest, or other particular matter, and

(3)   which is pending before such department or agency or in which such department or agency has a direct and substantial interest — shall be fined not more than $10,000 or imprisoned for not more than two years, or both.

(d) (1) Subsection (c) of this section shall apply to a person employed —

(A)   at a rate of pay specified in or fixed according to subchapter II of chapter 53 of title 5, United States Code, or a comparable or greater rate of pay under other authority;

(B)   on active duty as a commissioned officer of a uniformed service assigned to pay grade of 0-9 or above as described in section 201 of title 37, United States Code; or

(C)   in a position which involves significant decision-making or supervisory responsibility, as designated under this subparagraph by the Director of the Office of Government Ethics, in consultation with the department or agency concerned. Only positions which are not covered by subparagraphs (A) and (B) above, and for which the basic rate of pay is equal to or greater than the basic rate of pay for GS-17 of the General Schedule prescribed by section 5332 of title 5, United States Code, or positions which are established within the Senior Executive Service pursuant to the Civil Service Reform Act of 1978, or positions of active duty commissioned officers of the uniformed services assigned to pay 0-7 or 0-8, as described in section 201 of title 37, United States Code, may be designated. As to persons in positions designated under this subparagraph, the Director may limit the restrictions of subsection (c) to permit a former officer or employee, who served in a separate agency or bureau within a department or agency, to make appearances before or communications to persons in an unrelated agency or bureau, within the same department or agency, having separate and distinct subject matter jurisdiction, upon a determination by the Director that there exists no potential for use of undue influence or unfair advantage based on past government service. On an annual basis, the Director of the Office of Government Ethics shall review the designations and determinations made under this subparagraph and, in consultation with the department or agency concerned, make such additions and deletions as are necessary. Departments and agencies shall cooperate to the fullest extent with the Director of the Office of Government Ethics in the exercise of his responsibilities under this paragraph.

(2)   The prohibition of subsection (c) shall not apply to appearances, communications, or representation by a former officer or employee, who is—

(A)   an elected official of a State or local government, or

(B)   whose principal occupation or employment is with (i) an agency or instrumentality of a State or local government, (ii) an accredited, degree-granting institution of higher education, as defined in section 1201(a) of the Higher Education Act of 1965, or (iii) a hospital or medical research organization, exempted and defined under section 501 (c) (3) of the Internal Revenue Code of 1954, and the appearance, communication, or representation is on behalf of such government, institution, hospital, or organization.

(e)   For the purposes of subsection (c), whenever the Director of the Office of Government Ethics determines that a separate statutory agency or bureau within a department or agency exercises functions which are distinct and separate from the remaining functions of the department or agency, the Director shall by rule designate such agency or bureau as a separate department or agency; exept that such designation shall not apply to former heads of designated bureaus or agencies, or former officers and employees of the department or agency whose official responsibilities included supervision of said agency or bureau.

(f)   The prohibitions of subsections (a), (b), and (c) shall not apply with respect to the making of communications solely for the purpose of furnishing scientific or technological information under procedures acceptable to the department or agency concerned, or if the head of the department or agency concerned with the particular matter, in consultation with the Director of the Office of Government Ethics, makes a certification, published in the Federal Register, that the former officer or employee has outstanding qualifications in a scientific, technological, or other technical discipline, and is acting with respect to a particular matter which requires such qualifications, and that the national interest would be served by the participation of the former officer or employee.

(g)   Whoever, being a partner of an officer or employee of the executive branch of the United States Government, of any independent agency of the United States, or of the District of Columbia, including a special Government employee, acts as agent or attorney for anyone other than the United States before any department, agency, court, court-martial, or any civil, military, or naval commission of the United

States or the District of Columbia, or any officer or employee thereof, in connection with any judicial or other proceeding, application, request for a ruling or other determination, contract, claim, controversy, investigation, charge, accusation, arrest, or other particular matter in which the United States or the District of Columbia is a party or has a direct and substantial interest and in which such officer or employee or special Government employee participates or has participated personally and substantially as an officer or employee through decision, approval, disapproval, recommendation, the rendering of advice, investigation, or otherwise, or which is the subject of his official responsibility, shall be fined not more than $5,000, or imprisoned for not more than one year, or both.

(h) Nothing in this section shall prevent a former officer or employee from giving testimony under oath, or from making statements required to be made under penalty of perjury.

(i) The prohibition contained in subsection (c) shall not apply to appearances or communications by a former officer or employee concerning matters of a personal and individual nature, such as personal income taxes or pension benefits; nor shall the prohibition of that subsection prevent a former officer or employee from making or providing a statement, which is based on the former officer's or employee's own special knowledge in the particular area that is the subject of the statement, provided that no compensation is thereby received, other than that regularly provided for by law or regulation for witnesses.

(j) If the head of the department or agency in which the former officer or employee served finds, after notice and opportunity for a hearing, that such former officer or employee violated subsection (a), (b), or (c) of this section, such department or agency head may prohibit that person from making, on behalf of any other person (except the United States), any informal or formal appearance before, or, with the intent to influence, any oral or written communication to, such department or agency on a pending matter of business for a period not to exceed five years, or may take other appropriate disciplinary action. Such disciplinary action shall be subject to review in an appropriate United States district court. No later than six months after the effective date of this Act, departments and agencies shall, in consultation with the Director of the Office of Government Ethics, establish procedures to carry out this subsection.

§208. Acts affecting a personal financial interest

(a) Except as permitted by subsection (b) hereof, whoever, being an officer or employee of the executive branch of the United States Government, of any independent agency of the United States, a Federal Reserve bank director, officer, or employee, or of the District of Columbia, including a special Government employee, participates personally and substantially as a Government officer or employee, through decision, approval, disapproval, recommendation, the rendering of advice, investigation, or otherwise, in a judicial or other proceeding, application, request for a ruling or other determination, contract, claim, controversy, charge, accusation, arrest, or other particular matter in which, to his knowledge, he, his spouse, minor child, partner, organization in which he is serving as officer, director, trustee, partner or employee, or any person or organization with whom he is negotiating or has any arrangement concerning prospective employment, has a financial interest —

Shall be fined not more than $10,000, or imprisoned not more than two years, or both.

(b)   Subsection (a) hereof shall not apply (1) if the officer or employee first advises the Government official responsible for appointment to his position of the nature and circumstances of the judicial or other proceeding, application, request for a ruling or other determination, contract, claim, controversy, charge, accusation, arrest, or other particular matter and makes full disclosure of the financial interest and receives in advance a written determination made by such official that the interest is not so substantial as to be deemed likely to affect the integrity of the services which the Government may expect from such officer or employee, or (2) if, by general rule or regulation published in the Federal Register, the financial interest has been exempted from the requirements of clause (1) hereof as being too remote or too inconsequential to affect the integrity of Government officers' or employees' services. In the case of class A and B directors of Federal Reserve banks, the Board of Governors of the Federal Reserve System shall be the Government official responsible for appointment.

§209.   Salary of Government officials and employees payable only by United States

(a)   Whoever receives any salary, or any contribution to or supplementation of salary, as compensation for his services as an officer or employee of the executive branch of the United States Government, of any independent agency of the United States, or of the District of Columbia, from any source other than the Government of the United States, except as may be contributed out of the treasury of any State, county, or municipality; or

Whoever, whether an individual, partnership, association, corporation, or other organization pays, or makes any contribution to, or in any way supplements the salary of, any such officer or employee under circumstances which would make its receipt a violation of this subsection —

Shall be fined not more than $5,000 or imprisoned not more than one year, or both.

(b) Nothing herein prevents an officer or employee of the executive branch of the United States Government, or of any independent agency of the United States or of the District of Columbia, from continuing to participate in a bona fide pension, retirement, group life, health or accident insurance, profit-sharing, stock bonus, or other employee welfare or benefit plan maintained by a former employer.

(c) This section does not apply to a special Government employee or to an officer or employee of the Government serving without compensation, whether or not he is a special Government employee, or to any person paying, contributing to, or supplementing his salary as such.

(d) This section does not prohibit payment or acceptance of contributions, awards, or other expenses under the terms of the Government Employees Training Act.

(e) This section does not prohibit the payment of actual relocation expenses incident to participation, or the acceptance of same by a participant in an executive exchange or fellowship program in an executive agency: *Provided*, That such program has been established by statute or Executive order of the President, offers appointments not to exceed three hundred and sixty-five days, and permits no extensions in excess of ninety additional days.

§210. Offer to procure appointive public office

Whoever pays or offers or promises any money or thing of value, to any person, firm, or corporation in consideration of the use or promise to use any influence to procure any appointive office or place under the United States for any person, shall be fined not more than $1,000 or imprisoned not more than one year, or both.

§211. Acceptance or solicitation to obtain appointive public office

Whoever solicits or receives, either as a political contribution, or for personal emolument, any money or thing of value, in consideration of the promise of support or use of influence in obtaining for any person any appointive office or place under the United States, shall be fined not more than $1,000 or imprisoned not more than one year, or both.

Whoever solicits or receives any thing of value in consideration of aiding a person to obtain employment under the United States either by referring his name to an executive department or agency of the United States or by requiring the payment of a fee because such person has secured such employment shall be fined not more than $1,000, or imprisoned not more than one year, or both. This section shall not apply to such services rendered by an employment agency pursuant to the written request of an executive department or agency of the United States. . . .

DISCLOSURE OF CONFIDENTIAL INFORMATION
18 U.S.C.A. §1905

Whoever, being an officer or employee of the United States or of any department or agency thereof, or agent of the Department of Justice as defined in the Antitrust Civil Process Act (15 U.S.C. 1311-1314), publishes, divulges, discloses, or makes known in any manner or to any extent not authorized by law any information coming to him in the course of his employment or official duties or by reason of any examination or investigation made by, or return, report or record made to or filed with, such department or agency or officer or employee thereof, which information concerns or relates to the trade secrets, processes, operations, style of work, or apparatus, or to the identity, confidential statistical data, amount or source of any income, profits, losses, or expenditures of any person, firm, partnership, corporation, or association; or permits any income return or copy thereof or any book containing any abstract or particulars thereof to be seen or examined by any person except as provided by law; shall be fined not more than $1,000, or imprisoned not more than one year, or both; and shall be removed from office or employment.

CALIFORNIA RULES OF PROFESSIONAL CONDUCT*

In Effect January 1, 1975

Revised Rules Approved by Order of the Supreme Court Filed December 31, 1974 together with subsequent revisions.

The following revision constitutes the first complete revision of the Rules of Professional Conduct. The first set of Rules of Professional Conduct were approved by the Supreme Court effective May 24, 1928. For the last official printing of the former revision of the Rules, see (1969) 1 Cal. 3d Rules amended 1972 and 1973.

Rule 1-100.   Rules of Professional Conduct, In General

These rules of professional conduct, adopted by the Board of Governors of the State Bar of California, pursuant to the provisions of the State Bar Act, shall become effective upon approval by the Supreme Court of California. When so approved, these rules shall be binding upon all members of the State Bar, and the wilful breach of any of these rules shall be punishable as provided by law. Nothing in these rules is intended to limit or supersede any provision of law relating to the duties and obligations of attorneys or the consequences of a violation thereof. The prohibition of certain conduct in these rules is not to be interpreted as an approval of conduct not specifically mentioned. These rules may be cited and referred to as "Rules of Professional Conduct of the State Bar of California".

Wherever in these rules reference is made to a law firm or association, such reference shall also apply to a law corporation.

---

* NOTE: As adopted and approved, the new rules are prospective in application but neither their adoption nor anything in their provisions will constitute a bar to a disciplinary proceeding in progress or later commenced for an alleged violation of the Rules of Professional Conduct in effect prior to January 1, 1975. For this purpose, the prior rules are continued.

Rule 1-101. Maintaining Integrity and Competence of the Legal Profession

A member of the State Bar shall not further the application for admission to practice law of another person known by him to be unqualified in respect to character, education, or other relevant attribute. This rule shall not prevent a member from serving as counsel of record for an applicant for admission to practice in proceedings related to such admission.

Rule 2-101. General Prohibition Against Solicitation of Professional Employment

(Repealed by order of Supreme Court, effective April 1, 1979.)

Rule 2-101. Professional Employment

This rule is adopted to foster and encourage the free flow of truthful and responsible information to assist the public in recognizing legal problems and in making informed choices of legal counsel.

Accordingly, a member of the State Bar may seek professional employment from a former, present or potential client by any means consistent with these rules.

(A) A "communication" is a message concerning the availability for professional employment of a member or a member's firm. A "communication" made by or on behalf of a member shall not:

    (1) Contain any untrue statement; or

    (2) Contain any matter, or present or arrange any matter in a manner or format which is false, deceptive, or which tends to confuse, deceive or mislead the public; or

    (3) Omit to state any fact necessary to make the statements made, in the light of the circumstances under which they are made, not misleading to the public; or

    (4) Fail to indicate clearly, expressly or by context, that it is a "communication"; or

    (5) State that a member is a certified specialist unless the member holds a current certificate as a specialist issued by the California Board of Legal Specialization pursuant to a plan for specialization approved by the Supreme Court; or

    (6) Be transmitted in any manner which involves intrusion, coercion, duress, compulsion, intimidation, threats or vexatious or harassing conduct.

(B) No solicitation or "communication" seeking professional employment from a potential client for pecuniary gain shall be delivered by a member or a member's agent in person or by telephone to the potential client, nor shall a solicitation or "communication" specifically directed to a particular potential client regarding that potential client's particular case or matter and seeking professional employment for pecuniary gain be delivered by any other means, unless the solicitation or "communication" is protected from abridgment by the Constitution of the United States or by the Constitution of the State of California. A potential client includes a former or present client.

Notwithstanding the foregoing, nothing in this subdivision (B) shall limit or negate the continuing professional duties of a member or a member's firm to former or present clients, or a member's right to respond to inquiries from potential clients.

(C)   A member or member's firm shall not solicit or accept professional employment offered or obtained through the acts of an agent, runner or capper, which acts would be in violation of law, or which, if performed by a member of the State Bar, would be in violation of subdivisions (A) or (B) of this rule 2-101.

*(D)   The Board of Governors of the State Bar shall formulate and adopt standards as to what "communications" will be presumed to violate subdivisions (A) or (B) of this rule 2-101. The standards shall have effect exclusively in disciplinary proceedings involving alleged violations of these rules as presumptions affecting the burden of proof. "Presumption affecting the burden of proof" means that presumption defined in Evidence Code sections 605 and 606. The standards formulated and adopted by the Board, as from time to time amended, shall be effective and binding on members of the State Bar.

(E)   The member shall retain for one year a true and correct copy or recording of any "communication" made by written or electronic media pertaining to the member or the member's firm. Upon written request, the member or the member's firm shall make any such copy or recording available to the State Bar, and, if requested, shall provide to the State Bar the evidence of the facts upon which any factual or objective claims contained in the "communication" are based. (Adopted by order of Supreme Court, effective April 1, 1979.)

---

* Pursuant to rule 2-101(D) the Board of Governors of the State Bar has adopted the following standards; effective May 25, 1979.

(1)   A "communication" which contains guarantees, warranties or predictions regarding the result of legal action is presumed to violate rule 2-101, Rules of Professional Conduct.

(2)   A "communication" which contains testimonials about or endorsements of a member is presumed to violate rule 2-101, Rules of Professional Conduct.

(3)   A "communication" which is delivered in person or by telephone to a potential client who is in such a physical, emotional or mental state that he or she would not be expected to exercise reasonable judgment as to the retention of counsel, is presumed to violate rule 2-101, Rules of Professional Conduct.

(4)   A "communication" which is transmitted at the scene of an accident or at or en route to a hospital, emergency care center or other health care facility is presumed to violate rule 2-101, Rules of Professional Conduct.

Rule 2-102.   Publicity in General

(Repealed by order of Supreme Court, effective April 1, 1979.)

Rule 2-102.   Legal Service Programs

(A)   The participation of a member or a member's firm in a bona fide program, activity or organization that furnishes, recommends, or pays for legal services, including but not limited to group, prepaid and voluntary legal service organizations, programs or activities is encouraged, and is not, of itself, a violation of these rules. A program or activity is not bona fide if its organization or operation allows any third person, organization or group to interfere with or control the performance of the member's duties to his or her clients; or allows unlicensed persons to practice law; or allows any third person, organization or group to receive directly or indirectly any part of the consideration paid to the member of the State Bar except as permitted by these rules; or would violate rule 2-101.

(B)   The participation of a member of the State Bar in a lawyer referral service established, sponsored, supervised and operated in conformity with the Minimum Standards for a Lawyer Referral Service in California (hereinafter "Standards") is encouraged, and is not, of itself, a violation of these rules. The Board of Governors of the State Bar shall formulate and adopt the Standards, which, as from time to time amended, shall be effective and binding on members of the State Bar. (Amended by order of Supreme Court, effective April 1, 1979.)*

Rule 2-103.   Professional Notices, Letterheads, Offices
and Law Lists

(Repealed by order of Supreme Court, effective April 1, 1979.)

Rule 2-104.   Recommendation of Professional
Employment

(Repealed by order of Supreme Court, effective April 1, 1979.)

Rule 2-105.   Advising Inquirers Through the Media on
Specific Legal Problems

A member of the State Bar shall not advise inquirers or render opinions to them through or in connection with a newspaper, radio or other publicity medium of any kind in respect to their specific legal problems, whether or not such attorney shall be compensated for his or her services. (Amended by order of Supreme Court, effective April 1, 1979.)

Rule 2-106.   Specialization

(Repealed by order of Supreme Court, effective April 1, 1979.)

Rule 2-107.   Fees for Legal Services

(A)   A member of the State Bar shall not enter into an agreement for, charge or collect an illegal or unconscionable fee.

(B)   A fee is unconscionable when it is so exorbitant and wholly disproportionate to the services performed as to shock the conscience of lawyers of ordinary prudence practicing in the same community. Reasonableness shall be determined on the basis of circumstances existing at the time the agreement is entered into except where the parties contemplate that the fee will be affected by later events. Among the factors to be considered, where appropriate, in determining the reasonableness of a fee are the following:

   (1)   The novelty and difficulty of the questions involved and the skill requisite to perform the legal service properly.
   (2)   The likelihood, if apparent to the client, that the acceptance of the particular employment will preclude other employment by the lawyer.
   (3)   The amount involved and the results obtained.
   (4)   The time limitations imposed by the client or by the circumstances.
   (5)   The nature and length of the professional relationship with the client.
   (6)   The experience, reputation, and ability of the lawyer or lawyers performing the services.
   (7)   Whether the fee is fixed or contingent.
   (8)   The time and labor required.
   (9)   The informed consent of the client to the fee agreement.

Rule 2-108.   Financial Arrangements Among Lawyers

(A)   A member of the State Bar shall not divide a fee for legal services with another person licensed to practice law who is not a partner or associate in the member's law firm or law office, unless:

   (1)   The client consents in writing to employment of the other person licensed to practice law after a full disclosure has been made in writing that a division of fees will be made and the terms of such division; and

245

    (2)   The total fee charged by all persons licensed to practice law is not increased solely by reason of the provision for division of fees and does not exceed reasonable compensation for all services they render to the client.

    (B)   Except as permitted in subdivision (A), a member of the State Bar shall not compensate, give or promise anything of value to any person licensed to practice law for the purpose of recommending or securing employment of the member or the member's firm by a client, or as a reward for having made a recommendation resulting in employment of the member or the member's firm by a client. A member's offering of or giving a gift or gratuity to any person licensed to practice law, who has made a recommendation resulting in the employment of the member or the member's firm, shall not of itself violate this rule, provided that the gift or gratuity was not offered in consideration of any promise, agreement or understanding that such a gift or gratuity would be forthcoming or that referrals would be made or encouraged in the future. (Amended by order of Supreme Court, effective October 1, 1979.)

Rule 2-109.   Agreements Restricting the Practice of a Member of the State Bar

    (A)   A member of the State Bar shall not be a party to or participate in an agreement, whether in connection with the settlement of a lawsuit or otherwise, if the agreement restricts the right of a member of the State Bar to practice law.

    (B)   Nothing in subdivision (A) of this rule shall be construed as prohibiting such a restrictive agreement which:

    (1)   is a part of an employment or partnership agreement between members of the State Bar provided said restrictive agreement does not survive the term of said partnership or employment; or

    (2)   requires payments to a member of the State Bar upon his permanent retirement from the practice of law.

Rule 2-110.   Acceptance of Employment

    A member of the State Bar shall not seek or accept employment to accomplish any of the following objectives, nor shall the member do so if he knows or should know that the person solicited for or offering the employment wishes to accomplish any of the following objectives:

    (A)   Bring a legal action, conduct a defense, or assert a position in litigation, or otherwise take steps, solely for the purpose of harassing or maliciously injuring any person or to prosecute or defend a case solely out of spite.

(B)   Present a claim or defense in litigation that is not warranted under existing law, unless it can be supported by good faith argument for an extension, modification or reversal of existing law.

(C)   Take or prosecute an appeal solely for delay, or for any other reason not in good faith. (Amended by order of Supreme Court, effective April 1, 1979.)

Rule 2-111.   Withdrawal from Employment

(A)   **In general.**

   (1)   If permission for withdrawal from employment is required by the rules of a tribunal, a member of the State Bar shall not withdraw from employment in a proceeding before that tribunal without its permission.

   (2)   In any event, a member of the State Bar shall not withdraw from employment until he has taken reasonable steps to avoid forseeable prejudice to the rights of his client, including giving due notice to his client, allowing time for employment of other counsel, delivering to the client all papers and property to which the client is entitled, and complying with applicable laws and rules.

   (3)   A member of the State Bar who withdraws from employment shall refund promptly any part of a fee paid in advance that has not been earned. However, this rule shall not be applicable to a true retainer fee which is paid solely for the purpose of insuring the availability of the attorney for the matter.

   (4)   If upon or after undertaking employment, a member of the State Bar knows or should know that the member ought to be called as a witness on behalf of the member's client in litigation concerning the subject matter of such employment, the member may continue employment only with the written consent of the client given after the client has been fully advised regarding the possible implications of such dual role as to the outcome of the client's cause and has had a reasonable opportunity to seek the advice of independent counsel on the matter. In civil proceedings, the written consent of the client shall be filed with the court not later than the commencement of trial. In criminal proceedings, the written consent need not be filed with the court but the member has the duty, before testifying, of satisfying the court that such consent has been obtained from the client if representing the defendant. The member may continue employment and the client's consent need not be obtained in the following circumstances.

(a) If the member's testimony will relate solely to an uncontested matter; or

(b) If the member's testimony will relate solely to a matter of formality and there is not reason to believe that substantial evidence will be offered in opposition to the testimony; or

(c) If the member's testimony will relate solely to the nature and value of legal services rendered in the case by the lawyer or his firm to the client; or

(d) If the member is representing the People, if the member obtains the consent of the head of the particular office representing the People, and if the member's continued representation is not inconsistent with the principles of recusal. (Amended by order of the Supreme Court, effective November 1, 1979.)

(5) If, after undertaking employment in contemplated or pending litigation, a member of the State Bar learns or it is obvious that he or a lawyer in his firm may be called as a witness other than on behalf of his client, he may continue the representation until it is apparent that his testimony is or may be prejudicial to his client.

(B) **Mandatory Withdrawal.** A member of the State Bar representing a client before a tribunal, with its permission if required by its rules, shall withdraw from employment, and a member of the State Bar representing a client in other matters shall withdraw from employment, if:

(1) He knows or should know that his client is bringing a legal action, conducting a defense, asserting a position in litigation, or otherwise having steps taken for him solely for the purpose of harassing or maliciously injuring any person or solely out of spite, or is taking or prosecuting an appeal merely for delay, or for any other reason not in good faith; or

(2) He knows or should know that his continued employment will result in violation of these Rules of Professional Conduct or of the State Bar Act; or

(3) His mental or physical condition renders it unreasonably difficult for him to carry out the employment effectively.

(C) **Permissive Withdrawal.** If Rule 2-111(B) is not applicable, a member of the State Bar may not request permission to withdraw in matters pending before a tribunal and may not withdraw in other matters, unless such request or such withdrawal is because:

(1) His client:

(a) Insists upon presenting a claim or defense that is not warranted under existing law and cannot be supported by good faith argument for an extension, modification, or reversal of existing law; or

(b)   Personally seeks to pursue an illegal course of conduct; or

(c)   Insists that the member of the State Bar pursue a course of conduct that is illegal or that is prohibited under these Rules of Professional Conduct or the State Bar Act; or

(d)   By other conduct renders it unreasonably difficult for the member of the State Bar to carry out his employment effectively; or

(e)   Insists, in a matter not pending before a tribunal, that the member of the State Bar engage in conduct that is contrary to the judgment and advice of the member of the State Bar but not prohibited under these Rules of Professional Conduct or the State Bar Act; or

(f)   Deliberately disregards an agreement or obligation to the member of the state Bar as to expenses or fees; or

(2)   His continued employment is likely to result in a violation of these Rules of Professional Conduct or of the State Bar Act; or

(3)   His inability to work with co-counsel indicates that the best interests of the client likely will be served by withdrawal; or

(4)   His mental or physical condition renders it difficult for him to carry out the employment effectively; or

(5)   His client knowingly and freely assents to termination of his employment; or

(6)   He believes in good faith, in a proceeding pending before a tribunal, that the tribunal will find the existence of other good cause for withdrawal.

Rule 3-101.   Aiding Unauthorized Practice of Law

(A)   A member of the State Bar shall not aid any person, association, or corporation in the unauthorized practice of law.

(B)   A member of the State Bar shall not practice law in a jurisdiction where to do so would be in violation of regulations of the profession in that jurisdiction.

Rule 3-102.   Financial Arrangements with Non-Lawyers

(A)   A member of the State Bar or the member's firm shall not directly or indirectly share legal fees except with a person licensed to practice law except that:

(1)   An agreement by a member of the State Bar with member's firm, partner, or associate may provide for the payment of money, over a reasonable period of time after the member's death, to his or her estate or to one or more specified persons.

(2) A member of the State Bar who undertakes to complete unfinished legal business of a deceased member of the State Bar may pay to the estate of the deceased member of the State Bar or other person legally entitled thereto that proportion of the total compensation which fairly represents the services rendered by the deceased member of the State Bar.

(3) A member of the State bar or the member's firm may include employees not members of the State Bar in a retirement plan, even though the plan is based in whole or in part on a profit-sharing arrangement.

(B) A member of the State Bar shall not compensate or give or promise anything of value to any person or entity for the purpose of recommending or securing employment of the member or the member's firm by a client, or as a reward for having made a recommendation resulting in employment of the member of the member's firm by a client. A member's offering of or giving a gift or gratuity to any person or entity, which has made a recommendation resulting in employment of the member or the member's firms, shall not of itself violate this rule, provided that the gift or gratuity was not offered in consideration of any promise, agreement or understanding that such a gift or gratuity would be forthcoming or that referrals would be made or encouraged in the future. (Amended by order of Supreme Court, effective October 1, 1979.)

(C) A member of the State Bar shall not compensate or give or promise anything of value to any representative of the press, radio, television or other communication medium in anticipation of or in return for publicity of the member, the member's firm, or any other attorney as such in a news item, but the incidental provision of food or beverages shall not of itself violate this subdivision. (Amended by order of Supreme Court, effective April 1, 1979.)

Rule 3-103.   Forming a Partnership with a Non-Lawyer

A member of the State Bar shall not form a partnership with a person not licensed to practice law if any of the activities of the partnership consist of the practice of law.

Rule 4-101.   Accepting Employment Adverse to a Client

A member of the State Bar shall not accept employment adverse to a client or former client, without the informed and written consent of the client or former client, relating to a matter in reference to which he has obtained confidential information by reason of or in the course of his employment by such client or former client.

Rule 5-101. Avoiding Adverse Interests

A member of the State Bar shall not enter into a business transaction with a client or knowingly acquire an ownership, possessory, security or other pecuniary interest adverse to a client unless (1) the transaction and terms in which the member of the State Bar acquires the interest are fair and reasonable to the client and are fully disclosed and transmitted in writing to the client in manner and terms which should have reasonably been understood by the client, (2) the client is given a reasonable opportunity to seek the advice of independent counsel of the client's choice on the transaction, and (3) the client consents in writing thereto.

Rule 5-102. Avoiding the Representation of Adverse Interests

(A)   A member of the State Bar shall not accept professional employment without first disclosing his relation, if any, with the adverse party, and his interest, if any, in the subject matter of the employment. A member of the State Bar who accepts employment under this rule shall first obtain the client's written consent to such employment.

(B)   A member of the State Bar shall not represent conflicting interests, except with the written consent of all parties concerned.

Rule 5-103. Purchasing Property at a Probate, Foreclosure or Judicial Sale

A member of the State Bar shall not directly or indirectly purchase property at a probate, foreclosure or judicial sale in an action or proceeding in which such member or any partner or associate of such member appears as attorney for a party or is acting as executor, trustee, administrator, guardian or conservator.

As used in this rule, the term "associate" means an employee or fellow employee who is a member of the State Bar.

Rule 5-104. Payment of Personal or Business Expenses Incurred by or for a Client

(A)   A member of the State Bar shall not directly or indirectly pay or agree to pay, guarantee, or represent or sanction the representation that he will pay personal or business expenses incurred by or for a client, prospective or existing and shall not prior to his employment enter into any discussion or other communication with a prospective client regarding any such payments or agreements to pay; provided this rule shall not prohibit a member:

    (1)   with the consent of the client, from paying or agreeing to pay to third persons such expenses from funds collected or to be collected for the client; or

    (2)   after he has been employed, from lending money to his client upon the client's promise in writing to repay such loan; or

    (3)   from advancing the costs of prosecuting or defending a claim or action or otherwise protecting or promoting the client's interests. Such costs within the meaning of this subparagraph (3) shall be limited to all reasonable expenses of litigation or reasonable expenses in preparation for litigation or in providing any legal services to the client.

  (B)   Nothing in Rule 5-104 shall be deemed to abrogate any of the provisions set forth in Rules 5-101 through 5-103.

  (C)   Nothing in this Rule 5-104 shall prohibit a member of the State Bar from reading or showing this Rule to a prospective client and describing the nature and extent of the conduct prohibited by this rule.

Rule 5-105.   Communication of Written Settlement Offer

A member of the State Bar shall promptly communicate to the member's client all amounts, terms and conditions of any written offer of settlements made by or on behalf of an opposing party. As used in this rule, "client" includes a person employing the member of the State Bar who possesses the authority to accept an offer of settlement, or, in a class action, who is a representative of the class. (Added by order of Supreme Court, effective March 15, 1979.)

Rule 6-101.   Failing to Act Competently

A member of the State Bar shall not willfully or habitually

    (1)   Perform legal services for a client or clients if he knows or reasonably should know that he does not possess the learning and skill ordinarily possessed by lawyers in good standing who perform, but do not specialize in, similar services practicing in the same or similar locality and under similar circumstances unless he associates or, where appropriate, professionally consults another lawyer who he reasonably believes does possess the requisite learning and skill;

    (2)   Fail to use reasonable diligence and his best judgment in the exercise of his skill and in the application of his learning in an

effort to accomplish, with reasonable speed, the purpose for which he is employed.

The good faith of an attorney is a matter to be considered in determining whether acts done through ignorance or mistake warrant imposition of discipline under Rule 6-101.

Rule 6-102. Limiting Liability to Client

A member of the State Bar shall not attempt to exonerate himself from or limit his liability to his client for his personal malpractice. This rule shall not prevent a member of the State Bar from settling or defending a malpractice claim.

Rule 7-101. Advising the Violation of Law

A member of the State Bar shall not advise the violation of any law, rule or ruling of a tribunal unless he believes in good faith that such law, rule or ruling is invalid. A member of the State Bar may take appropriate steps in good faith to test the validity of any law, rule or ruling of a tribunal.

Rule 7-102. Performing the Duty of Member of the State Bar in Government Service

A member of the State Bar in government service shall not institute or cause to be instituted criminal charges when he knows or should know that the charges are not supported by probable cause. If, after the institution of criminal charges, a member of the State Bar in government service having responsibility for prosecuting the charges becomes aware that those charges are not supported by probable cause, he shall promptly so advise the court in which the criminal matter is pending.

Rule 7-103. Communicating with an Adverse Party Represented by Counsel

A member of the State Bar shall not communicate directly or indirectly with a party whom he knows to be represented by counsel upon a subject of controversy, without the express consent of such counsel. This rule shall not apply to communcations with a public officer, board, committee or body.

Rule 7-104.   Threatening Criminal Prosecution

A member of the State Bar shall not threaten to present criminal, administrative or disciplinary charges to obtain an advantage in a civil action nor shall he present or participate in presenting criminal, administrative or disciplinary charges solely to obtain an advantage in a civil matter.

Rule 7-105.   Trial Conduct

In presenting a matter to a tribunal, a member of the State Bar shall:
   (1)   Employ, for the purpose of maintaining the causes confided to him such means only as are consistent with truth, and shall not seek to mislead the judge, judicial officer or jury by an artifice or false statement of fact or law. A member of the State Bar shall not intentionally misquote to a judge or judicial officer the language of a book, statute or decision; nor shall he, with knowledge of its invalidity and without disclosing such knowledge, cite as authority a decision that has been overruled or a statute that has been repealed or declared unconstitutional. A member of the State Bar shall refrain from asserting his personal knowledge of the facts at issue, except when testifying as a witness.
   (2)   Disclose, unless privileged or irrelevant, the identities of the clients he represents.

Rule 7-106.   Communication with or Investigation of Jurors

(A)   Before the trial of a case, a member of the State bar connected therewith shall not communicate directly or indirectly with anyone he knows to be a member of the venire from which the jury will be selected for the trial of the case.

(B)   During the trial of a case:
   (1)   A member of the State Bar connected therewith shall not communicate directly or indirectly with any member of the jury.
   (2)   A member of the State Bar who is not connected therewith shall not communicate directly or indirectly with a juror concerning the case.

(C)   Rule 7-106(A) and (B) do not prohibit a member of the State Bar from communicating with veniremen or jurors as a part of the official proceedings.

(D)   After discharge of the jury from further consideration of a case with which the member of the State Bar was connected, the member of the State Bar shall not ask questions of or make comments to a member of that jury that are intended to harass or embarass the juror or to influence the juror's actions in future jury service.

(E)   A member of the State Bar shall not conduct directly or indirectly an out of court investigation of either a venireman or a juror of a type likely to influence the state of mind of such venireman or juror in present or future jury service.

(F)   All restrictions imposed by Rule 7-106 upon a member of the State Bar also apply to communications with or investigations of members of a family of a venireman or a juror.

(G)   A member of the State Bar shall reveal promptly to the court improper conduct by a venireman or a juror, or by another toward a venireman or a juror or a member of his family of which the member of the State Bar has knowledge.

Rule 7-107.   Contact with Witnesses

A member of the State Bar shall not:

(A)   Suppress any evidence that he or his client has a legal obligation to reveal or produce.

(B)   Advise or directly or indirectly cause a person to secrete himself or to leave the jurisdiction of a tribunal for the purpose of making him unavailable as a witness therein.

(C)   Directly or indirectly pay, offer to pay, or acquiesce in the payment of compensation to a witness contingent upon the content of his testimony or the outcome of his case. Except where prohibited by law, a member of the State Bar may advance, guarantee or acquiesce in the payment of:

   (1)   Expenses reasonably incurred by a witness in attending or testifying.
   (2)   Reasonable compensation to a witness for his loss of time in attending or testifying.
   (3)   A reasonable fee for the professional services of an expert witness.

Rule 7-108.   Contact with Officials

(A)   A member of the State Bar shall not directly or indirectly give or lend anything of value to a judge, official, or employee of a tribunal unless the personal or family relationship between the member and the judge, official or employee is such that gifts are customarily given and exchanged.

(B)   A member of the State Bar shall not directly or indirectly, in the absence of opposing counsel, communicate with or argue to a judge or judicial officer, upon the merits of a contested matter pending before such judge or judicial officer, except in open court; nor shall he, without furnishing opposing counsel with a copy thereof, address a written communication to a judge or judicial officer concerning the merits of a contested matter pending before such judge or judicial officer. The rule shall not apply to ex parte matters.

Rule 8-101.   Preserving Identity of Funds and Property of a Client

(A)   All funds received or held for the benefit of clients by a member of the State Bar or firm of which he is a member, including advances for costs and expenses, shall be deposited in one or more identifiable bank accounts labelled "Trust Account," "Client's Funds Account" or words of similar import, maintained in the State of California, or, with written consent of the client, in such other jurisdiction where there is a substantial relationship between his client or his client's business and the other jurisdiction and no funds belonging to the member of the State Bar or firm of which he is a member shall be deposited therein or otherwise commingled therewith except as follows:

      (1)   Funds reasonably sufficient to pay bank charges may be deposited therein.

      (2)   Funds belonging in part to a client and in part presently or potentially to the member of the State Bar or firm of which he is a member must be deposited therein and the portion belonging to the member of the State Bar or firm of which he is a member must be withdrawn at the earliest reasonable time after the member's interest in that portion becomes fixed. However, when the right of the member of the State Bar or firm of which he is a member to receive a portion of trust funds is disputed by the client, the disputed portion shall not be withdrawn until the dispute is finally resolved.

(B)   A member of the State Bar shall:

      (1)   Promptly notify a client of the receipt of his funds, securities, or other properties.

      (2)   Identify and label securities and properties of a client promptly upon receipt and place them in a safe deposit box or other place of safekeeping as soon as practicable.

      (3)   Maintain complete records of all funds, securities, and other properties of a client coming into the possession of the member of the State Bar and render appropriate accounts to his client regarding them.

      (4)   Promptly pay or deliver to the client as requested by a client the funds, securities, or other properties in the possession of the member of the State Bar which the client is entitled to receive.

PART II

STANDARDS FOR JUDGES

A.B.A. CODE OF JUDICIAL CONDUCT*

PREFACE

Almost fifty years ago the American Bar Association formulated the original *Canons of Judicial Ethics*. Those Canons, occasionally amended, have been adopted in most states. In 1969 the association determined that current needs and problems required revision of the Canons. In the revision process, the Association has sought and considered the views of the Bench and Bar and other interested persons. In the judgment of the Association this Code, consisting of statements of norms denominated canons, the accompanying text setting forth specific rules, and the commentary, states the standards that judges should observe. The canons and text establish mandatory standards unless otherwise indicated. It is hoped that all jurisdictions will adopt this Code and establish effective disciplinary procedures for its enforcement.

CANON 1
A JUDGE SHOULD UPHOLD THE INTEGRITY AND INDEPENDENCE OF THE JUDICIARY

An independent and honorable judiciary is indispensable to justice in our society. A judge should participate in establishing, maintaining, and enforcing, and should himself observe, high standards of conduct so that the integrity and independence of the judiciary may be preserved. The provisions of this Code should be construed and applied to further that objective.

---

* The Code of Judicial Conduct was adopted by the House of the Delegates of the American Bar Association on August 16, 1972. Copyright © 1972 by the American Bar Association. All Rights reserved. Reprinted with permission of the American Bar Association.

CANON 2
A JUDGE SHOULD AVOID IMPROPRIETY
AND THE APPEARANCE OF
IMPROPRIETY IN ALL HIS ACTIVITIES

A.   A judge should respect and comply with the law and should conduct himself at all times in a manner that promotes public confidence in the integrity and impartiality of the judiciary.

B.   A judge should not allow his family, social, or other relationships to influence his judicial conduct or judgment. He should not lend the prestige of his office to advance the private interests of others; nor should he convey or permit others to convey the impression that they are in a special position to influence him. He should not testify voluntarily as a character witness.

Commentary

Public confidence in the judiciary is eroded by irresponsible or improper conduct by judges. A judge must avoid all impropriety and appearance of impropriety. He must expect to be the subject of constant public scrutiny. He must therefore accept restrictions on his conduct that might be viewed as burdensome by the ordinary citizen and should do so freely and willingly.

The testimony of a judge as a character witness injects the prestige of his office into the proceeding in which he testifies and may be misunderstood to be an official testimonial. This Canon, however, does not afford him a privilege against testifying in response to an official summons.

CANON 3
A JUDGE SHOULD PERFORM THE
DUTIES OF HIS OFFICE IMPARTIALLY
AND DILIGENTLY

The judicial duties of a judge take precedence over all his other activities. His judicial duties include all the duties of his office prescribed by law. In the performance of these duties, the following standards apply:

A.   ADJUDICATIVE RESPONSIBILITIES

(1)   A judge should be faithful to the law and maintain professional competence in it. He should be unswayed by partisan interests, public clamor, or fear of criticism.

(2) A judge should maintain order and decorum in proceedings before him.

(3) A judge should be patient, dignified, and courteous to litigants, jurors, witnesses, lawyers, and others with whom he deals in his official capacity, and should require similar conduct of lawyers, and of his staff, court officials, and others subject to his direction and control.

Commentary

The duty to hear all proceedings fairly and with patience is not inconsistent with the duty to dispose promptly of the business of the court. Courts can be efficient and business-like while being patient and deliberate.

(4) A judge should accord to every person who is legally interested in a proceeding, or his lawyer, full right to be heard according to law, and, except as authorized by law, neither initiate nor consider *ex parte* or other communications concerning a pending or impending proceeding. A judge, however, may obtain the advice of a disinterested expert on the law applicable to a proceeding before him if he gives notice to the parties of the person consulted and the substance of the advice, and affords the parties reasonable opportunity to respond.

Commentary

The proscription against communications concerning a proceeding includes communications from lawyers, law teachers, and other persons who are not participants in the proceeding, except to the limited extent permitted. It does not preclude a judge from consulting with other judges, or with court personnel whose function is to aid the judge in carrying out his adjudicative responsibilities.

An appropriate and often desirable procedure for a court to obtain the advice of a disinterested expert on legal issues is to invite him to file a brief *amicus curiae*.

(5) A judge should dispose promptly of the business of the court.

Commentary

Prompt disposition of the court's business requires a judge to devote adequate time to his duties, to be punctual in attending court and expeditious in determining matters under submission, and to insist that court officials, litigants and their lawyers cooperate with him to that end.

(6) A judge should abstain from public comment about a pending or impending proceeding in any court, and should require similar abstention on the part of court personnel subject to his direction and control. This subsection does not prohibit judges from making public statements in the course of their official duties or from explaining for public information the procedures of the court.

Commentary

"Court personnel" does not include the lawyers in a proceeding before a judge. The conduct of lawyers is governed by DR7-107 of the *Model Code of Professional Responsibility.*

(7) A judge should prohibit broadcasting, televising, recording, or taking photographs in the courtroom and areas immediately adjacent thereto during sessions of court or recesses between sessions, except that a judge may authorize:

    (a)   the use of electronic or photographic means for the presentation of evidence, for the perpetuation of a record, or for other purposes of judicial administration;

    (b)   the broadcasting, televising, recording, or photographing of investitive, ceremonial, or naturalization proceedings;

    (c)   the photographic or electronic recording and reproduction of appropriate court proceedings under the following conditions:

        (i)   the means of recording will not distract participants or impair the dignity of the proceedings;

        (ii)   the parties have consented, and the consent to being depicted or recorded has been obtained from each witness appearing in the recording and reproduction;

        (iii)   the reproduction will not be exhibited until after the proceeding has been concluded and all direct appeals have been exhausted; and

        (iv)   the reproduction will be exhibited only for instructional purposes in educational institutions.

Commentary

Temperate conduct of judicial proceedings is essential to the fair administration of justice. The recording and reproduction of a proceeding should not distort or dramatize the proceeding.

B. ADMINISTRATIVE RESPONSIBILITIES

(1)   A judge should diligently discharge his administrative responsibilities, maintain professional competence in judicial administration, and facilitate the performance of the administrative responsibilities of other judges and court officials.

(2)   A judge should require his staff and court officials subject to his direction and control to observe the standards of fidelity and diligence that apply to him.

(3)   A judge should take or initiate appropriate disciplinary measures against a judge or lawyer for unprofessional conduct of which the judge may become aware.

Commentary

Disciplinary measures may include reporting a lawyer's misconduct to an appropriate disciplinary body.

(4)   A judge should not make unnecessary appointments. He should exercise his power of appointment only on the basis of merit, avoiding nepotism and favoritism. He should not approve compensation of appointees beyond the fair value of services rendered.

Commentary

Appointees of the judge include officials such as referees, commissioners, special masters, receivers, guardians and personnel such as clerks, secretaries, and bailiffs. Consent by the parties to an appointment or an award of compensation does not relieve the judge of the obligation prescribed by this subsection.

C. DISQUALIFICATION

(1)   A judge should disqualify himself in a proceeding in which his impartiality might reasonably be questioned, including but not limited to instances where:

   (a)   he has a personal bias or prejudice concerning a party, or personal knowledge of disputed evidentiary facts concerning the proceeding;

   (b)   he served as lawyer in the matter in controversy, or a lawyer with whom he previously practiced law served during such association as a lawyer concerning the matter, or the judge or such lawyer has been a material witness concerning it;

Commentary

A lawyer in a governmental agency does not necessarily have an association with other lawyers employed by that agency within the meaning of this subsection; a judge formerly employed by a governmental agency, however, should disqualify himself in a proceeding if his impartiality might reasonably be questioned because of such association.

    (c)   he knows that he, individually or as a fiduciary, or his spouse or minor child residing in his household, has a financial interest in the subject matter in controversy or in a party to the proceeding, or any other interest that could be substantially affected by the outcome of the proceeding;

    (d)   he or his spousue, or a person within the third degree of relationship to either of them, or the spouse of such a person:
        (i)   is a party to the proceeding, or an officer, director, or trustee of a party;
        (ii)   is acting as a lawyer in the proceeding;

Commentary

The fact that a lawyer in a proceeding is affiliated with a law firm with which a lawyer-relative of the judge is affiliated does not of itself disqualify the judge. Under appropriate circumstances, the fact that "his impartiality might reasonably be questioned" under Canon 3C(1), or that the lawyer-relative is known by the judge to have an interest in the law firm that could be "substantially affected by the outcome of the proceeding" under Canon 3C(1) (d) (iii) may require his disqualification.

        (iii)   is known by the judge to have an interest that could be substantially affected by the outcome of the proceeding;
        (iv)   is to the judge's knowledge likely to be a material witness in the proceeding;

(2)   A judge should inform himself about his personal and fiduciary financial interests, and make a reasonable effort to inform himself about the personal financial interests of his spouse and minor children residing in his household.

(3)   For the purposes of this section:
    (a)   the degree of relationship is calculated according to the civil law system;

Commentary

According to the civil law system, the third degree of relationship test would, for example, disqualify the judge if his or his spouse's father, grandfather, uncle, brother, or niece's husband were a party or lawyer in the proceeding, but would not disqualify him if a cousin were a party or lawyer in the proceeding.

    (b) "fiduciary" includes such relationships as executor, administrator, trustee, and guardian;

    (c) "financial interest" means ownership of a legal or equitable interest, however small, or a relationship as director, advisor, or other active participant in the affairs of a party, except that:

        (i) ownership in a mutual or common investment fund that holds securities is not a "financial interest" in such securities unless the judge participates in the management of the fund;

        (ii) an office in an educational, religious, charitable, fraternal, or civic organization is not a "financial interest" in securities held by the organization;

        (iii) the proprietary interest of a policy holder in a mutual insurance company, of a depositor in a mutual savings association, or a similar proprietary interest, is a "financial interest" in the organization only if the outcome of the proceeding could substantially affect the value of the interest;

        (iv) ownership of government securities is a "financial interest" in the issuer only if the outcome of the proceeding could substantially affect the value of the securities.

D. REMITTAL OF DISQUALIFICATION

A judge disqualified by the terms of Canon 3C(1) (c) or Canon 3C(1) (d) may, instead of withdrawing from the proceeding, disclose on the record the basis of his disqualification. If, based on such disclosure, the parties and lawyers, independently of the judge's participation, all agree in writing that the judge's relationship is immaterial or that his financial interest is insubstantial, the judge is no longer disqualified, and may participate in the proceeding. The agreement, signed by all parties and lawyers, shall be incorporated in the record of the proceeding.

Commentary

This procedure is designed to minimize the chance that a party or lawyer will feel coerced into an agreement. When a party is not immediately available, the judge without violating this section may proceed on the written assurance of the lawyer that his party's consent will be subsequently filed.

CANON 4
A JUDGE MAY ENGAGE IN ACTIVITIES TO IMPROVE THE LAW, THE LEGAL SYSTEM, AND THE ADMINISTRATION OF JUSTICE

A judge, subject to the proper performance of his judicial duties, may engage in the following quasi-judicial activities, if in doing so he does not cast doubt on his capacity to decide impartially any issue that may come before him:

A. He may speak, write, lecture, teach, and participate in other activities concerning the law, the legal system, and the administration of justice.

B. He may appear at a public hearing before an executive or legislative body or official on matters concerning the law, the legal system, and the administration of justice, and he may otherwise consult with an executive or legislative body or official, but only on matters concerning the administration of justice.

C. He may serve as a member, officer, or director of an organization or governmental agency devoted to the improvement of the law, the legal system, or the administration of justice. He may assist such an organization in raising funds and may participate in their management and investment, but should not personally participate in public fund raising activities. He may make recommendations to public and private fund-granting agencies on projects and programs concerning the law, the legal system, and the administration of justice.

Commentary

As a judicial officer and person specially learned in the law, a judge is in a unique position to contribute to the improvement of the law, the legal system, and the administration of justice, including revision of substantive and procedural law and improvement of criminal and juvenile justice. To the extent that his time permits, he is encouraged to do so, either independently or through a bar association, judicial conference, or other organization dedicated to the improvement of the law.

Extra-judicial activities are governed by Canon 5.

CANON 5
A JUDGE SHOULD REGULATE HIS EXTRA-JUDICIAL ACTIVITIES TO MINIMIZE THE RISK OF CONFLICT WITH HIS JUDICIAL DUTIES

A. Avocational Activities. A judge may write, lecture, teach, and speak on non-legal subjects, and engage in the arts, sports, and other social and recreational activities, if such avocational activities do not detract from the dignity of his office or interfere with the performance of his judicial duties.

Commentary

Complete separation of a judge from extra-judicial activities is neither possible nor wise; he should not become isolated from the society in which he lives.

B. Civic and Charitable Activities. A judge may participate in civic and charitable activities that do not reflect adversely upon his impartiality or interfere with the performance of his judicial duties. A judge may serve as an officer, director, trustee, or non-legal advisor of an educational, religious, charitable, fraternal, or civic organization not conducted for the economic or political advantage of its members, subject to the following limitations:

(1) A judge should not serve if it is likely that the organization will be engaged in proceedings that would ordinarily come before him or will be regularly engaged in adversary proceedings in any court.

Commentary

The changing nature of some organizations and of their relationship to the law makes it necessary for a judge regularly to reexamine the activities of each organization with which he is affiliated to determine if it is proper for him to continue his relationship with it. For example, in many jurisdictions charitable hospitals are now more frequently in court than in the past. Similarly, the boards of some legal aid organizations now make policy decisions that may have political significance or imply commitment to causes that may come before the courts for adjudication.

(2)   A judge should not solicit funds for any educational, religious, charitable, fraternal, or civic organization, or use or permit the use of the prestige of his office for that purpose, but he may be listed as an officer, director, or trustee of such an organization. He should not be a speaker or the guest of honor at an organization's fund raising events, but he may attend such events.

(3)   A judge should not give investment advice to such an organization, but he may serve on its board of directors or trustees even though it has the responsibility for approving investment decisions.

Commentary

A judge's participation in an organization devoted to quasi-judicial activities is governed by Canon 4.

C.   FINANCIAL ACTIVITIES

(1)   A judge should refrain from financial and business dealings that tend to reflect adversely on his impartiality, interfere with the proper performance of his judicial duties, exploit his judicial position, or involve him in frequent transactions with lawyers or persons likely to come before the court on which he serves.

*(2)   Subject to the requirements of subsection (1), a judge may hold and manage investments, including real estate, and engage in other remunerative activity, but should not serve as an officer, director, manager, advisor, or employee of any business.

Commentary

The Effective Date of Compliance provision of this Code qualifies this subsection with regard to a judge engaged in a family business at the time this Code becomes effective.

Canon 5 may cause temporary hardship in jurisdictions where judicial salaries are inadequate and judges are presently supplementing their income through commercial activities. The remedy, however, is to secure adequate judicial salaries.

[Canon 5C(2)   sets the minimum standard to which a full-time judge should adhere. Jurisdictions that do not provide adequate judicial salaries but are willing to allow full-time judges to supplement their incomes through commercial activities may adopt the following substitute until such time as adequate salaries are provided:

*(2)   Subject to the requirement of subsection (1), a judge may hold and manage investments, including real estate, and engage in other remunerative activity including the operation of a business.

Jurisdictions adopting the foregoing substitute may also wish to prohibit a judge from engaging in certain types of businesses such as that of banks, public utilities, insurance companies, and other businesses affected with a public interest.]

(3)   A judge should manage his investments and other financial interests to minimize the number of cases in which he is disqualified. As soon as he can do so without serious financial detriment, he should divest himself of investments and other financial interests that might require frequent disqualification.

(4)   Neither a judge nor a member of his family residing in his household should accept a gift, bequest, favor, or loan from anyone except as follows:

   (a)   a judge may accept a gift incident to public testimonial to him; books supplied by publishers on a complimentary basis for official use; or an invitation to the judge and his spouse to attend a bar-related function or activity devoted to the improvement of the law, the legal system, or the administration of justice;

   (b)   a judge or a member of his family residing in his household may accept ordinary social hospitality; a gift, bequest, favor, or loan from a relative; a wedding or engagement gift; a loan from a lending institution in its regular course of business on the same terms generally available to persons who are not judges; or a scholarship or fellowship awarded on the same terms applied to other applicants;

   (c)   a judge or a member of his family residing in his household may accept any other gift, bequest, favor, or loan only if the donor is not a party or other person whose interests have come or are likely to come before him, and, if its value exceeds $100, the judge reports it in the same manner as he reports compensation in Canon 6C.

Commentary

This subsection does not apply to contributions to a judge's campaign for judicial office, a matter governed by Canon 7.

(5)   For the purposes of this section "member of his family residing in his household" means any relative of a judge by blood or marriage, or a person treated by a judge as a member of his family, who resides in his household.

(6)   A judge is not required by this Code to disclose his income, debts, or investments, except as provided in this Canon and Canons 3 and 6.

Commentary

Canon 3 requires a judge to disqualify himself in any proceeding in which he has a financial interest, however small; Canon 5 requires a judge to refrain from engaging in business and from financial activities that might interfere with the impartial performance of his judicial duties; Canon 6 requires him to report all compensation he receives for activities outside his judicial office. A judge has the rights of an ordinary citizen, including the right to privacy of his financial affairs, except to the extent that limitations thereon are required to safeguard the proper performance of his duties. Owning and receiving income from investments do not as such affect the performance of a judge's duties.

(7)   Information acquired by a judge in his judicial capacity should not be used or disclosed by him in financial dealings or for any other purpose not related to his judicial duties.

D.   Fiduciary Activities. A judge should not serve as the executor, administrator, trustee, guardian, or other fiduciary, except for the estate, trust, or person of a member of his family, and then only if such service will not interfere with the proper performance of his judicial duties. "Member of his family" includes a spouse, child, grandchild, parent, grandparent, or other relative or person with whom the judge maintains a close familial relationship. As a family fiduciary a judge is subject to the following restrictions:

(1)   He should not serve if it is likely that as a fiduciary he will be engaged in proceedings that would ordinarily come before him, or if the estate, trust, or ward becomes involved in adversary proceedings in the court on which he serves or one under its appellate jurisdiction.

Commentary

The Effective Date of Compliance provision of this Code qualifies this subsection with regard to a judge who is an executor, administrator, trustee, or other fiduciary at the time this Code becomes effective.

(2)   While acting as a fiduciary a judge is subject to the same restrictions on financial activities that apply to him in his personal capacity.

Commentary

A judge's obligation under this Canon and his obligation as a fiduciary may come into conflict. For example, a judge should resign as trustee if it would result in detriment to the trust to divest it of holdings whose retention would place the judge in violation of Canon 5C(3).

E.   Arbitration. A judge should not act as an arbitrator or mediator.

F.   Practice of Law. A judge should not practice law.

G.   Extra-judicial Appointments. A judge should not accept appointment to a governmental committee, commission, or other position that is concerned with issues of fact or policy on matters other than the improvement of the law, the legal system, or the administration of justice. A judge, however, may represent his country, state, or locality on ceremonial occasions or in connection with historical, educational, and cultural activities.

Commentary

Valuable services have been rendered in the past to the states and the nation by judges appointed by the executive to undertake important extra-judicial assignments. The appropriateness of conferring these assignments on judges must be reassessed, however, in light of the demands on judicial manpower created by today's crowded dockets and the need to protect the courts from involvement in extra-judicial matters that may prove to be controversial. Judges should not be expected or permitted to accept governmental appointments that could interfere with the effectiveness and independence of the judiciary.

CANON 6
A JUDGE SHOULD REGULARLY FILE REPORTS OF COMPENSATION RECEIVED FOR QUASI-JUDICIAL AND EXTRA-JUDICIAL ACTIVITIES

A judge may receive compensation and reimbursement of expenses for the quasi-judicial and extra-judicial activities permitted by this Code, if the source of such payments does not give the appearance of influencing the judge in his judicial duties or otherwise give the appearance of impropriety, subject to the following restrictions:

A.   Compensation. Compensation should not exceed a reasonable amount nor should it exceed what a person who is not a judge would receive for the same activity.

B.   Expense Reimbursement. Expense reimbursement should be limited to the actual cost of travel, food, and lodging reasonably incurred by the judge and, where appropriate to the occasion, by his spouse. Any payment in excess of such an amount is compensation.

C.   Public Reports. A judge should report the date, place, and nature of any activity for which he received compensation, and the name of the payor and the amount of compensation so received. Compensation or income of a spouse attributed to the judge by operation of a community property law is not extra-judicial compensation to the judge. His report should be made at least annually and should be filed as a public document in the office of the clerk of the court on which he serves or other office designated by rule of court.

CANON 7
A JUDGE SHOULD REFRAIN FROM POLITICAL ACTIVITY INAPPROPRIATE TO HIS JUDICIAL OFFICE

A. POLITICAL CONDUCT IN GENERAL

(1) A judge or a candidate for election to judicial office should not:
  (a) act as a leader or hold any office in a political organization;
  (b) make speeches for a political organization or candidate or publicly endorse a candidate for public office;

Commentary

A candidate does not publicly endorse another candidate for public office by having his name on the same ticket.

  (c) solicit funds for or pay an assessment or make a contribution to a political organization or candidate, attend political gatherings, or purchase tickets for political party dinners, or other functions, except as authorized in subsection A(2).
(2) A judge holding an office filled by public election between competing candidates, or a candidate for such office, may, only insofar as permitted by law, attend political gatherings, speak to such gatherings on his own behalf when he is a candidate for election or re-election, identify himself as a member of a political party, and contribute to a political party or organization.
(3) A judge should resign his office when he becomes a candidate either in a party primary or in a general election for a non-judicial office, except that he may continue to hold his judicial office while being a candidate for election to or serving as a delegate in a state constitutional convention, if he is otherwise permitted by law to do so.
(4) A judge should not engage in any other political activity except on behalf of measures to improve the law, the legal system, or the administration of justice.

B.   CAMPAIGN CONDUCT

(1)   A candidate, including an incumbent judge, for a judicial office that is filled either by public election between competing candidates or on the basis of a merit system election:

    (a)   should maintain the dignity appropriate to judicial office, and should encourage members of his family to adhere to the same standards of political conduct that apply to him;

    (b)   should prohibit public officials or employees subject to his direction or control from doing for him what he is prohibited from doing under this Canon; and except to the extent authorized under subsection B(2) or B(3), he should not allow any other person to do for him what he is prohibited from doing under this Canon;

    (c)   should not make pledges or promises of conduct in office other than the faithful and impartial performance of the duties of the office; announce his views on disputed legal or political issues; or misrepresent his identity, qualifications, present position, or other fact.

(2)   A candidate, including an incumbent judge, for a judicial office that is filled by public election between competing candidates should not himself solicit or accept campaign funds, or solicit publicly stated support, but he may establish committees of responsible persons to secure and manage the expenditure of funds for his campaign and to obtain public statements of support for his candidacy. Such committees are not prohibited from soliciting campaign contributions and public support from lawyers. A candidate's committees may solicit funds for his campaign no earlier than [90] days before a primary election and no later than [90] days after the last election in which he participates during the election year. A candidate should not use or permit the use of campaign contributions for the private benefit of himself or members of his family.

Commentary

Unless the candidate is required by law to file a list of his campaign contributors, their names should not be revealed to the candidate.

[Each jurisdiction adopting this Code should prescribe a time limit on soliciting campaign funds that is appropriate to the elective process therein.]

(3)   An incumbent judge who is a candidate for retention in or re-election to office without a competing candidate, and whose candidacy has drawn active opposition, may campaign in response thereto and may obtain publicly stated support and campaign funds in the manner provided in subsecion B(2).

COMPLIANCE WITH THE CODE OF JUDICIAL CONDUCT

Anyone, whether or not a lawyer, who is an officer of a judicial system performing judicial functions, including an officer such as a referee in bankruptcy, special master, court commissioner, or magistrate, is a judge for the purpose of this Code. All judges should comply with this Code except as provided below.

A.   Part-time Judge. A part-time judge is a judge who serves on a continuing or periodic basis, but is permitted by law to devote time to some other profession or occupation and whose compensation for that reason is less than that of a full-time judge. A part-time judge:

(1)   is not required to comply with Canon 5C(2), D, E, F, and G, and Canon 6C;

(2)   should not practice law in the court on which he serves or in any court subject to the appellate jurisdiction of the court on which he serves, or act as a lawyer in a proceeding in which he has served as a judge or in any other proceeding related thereto.

B.   Judge Pro Tempore. A judge *pro tempore* is a person who is appointed to act temporarily as a judge.

(1)   While acting as such, a judge *pro tempore* is not required to comply with Canon 5C(2), (3), D, E, F, and G, and Canon 6C.

(2)   A person who has been a judge *pro tempore* should not act as a lawyer in a proceeding in which he has served as a judge or in any other proceeding related thereto.

C.   Retired Judge. A retired judge who receives the same compensation as a full-time judge on the court from which he retired and is eligible for recall to judicial service should comply with all the provisions of this Code except Canon 5G, but he should refrain from judicial service during the period of an extra-judicial appointment not sanctioned by Canon 5G. All other retired judges eligible for recall to judicial service should comply with the provisions of this Code governing part-time judges.

EFFECTIVE DATE OF COMPLIANCE

A person to whom this Code becomes applicable should arrange his affairs as soon as reasonably possible to comply with it. If, however, the demands on his time and the possibility of conflicts of interest are not substantial, a person who holds judicial office on the date this Code becomes effective may:

(a)   continue to act as an officer, director, or non-legal advisor of a family business;

(b)   continue to act as an executor, administrator, trustee, or other fiduciary for the estate or person of one who is not a member of his family.

RETIREMENT FOR DISABILITY AND PROCEDURES FOR DISCIPLINE OF FEDERAL JUDGES

28 U.S.C.A. §372

§372. Retirement for disability; substitute judge on failure to retire; judicial discipline

(a) Any justice or judge of the United States appointed to hold office during good behavior who becomes permanently disabled from performing his duties may retire from regular active service, and the President shall by and with the advice and consent of the Senate, appoint a successor.

Any justice or judge of the United States desiring to retire under this section shall certify to the President his disability in writing.

Whenever an associate justice of the Supreme Court, a chief judge of a circuit or the chief judge of the Court of Claims, Court of Customs and Patent Appeals, or Court of International Trade, desires to retire under this section, he shall furnish to the President a certificate of disability signed by the Chief Justice of the United States.

A circuit or district judge, desiring to retire under this section, shall furnish to the President a certificate of disability signed by the chief judge of his circuit.

A judge of the Court of Claims, Court of Customs and Patent Appeals, or Court of International Trade desiring to retire under this section, shall furnish to the President a certificate of disability signed by the chief judge of his court.

Each justice or judge retiring under this section after serving ten years continuously or otherwise shall, during the remainder of his lifetime, receive the salary of the office. A justice or judge retiring under this section who has served less than ten years in all shall, during the remainder of his lifetime, receive one-half the salary of the office.

(b) Whenever any judge of the United States appointed to hold office during good behavior who is eligible to retire under this section does not do so and a certificate of his disability signed by a majority of the members of the Judicial Council of his circuit* in the case of a circuit or district judge, or by the Chief Justice of the United States in the case of the Chief Judge of the Court of Claims, Court of Customs and Patent Appeals, or Court of International Trade, or by the chief judge of his court in the case of a judge of the Court of Claims, Court of Customs and Patent Appeals, or Court of International Trade, is presented to the President and the President finds that such judge is unable to discharge efficiently all the duties of his office by reason of permanent mental or physical disability and that the appointment of an additional judge is necessary for the efficient dispatch of business, the President may make such appointment by and with the advice and consent of the Senate. Whenever any such additional judge is appointed, the vacancy subsequently caused by the death, resignation, or retirement of the disabled judge shall not be filled. Any judge whose disability causes the appointment of an additional judge shall, for purpose of precedence, service as chief judge, or temporary performance of the duties of that office, be treated as junior in commission to the other judges of the circuit, district, or court.

(c)(1)   Any person alleging that a circuit, district, or bankruptcy judge, or a magistrate, has engaged in conduct prejudicial to the effective and expeditious administration of the business of the courts, or alleging that such a judge or magistrate is unable to discharge all the duties of office by reason of mental or physical disability, may file with the clerk of the court of appeals for the circuit a written complaint containing a brief statement of the facts constituting such conduct.

(2)   Upon receipt of a complaint filed under paragraph (1) of this subsection, the clerk shall promptly transmit such complaint to the chief judge of the circuit, or, if the conduct complained of is that of the chief judge, to that circuit judge in regular active service next senior in date of commission (hereafter, for purposes of this subsection only, included in the term "chief judge"). The clerk shall simultaneously transmit a copy of the complaint to the judge or magistrate whose conduct is the subject of the complaint.

(3)   After expeditiously reviewing a complaint, the chief judge, by written order stating his reasons, may—

    (A)   dismiss the complaint, if he finds it to be (i) not in conformity with paragraph (1) of this subsection, (ii) directly related to the merits of a decision or procedural ruling, or (iii) frivolous; or

    (B)   conclude the proceeding if he finds that appropriate corrective action has been taken.

The chief judge shall transmit copies of his written order to the complainant and to the judge or magistrate whose conduct is the subject of the complaint.

[*See 28 U.S.C.A. Sec. 332 for composition of Judicial Councils of the Circuit Courts]

(4)   If the chief judge does not enter an order under paragraph (3) of this subsection, such judge shall promptly—

    (A)   appoint himself and equal numbers of circuit and district judges of the circuit to a special committee to investigate the facts and allegations contained in the complaint;

    (B)   certify the complaint and any other documents pertaining thereto to each member of such committee; and

    (C)   provide written notice to the complainant and the judge or magistrate whose conduct is the subject of the complaint of the action taken under this paragraph.

(5)   Each committee appointed under paragraph (4) of this subsection shall conduct an investigation as extensive as it considers necessary, and shall expeditiously file a comprehensive written report thereon with the judicial council of the circuit. Such report shall present both the findings of the investigation and the committee's recommendations for necessary and appropriate action by the judicial council of the circuit.

(6)   Upon receipt of a report filed under paragraph (5) of this subsection, the judicial council—

    (A)   may conduct any additional investigation which it considers to be necessary;

    (B)   shall take such action as is appropriate to assure the effective and expeditious administration of the business of the courts within the circuit, including, but not limited to, any of the following actions:

        (i)   directing the chief judge of the district of the magistrate whose conduct is the subject of the complaint to take such action as the judicial council considers appropriate;

        (ii)   certifying disability of a judge appointed to hold office during good behavior whose conduct is the subject of the complaint, pursuant to the procedures and standards provided under subsection (b) of this section;

        (iii)   requesting that any such judge appointed to hold office during good behavior voluntarily retire, with the provision that the length of service requirements under section 371 of this title shall not apply;

        (iv)   ordering that, on a temporary basis for a time certain, no further cases be assigned to any judge or magistrate whose conduct is the subject of a complaint;

        (v)   censuring or reprimanding such judge or magistrate by means of private communication;

        (vi)   censuring or reprimanding such judge or magistrate by means of public announcement; or

        (vii)   ordering such other action as it considers appropriate under the circumstances, except that (I) in no circumstances may the council order removal from office of any judge appointed to hold office during good behavior, and (II) any removal of a magistrate shall be in accordance with section 631 of this title and any removal of a bankruptcy judge shall be in accordance with section 153 of this title; and

(C)   shall immediately provide written notice to the complainant and to such judge or magistrate of the action taken under this paragraph.

(7)   (A)   In addition to the authority granted under paragraph (6) of this subsection, the judicial council may, in its discretion, refer any complaint under this subsection, together with the record of any associated proceedings and its recommendations for appropriate action, to the Judicial Conference of the United States.*

(B)   In any case in which the judicial council determines, on the basis of a complaint and an investigation under this subsection, or on the basis of information otherwise available to the council, that a judge appointed to hold office during good behavior has engaged in conduct—

(i)   which might constitute one or more grounds for impeachment under article I of the Constitution; or

(ii)   which, in the interest of justice, is not amenable to resolution by the judicial council,

the judicial council shall promptly certify such determination, together with any complaint and a record of any associated proceedings, to the Judicial Conference of the United States.

(C)   A judicial council acting under authority of this paragraph shall, unless contrary to the interests of justice, immediately submit written notice to the complainant and to the judge or magistrate whose conduct is the subject of the action taken under this paragraph.

(8)   Upon referral or certification of any matter under paragraph (7) of this subsection, the Judicial Conference, after consideration of the prior proceedings and such additional investigation as it considers appropriate, shall by majority vote take such action, as described in paragraph (6) (B) of this subsection, as it considers appropriate. If the Judicial Conference concurs in the determination of the council, or makes its own determination, that consideration of impeachment may be warranted, it shall so certify and transmit the determination and the record of proceedings to the House of Representatives for whatever action the House of Representatives considers to be necessary.

[*See 28 U.S.C.A. Sec. 331 for composition of Judicial Conference of the United States]

(9) (A) In conducting any investigation under this subsection, the judicial council, or a special committee appointed under paragraph (4) of this subsection, shall have full subpoena powers as provided in section 332 (d) of this title.

> (B) In conducting any investigation under this subsection, the Judicial Conference, or a standing committee appointed by the Chief Justice under section 331 of this title, shall have full subpoena powers as provided in that section.

(10) A complainant, judge, or magistrate aggrieved by a final order of the chief judge under paragraph (3) of this subsection may petition the judicial council for review thereof. A complainant, judge, or magistrate aggrieved by an action of the judicial council under paragraph (6) of this subsection may petition the Judicial Conference of the United States for review thereof. The Judicial Conference, or the standing committee established under section 331 of this title, may grant a petition filed by a complainant, judge, or magistrate under this paragraph. Except as expressly provided in this paragraph, all orders and determinations, including denials of petitions for review, shall be final and conclusive and shall not be judicially reviewable on appeal or otherwise.

(11) Each judicial council and the Judicial Conference may prescribe such rules for the conduct of proceedings under this subsection, including the processing of petitions for review, as each considers to be appropriate. Such rules shall contain provisions requiring that—

> (A) adequate prior notice of any investigation be given in writing to the judge or magistrate whose conduct is the subject of the complaint;
>
> (B) the judge or magistrate whose conduct is the subject of the complaint be afforded an opportunity to appear (in person or by counsel) at proceedings conducted by the investigating panel, to present oral and documentary evidence, to compel the attendance of witnesses or the production of documents, to cross-examine witnesses, and to present argument orally or in writing; and
>
> (C) the complainant be afforded an opportunity to appear at proceedings conducted by the investigating panel, if the panel concludes that the complainant could offer substantial information.

Any rule promulgated under this subsection shall be a matter of public record, and any such rule promulgated by a judicial council may be modified by the Judicial Conference.

(12) No judge or magistrate whose conduct is the subject of an investigation under this subsection shall serve upon a special committee appointed under paragraph (4) of this subsection, upon a judicial council, upon the Judicial Conference, or upon the standing committee established under section 331 of this title, until all related proceedings under this subsection have been finally terminated.

(13) No person shall be granted the right to intervene or to appear as amicus curiae in any proceeding before a judicial council or the Judicial Conference under this subsection.

(14) All papers, documents, and records of proceedings related to investigations conducted under this subsection shall be confidential and shall not be disclosed by any person in any proceeding unless—

  (A) the judicial council of the circuit, the Judicial Conference of the United States, or the Senate or the House of Representatives by resolution, releases any such material which is believed necessary to an impeachment investigation or trial of a judge under article I of the Constitution; or

  (B) authorized in writing by the judge or magistrate who is the subject to the complaint and by the chief judge of the circuit, the Chief Justice, or the chairman of the standing committee established under section 331 of this title.

(15) Each written order to implement any action under paragraph (6)(B) of this subsection, which is issued by a judicial council, the Judicial Conference, or the standing committee established under section 331 of this title, shall be made available to the public through the appropriate clerk's office of the court of appeals for the circuit. Unless contrary to the interests of justice, each such order issued under this paragraph shall be accompanied by written reasons therefor.

(16) Except as expressly provided in this subsection, nothing in this subsection shall be construed to affect any other provision of this title, the Federal Rules of Civil Procedure, the Federal Rules of Criminal Procedure, the Federal Rules of Appellate Procedure, or the Federal Rules of Evidence.

(17) The Court of Claims, the Court of Customs and Patent Appeals, and the Customs Court shall each prescribe rules, consistent with the foregoing provisions of this subsection, establishing procedures for the filing of complaints with respect to the conduct of any judge of such court and for the investigation and resolution of such complaints. In investigating and taking action with respect to any such complaint, each such court shall have the powers granted to a judicial council under this subsection.

JUDICIAL PERSONNEL FINANCIAL DISCLOSURE REQUIREMENTS

28 U.S.C.A. §§301-309 (excerpts)

§301. Persons required to file

(a) Within thirty days of assuming the position of a judicial employee, an individual shall file a report containing the information described in section 302(b).

(b) Within five days of the transmittal by the President to the Senate of the nomination of an individual to be a judicial officer, such individual shall file a report containing the information described in section 302(b). Nothing in this Act shall prevent any Congressional committee from requesting, as a condition of confirmation, any additional financial information from any Presidential nominee whose nomination has been referred to that committee.

(c) Any individual who is a judicial officer or employee during any calendar year and performs the duties of his position or office for a period in excess of sixty days in that calendar year shall file on or before May 15 of the succeeding year a report containing the information described in section 302(a)....

§302. Contents of reports

(a) Each report filed pursuant to section 301(c) shall include a full and complete statement with respect to the following:

    (1)(A) The source, type, and amount or value of income (other than income referred to in subparagraph (B)) from any source (other than from current employment by the United States Government), and the source, date, and amount of honoraria from any source, received during the preceding calendar year, aggregating $100 or more in value.

    (B) The source and type of income which consists of dividends, rent, interest, and capital gains received during the preceding calendar year which exceeds $100 in amount or value, and an indication of which of the following categories the amount or value of such item of income is within —

    (i)   not more than $1,000,
    (ii) greater than $1,000 but not more than $2,500,
    (iii) greater than $2,500 but not more than $5,000,
    (iv) greater than $5,000 but not more than $15,000,
    (v) greater than $15,000 but not more than $50,000,
    (vi) greater than $50,000 but not more than $100,000, or
    (vii) greater than $100,000.

(2)(A) The identity of the source and a brief description of any gifts of transportation, lodging, food, or entertainment aggregating $250 or more in value received from any source other than a relative of the reporting individual during the preceding calendar year, except that any food, lodging, or entertainment received as personal hospitality of any individual need not be reported, and any gift with a fair market value of $35 or less need not be aggregated for purposes of this subparagraph.

(B) The identity of the source, a brief description, and the value of all gifts other than transportation, lodging, food, or entertainment aggregating $100 or more in value received from any source other than a relative of the reporting individual during the preceding calendar year, except that any gift with a fair market value of $35 or less need not be aggregated for purposes of this subparagraph.

(C) The identity of the source and a brief description of reimbursements received from any source aggregating $250 or more in value and received during the preceding calendar year.

(D) In an unusual case, a gift need not be aggregated under subparagraph (A) or (B) if a publicly available request for a waiver is granted.

(3) The identity and category of value of any interest in property held during the preceding calendar year in a trade or business, or for investment or the production of income, which has a fair market value which exceeds $1,000 as of the close of the preceding calendar year, excluding any personal liability owed to the reporting individual by a relative or any deposits aggregating $5,000 or less in a personal savings account. For purposes of this paragraph, a personal savings account shall include any certificate of deposit or any other form of deposit in a bank, savings and loan association, credit union, or similar financial institution.

(4) The identity and category of value of the total liabilities owed to any creditor other than a relative which exceeds $10,000 at any time during the preceding calendar year, excluding —

    (A)   any mortgage secured by real property which is a personal residence of the reporting individual or his spouse; and

    (B)   any loan secured by a personal motor vehicle, household furniture, or appliances, which loan does not exceed the purchase price of the item which secures it.

With respect to revolving charge accounts, only those with an outstanding liability which exceeds $10,000 as of the close of the preceding calendar year need be reported under this paragraph.

    (5)   Except as provided in this paragraph, a brief description, the date, and category of value of any purchase, sale, or exchange during the preceding calendar year exceeds $1,000 —

    (A)   in real property, other than property used solely as a personal residence of the reporting individual or his spouse; or

    (B)   in stocks, bonds, commodities futures, and other forms of securities.

Reporting is not required under this paragraph of any transactions solely by and between the reporting individual, his spouse, or dependent children.

    (6)   The identity of all positions held on or before the date of filing during the current calendar year as an officer, director, trustee, partner, proprietor, representative, employee, or consultant of any corporation, company, firm, partnership, or other business enterprise, any nonprofit organization, any labor organization, or any educational or other institution other than the United States. This paragraph shall not require the reporting of positions held in any religious, social, fraternal, or political entity and positions solely of an honorary nature.

    (7)   A description of the date, parties to, and terms of any agreement or arrangement with respect to (A) future employment; (B) a leave of absence during the period of the reporting individual's Government service; (C) continuation of payments by a former employer other than the United States Government; and (D) continuing participation in an employee welfare or benefit plan maintained by a former employee.

    (b)   Each report filed pursuant to subsections (a) and (b) of section 301 shall include a full and complete statement with respect to the information required by —

    (1)   paragraph (1) of subsection (a) of this section for the year of filing and the preceding calendar year,

    (2)   paragraphs (3) and (4) of subsection (a) of this section as of the date specified in the report but which is less than thirty-one days before the filing date, and

    (3)   paragraph (6) and (7) of subsection (a) of this section as of the filing date but for periods described in such paragraphs.

    (c)   In the case of any individual described in section 301(d) of this title, any reference to the preceding calendar year shall be considered also to include that part of the calendar year of filing up to the date of the termination of employment.

(d)(1)   The categories for reporting the amount or value of the items covered in paragraphs (3), (4), and (5) of subsection (a) of this section are as follows:

     (A)   not more than $5,000;

     (B)   greater than $5,000 but not more than $15,000;

     (C)   greater than $15,000 but not more than $50,000;

     (D)   greater than $50,000 but not more than $100,000;

     (E)   greater than $100,000 but not more than $250,000; and

     (F)   greater than $250,000.

(2)   For the purposes of paragraph (3) of subsection (a) of this section if the current value of an interest in real property (or an interest in a real estate partnership) is not ascertainable without an appraisal, an individual may list (A) the date of purchase and the purchase price of the interest in the real property, or (B) the assessed value of the real property for tax purposes, adjusted to reflect the market value of the property used for the assessment if the assessed value is computed at less than 100 percent of such market value, but such individual shall include in his report a full and complete description of the method used to determine such assessed value, instead of specifiying a category of value pursuant to paragraph (1) of this subsection. If the current value of any other item required to be reported under paragraph (3) of subsection (a) of this section is not ascertainable without an appraisal, such individual may list the book value of a corporation whose stock is not publicly traded, the net worth of a business partnership, the equity value of an individually owned business, or with respect to other holdings, any recognized indication of value, but such individual shall include in his report a full and complete description of the method used in determining such value. In lieu of any value referred to in the preceding sentence, an individual may list the assessed value of the item for tax purposes, adjusted to reflect the market value of the item used for the assessment if the assessed value is computed at less than 100 percent of such market value, but a full and complete description of the method used in determining such assessed value shall be included in the report.

(e)(1)   Except as provided in the last sentence of this paragraph, each report required by subsection (a), (b), or (c) of this section shall also contain information listed in paragraphs (1) through (5) of subsection (a) of this section respecting the spouse or dependent child of the reporting individual as follows:

     (A)   The source of items of earned income earned by a spouse from any person which exceed $1,000 and, with respect to his spouse or dependent child, all information required to be reported in subsection (a)(1)(B) of this section with respect to income derived from any asset held by the spouse or dependent child and reported pursuant to paragraph (3). With respect to earned income, if the spouse is self-employed in business or a profession, only the nature of such business or profession need be reported.

  (B) In the case of any gifts received by a spouse which are not received totally independent of the spouse's relationship to the reporting individual, the identity of the source and a brief description of gifts of transportation, lodging, food, or entertainment or the value of other gifts.

  (C) In the case of any reimbursements received by a spouse which are not received totally independent of the spouse's relationship to the reporting individual, the identity of the source and a brief description of each such reimbursement.

  (D) In the case of items described in paragraphs (3) through (5), all information required to be reported under these paragraphs other than items (1) which the reporting individual certifies represent the spouse's or dependent child's sole financial interest or responsibility and which the reporting individual has no knowledge of, (ii) which are not in any way, past or present, derived from the income, assets, or activities of the reporting individual, and (iii) from which the reporting individual neither derives, nor expects to derive, any financial or economic benefit.

Each report referred to in subsection (b) of this section shall, with respect to the spouse and dependent child of the reporting individual, only contain information listed in paragraphs (1), (3), and (4) of subsection (a) of this section, as specified in this paragraph.

 (2) No report shall be required with respect to a spouse living separate and apart from the reporting individual with the intention of terminating the marriage or providing for permanent separation; or with respect to any income or obligations of an individual arising from the dissolution of his marriage or the permanent separation from his spouse.

 (f)(1) Except as provided in paragraph (2), each reporting individual shall report the information required to be reported pursuant to subsections (a), (b), and (c) of this section with respect to the holdings of and the income from a trust or other financial arrangement from which income is received by, or with respect to which a beneficial interest in principal or income is held by, such individual, his spouse, or any dependent child.

 (2) A reporting individual other than a judicial officer of the United States need not report the holdings of or the source of income from any of the holdings of —

  (A) any qualified blind trust (as defined in paragraph (3)); or

  (B) a trust —

   (i) which was not created directly by such individual, his spouse, or any dependent child, and

   (ii) the holding or sources of income of which such individual, his spouse, and any dependent child have no knowledge of, but such individual shall report the category of the amount of income received by him, his spouse, or any dependent child from the trust under subsection (a)(1)(B) of this section.

(3) [Sections on Blind Trusts Omitted]

(g) Political campaign funds, including campaign receipts and expenditures, need not be included in any report filed pursuant to this title.

(h) A report filed pursuant to subsection (c) or (d) of section 301 need not contain the information described in subparagraphs (A), (B), and (C) of subsection (a)(2) of this section with respect to gifts and reimbursements received in a period when the reporting individual was not an officer or employee of the Federal Government.

§303. Filing of reports

(a) The Judicial Conference of the United States shall establish a Judicial Ethics Committee which shall be responsible for developing the forms for reporting the information required by this title and for receiving and making available, in accordance with the provisions of this title, the reports described in section 301.

(b) Each judicial officer and judicial employee shall file the report required by this title with the Committee and shall file a copy of such report as a public document with the clerk of the court on which he sits or serves.

(c) In the performance of its functions under this title, the Committee, with the approval of the Judicial Conference of the United States, shall —

    (1) develop the necessary forms and promulgate such rules and regulations as may be necessary;

    (2) monitor and investigate compliance with the requirements of this title;

    (3) provide for the availability or reports as required by section 305;

    (4) conduct, or cause to be conducted, the review required by section 306;

    (5) cooperate with the Attorney General in enforcing the requirements of this title;

    (6) submit to the Congress and the President recommendations for legislative revision of this title; and

    (7) perform such other functions as may be assigned by the Judicial Conference of the United States. . . .

§304. Failure to file or falsifying reports

(a) The Attorney General may bring a civil action in any appropriate United States District Court against any individual who knowingly and willfully falsifies or who knowingly or willfully fails to file or report any information that such individual is required to report pursuant to section 302. The court in which such action is brought may assess against such individual a civil penalty in any amount not to exceed $5,000.

(b)   The Committee shall refer to the Attorney General the name of any individual the Committee has reasonable cause to believe has willfully failed to file a report or has willfully falsified or failed to file information required to be reported.

§305.   Custody of and public access to reports

(a)   The Committee shall make each report filed with it under this title available to the public in accordance with subsection (b) of this section.

(b)(1)   The Committee shall, within fifteen days after any report is received by the Committee under this title, permit inspection by or furnish a copy of such report to any person requesting such inspection or copy. The Committee may require the requesting person to pay a reasonable fee in any amount which is found necessary to recover the cost of reproduction or mailing of such report excluding any salary of any employee involved in such reproduction or mailing. A copy of such report may be furnished without charge or at a reduced charge if it is determined that waiver or reduction of the fee is in the public interest.

(2)   Notwithstanding paragraph (1), a report may not be made available under this section to any person nor may any copy thereof be provided under this section to any person except upon a written application by such person stating —

    (A)   that person's name, occupation and address;

    (B)   the name and address of any other person or organization on whose behalf the inspection or copy is requested; and

    (C)   that such person is aware of the prohibitions on the obtaining or use of the report.

Any such application shall be made available to the public throughout the period during which the report is made available to the public.

(c)(1)   It shall be unlawful for any person to obtain or use a report —

    (A)   for any unlawful purpose;

    (B)   for any commercial purpose other than by news and communications media for dissemination to the general public;

    (C)   for determining or establishing the credit rating of any individual; or

    (D)   for use, directly or indirectly, in the solicitation of money for any political, charitable, or other purpose.

(2) The Attorney General may bring a civil action against any person who obtains or uses a report for any purpose prohibited in paragraph (1). The court in which such action is brought may assess against such person a pen-

alty in any amount not to exceed $5,000. Such remedy shall be in addition to any other remedy available under statutory or common law.

(d)   Any report received by the Committee shall be held in its custody and be made available to the public for a period of six years after receipt of the report. After such six-year period the report shall be destroyed unless needed in an ongoing investigation, except that in the case of an individual who filed the report pursuant to section 301(b) and was not subsequently confirmed by the Senate, such reports shall be destroyed one year after the individual is no longer under consideration by the Senate unless needed in an ongoing investigation.

§306.   Compliance procedures

(a)   The Committee shall establish procedures for the review of reports filed with it under this title to determine whether the reports are filed in a timely manner, are complete, and are in proper form. In the event a determination is made that a report is not so filed, the Committee shall so inform the reporting individual and direct him to take all necessary corrective action.

(b)   Such procedures shall include provisions for conducting a review each year of financial statements filed in that year by judicial officers and employees to determine whether such statements reveal possible violations of applicable conflict of interest laws or regulations and recommending appropriate action to correct any conflict of interest or ethical problems revealed by such review.

§307.   Additional requirements

(a)   Nothing in this title shall be construed to prevent the Committee, with the approval of the Judicial Conference of the United States, from requiring officers or employees of the judicial branch not covered by this title to submit confidential financial statements.

(b)   The Committee, with the approval of the Judicial Conference, may require disclosure, in the reports filed pursuant to subsections (a) and (c) of section 302, of gifts received by a dependent child of a reporting individual if the information required to be disclosed does not exceed that which must be reported by a spouse of a reporting individual under this title.

(c)   Nothing in this Act requiring reporting of information shall be deemed to authorize the receipt of income, gifts, or reimbursements; the holding of assets, liabilities, or positions; or the particpation in transactions that are prohibited by law or regulation.

(d)   The provisions of this title requiring the reporting of information shall not supersede the requirements of section 7342 of Title 5.

§308.   Definitions

For the purposes of this title, the term —

(1) "income" means all income from whatever source derived, including but not limited to the following items: compensation for services, including fees, commissions, and similar items; gross income derived from business (and net income if the individual elects to include it); gains derived from dealings in property; interest; rents; royalties, dividends; annuities; income from life insurance and endowment contracts; pensions; income from discharge of indebtedness; distributive share of partnership income; and income from an interest in an estate or trust;

(2) "relative" means an individual who is related to the reporting individual, as father, mother, son, daughter, brother, sister, uncle, aunt, great aunt, great uncle, first cousin, nephew, niece, husband, wife, grandfather, grandmother, grandson, granddaughter, father-in-law, mother-in-law, son-in-law, daughter-in-law, brother-in-law, sister-in-law, stepfather, stepmother, stepson, stepdaughter, stepbrother, stepsister, half brother, half sister, or who is the grandfather or grandmother of the spouse of the reporting individual, and shall be deemed to include the fiance or fiancee of the reporting individual;

(3) "gift" means a payment, advance, forebearance, rendering, or deposit of money, or any thing of value, unless consideration of equal or greater value is received by the donor, but does not include —

    (A)   bequest and other forms of inheritance;

    (B)   suitable mementos of a function honoring the reporting individual;

    (C)   food, lodging, transportation, and entertainment provided by a foreign government within a foreign country or by the United States Government;

    (D)   food and beverages consumed at banquets, receptions, or similar events; or

    (E)   communications to the offices of a reporting individual including subscriptions to newspapers and periodicals;

(4) "honoraria" has the meaning given such term in the Federal Election Campaign Act of 1971;

(5) "value" means a good faith estimate of the dollar value if the exact value is neither known nor easily obtainable by the reporting individual;

(6) "personal hospitality of any individual" means hospitality extended for a nonbusiness purpose by an individual, not a corporation or organization, at the personal residence of that individual or his family or on property or facilities owned by that individual or his family;

(7) "dependent child" means, when used with respect to any reporting individual, any individual who is a son, daughter, stepson, or stepdaughter and who —

      (A)   is unmarried and under age 21 and is living in the household of such reporting individual; or

      (B)   is a dependent of such reporting individual within the meaning of section 152 of Title 26;

(8)   "reimbursement" means any payment or other thing of value received by the reporting individual, other than gifts, to cover travel-related expenses of such individual other than those which are —

      (A)   provided by the United States Government;

      (B)   required to be reported by the reporting individual under section 7342 of Title 5; or

      (C)   required to be reported under section 434 of Title 2;

(9)   "judicial officer" means the Chief Justice of the United States, the Associate Justices of the Supreme Court, and the judges of the United States courts of appeals; United States district courts, including the district courts in the Canal Zone, Guam, and the Virgin Islands; Court of Claims; Court of Customs and Patent Appeals; Court of International Trade; Tax Court; United States Court of Military Appeals; courts of the District of Columbia and any court created by Act of Congress, the judges of which are entitled to hold office during good behavior; and

(10)   "judicial employee" means any employee of the judicial branch of the Government, of the Tax Court, or of the United States Court of Military Appeals who is not a judicial officer and who is authorized to perform adjudicatory functions with respect to proceedings in the judicial branch, or who receives compensation at a rate at or in excess of the minimum rate prescribed for grade 16 of the General Schedule under section 5332 of Title 5.

§309.   Effective date

This title shall take effect on January 1, 1979, and the reports filed under section 301(c) on May 15, 1979, shall include information for calendar year 1978.

A.B.A. STANDARDS FOR CRIMINAL JUSTICE*

CHAPTER 6
SPECIAL FUNCTIONS OF
THE TRIAL JUDGE

Standard 6-1.1. General responsibility of the trial judge

(a) The trial judge has the responsibility for safeguarding both the rights of the accused and the interests of the public in the administration of criminal justice. The adversary nature of the proceedings does not relieve the trial judge of the obligation of raising on his or her initiative, at all appropriate times and in an appropriate manner, matters which may significantly promote a just determination of the trial. The only purpose of a criminal trial is to determine whether the prosecution has established the guilt of the accused as required by law, and the trial judge should not allow the proceedings to be used for any other purpose.

(b) The trial judge should require that every proceeding before him or her be conducted with unhurried and quiet dignity and should aim to establish such physical surroundings as are appropriate to the administration of justice. The trial judge should give each case individual treatment; and the judge's decisions should be based on the particular facts of that case. The trial judge should conduct the proceedings in clear and easily understandable language, using interpreters when necessary.

(c) The trial judge should be sensitive to the important roles of the prosecutor and defense counsel; and the judge's conduct toward them should manifest professional respect, courtesy, and fairness.

Standard 6-1.2. Adherence to standards

The trial judge should be familiar with and adhere to the canons and codes applicable to the judiciary, the code of professional responsibility applicable to the legal profession, and standards concerning the proper administration of criminal justice.

Standard 6-1.3.   Appearance and demeanor of the judge

The trial judge's appearance and demeanor should reflect the dignity of the judicial office and enhance public confidence in the administration of justice. The wearing of the judicial robe in the courtroom will contribute to these goals.

Standard 6-1.4.   Obligation to use judicial time effectively

The trial judge has the obligation to avoid delays, continuances, and extended recesses, except for good cause. In the matter of punctuality, the observance of scheduled court hours, and the use of working time, the trial judge should be an exemplar for all other persons engaged in the criminal case. The judge should require punctuality and optimum use of working time from all such persons.

Standard 6-1.5.   Duty to maintain impartiality

The trial judge should avoid impropriety and the appearance of impropriety in all activities, and should conduct himself or herself at all times in a manner that promotes public confidence in the integrity and impartiality of the judiciary. The judge should not allow family, social, or other relationships to influence judicial conduct or judgment.

Standard 6-1.6.   Judge's duty concerning record of judicial proceedings

The trial judge has a duty to see that the reporter makes a true, complete, and accurate record of all proceedings. The judge should at all times respect the professional independence of the reporter, but may challenge the accuracy of the reporter's record of the proceedings. The trial judge should not change the transcript without notice to the prosecution, the defense, and the reporter, with opportunity to be heard. The trial judge should take steps to ensure that the reporter's obligation to furnish transcripts of court proceedings is promptly met.

Standard 6-1.7. Circumstances requiring recusation

The trial judge should recuse himself or herself whenever the judge has any doubt as to his or her ability to preside impartially in a criminal case or whenever the judge believes his or her impartiality can reasonably be questioned.

Standard 6-1.8. Issuance of review of warrants

Whenever a trial judge is called upon to issue a warrant for arrest or for search, or to review the issuance of such a warrant or the execution thereof, the judge should carefully observe constitutional and statutory norms and not permit these procedures to become mechanical or perfunctory. Where the trial court has supervisory jurisdiction over other judicial officers who perform these functions, the court should ensure that this standard is observed.

Standard 6-1.9. Inquiries concerning jail population

The trial judge should periodically make careful inquiry concerning persons held in jail awaiting formal charge, trial, or sentence. The judge should take appropriate corrective action when required.

Standard 6-2.1. Duty to prevent ex parte discussions of a pending case

The trial judge should insist that neither the prosecutor nor the defense counsel nor any other person discuss a pending case with the judge ex parte, except after adequate notice to all other parties and when authorized by law or in accordance with approved practice.

Standard 6-2.2. Duty to protect witnesses

(a) The trial judge should permit full and proper examination and cross-examination of witnesses, but should require the interrogation to be conducted fairly and objectively and with due regard for the dignity and legitimate privacy of the witnesses and without seeking to intimidate or humiliate them.

(b) The trial judge should not permit examination or cross-examination of witnesses at the witness stand, but should require counsel to examine from the counsel table or the lectern or other designated location, except as permission is granted for counsel to present a document or an object to the witness for observation or inspection.

Standard 6-2.3. Duty to control length and scope of examination

The trial judge should permit reasonable latitude to counsel in the examination and cross-examination of witnesses, but should not permit unreasonable repetition or permit counsel to pursue clearly irrelevant lines of inquiry.

Standard 6-2.4. Duty of judge on counsel's objections and requests for rulings

The trial judge should respect the obligation of counsel to present objections to procedures and to admissibility of evidence, to request rulings on motions, to make offers of proof, and to have the record show adverse rulings and reflect conduct of the judge which counsel considers prejudicial. Counsel should be permitted to state succinctly the grounds of his or her objections or requests; but the judge should nevertheless control the length and manner of argument.

Standard 6-2.5. Duty of judge to respect attorney-client relationship

The trial judge should respect the obligation of counsel to refrain from speaking on privileged matters and should avoid putting counsel in a position where counsel's adherence to the obligation, such as by a refusal to answer, may tend to prejudice the client. Unless the privilege is waived, the trial judge should not request counsel to comment on evidence or other matters where counsel's knowledge is likely to be gained from privileged communications.

Standard 6-3.1. Special rules for order in the courtroom

The trial judge, either before a criminal trial or at its beginning, should prescribe and make known the ground rules relating to conduct which the parties, the prosecutor, the defense counsel, the witnesses, and others will be expected to follow in the courtroom, and which are not set forth in the code of criminal procedure or in the published rules of court.

Standard 6-3.2. Colloquy between counsel

The trial judge should make known before trial that no colloquy, argument, or discussion directly between counsel in the presence of the judge or jury will be permitted, except that, if a brief conference between counsel might tend to expedite the trial, the judge will grant them leave to confer.

Standard 6-3.3. Judge's use of powers to maintain order

The trial judge has the obligation to use his or her judicial power to prevent distractions from and disruptions of the trial. If the judge determines to impose sanctions for misconduct affecting the trial, the judge should ordinarily impose the least severe sanction appropriate to correct the abuse and to deter repetition. In weighing the severity of a possible sanction for disruptive courtroom conduct to be applied during the trial, the judge should consider the risk of further disruption, delay, or prejudice that might result from the character of the sanction or the time of its imposition.

Standard 6-3.4. Judge's responsibility for self-restraint

The trial judge should be the exemplar of dignity and impartiality. The judge should exercise restraint over his or her conduct and utterances. The judge should suppress personal predilections, and control his or her temper and emotions. The judge should not permit any person in the courtroom to embroil him or her in conflict, and should otherwise avoid personal conduct which tends to demean the proceedings or to undermine judicial authority in the courtroom. When it becomes necessary during the trial for the judge to comment upon the conduct of witnesses, spectators, counsel, or others, or upon the testimony, the judge should do so in a firm, dignified, and restrained manner, avoiding repartee, limiting comments and rulings to what is reasonably required for the orderly progress of the trial, and refraining from unnecessary disparagement of persons or issues.

Standard 6-3.5. Deterring and correcting misconduct of attorneys

The trial judge should require attorneys to respect their obligations as officers of the court to support the authority of the court and enable the trial to proceed with dignity. When an attorney causes a significant disruption in a criminal proceeding, the trial judge, having particular regard to the provisions of standard 6-3.3, should correct the abuse, and if necessary, discipline the attorney by use of one or more of the following sanctions:

(a) censure or reprimand;

(b) citation or punishment for contempt;

(c) removal from the courtroom;

(d) suspension for a limited time of the right to practice in the court where the misconduct occurred if such sanction is permitted by law; and

(e) informing the appropriate disciplinary bodies in every jurisdiction where the attorney is admitted to practice of the nature of the attorney's misconduct and of any sanction imposed.

Standard 6-3.6. The defendant's election to represent himself or herself at trial

(a) A defendant should be permitted at the defendant's election to proceed in the trial of his or her case without the assistance of counsel only after the trial judge makes thorough inquiry and is satisfied that the defendant:

(i) has been clearly advised of the right to the assistance of counsel, including the right to the assignment of counsel when the defendant is so entitled;

(ii) possesses the intelligence and capacity to appreciate the consequences of this decision; and

(iii) comprehends the nature of the charges and proceedings, the range of permissible punishments, and any additional facts essential to a broad understanding of the case.

(b) When a litigant undertakes to represent himself or herself, the court should take whatever measures may be reasonable and necessary to ensure a fair trial.

Standard 6-3.7. Standby counsel for pro se defendant

When a defendant has been permitted to proceed without the assistance of counsel, the trial judge should consider the appointment of standby counsel to assist the defendant when called upon and to call the judge's attention to matters favorable to the accused upon which the judge should rule on his or her motion. Standby counsel should always be appointed in cases expected to be long or complicated or in which there are multiple defendants.

Standard 6-3.8. The disruptive defendant

A defendant may be removed from the courtroom during trial when the defendant's conduct is so disruptive that the trial cannot proceed in an orderly manner. Removal is preferable to gagging or shackling the disruptive defendant. If removed, the defendant should be required to be present in the court building while the trial is in progress, be given the opportunity of learning of the trial proceedings through defense counsel at reasonable intervals, and be given a continuing opportunity to return to the courtroom during the trial upon assurance from the defendant of good behavior. The removed defendant should be summoned to the courtroom at appropriate intervals and invited to remain, with the offer to remain repeated in open court each time.

Standard 6-3.9.   Misconduct of pro se defendant

If a defendant who is permitted to proceed without the assistance of counsel engages in conduct which is so disruptive that the trial cannot proceed in an orderly manner, the court should, after appropriate warnings, revoke the permission and require representation by counsel. If standby counsel has previously been appointed, the counsel should be asked to represent the defendant. In any event, the trial should be recessed only long enough for counsel to make the necessary preparations to go forward with the trial.

Standard 6-3.10.   Misconduct of spectators and others

The right of the defendant to a public trial does not give particular members of the general public or of the news media a right to enter the courtroom or to remain there. Any person who engages in conduct which disturbs the orderly process of the trial may be admonished or excluded, and, if such conduct is intentional, may be punished for contempt. Any person whose conduct tends to menace a defendant, an attorney, a witness, a juror, a court officer, or the judge in a criminal proceeding may be removed from the courtroom.

Standard 6-3.11.   Attorneys from other jurisdictions

If an attorney who is not admitted to practice in the jurisdiction of the court petitions for permission to represent a defendant, the trial judge may:

(a)   deny such permission if the attorney has been held in contempt of court or otherwise formally disciplined for courtroom misconduct, or if it appears by reliable evidence that the attorney has engaged in courtroom misconduct sufficient to warrant disciplinary action; or

(b)   grant such permission on condition that:
    (i)   the petitioning attorney associate with him or her as cocounsel a local attorney admitted to practice in the jurisdiction;

(ii)   the local attorney will assume full responsibility for the defense if the petitioning attorney becomes unable or unwilling to perform his or her duties; and

(iii) the defendant consents to the foregoing conditions.

Standard 6-4.1.   Inherent power of the court

The court has the inherent power to punish any contempt in order to protect the rights of the defendant and the interests of the public by assuring that the administration of criminal justice shall not be thwarted. The trial judge has the power to cite and, if necessary, punish summarily anyone who, in the judge's presence in open court, willfully obstructs the course of criminal proceedings.

Standard 6-4.2.   Admonition and warning

No sanction other than censure should be imposed by the trial judge unless:

(a)   it is clear from the identity of the offender and the character of his or her acts that the disruptive conduct was willfully contemptuous; or

(b)   the conduct warranting the sanction was preceded by a clear warning that such conduct was impermissible and that specified sanctions might be imposed for its repetition.

Standard 6-4.3.   Notice of intent to use contempt power; postponement of adjudication

(a)   The trial judge should, as soon as practicable after he or she is satisfied that courtroom misconduct requires contempt proceedings, inform the alleged offender of the judge's intention to institute such proceedings.

(b)   The trial judge should consider the advisability of deferring adjudication of contempt for courtroom misconduct of a defendant, an attorney, or a witness until after the trial, and should defer such a proceeding unless prompt punishment is imperative.

Standard 6-4.4.   Notice of charges and opportunity to be heard

Before imposing any punishment for criminal contempt, the judge should give the offender notice of the charges and at least a summary opportunity to adduce evidence or argument relevant to guilt or punishment.

Standard 6-4.5.   Referral to another judge

The judge before whom courtroom misconduct occurs may impose appropriate sanctions, including punishment for contempt, but should refer the matter to another judge if the original judge's conduct was so integrated with the contempt so as to have contributed to it or was otherwise involved, or if the original judge's objectivity can reasonably be questioned.

FEDERAL STATUTES REGARDING BIAS AND DISQUALIFICATION OF FEDERAL JUDGES

BIAS OR PREJUDICE OF JUDGES
28 U.S.C.A. §144

Whenever a party to any proceeding in a district court makes and files a timely and sufficient affidavit that the judge before whom the matter is pending has a personal bias or prejudice either against him or in favor of any adverse party, such judge shall proceed no further therein, but another judge shall be assigned to hear such proceeding.

The affidavit shall state the facts and the reasons for the belief that bias or prejudice exists, and shall be filed not less than ten days before the beginning of the term at which the proceeding is to be heard, or good cause shall be shown for failure to file it within such time. A party may file only one such affidavit in any case. It shall be accompanied by a certificate of counsel of record stating that it is made in good faith.

DISQUALIFICATION OF JUSTICE, JUDGE, OR MAGISTRATE
28 U.S.C.A. §455

(a)   Any justice, judge, or magistrate of the United States shall disqualify himself in any proceeding in which his impartiality might reasonably be questioned.

(b)   He shall also disqualify himself in the following circumstances:

   (1)   Where he has a personal bias or prejudice concerning a party, or personal knowledge of disputed evidentiary facts concerning the proceeding;

   (2)   Where in private practice he served as lawyer in the matter in controversy, or a lawyer with whom he previously practiced law served during such association as a lawyer concerning the mat-

ter, or the judge or such lawyer has been a material witness concerning it;

(3) Where he has served in governmental employment and in such capacity participated as counsel, adviser or material witness concerning the proceeding or expressed an opinion concerning the merits of the particular case in controversy;

(4) He knows that he, individually or as a fiduciary, or his spouse or minor child residing in his household, has a financial interest in the subject matter in controversy or in a party to the proceeding, or any other interest that could be substantially affected by the outcome of the proceeding;

(5) He or his spouse, or a person within the third degree of relationship to either of them, or the spouse of such a person:

    (i) Is a party to the proceeding, or an officer, director, or trustee of a party;

    (ii) Is acting as a lawyer in the proceeding;

    (iii) Is known by the judge to have an interest that could be substantially affected by the outcome of the proceeding;

    (iv) Is to the judge's knowledge likely to be a material witness in the proceeding.

(c) A judge should inform himself about his personal and fiduciary financial interests, and make a reasonable effort to inform himself about the personal financial interests of his spouse and minor children residing in his household.

(d) For the purposes of this section the following words or phrases shall have the meaning indicated:

(1) "proceeding" includes pretrial, trial, appellate review, or other stages of litigation;

(2) the degree of relationship is calculated according to the civil law system;

(3) "fiduciary" includes such relationships as executor, administrator, trustee, and guardian;

(4) "financial interest" means ownership of a legal or equitable interest, however small, or a relationship as director, adviser, or other active participant in the affairs of a party, except that:

    (i) Ownership in a mutual or common investment fund that holds securities is not a "financial interest" in such securities unless the judge participates in the management of the fund;

    (ii) An office in an educational, religious, charitable, fraternal, or civic organization is not a "financial interest" in securities held by the organization;

    (iii) The proprietary interest of a policyholder in a mutual insurance company, of a depositor in a mutual savings association, or a similar proprietary interest, is a "financial

    interest" in the organization only if the outcome of the
    proceeding could substantially affect the value of the
    interest;

  (iv) Ownership of governmental securities is a "financial in-
    terest" in the issuer only if the outcome of the proceed-
    ing could substantially affect the value of the securities.

 (e) No justice, judge, or magistrate shall accept from the parties to the proceeding a waiver of any ground for disqualification enumerated in subsection (b). Where the ground for disqualification arises only under subsection (a), waiver may be accepted provided it is preceded by a full disclosure on the record of the basis for disqualification.

CALIFORNIA CODE OF JUDICIAL CONDUCT

PREFACE

Formal standards of judicial conduct have existed for more than fifty years. The original Canons of Judicial Ethics were modified and adopted in 1949 for application in California by the Conference of California Judges (California Judges Association).

In 1969 the American Bar Association determined the current needs and problems warranted revision of the Canons. In the revision process, a special American Bar Association committee, headed by former California Chief Justice Roger Traynor, sought and considered the views of the bench and bar and other interested persons. The American Bar Association Code of Judicial Conduct was adopted by the House of Delegates of the American Bar Association August 16, 1972.

The California Code of Judicial Conduct is adapted from the American Bar Association Code of Judicial Conduct of 1972 and supersedes all prior Canons. The Code was adopted on September 10, 1974 and became effective January 1, 1975. This edition includes all amendments made to the Code through the Association's 1981 Annual Meeting.

PREAMBLE

The California Judges Association, mindful that the character and conduct of a judge should never be objects of indifference, and that declared ethical standards should become habits of life, adopts these principles which should govern the personal practice of members of the judiciary. The administration of justice requires adherence by the judiciary to the highest ideals of personal and official conduct. The office of judge casts upon the incumbent duties in respect to his conduct which concern his relation to the state, its inhabitants, and all who come in contact with him. The Association adopts this Code of Judicial Conduct as a proper guide and reminder for justices and judges of courts in California and for aspirants to judicial office, and as indicating what the people have a right to expect from them.

CANON 1
A JUDGE SHOULD UPHOLD THE INTEGRITY AND INDEPENDENCE OF THE JUDICIARY

An independent and honorable judiciary is indispensable to justice in our society. A judge should participate in establishing, maintaining, and enforcing, and should himself observe, high standards of conduct so that the integrity and independence of the judiciary may be preserved. The provisions of this Code should be construed and applied to further that objective.

CANON 2
A JUDGE SHOULD AVOID IMPROPRIETY AND THE APPEARANCE OF IMPROPRIETY IN ALL HIS ACTIVITIES

A. A judge should respect and comply with the law and should conduct himself at all times in a manner that promotes public confidence in the integrity and impartiality of the judiciary.
B. A judge should not allow his family, social, or other relationships to influence his judicial conduct or judgment. He should not lend the prestige of his office to advance the private interests of others; nor should he convey or permit others to convey the impression that they are in a special position to influence him. He should not testify voluntarily as a character witness.

Commentary

Public confidence in the judiciary is eroded by irresponsible or improper conduct by judges. A judge must avoid all impropriety and appearance of impropriety. He must expect to be the subject of constant public scrutiny. He must therefore accept restrictions on his conduct that might be viewed as burdensome by the ordinary citizen and should do so freely and willingly.

The testimony of a judge as a character witness injects the prestige of his office into the proceeding in which he testifies and may be misunderstood to be an official testimonial. This Canon, however, does not afford him a privilege against testifying in response to an official summons.

CANON 3
A JUDGE SHOULD PERFORM THE DUTIES OF HIS OFFICE IMPARTIALLY AND DILIGENTLY

The judicial duties of a judge take precedence over all his other activities. His judicial duties include all the duties of his office prescribed by law. In the performance of these duties, the following standards apply:

A. Adjudicative Responsibilities

(1) A judge should be faithful to the law and maintain professional competence in it. He should be unswayed by partisan interests, public clamor, or fear of criticism.

(2) A judge should maintain order and decorum in proceedings before him.

(3) A judge should be patient, dignified, and courteous to litigants, jurors, witnesses, lawyers, and others with whom he deals in his official capacity, and should require similar conduct of lawyers, and of his staff, court officials, and others subject to his direction and control.

Commentary

The duty to hear all proceedings fairly and with patience is not inconsistent with the duty to dispose promptly of the business of the court. Courts can be efficient and business-like while being patient and deliberate.

(4) A judge should accord to every person who is legally interested in a proceeding, or his lawyer, full right to be heard according to law, and, except as authorized by law, neither initiate nor consider ex parte or other communications concerning a pending or impending proceeding. A judge, however, may obtain the advice of a disinterested expert on the law applicable to a proceeding before him if he gives notice to the parties of the person consulted and the substance of the advice, and affords the parties reasonable opportunity to respond.

Commentary

The proscription against communications concerning a proceeding includes communications from lawyers, law teachers, and other persons who are not participants in the proceeding, except to the limited extent permitted. It does not preclude a judge from consulting with other judges, or with court personnel whose function is to aid the judge in carrying out his adjudicative responsibilities.

An appropriate and often desirable procedure for a court to obtain the advice of a disinterested expert on legal issues is to invite him to file a brief amicus curiae.

(5)   A judge should dispose promptly of the business of the court.

Commentary

Prompt disposition of the court's business requires a judge to devote adequate time to his duties, to be punctual in attending court and expeditious in determining matters under submission, and to insist that court officials, litigants and their lawyers cooperate with him to that end.

(6)   A judge should abstain from public comment about a pending or impending proceeding in any court, and should require similar abstention on the part of court personnel subject to his direction and control. This subsection does not prohibit judges from making public statements in the course of their official duties or from explaining for public information the procedures of the court.

Commentary

"Court personnel" does not include the lawyers in a proceeding before a judge. The conduct of lawyers is governed by DR 7-107 of the Code of Professional Responsibility.

(7)   Unless otherwise provided by law or by California Rule of Court or Standards, a judge should prohibit broadcasting, televising, recording, or taking photographs in the courtroom during sessions of court or recesses between sessions, and also prohibit such activities in areas immediately adjacent thereto if such activities disturb or are likely to disturb the court proceedings, except that a judge may authorize:

    (a)   the use of electronic or photographic means for the presentation of evidence, for the perpetuation of a record, or for other purposes of judicial administration;

    (b)   the broadcasting, televising, recording, or photographing of investitive, ceremonial, or naturalization proceedings;

    (c)   the photographic or electronic recording and reproduction of appropriate court proceedings under the following conditions:

(i) the means of recording will not distract participants or impair the dignity of the proceedings;

(ii) the parties have consented, and the consent to being depicted or recorded has been obtained from each witness appearing in the recording and reproduction;

(iii) the reproduction will not be exhibited until after the proceeding has been concluded and all direct appeals have been exhausted; and

(iv) the reproduction will be exhibited only for instructional purposes in educational institutions.

(d) A judge should comply with any additional and more restrictive requirements of applicable statutes and California Rules of Court.

Commentary

Temperate conduct of judicial proceedings is essential to the fair administration of justice. The recording and reproduction of a proceeding should not distort or dramatize the proceeding.

B. Administrative Responsibilities

(1) A judge should diligently discharge his administrative responsibilities, maintain professional competence in judicial administration, and facilitate the performance of the administrative responsibilities of other judges and court officials.

(2) A judge should require his staff and court officials subject to his direction and control to observe the standards of fidelity and diligence that apply to him.

(3) A judge should take or initiate appropriate disciplinary measures against a judge or lawyer for unprofessional conduct of which the judge may become aware.

Commentary

Disciplinary measures may include reporting a lawyer's misconduct to an appropriate disciplinary body.

(4) A judge should not make unnecessary appointments. He should exercise his power of appointment only on the basis of merit, avoiding nepotism and favoritism. He should not approve compensation of appointees beyond the fair value of services rendered.

Commentary

Appointees of the judge include officials such as attorneys, referees, commissioners, special masters, receivers, guardians and personnel such as clerks, secretaries, and bailiffs. Consent by the parties to an appointment or an award of compensation does not relieve the judge of the obligation prescribed by this subsection.

C. Disqualification

(1) A judge should disqualify himself in a proceeding in which his disqualification is required by law, or his impartiality might reasonably be questioned, including but not limited to instances where:

    (a) he has a personal bias or prejudice concerning a party, or personal knowledge of disputed evidentiary facts concerning the proceeding;

California Commentary

CCP Section 170, subdivision 5, contains the comparable California statutory disqualification. Because the Code emphasizes the appearance as well as the fact of propriety, Canon 3C(1)(a) may require more disqualification than the statute requires. Section 170, subdivision 5, provides, in part, that no judge shall sit or act in any action or proceeding:

> When it is made to appear probable that, by reason of bias or prejudice of such justice or judge a fair and impartial trial cannot be had before him.
> Whenever a judge or justice shall have knowledge of any fact or facts, which under the provisions of this section, disqualify him to sit or act as such in any action or proceeding pending before him, it shall be his duty to declare the same in open court and cause a memorandum thereof to be entered in the minutes or docket.

    (b) he served as lawyer in the matter in controversy, or a lawyer with whom he previously practiced law served during such association as a lawyer concerning the matter, or the judge or such lawyer has been a material witness concerning it;

Commentary

A lawyer in a governmental agency does not necessarily have an association with other lawyers employed by that agency within the meaning of this subsection; a judge formerly employed by a governmental agency, however, should disqualify himself in a proceeding if his impartiality might reasonably be questioned because of such association.

California Commentary

Subdivision 4 of section 170 of the California Code of Civil Procedure contains disqualifications in addition to those enumerated in Canon 3C(1)(b). A California judge should carefully consider CCP section 170, subdivision 4, in connection with Canon 3C(1)(b).

CCP section 170, subdivision 4 provides for disqualification:

> When, in the action or proceeding, or in any previous action or proceeding involving any of the same issues, he has been attorney or counsel for any party; or when he has given advice to any party upon any matter involved in the action or proceeding; or when he has been retained or employed as attorney or counsel for any party within two years prior to the commencement of the action or proceeding.

(c) he knows that he, individually or as a fiduciary, or his spouse or minor child residing in his household, has a financial interest in the subject matter in controversy or in a party to the proceeding, or any other interest that could be substantially affected by the outcome of the proceeding;

California Commentary

Canon 3C(1)(c) contains more grounds for disqualification than does California Code of Civil Procedure section 170, subdivision 2, which provides that a judge shall not sit in an action:

> In which he is interested as a holder or owner of any capital stock of a corporation, or of any bond, note or other security issued by a corporation;

CCP section 170, subdivision 3(b), contains a disqualification not specifically enumerated in Canon 3C(1)(c). The statutory disqualification not included in the Canon is indebtedness of the judge:

> ... through money borrowed as a loan, to either party, or to an attorney, counsel or partner of either party, or when he is so indebted to an officer of a corporation or unincorporated association which is a party;

(d) he or his spouse, or a person within the third degree of relationship to either of them, or the spouse of such a person:

(i)   is a party to the proceeding, or an officer, director, or a trustee of a party;

(ii) is acting as a lawyer in the proceeding;

Commentary

The fact that a lawyer in a proceeding is affiliated with a law firm with which a lawyer-relative of the judge is affiliated does not of itself disqualify the judge. Under appropriate circumstances, the fact that "his impartiality might reasonably be questioned" under Canon 3C(1), or that the lawyer-relative is known by the judge to have an interest in the law firm that could be "substantially affected by the outcome of the proceeding" under Canon 3C(1)(d)(iii) may require his disqualification.

(iii) is known by the judge to have an interest that could be substantially affected by the outcome of the proceeding;

(iv)   is to the judge's knowledge likely to be a material witness in the proceeding;

(2) A judge should inform himself about his personal and fiduciary financial interests, and make a reasonable effort to inform himself about the personal financial interests of his spouse and minor children residing in his household.

(3) For the purposes of this section:

(a) the degree of relationship is calculated according to the civil law system;

Commentary

According to the civil law system, the third degree of relationship test would, for example, disqualify the judge if his or his spouse's father, grandfather, uncle, brother, or niece's husband were a party or lawyer in the proceeding, but would not disqualify him if a cousin were a party or lawyer in the proceeding.

California Commentary

Canon 3C(1)(d) contains more grounds for disqualification than does section 170 of the California Code of Civil Procedure, subdivision 3. The Canon extends the disqualifying relationships to spouses of persons related within the third degree, while CCP section 170, subdivision 3, provides for disqualification of the judge:

When he is related to either party, or to an officer of a corporation, which is a party, or to an attorney, counsel, or agent of either party, by consanguinity or affinity within the third degree computed according to the rules of law . . .

    (b) "fiduciary" includes such relationships as executor, administrator, trustee, and guardian;

    (c) "financial interest" means ownership of a legal or equitable interest, however small, or a relationship as director, advisor, or other active participant in the affairs of a party, except that:

        (i) ownership in a mutual or common investment fund that holds securities is not a "financial interest" in such securities unless the judge participates in the management of the fund;

        (ii) an office in an educational, religious, charitable, fraternal, or civic organization is not a "financial interest" in securities held by the organization;

        (iii) the proprietary interest of a policy holder in a mutual insurance company, of a depositor in a mutual savings association, or a similar proprietary interest, is a "financial interest" in the organization only if the outcome of the proceeding could substantially affect the value of the interest;

California Commentary

CCP 170, subdivision 2, (previously quoted) may be more restrictive than Canon 3C(3)(iii). For example, if CCP section 170, subdivision 2, is interpreted to include holders of insurance policies in mutual insurance companies it would contain more disqualifications than Canon 3C(3)(iii). The Canon provides the disqualification only if the outcome would affect the value of the interest, where CCP section 170 provides that a holder of "any" capital stock is disqualified from the case.

        (iv) ownership of government securities is a "financial interest" in the issuer only if the outcome of the proceeding could substantially affect the value of the securities.

D. Remittal of Disqualification

A judge disqualified by the terms of Canon 3C(1)(c) or Canon 3C(1)(d) may, instead of withdrawing from the proceeding, disclose on the record the basis of his disqualification. If, based on such disclosure, the parties and lawyers, independently of the judge's participation, all agree in writing that the judge's relationship is immaterial or that his financial interest is insubstantial, the judge is no longer disqualified, and may participate in the proceeding. The agreement, signed by all parties and lawyers, shall be incorporated in the record of the proceeding.

Commentary

This procedure is designed to minimize the chance that a party or lawyer will feel coerced into an agreement. When a party is not immediately available, the judge without violating this section may proceed on the written assurance of the lawyer that his party's consent will be subsequently filed.

California Commentary

Canon 3D is more restrictive than CCP section 170, subdivision 3, in several respects. 1) The Canon permits waivers of disqualifications of the judge only in situations involving financial interest or relationship. CCP section 170, subdivision 3, also permits a waiver in a "former counsel" situation. 2) CCP 170 requires that the stipulation waiving the disqualification be signed by the party or his attorney, whereas the Canon requires the signatures of both parties and their counsel. 3) The Canon provides that the waiver agreement shall be entered into "independent of participation by the judge," whereas CCP section 170 has no such limitation.

CANON 4
A JUDGE MAY ENGAGE IN ACTIVITIES TO IMPROVE THE LAW, THE LEGAL SYSTEM, AND THE ADMINISTRATION OF JUSTICE

A judge, subject to the proper performance of his judicial duties, may engage in the following quasi-judicial activities, if in doing so he does not cast doubt on his capacity to decide impartially any issue that may come before him:

A. He may speak, write, lecture, teach, and participate in other activities concerning the law, the legal system, and the administration of justice.
B. He may appear at a public hearing before an executive or legislative body or official on matters concerning the law, the legal system, and the administration of justice, and he may otherwise consult with an executive or legislative body or official, but only on matters concerning the administration of justice.

California Commentary

This Canon is not intended to prevent the judge from making an appearance in the management of his personal affairs, provided he does not exploit his judicial position; for example, a judge may properly appear before a zoning board acting with respect to property in which he owns an interest.

C. He may serve as a member, officer, or director of an organization or governmental agency devoted to the improvement of the law, the legal system, or the administration of justice. He may assist such an organization in raising funds and may participate in their management and investment, but should not personally participate in public fund raising activities. He may make recommendations to public and private fund granting agencies on projects and programs concerning the law, the legal system, and the administration of justice.

Commentary

As a judicial officer and person specially learned in the law, a judge is in a unique position to contribute to the improvement of the law, the legal system, and the administration of justice, including revision of substantive and procedural law and improvement of criminal and juvenile justice. To the extent that his time permits, he is encouraged to do so, either independently or through a bar association, judicial conference, or other organization dedicated to the improvement of the law.

Extra-judicial activities are governed by Canon 5.

CANON 5
A JUDGE SHOULD REGULATE HIS EXTRA-JUDICIAL ACTIVITIES TO MINIMIZE THE RISK OF CONFLICT WITH HIS JUDICIAL DUTIES

A. Avocational Activities

A judge may write, lecture, teach, and speak on non-legal subjects, and engage in the arts, sports, and other social and recreational activities, if such avocational activities do not detract from the dignity of his office or interfere with the performance of his judicial duties.

315

Commentary

Complete separation of a judge from extra-judicial activities is neither possible nor wise; he should not become isolated from the society in which he lives.

B. Civic and Charitable Activities

A judge may participate in civic and charitable activities that do not reflect adversely upon his impartiality or interfere with the performance of his judicial duties. A judge may serve as an officer, director, trustee, or non-legal advisor of an educational, religious, charitable, fraternal, or civic organization not conducted for the economic or political advantage of its members, subject to the following limitations:

(1) A judge should not serve if it is likely that the organization will be engaged in proceedings that would ordinarily come before him or will be regularly engaged in adversary proceedings in any court.

Commentary

The changing nature of some organizations and of their relationship to the law makes it necessary for a judge regularly to reexamine the activities of each organization with which he is affiliated to determine if it is proper for him to continue his relationship with it. For example, in many jurisdictions charitable hospitals are now more frequently in court than in the past. Similarly, the boards of some legal aid organizations now make policy decisions that may have political significance or imply commitment to causes that may come before the courts for adjudication.

(2) A judge should not solicit funds for any educational, religious, charitable, fraternal, or civic organization, or use or permit the use of the prestige of his office for that purpose, but he may be listed as an officer, director, or trustee of such an organization. He should not be the principal speaker or the guest of honor at an organization's fund raising events, but he may attend such events.

(3) A judge should not give investment advice to such an organization, but he may serve on its board of directors or trustees even though it has the responsibility for approving investment decisions.

Commentary

A judge's participation in an organization devoted to quasi-judicial activities is governed by Canon 4.

C. Financial Activities

(1) A judge should refrain from financial and business dealings that tend to reflect adversely on his impartiality, interfere with the proper performance of his judicial duties, exploit his judicial position, or involve him in frequent transactions with lawyers or persons likely to come before the court on which he serves.

(2) Subject to the requirements of subsection (1), a judge may hold and manage investments, including real estate, and engage in other remunerative activities, but should not participate in, nor permit his name to be used in connection with, any business venture or commercial advertising program, with or without compensation, in such a way as would justify a reasonable inference that the power or prestige of his office is being utilized to promote a business or commercial product. A judge should not serve as an officer, director, manager or employee of a business affected with a public interest including, without limitation, a financial institution, insurance company, or public utility.

(3) A judge should manage his investments and other financial interests to minimize the number of cases in which he is disqualified. As soon as he can do so without serious financial detriment, he should divest himself of investments and other financial interests that might require frequent disqualification.

(4) Neither a judge nor a member of his family residing in his household should accept a gift, bequest, favor, or loan from anyone except as follows:

(a) a judge may accept a gift incident to a public testimonial to him; books supplied by publishers on a complimentary basis for official use; or an invitation to the judge and his spouse to attend a bar-related function or activity devoted to the improvement of the law, the legal system, or the administration of justice;

(b) a judge or a member of his family residing in his household may accept ordinary social hospitality; a gift, bequest, favor, or loan from a relative; a wedding or engagement gift; a loan from a lending institution in its regular course of business on the same terms generally available to persons who are not judges; or a scholarship or fellowship awarded on the same terms applied to other applicants;

(c)   a judge or a member of his family residing in his household may accept any other gift, bequest, favor, or loan only if the donor is not a party or other person whose interests have come or are likely to come before him.

Commentary

This subsection does not apply to contributions to a judge's campaign for judicial office, a matter governed by Canon 7.

(5)   For the purposes of this section "member of his family residing in his household" means any relative of a judge by blood or marriage, or a person treated by a judge as a member of his family, who resides in his household.

(6)   A judge is not required by this Code to disclose his income, debts, or investments.

Commentary

Canon 3 requires a judge to disqualify himself in any proceeding in which he has a financial interest, however small; Canon 5 requires a judge to refrain from engaging in business and from financial activities that might interfere with the impartial performance of his judicial duties. A judge has the rights of an ordinary citizen, including the right to privacy of his financial affairs. Owning and receiving income from investments do not as such affect the performance of a judge's duties.

(7)   Neither confidential information acquired by a judge in his official capacity nor his intentions with respect to rulings to be made by him should be used or disclosed by him in financial dealings or for any other purpose until such information is a matter of public record.

D.   Fiduciary Activities

A judge should not serve as the executor, administrator, trustee, guardian, or other fiduciary, except for the estate, trust, or person of a member of his family, and then only if such service will not interfere with the proper performance of his judicial duties. "Member of his family" includes a spouse, child, grandchild, parent, grandparent, or other relative or person with whom the judge maintains a close family-like relationship. As a family fiduciary a judge is subject to the following restrictions:

(1) He should not serve if it is likely that as a fiduciary he will be engaged in proceedings that would ordinarily come before him.

Commentary

The Effective Date of Compliance provision of this Code qualifies this subsection with regard to a judge who is an executor, administrator, trustee, or other fiduciary at the time this Code becomes effective.

(2) While acting as a fiduciary a judge is subject to the same restrictions on financial activities that apply to him in his personal capacity.

Commentary

A judge's obligation under this Canon and his obligation as a fiduciary may come into conflict. For example, a judge should resign as trustee if it would result in detriment to the trust to divest it of holdings whose retention would place the judge in violation of Canon 5C(3).

E. Arbitration

A judge should not act as an arbitrator or mediator, other than in his official capacity as a judge.

F. Practice of Law

A judge should not practice law.

G. Extra-judicial Appointments

A judge should not accept appointment to a governmental committee, commission, or other position that is concerned with issues of fact or policy on matters other than the improvement of the law, the legal system, or the administration of justice. A judge, however, may represent his country, state, or locality on ceremonial occasions or in connection with historical, educational, and cultural activities.

Commentary

Valuable services have been rendered in the past to the states and the nation by judges appointed by the executive to undertake important extra-judicial assignments. The appropriateness of conferring these assignments on judges must be reassessed, however, in light of the demands on judicial manpower created by today's crowded dockets and the need to protect the courts from involvement in extra-judicial matters that may prove to be controversial. Judges should not be expected or permitted to accept governmental appointments that could interfere with the effectiveness and independence of the judiciary.

CANON 6
COMPENSATION AND EXPENSE REIMBURSEMENT FOR QUASI-JUDICIAL AND EXTRA-JUDICIAL ACTIVITIES

A judge may receive compensation and reimbursement of expenses for the quasi-judicial and extra-judicial activities permitted by this Code, if the source of such payments does not give the appearance of influencing the judge in his judicial duties or otherwise give the appearance of impropriety, subject to the following restrictions:

A. Compensation

Compensation should not exceed a reasonable amount nor should it exceed what a person who is not a judge would receive for the same activity.

B. Expense Reimbursement

Expense reimbursement should be limited to the actual cost of travel, food, and lodging reasonably incurred by the judge and, where appropriate to the occasion, by his spouse. Any payment in excess of such an amount is compensation.

Commentary

Subject to Canon 5C(1), the foregoing restrictions shall not apply to the sale or distribution of publications authored by a judge which are available to the general public.

CANON 7
A JUDGE SHOULD REFRAIN FROM POLITICAL ACTIVITY INAPPROPRIATE TO HIS JUDICIAL OFFICE

A judge is entitled to entertain his personal views on political questions. He is not required to surrender his rights or opinions as a citizen. He should avoid political activity which may give rise to a suspicion of political bias or impropriety.

A. Political Conduct in General

(1) A judge or a candidate for election to judicial office should not:
   (a) act as a leader or hold any office in a political organization;
   (b) make speeches for a political organization or candidate for non-judicial office or publicly endorse a candidate for non-judicial office;
   (c) personally solicit funds for or pay an assessment to a political organization or non-judicial candidate; make contributions to a political party or organization or to a non-judicial candidate in excess of one hundred dollars per year per political party or organization or candidate, or in excess of an aggregate of five hundred dollars per year for all political parties or organizations or candidates.

California Commentary

Although attendance at political gatherings is not prohibited, any such attendance should be restricted in such a manner as not to constitute a public endorsement of a cause or candidate otherwise prohibited by these Canons.

Subject to the monetary limitation herein to political contributions, a judge may purchase tickets for political dinners or other similar functions. Any admission price to such a political dinner or function, in excess of the actual cost of the meal shall be considered a political contribution. The prohibition in 7A(1) (c) does not preclude judges from contributing to a campaign fund for distribution among judges who are candidates for re-election or retention.

(2) A judge who is a candidate for election or reelection or a non-judge who is a candidate for judicial office, may speak to political gatherings only on his own behalf.

(3) Except as otherwise permitted in this Code, a judge should not engage in any political activity, other than on behalf of measures to improve the law, the legal system or the administration of justice.

California Commentary

The term "political activity" should not be construed so narrowly as to prevent private comment.

This provision does not prohibit a judge from signing a petition to qualify a measure for the ballot without the use of the judge's official title.

B. Judicial Campaign Conduct. INDEFINITELY SUSPENDED (9/21/76)

(1) A candidate, including an incumbent judge, for a judicial office that is filled either by public election between competing candidates or on the basis of a merit system election:

  (a) should maintain the dignity appropriate to judicial office, and should encourage members of his family to adhere to the same standards of political conduct that apply to him;

  (b) should prohibit public officials or employees subject to his direction or control from doing for him what he is prohibited from doing under this Canon; and except to the extent authorized under subsection B(2) or B(3), he should not allow any other person to do for him what he is prohibited from doing under this Canon;

  (c) should not make pledges or promises of conduct in office other than the faithful and impartial performance of the duties of the office; should not announce his views on disputed political or legal issues, or refer publicly to pending litigation; and should not misrepresent his identity, qualifications, present position or other fact.

California Commentary

Litigation on appeal is pending litigation.

(2) A candidate, including an incumbent judge, for a judicial office that is filled by public election between competing candidates, should not himself solicit campaign funds, but he may establish committees of responsible persons to secure and manage the expenditure of funds for his campaign. Such committees are not prohibited from

soliciting campaign contributions and public support from lawyers. A candidate's committees may solicit funds for his campaign no earlier than such time as an announcement of a potential candidacy against the incumbent judge has been made, and then no later than 120 days after the last election in which he participates during the election year. A candidate should not use or permit the use of campaign contributions for the private benefit of himself or members of his family.

(3)   An incumbent judge who is a candidate for retention in or reelection to office without a competing candidate, and whose candidacy has drawn active opposition, may campaign in response thereto; may obtain publicly stated support; and in the manner provided in subsection B(2) may obtain campaign funds.

COMPLIANCE WITH THE CODE OF JUDICIAL CONDUCT

Anyone, whether or not a lawyer, who is an officer of a judicial system performing judicial functions, including an officer such as a referee in bankruptcy, special master, court commissioner, or magistrate, is a judge for the purpose of this Code. All judges should comply with this Code except as provided below.

A.   Part-time Judge

A part-time judge is a judge who serves on a continuing or periodic basis, but is permitted by law to devote time to some other profession or occupation and whose compensation for that reason is less than that of a full-time judge. A part-time judge:

(1)   is not required to comply with Canon 5C(2), D, E, F, and G.
(2)   should not practice law in the court on which he serves or in any court subject to the appellate jurisdiction of the court on which he serves, or act as a lawyer in a proceeding in which he has served as a judge or in any other proceeding related thereto.

B.   Judge Pro Tempore

A judge pro tempore is a person appointed to act temporarily as a judge, except that officers of the judicial system performing judicial functions, as defined above, shall not be deemed judges pro tempore qualifying for the exceptions contained herein.

(1)   While acting as such, a judge pro tempore is not required to comply with Canon 5C(2), (3), D, E, F, and G.

(2)   A person who has been a judge pro tempore should not act as a lawyer in a proceeding in which he has served as a judge or in any other proceeding related thereto.

C.   *Retired Judge*

A retired judge, upon recall to judicial service, during such service or prior to such service if he/she considers himself/herself available for such service, shall comply with all the provisions of this Code. However, he/she shall not be required to comply with 5C(2), 5D, 5E, and 5G.

EFFECTIVE DATE OF COMPLIANCE

A person to whom this Code becomes applicable should arrange his affairs as soon as reasonably possible to comply with it. If, however, the demands on his time and the possibility of conflicts of interest are not substantial, a person who holds judicial office on the date this Code becomes effective may continue to act as an executor, administrator, trustee, or other fiduciary for the estate or person of one who is not a member of his family.